LOBEL'S
MEAT BIBLE

LOBEL'S

MEAT BIBLE

ALL YOU NEED TO KNOW ABOUT
MEAT AND POULTRY FROM AMERICA'S
MASTER BUTCHERS

by Stanley, Evan, Mark, and David Lobel,
with Mary Goodbody and David Whiteman
Photographs by Lucy Schaeffer

CHRONICLE BOOKS
SAN FRANCISCO

ACKNOWLEDGMENTS

Writing this book has given us immense satisfaction. It is a logical step for us to come out with an inclusive meat book in the 21st century, as so much about butchery and meat and poultry in general has changed over the years, and certainly since the 1970s when we published *Meat*. This new book, *Lobel's Meat Bible*, would not have been completed without the help of many people. Our great thanks to Mary Goodbody and David Whiteman, whose collaboration with us made this book possible, and to Lisa Thornton for help with the manuscript. Thanks, also, to our agent Jane Dystel, who never loses faith in us and who saw this project through from start to finish. A big thanks to Bill LeBlond, Amy Treadwell, Sarah Billingsley, Michael Morris, Ben Kasman, Molly Jones, Doug Ogan, and the rest of the team at Chronicle who worked tirelessly with us to turn our manuscript into a beautiful book. We also would be remiss if we did not thank our employees, customers, and friends who make practicing the art of butchery a daily pleasure for us. And, of course, everything we do is especially gratifying because of the loving support of our families.

Library of Congress Cataloging-in-Publication Data available.

ISBN 978-0-8118-5826-7

Manufactured in China.

Designed by MICHAEL MORRIS
Prop styling by ALISTAIR TURNBULL
Food styling by ALISON ATTENBOROUGH

Front cover image supplied by Corbis Images, photographed by Olivier Pojzman

10 9 8 7 6 5 4 3 2 1

Chronicle Books LLC
680 Second Street
San Francisco, California 94107
www.chroniclebooks.com

DEDICATION

To my dear wife, Evelyn, my partner in life, who makes each day brighter than the day before; to my wonderful children, David, Mark, and Carla, of whom I am very proud; and to my dear, sweet grandchildren, Brian, Jessica, Michael, and Scotty. I dedicate this book to you all with enormous love and devotion. To my brother Leon, whom I worked so closely with for more than 50 years and whose loving memory will stay with me forever. I miss you.

–STANLEY LOBEL

My wife, Tamie, and my three wonderful girls, Joey, Cori, and Haley, have been a huge inspiration in my life. You make the cloudy days seem sunny and make the cold days of winter feel warm. You are my life . . . 143 forever.

–EVAN LOBEL

To my dear wife, Carla, my best friend and inspiration in life. To my dear children, Brian and Scotty, whom I cherish with all my heart. You bring so much joy and laughter into my world. To my wonderful parents, Evelyn and Stanley, whose love and support are endless. And to my Uncle Leon, whose love, guidance, and support I so sadly miss but will remember fondly forever.

–MARK LOBEL

I dedicate this book to my precious children, Jessica and Michael, who fill my heart with love and make each day of my life uniquely enjoyable. To my extraordinary parents, Stanley and Evelyn, whose invaluable and unending love, guidance, understanding, and wisdom have been the cornerstone of my life.

–DAVID LOBEL

EARNAISE SAUCE

Brine FOR PORK OR POULTRY

Cilantro-Lime CHUTNEY

MAYONNAISE

TOMATI SALS

QUICK TOMATO SAUCE

CHICKEN STOCK

GREEN OLIVE, WALNUT & POMEGRANATE RELISH

Salsa Mexican

Mustard Seed VINAIGRETTE

GARAM MAS SPICE BLE

AUCES, HUTNEYS, ON DIMENTS, ND STOCKS

ROASTED RED PEPPERS

BEEF STOCK

OSTRICH

PHEASANT

PARTRIDGE

SQUIRREL

COTCH ROUSE

VENISON

ELK

QUAIL

"GLOVE BONED" QUAIL

"quack!"

DUCK

WILD DUCK

BUFFALO

REINDEER

WILD TURKEY

MUSKRA

WOOD PIGEON

GOOSE

Wild Goose

AM BIRDS

WILD BOAR

Contents

Introduction

For generations, our family has been supplying our New York customers with the highest quality meats and poultry and, over the years, we have become recognized experts in our field. We have written a number of cookbooks, including one that focuses on grilling and another that examines cooking meat and poultry with wine. Through our Web site, we sell meat to home cooks across the country and also offer great tips and guidance. Closer to home, it's not unusual to get a phone call from a customer with a question, even as he or she is in the middle of cooking! We stop what we're doing, often with meat cleaver in hand, to give an answer. With this book, we hope to give our readers the same care and consideration.

We want nothing more than to help meat lovers get the most from their purchases. Few things are more discouraging than choosing the wrong cut of beef or pork for a dish you labor over, or cooking a fine steak until it's dry and gray.

We realize home cooks are baffled by the array of cuts covered tightly in plastic wrap and displayed on refrigerated shelves in the supermarket. The bright red, plump steak looks good . . . but should you buy it? Probably not. Instead, you should buy a darker red steak webbed with streaks of ivory-colored fat. This is the steak that will taste juicy and tender after you grill it; the steak without the fat will be tasteless and tough.

When a recipe calls for a loin lamb chop, what do you look for? Or how about a butterflied leg of lamb? Pork loin? St. Louis ribs? What is entrecôte? Is there a difference between club steak and strip steak? You may have heard of hanger steak but haven't a clue what it is.

This is precisely why we wrote this book. These are the questions we field daily from customers in our Madison Avenue shop on New York's Upper East Side. They are the questions we get from our many Web users who rely on us to ship top-quality meat and poultry to all reaches of the United States.

We decided the time was right for a careful look at the cuts of meat available in our market, at other butcher shops, and in supermarkets across the country. It's not unusual for a cut of meat to be called one thing in one part of the country and something quite different someplace else. This is most common among cuts of beef: Flat iron steak is also known as chuck top blade; skirt steak may be known as fajita steak; shell steak is also called Kansas City strip and New York strip.

There may not be as many of these differences with other meats, but it's useful to know that ham shank is another name for pork shank, that pork steaks and blade pork steaks are the same thing (cut from the

Boston butt). Any lamb chop labeled "bone-in lamb shoulder chop," "blade chop," "flat-bone chop," or "round-bone chop" works in any recipe that calls for shoulder lamb.

We want meat buyers to know what they are looking for, and once they make the purchase to take proper care of the meat at home. And we couldn't write this book without supplying one delicious recipe after another for beef, veal, pork, lamb, poultry, and game.

With *Lobel's Meat Bible* in your kitchen, you won't ever need another meat book! It's all here. Sit back, read about great meat, and then have a lot of fun cooking it to perfection. We're with you every step of the way.

LET US INTRODUCE OURSELVES

We run a family-owned business in the heart of Manhattan that is open six days a week. Never a day goes by without at least one Lobel on the premises. Stanley and his late brothers Leon and Nathan took over the business from their father, Morris, years ago. The next generation currently works in the business with Stanley: Leon's son Evan and Stanley's sons, Mark and David.

Stanley's great-grandfather and grandfather farmed beef cattle near Czernowitz, part of the Austrian Empire from 1775 to 1918. His grandfather added a processing facility to the business and because he knew so much about cattle in general was able to apply this knowledge to the art of butchering. His son, Morris, learned the business from him, so that by the time he was 14 years old, Morris was buying and selling his own cattle. At the age of 17, Morris, like so many other young men of the era, emigrated to the United States to start life in the New World.

Morris's career began in Boston. He eventually found his way to New York where he established a butcher shop first in the Bronx, and later on the West Side on Broadway. Then, in 1954, he opened the shop on the Upper East Side of Manhattan where we do business today at 1096 Madison Avenue, near the corner of East Eighty-second Street.

Butchering is a lost art. Today, most meat is butchered at a wholesale location, wrapped in Cryovac (air-tight plastic), and shipped to its destination. Hanging meat for aging seems to be a thing of the past, except among a small group of dedicated butchers. Aging itself is an art and can mean the difference between a good and a great tasting piece of meat. We age our meat for four to six weeks in our own patented coolers where the environment is meticulously maintained for the perfect temperature (between 34° and 36°F), humidity (kept at approximately 70 percent), and air circulation. Finally, our extensive knowledge and wisdom from years of experience tells us when a piece of meat reaches perfection and is ready to sell.

We respect these time-tested traditions and deliberately take the best of the old and combine it with the requirements of the present and future. We also believe it is crucial to treat our customers fairly and pleasantly, to sell only quality meat, and to answer every question.

Which brings us back to the reason for this book!

HANDLE WITH CARE

In the beginning of every chapter, we discuss what to look for when you buy beef, veal, pork, lamb, poultry, or game. All meat should be nice and cold when you buy it and then refrigerated as soon as possible.

To avoid unnecessary exposure to the air, which can trigger a process that breaks down the meat, it's a good idea to keep it wrapped in its protective paper until you are ready to begin prepping it for cooking. Store the meat or poultry in the coldest part of the refrigerator, which is a chill drawer or the rear of the box. Cook it as soon after purchase as you can-preferably on the day it's bought.

On the other hand, meat and poultry freeze well. We never sell meat that has been frozen, but we are well aware that our customers often freeze it. It's a marvelous convenience. If you plan to freeze it, do so as soon as you get the meat or poultry home from the market. Whether wrapped in plastic from the supermarket or butcher paper, the meat should be kept in its original wrapping. Protect it with another layer of plastic wrap. (Do not use foil, which becomes brittle in the freezer and tears.) Finally, enclose the protected meat in a plastic zippered freezer bag, pressing on the bag to expel as much air as you can. Date and identify the bag and put it as far back in the freezer as you can, where it's coldest.

Many people think once their meat or poultry is frozen rock hard, it will last for months, even years. Not so. We suggest never leaving meat in the freezer for more than a month (half that time during the hot summer months). Any longer and the texture and flavor can suffer.

Let the meat thaw slowly in the refrigerator, which can take a day or two depending on the cut. If you feel confident doing so, you can hasten this process in the microwave but take care not to "cook" the meat instead of thawing it. If you plan to cut the meat when it's raw (for stews or kababs, for instance), do so while the meat is partially frozen. It's much easier.

Many recipes call for seasoning the meat or marinating it. When you do, return the meat or poultry to the refrigerator as soon as you can. The trick is to keep the meat cold for as long as you can before cooking.

As critical as it is to keep the meat cold, it's equally important to let it come to room temperature right before you put it on the fire or in the oven. This insures the meat cooks evenly. Let the meat sit on the countertop for 30 to 40 minutes before cooking it—half that time if the day is very warm. The exception to this is chopped meat, which should be kept cold right up until it's cooked.

THE CORRECT TEMPERATURE

As do most professionals, we believe the best way to determine if a cut of meat is ready for serving is by feel, aroma, and appearance. Once you master these fairly simple techniques, never again will you find it necessary to slice into meat to tell if it's cooked to your liking, and lose valuable juices at the same time.

When you grill or broil steak, for instance, you want to char the outside but not let the meat turn black. If the fire is too hot, this will happen. The goal is to cook it just until the char is crispy and light. The meat's surface should not turn black and if it starts to, move the steak to a cool part of the grill. When the meat begins to separate from the bone, the steak is medium-rare and it's time to take it from the fire. Small, whitish deposits of liquid on the top of the steak indicate the meat is nearly medium.

To test for doneness by feel, start with your own hand.

- If the meat feels like the pad of flesh at the base of your thumb when your hand is held loosely open, it's rare.
- If the meat feels like the area between the thumb pad and the center of the palm, it's medium-rare.
- If the meat feels like the middle of the palm, it's medium.
- If the meat feels like the base of your little finger (pinkie), it's well-done.

Home cooks may feel more secure using an instant-read thermometer to gauge the degree of doneness when cooking meat. We love these little gizmos that allow us to poke a piece of meat near the end of cooking and determine in seconds if it's ready to remove from the heat. It's reassuring to know that the interior of the chicken has reached 170°F for white meat, or the pork is indeed 150° to 155°F, which means it will reach 160°F after it rests for a few minutes. These thermometers are sold everywhere: in supermarkets, in hardware and cookware stores, and through cooking catalogs and Web sites. They are made of sturdy metal or plastic, and have a sharp point for inserting in the meat. Using these thermometers to test for doneness is far, far better than slicing meat open to judge its doneness. Less juice escapes, and with it moisture and flavor. In all our recipes, we also provide approximate times and often visual tests for doneness, so that you don't have to rely on the thermometer alone.

USDA-APPROVED INTERNAL TEMPERATURES FOR MEAT AND POULTRY

CHICKEN:	170°F for white meat 180°F for dark meat
TURKEY:	170°F for white meat 180°F for dark meat
PORK:	160°F; cook until temperature is 150°F to 155°F and then let the meat rest for 5 to 10 minutes. The internal temperature will rise to 160°F but the meat will not be overcooked.
LAMB:	140°F for rare meat 150°F for medium meat 160°F for well-done meat
BEEF:	130°F for rare meat 140°F for medium-rare meat 150°F for medium meat 160°F for well-done meat

OUR MOST VALUABLE TOOLS

Knives are a butcher's most important tools, and are equally essential for the home cook. This means that when you buy a knife, you should buy the best you can afford. There is no reason to buy an expensive set of knives all at once, you can build on the collection as the years go by. If you care for your knives properly, they will last a lifetime—and become trusted companions in the kitchen.

Start with a paring knife, an 8- or 10-inch chef's knife, a bread knife, and a cleaver. You might also want a 12-inch chef's knife, a boning knife, and a slicing knife. Invest in a pair of good-quality poultry shears; they make quick work of cutting up a chicken.

Dull knives are not worth much and so it's important to keep the blades sharp and honed and to do this, we recommend a honing stone and sharpening steel used in tandem. (It's been our experience that electric sharpeners, metal disks, wall holders, and abrasive wheels don't do a particularly good job.) Sharp knives also are safer than dull knives as they work efficiently and won't slip.

Honing stones are most commonly made of carborundum stone, but you can also find some made of silicon carbide, sandstone, aluminum oxide, and other materials. Although these stones may be coarse, medium, or fine, you can rely on the medium grade to keep knives sharp. Most have a coarse side and a finer side. Some are lubricated with water and others with oil. If your knives are very dull, you might want a coarse stone; if you prefer a super keen edge, a fine stone will give you one every time.

Hold the stone in its box or on a damp towel and hold the knife blade at a 20-degree angle to the stone. Sharpen in the same direction using the same number of strokes on both sides of the blade. Carefully wipe the edge with a damp towel and then use the steel.

While you only need to use the honing stone when the knives need sharpening, you should use the steel every day. Steels are the long tapered rods that come with knife sets; we usually hold them at a 45-degree angle in one hand, the knife in the other hand, and draw the blade first down one side of the steel and then down the other. While they are not sharpeners, using one keeps the blade sharp and ready. Some chefs use the steel between every cut but if you get in the habit of using it frequently, your knives will hold their edge for a long time.

When you buy a knife, make sure it feels good in your hand. The handle can be wood, a plastic compound, or a rubberized material, but the blade should run all the way to the end of the handle. This part of the blade is called the tang. Most people like high-carbon stainless-steel blades because they won't rust or stain.

Treat your knives with great care and respect. Wash them by hand and dry them right away. Store them in a knife block, specially designed drawer, or sheaths. The blades can get nicked and scratched in the dishwasher or in a drawer with a jumble of other utensils.

Use cutting boards—wood, plastic, or rubber—when you cut meat and other foods. Do not cut them on the countertop, as this can dull the knives, and might be dangerous if the knife slips off the food. Stabilize your cutting board with a damp towel or mat.

FINALLY, A WORD ABOUT CHOPPED MEAT

Chopped meat can mean beef, lamb, pork, chicken, or turkey, and we recommend that you buy it from a butcher, if you possibly can. When this is not possible, ask the butcher at the supermarket to grind it for you. If he cannot, ask him when the meat you plan to purchase was ground. You want to make sure it was ground in a clean machine, and never mingled with other meat or any part of the animal that should not be in the mixture. Most butchers will appreciate your care.

If the butcher can grind the meat for you, ask him to trim most of the fat before he puts the meat through the grinder. Let him know how you will be using the meat. If it's for hamburgers, for example, you want it quite fine so that it can be formed into compact patties; for meatloaf, it can be a coarser grind.

If you buy packaged ground beef or other meat, make sure it is rosy colored, without browned sections, and evenly mixed with creamy white particles of fat.

To grind your own beef, pork, lamb, or poultry, trim it of all fat (including chicken skin) and grind it in a meat grinder or a food processor fitted with a metal blade just until finely ground. If you use a meat grinder, pass the meat through the grinder three times until finely ground. A food processor can pulverize the meat, so take care that it does not turn mushy if you use one.

All ground meat should be kept refrigerated until cooking. Keep it wrapped in its original packaging. Try to cook the ground meat within a day. To freeze it, put the meat, still in its original wrapping, in a plastic freezer bag, and let it freeze solid in the coldest part of the freezer.

WHAT WE DO BEST

Selecting and cooking meat is what we do best and because we want our readers and our customers to get the most from their purchases, we decided to write this book. We hope it will help both home cooks and professionals choose the right cut for a specific dish. We also hope it will encourage you to try cuts of meat you may never have considered before, such as breast of veal or pork shoulder. Our recipes, created with the help of David Whiteman, are wonderful ways to explore the world of meat cookery. For a winning meal every time, we advise you to take your time when you pick out meat, prep it, and cook it. You won't go wrong.

We organized each chapter so that the animal is divided into logical cuts and sections (such as steaks, roasts, hind section, and so forth). This is a commonsensical way to view butchering—and since the neighborhood butcher is almost an endangered species, we hope that with *Lobel's Meat Bible*, we can take his place and help you become an even better meat cook.

SPECIAL

STEAK

Top Round

LONDON BROIL

POT ROAST

PRIME RIB

Châteaubriand

Flank BRISKET

RIBS

BEEF

TENDERLOIN

RIB-EYE

T-Bo

STE

DELM

Chuc

FLA

IRO

Sale! EYE OF ROUND

Quality Beef Shank

ne
AK

SKIRT STEAK

PORTERHOUSE

Jerky

ILET MIGNON

CHOPS

ONICO STEAK

CORNED BEEF

T
U

TRI-TIP

Filet

one
EAK
SKIRT STEAK
FILET MIGNON
MONICO STEAK
ck
CORNED BEEF
AT
ON
TRI-TIP

CHAPTER ONE

Beef

We love beef, which puts us in good company. Most meat eaters favor it. Let's face it—few things beat a plump burger sizzling on the grill, a thick steak and a glass of red wine, or a warm and comforting beef stew on a cold night.

American beef producers say that nearly 40 percent of all meat and poultry sold in the United States is beef. Clearly, as a nation we love our beef, and buy more ground beef than any other beef product, followed by steaks, deli beef items, roasts, and cubed beef.

With so much beef being marketed, and with its price so high, we believe it's only fair that consumers know what to look for when they buy it. So we have identified the most popular cuts of beef sold in America's butcher shops and supermarkets and described them so that never again will you be confused at the market. At least we hope not!

Whatever beef you buy, look for meat with a minimum of outer creamy white fat and soft-looking bones with red coloration. The meat should be firm, fine textured, and, in most instances, a light cherry red. Avoid beef with excessively heavy marbling (thick ropes of fat) or no marbling at all. Inexperienced meat buyers are drawn to bright red slices of beef without any visible fat, but this is a mistake. The fat gives the meat flavor and moisture. On the other hand, the fat should never be yellowed and the meat should never be two-toned, or have a deep, dark red color or a coarse texture.

Beef is graded by the USDA before it gets to the wholesaler. Most is graded prime, choice, or select, but other grades exist: standard, commercial, utility, cutter, and canner. These lesser grades are very rarely available to the ordinary consumer. The grade is based on the marbling and the approximate age of the animal from which it came. Most purveyors select prime or choice meat, with choice being the most commonly sold. Select beef, which has less marbling than choice, is also available. Even within a graded category variations exist.

We buy only prime beef for our shop and for our customers. At the wholesale level, we might examine 100 sides of beef graded as USDA prime and will choose only two or three for Lobel's. Admittedly, we are picky, picky, picky, particularly when you consider that less than 2 percent of all the beef produced in this country falls into the prime category. We look for graining (marbling) and at the color of the meat and the color of the fat. All indicate the age of the animal and its quality. What might be very good prime beef, as graded by the USDA, is not necessarily good enough for our customers. Over the years, we have all developed an eye for outstanding beef, and rarely are we wrong.

Our customers may be spoiled by our product, and not every butcher in every market can stock prime beef. If you can't get prime, go for choice and Certified Black Angus beef (which is high-end choice beef, and usually the best of the USDA choice beef, closest in quality to prime beef). This will be beautifully marbled, too. The best steaks will have a delicate marbling, called fine-needle marbling, or graining that runs through the meat like a web.

The marbled fat is a lubricant that dissolves as the meat cooks to give it that distinctive flavor and texture we all love so much in a good steak. Fine, uniformly marbled fat melts evenly and leaves meat juicy and tender. Conversely, chunky ropes of fat don't melt at the same rate as the meat cooks and will leave it tough and tasting fatty.

We age prime beef at Lobel's. Most good butchers age meat, although what you buy in the supermarket arrives a bare six to ten days after slaughter. We hang the beef in our coolers, which are maintained at 34° to 36°F, for four to six weeks after we purchase it, until it reaches what we consider perfection. Our customers expect and appreciate this quality. Talk to your butcher about how he ages the meat. It's a good way to start building a relationship with him and he will appreciate an interested customer.

A growing number of ranchers and farmers raise beef that is labeled "natural," "organic," and "grass-fed." Natural beef comes from cattle that are raised without antibiotics or growth hormones but may be fed grain on a feedlot. The USDA has instituted guidelines for all organic food products in its National Organic Program. Organically raised beef is not given antibiotics or growth hormones and is fed certified-organic feed from birth. It is processed at a certified-organic packing plant. Grass-fed beef cattle spend their entire lives eating grasses. They tend to be slaughtered at a slightly later age than other cattle; without corn in their diet, it takes them longer to reach the optimal weight. This results in leaner meat with a slightly different but equally appealing flavor, some say, from grain-fed beef.

STEAKS

PORTERHOUSE STEAK

Porterhouse is one of the most popular cuts of steak, perhaps because it has a generous section of tenderloin. The porterhouse is cut from the short loin, nearest the sirloin, and is a fine-grained steak with a characteristic portion of fat. It is usually cut nice and thick to be broiled or grilled, although thinner porterhouses can be pan-broiled. A good porterhouse ranges in thickness from 1½ to 3 inches.

Some of our customers ask us to remove the tenderloin so that they can serve it separately as a filet mignon. The tail of the meat may also be removed, ground to make a patty (which is cooked separately), tucked into the steak where the tenderloin was, which is tucked between the bone and the fillet. The tail is often referred to as the flap or flap meat.

T-BONE STEAK

A T-bone steak is easily identified by the shape of its bone, which looks like a "T." It comes from the center section of the short loin, between the porterhouse and the club steak. Very similar to the porterhouse, the T-bone has a smaller tail and a smaller section of tenderloin. It has a finely grained shell and should be 1 to 3 inches thick. These steaks are great on the grill or under the broiler, although the thinner ones do well when pan-broiled.

CLUB STEAK

Club steaks are triangular in shape and are smaller than T-bones. They are cut from the short loin, next to the rib end, and when properly cut are tender and delicious. They are also known as boneless top loin steaks when they are boned. But beware: Some butchers have been known to pass off less-expensive rib steaks as club steaks.

When you buy a club steak, take a good look at the steak's "eye," which is the meat in the center of the cut. It should be fine in texture with delicate marbling. If the meat appears coarse or contains visible chunks or deposits of fat, you will know it's not the quality you want. Another indication is heavier graining in the rib area.

Our customers ask us to cut club steaks as minute steaks, or "beef scalps." This means the steak is only about 1 inch thick and so cooks quickly. We also sell club steaks that are 2 or 3 inches thick, and may have the bone removed. This makes an excellent steak when grilled or broiled and then cut on the diagonal for serving.

Club steaks are also called "Delmonico steaks". This cut was made famous by the historic Delmonico's restaurant. While we have come to believe that the original Delmonico's steak was a club steak, we know others maintain that it was a boneless top loin, which is a boneless club steak, or even a sirloin steak.

Whatever was served at the popular eatery, probably it was very good, and today the term implies a great steak.

Delmonico's claims to have been the first restaurant in the United States. It was founded in downtown New York City in 1830 by Giovanni Del Monico and his brother Pietro and soon gained a reputation for serving the "best steak in town." Delmonico's is still located downtown, and while it's not the same restaurant that was founded by the Del Monico brothers, the modern-day eatery claims to celebrate the tradition of the original.

SHELL STEAK

When the tenderloin is removed from the short loin, the remaining meat is then cut into individual bone-in steaks of desired thickness. These are often called boneless top loin steaks. The term "shell steak" evolved because they are cut from the meat that encases the tenderloin. For some reason, the tasty shell steak is known by many names: New York strip, Kansas City strip, strip steak, or sirloin. When a shell steak is aged on the bone for more than four weeks, we suggest that you remove the bone to avoid a strong, aged flavor. Of course, some people like this flavor and seek out aged shell steak on the bone for just this reason.

A shell steak is easily identifiable in the meat market: It looks exactly like a porterhouse or T-bone but without the tenderloin. These steaks can be cut to any width, though most are from 1 to 2½ inches thick. If they are sold off the bone, they should be cut on the diagonal for serving. For more information, see Shell Roast, page 22.

At Lobel's, we call boneless shell steak "entrecôte" because we think it's such an outstanding cut. We remove all sinews, excess fat, and gristle and when it's cooked, it's simply delicious. For more information, see Rib-Eye Steak. The word *entrecôte* officially means "between the ribs," and traditionally these tender steaks are cut from the rib section and are sold as boneless rib steaks, or rib-eye steaks. We prefer our boned shell steaks.

TENDERLOIN STEAK

The better-known name for this steak is filet mignon. As we mentioned, some customers ask us to remove the tenderloin section from their porterhouse steaks to make individual fillets. But more often these days, we have requests for a complete fillet strip, or whole tenderloin, which is not a steak when left whole but a roast. When sliced into steaks, the tenderloin (or filet mignon) makes the most tender of all steaks, and yet no matter how delicious and tender, some find the texture too soft. For more information, see Filet Mignon, below, and Whole Fillet Roast (page 22).

FILET MIGNON

Filet mignon is the French term for those tenderloin steaks cut from the center of the tenderloin. They are individual steaks, generally cut about 2 inches thick and served as individual portions. These steaks are most often broiled, grilled, or pan-fried.

TORNEDOS AND PETITE FILETS

These terms are used to describe steaks cut from the narrower portion of the tenderloin toward its "tail."

TRI-TIP STEAK

The tri-tip gets its name from its shape, with its ends looking somewhat like a triangle. It is cut from the bottom of the sirloin and is far more popular in western regions of the country than elsewhere. The tri-tip is also referred to as the "culotte" steak.

SIRLOIN STEAK

The sirloin steak is a large steak, which makes it suitable for families and parties. A typical sirloin is usually cut from 1¾ to 2½ inches thick, although some are as thick as 3½ inches. It is cut from the end of the short loin where it meets the rump.

The most flavorful sirloin steak is on the bone, although in many supermarkets and butcher shops it is sold boneless. All high-grade sirloin steak is tender, delicious, and excellent when broiled or grilled. Of course, the thinner cuts may be pan-broiled.

SIRLOIN TIP STEAK

Sirloin tips are also referred to as "boneless sirloin steaks." The tip comes from the bottom tip of the sirloin section. It is not quite as tender as bone-in sirloin steaks, but has delicious flavor. We usually cut sirloin tips to about 2 inches thick and suggest you braise it for a short time.

TOP SIRLOIN STEAK

This cut is commonly sold in chain and casual dining restaurants where it is often called "sirloin steak." Depending on which part of the top sirloin section the steak is cut from, it can be very good, or quite tough. The top sirloin is the part of the sirloin section nearest the rump or the leg. Like any steak, it can be cut to various thicknesses, and if it's the first cut, rather than one of the end cuts, it will be tasty. It makes a good London broil.

HANGER STEAK

Hanger steaks, favored for their great rich flavor, are thicker than skirt steaks and lie next to the kidney and the short loin—or actually "hang" between the rib cage and loin cage. They are nice and juicy, especially when cut from prime beef; unless the hanger steak is prime beef, we believe it should be marinated. It's excellent on the grill, but can also be cooked in the broiler. Its uneven, tapered shape makes it ideal for families who like their meat cooked to different degrees of doneness.

These steaks are also called "butcher's tenderloin" or "butcher's steak" because before this cut was "discovered" by the general public, butchers very often held back the tasty but homely cuts for themselves and their families. In France, hanger steak is known as *onglet.* Since chefs and steak lovers made hanger steaks popular, they have acquired a degree of panache.

There is only one hanger steak in each steer. It is a chunk of beef that measures 3½ inches at its thickest point. A thick vein or sinew runs through the center of the meat, which should be removed by a butcher, as it is unpleasantly tough and chewy. This means you will end up with two pieces. If you can bear to grind it, hanger steaks make incredibly juicy hamburgers. We like to make huge, 12-ounce burgers and char them on the grill. They are about as succulent as it gets!

SKIRT STEAK

There are two cuts of skirt steak: the inside and the outside skirt and both are cut from under the breast. The outside skirt steak is preferred, because it is more tender, juicy, and flavorful. Typically, this skirt steak is about ¾ inch thick and is terrific for broiling, grilling, and pan-broiling. It benefits from a marinade, too. When we prepare skirt steaks for sale, we usually score the meat to allow the flavors from marinades or spice mixtures to permeate it.

The inside skirt steak is similar in texture and size, but is generally far less tender. This might explain why inside skirts are very often cooked for fajitas, although outside skirts make great fajitas, too.

RIB STEAK

Rib steaks, which are cut from the rib section of the steer, are also known as prime ribs. They are usually cut to be 1 or 2 inches thick and have excellent flavor; when well cooked, they have a pleasing texture, although they are not the most tender beef. As with all steaks, grade will affect the eating experience. Because the rib steak is cut from the front portion, or forequarter (in accordance with Jewish dietary laws), it is often sold in kosher butcher shops as their signature steak. When a rib steak is cut very thick, approximately 2½ to 3 inches, and the bones are frenched, it is known as a cowboy steak.

RIB-EYE STEAK

This is the rib steak without the bone.

CHUCK STEAK

Sometimes called "blade chuck," this steak comes from the shoulder, or chuck, section of the animal. It is an economical cut with well-developed flavor; it varies in texture and while very good, it is not the most tender cut. We consider the meat on the first three bones of the chuck section to be the most tender. These are adjacent to the rib roast and contain a sizable extension of rib eye; we recommend these for grilling. Chuck from the neck is nicely marbled, moist, and wonderfully flavorful, and is very good for braising.

The next three cuts, which are farther down the shoulder, are less tender and should be braised so that they will not be tough. Even though they require moist cooking, they are known as chuck steaks. When you buy chuck steaks, try to determine where the cut comes from on the chuck and request steaks cut from the first three ribs. Boneless chuck is as flavorful as meat on the bone, so we recommend buying it, simply because it is so easy to work with.

SHOULDER STEAK

Shoulder steaks are cut from the forequarter, so they are typically found in kosher meat markets. The first cuts from the shoulder make excellent thin steaks, also called minute steaks, mock sirloin steak, or London broil. For more information, see Shoulder Roast, page 23.

FLANK STEAK

This is a lean, flat muscle with no bone at all, cut from the lower section of the short loin, in which the meat fibers run lengthwise. There is only one flank steak to a side of beef. Flank steak has a lovely flavor and a tender texture when thinly and properly sliced for serving. For best results, this steak should be quickly broiled or grilled and then sliced on a diagonal, or the bias. It also benefits from marinating, which accentuates its flavor and makes it even more tender.

FLAT IRON STEAK

The flat iron, cut from the chuck, is also known as "chuck top blade." This popular steak is considered a "value cut" that we find does well when braised. For a palatable texture, its center vein should be removed, which the butcher will do for you. But if it's not removed, the vein will soften during slow, moist cooking and the meat will develop really good flavor. It is also very good grilled.

ROUND STEAK

The round steak is cut from the rump, or round, section of the hindquarter. Its shape is oval and it has a small, round bone, which explains its name. We usually sell it without this bone. Round steak has practically no fat, and because it is so lean it is excellent for steak tartare. It also makes a fine London broil if it is from one of the first three cuts off the rump. Cut thick, it can also be served as a roast. Round steaks have very little waste, which makes them an economical buy, but because they lack marbling, they are not as flavorful or juicy as other cuts.

LONDON BROIL

"London broil" is not a specific cut of beef but instead is the name given to a lean, flat steak with fibers that run lengthwise down the meat. London broil is most often cut from flank steak, although it may also be cut from top round, flat iron, shell steak, or any other steak that, once cooked, can be sliced on the bias (diagonal). The fact that it may be cut from a variety of steaks explains the differences in London broils from restaurant to restaurant, butcher to butcher, and home kitchen to home kitchen.

MINUTE STEAK

"Minute steak" is a term that refers to any boneless steak from any number of cuts, ranging from shell steaks to round steaks to shoulder steaks. In supermarkets, minute steaks are usually cut from the flat iron. These steaks are cut ¼ to ½ inch thick and earn their name because they cook very quickly, usually in a skillet or on a grill.

Minute steaks also are called Swiss steaks.

CUBE STEAK

Cube steaks are usually formed from tough cuts of meat, such as the shoulder, the chuck, and the bottom round. The meat is passed through a cuber, which is a machine fitted with numerous needles that score the meat deeply to tenderize and then cut the steaks very thin. These economical steaks are good for sandwiches and quick meals.

ROASTS

PRIME RIBS OF BEEF

This is traditional roast beef, the cut a lot of people expect on the holiday table. It is flavorful and impressive, cut as it is from the rib section of the forequarter, and depending on the size needed, can be as small as a two-bone rib roast, which is enough for three or four servings, and as large as a seven-rib roast, which is enough for fourteen and requires a large roasting pan for cooking.

The meat is very juicy and is well marbled throughout. It also has an exterior layer of fat. Don't be deceived by the word "prime." This is not an indicator of its grade, which may or may not be prime. Prime ribs can be cut from choice and select grades of beef, too. Other names for prime ribs are rib roast and standing rib roast.

There are four ways to prepare prime rib:

STANDING RIB ROAST: The roast is lightly trimmed and the short ribs are cracked.

HALF STANDING RIB ROAST #1: This is also lightly trimmed, but the short ribs are completely removed.

HALF STANDING RIB ROAST #2: The roast is lightly trimmed and the short ribs are removed. All other bones are cut from the meat and then tied back in place. After roasting, the strings are cut, bones are removed, and slicing is done with ease. The reason for this is to get the flavor provided by the bones without the annoyance of cutting meat from the bone for serving. You should ask a good butcher to prepare the roast like this for you.

ROLLED RIB ROAST: The rib roast is well trimmed and the short ribs are removed. The roast is completely boned and rolled and the outside layer of fat is tied around the meat, which adds flavor as the meat roasts and also acts to hold the juices in the meat during its time in the oven.

RIB-EYE ROAST

This is a boneless roast cut from the center of the rib section of the rib roast.

SHELL ROAST

When the tenderloin has been removed from the short loin, the remaining meat can be cut into individual shell steaks (page 19), or it can be cut into larger pieces to make roasts. These roasts are not as round and thick as other roasts, which means they can be cooked on a covered grill, as well as roasted in the oven.

Shell roasts are extremely popular in our shop, as our customers find they are excellent for parties and can be cut to the size dictated by your guest list. We sell them boned because otherwise they are difficult to slice. When boneless, this cut is known as a boneless shell roast or a New York strip roast. Whatever you call it, this is one of our favorites!

SIRLOIN ROAST

Like sirloin steaks, sirloin roasts are cut from the section of a steer where the meat is tender and delicious. When the first section of the sirloin is cut as a roast, it is flavorful and tender, although it doesn't compare to a rib roast.

WHOLE FILLET ROAST

The whole fillet is the tenderloin of the steer and is sometimes referred to as the butt end. It is cut from the loin and, before it is trimmed of fat, can weigh as much as 8 or 9 pounds. This tender, boneless roast is sold both trimmed and not, but we highly recommend you buy it trimmed, when it will weigh 3 to 5 pounds. Trimmed fillet costs more per pound, but at least you will know what and how much meat you are getting. Even when trimmed, the silverskin will still be attached to the meat and should be removed with a knife before the tenderloin is cooked. The silverskin is the thin membrane that separates the fat from the meat. Ask the butcher to remove the silverskin if you are not sure how to do it.

Whole fillets are oblong, about 2 to 2½ inches thick, with tapering ends called the head and the tail. The tail makes a great London broil, and both ends are good as minute (thin) steaks, cut into cubes for kababs, sliced paper-thin for carpaccio, or chopped and served raw for steak tartare. When the head and tail are removed from the fillet, the remaining center piece is called Châteaubriand, known as a particularly luxurious and tender roast. The whole fillet traditionally is wrapped in pastry for beef Wellington, a dish that is not as popular as it once was. When the tenderloin is cut into thick steaks, they are known as filet mignon.

Like all beef, fillet freezes nicely but because of its delicate texture, we don't recommend freezing it for longer than two or three weeks in the more humid summer and no longer than one month at other times of the year. It very easily develops freezer burn and loses flavor.

CHÂTEAUBRIAND

This is the center of the whole fillet, with the two uneven ends, called the head and the tail, removed. This is the finest part of the fillet. For more information, see Whole Fillet Roast above.

TRI-TIP ROAST

This roast is cut from the sirloin and usually weighs about 3 pounds. Like the tri-tip steak, it gets its name from its triangular shape and its flavor and texture are similar to a sirloin roast.

SHOULDER ROAST

Cut from the forequarter, the shoulder roast can be boned or not. It can be dry-roasted in the oven, similar to a rib roast, but it does better when braised as a pot roast. We suggest covering it with a layer of fat (available from the butcher) to keep it moist and flavorful if you dry-roast it. The fat is not necessary for braised dishes, although it adds flavor. This is a popular cut in kosher markets.

RUMP ROAST

The rump roast, more commonly known as "bottom round," is a great favorite for pot roast. It needs slow, moist cooking, and, when braised, is exceptionally tender and flavorful.

Like most braises, a pot roast made with rump roast is even better the second day.

CHUCK ROAST

Chuck roasts are usually sold with the bone in, although we sell them boneless as well. The bone adds flavor, but when it's removed, the roast is easier to serve. Chuck roasts are cut from the neck and shoulder of the steer.

Due to the relatively high proportion of marbling, chuck roasts have superb flavor and make outstanding pot roasts.

TENDERLOIN ROAST

See Whole Fillet Roast, page 22.

FLAT IRON ROAST

This soft, tender roast cut from the chuck makes a wonderful pot roast, but because it is a little thinner, will not take as much time to cook as other roasts recommended for similar braised preparations. The center vein becomes soft and gelatin-like during cooking, so that it's easy to cut around it during serving. Some folks like to eat this vein.

BRISKET

The brisket is located in front of the foreshank and below the chuck. Some people believe it makes the best pot roast ever, and we can't argue with them. It is also cured to make corned beef.

There are two cuts of brisket. The first cut is a little dry but lean, while the second is much fattier, and richer, and therefore juicier. Both cuts are great braised, but when preparing the first cut, let it first cool in the cooking liquid. When it reaches room temperature, refrigerate the pot roast for a day. This enhances its flavor and tenderness. To serve, reheat the roast and then cut it across the grain. When you braise the second cut, cut it across the grain as well.

In our grandparents' day when brisket was cooked frequently, careful housewives always asked for the leaner first cut. Nowadays when it's cooked infrequently, we urge you to buy the juicier second cut.

CORNED BEEF

Corned beef is commonly made from brisket, although it is also made from bottom round. The cuts of beef are "corned," or processed and pickled. Most people buy it already corned and vacuum-packed. You can also corn it yourself, as we describe on page 32.

TOP ROUND

Top round, which is cut from the front section of the hindquarter, is the roast that many delis and meat counters cook and slice for roast beef. We suggest braising it, however, because it's a lean roast. It's also a large roast and may not fit in everyone's oven, or may not meet everyone's needs. You can cut it in half horizontally and freeze half for later use. If you have a choice between braising or stewing top round and chuck, choose chuck. Round tends to be drier.

BOTTOM ROUND

The bottom round lies next to the top round but is from a different muscle. Because of its coarse grain (marbling), the relatively tough meat requires slow, moist cooking. The top and bottom round roasts got their names from the way butchers have traditionally cut them, rather than from their placement in the animal.

EYE OF ROUND

The eye of round lies next to the bottom round in the hindquarter and is a circular, log-shaped piece of meat about 3 inches in diameter. When it's cut into steaks, they are called "eye round steaks" and are tough and chewy and not too pleasant when grilled, broiled, or pan-broiled. Because of its dryness, we suggest pot roasting or stewing this cut of meat.

POT ROAST

Pot roast is a dish, not a cut of meat. Any relatively large cut of beef does well when pot roasted, or, to use an old-fashioned term, when it is "potted." We don't recommend using this method to cook the more tender roasts, such as rib roasts, sirloin roasts, or whole fillets. Instead, use tougher cuts that are improved by braising. In order of preference, we like the following cuts for pot roast: chuck, whole flat iron, brisket, bottom round, and eye of round. The long, slow braising tenderizes the meat and gives it and the other ingredients in the pot a deep, rich flavor. Pot roasts can be cooked in the oven or on top of the stove over low, steady heat. For the very best flavor, let the meat and other ingredients cool in the cooking liquid once cooked, and then refrigerate them. Reheat and serve the next day. This way, the meat absorbs all the good flavors in the liquid as it cools, and when reheated, tastes great.

OTHER CUTS OF BEEF

PLATE

Although the plate is composed of layers of fat and lean meat, it tends to be a little stringy—yet it has very good flavor. It enriches gravies, soups, and stews and, because of its texture, must be simmered slowly in liquid, usually water or stock, until tender. Plate is sold flat or rolled. It is cut from the forequarter and lies in the belly area behind the foreshank and brisket and below the short ribs.

SHORT RIBS

In our shop, we refer to short ribs by their German name, *flanken*. They are cut from the ends of the rib roast and the plate, which means they lie between these two parts of the animal.

Short ribs contain layers of lean meat and fat and have a flat rib bone. The ribs are about 8 inches long and are usually cut crosswise into three sections, each about 2½ inches long. These short "riblets" are called flanken, too. When short ribs are cut into 3- or 5-inch lengths or longer, they are called English style. Both these and flanken are good grilled or braised. See our recipe for Korean-Style Barbecued Short Ribs, page 69.

Short ribs make excellent boiled beef and enhance the flavor of soups and stews. Another popular way to cut these ribs is along the bone. These boneless ribs are best cut by the butcher, although home cooks equipped with a very sharp knife and some good skills can cut the meat from the bone. This meat, cut lengthwise from the bone, is wonderful when cooked in a flavorful stew.

BEEF SPARERIBS

Beef spareribs are the bones that come off the prime rib, and, as such, are very flavorful. When they are removed from the prime rib roast, what is left is a boneless prime rib roast. Spareribs are usually about 8 inches long but may be cut so that they are shorter. They are cut from the same bone as that for the bone-in rib steak and are great for grilling, broiling, and even for slow roasting.

CUBED MEAT FOR STEW

The most desirable meat for stewing is from the chuck portion cut from the neck, because the relatively high amount of fat makes it rich, juicy, and flavorful. When you buy chuck for stew meat, buy the first or center cut. Boneless is easier to work with, although it's equally delicious on the bone. But chuck is not the only meat that can be cut into cubes for stewing. In order of preference, we like: chuck, boneless short ribs, flap (which is the tail of the porterhouse), shoulder, top round, and bottom round or any bits and pieces of meat the butcher needs to use up.

Don't think that a more expensive cut of beef, such as sirloin or fillet, will produce a better stew. The long, slow cooking is better suited for tougher cuts that need to tenderize as they braise, while more tender cuts of beef tend to dry out when braised.

BEEF SHANK

Cut from both the forequarter and the hindquarter, beef shank is sometimes called "beef osso buco". It's the shin of the leg, which surrounds a small marrow bone, similar to veal osso buco. Our preference is the foreshank, which is moister than the hindshank. This cut makes great beef stock and soup, and is good for dishes that require long braising. Beef shank may not be easy to find and may have to be special ordered. For some recipes that call for beef shanks, you may substitute veal shanks—but it's usually not a good idea to replace veal shanks with beef shanks.

BEEF MARROWBONES

Beef marrowbones are from the hindlegs or forelegs and are usually cut crosswise to expose the marrow. We love the rich flavor of marrow and how it deepens the flavor of many dishes. Depending on where they are cut, marrowbones can be from ¾ to 2 inches in diameter. The marrow in the bone should be ivory white and firm, never yellowed or soft.

It's easy to extract the marrow if you chill the bones first and then push the firm marrow out with your thumb or forefinger. Some recipes call for marrow to be soaked in water and others call for it to be blanched.

Don't shy away from making a recipe calling for marrowbone. It's not hard to get from a good butcher and its flavor is wonderful.

BEEF CHEEKS

Although they are not expensive, beef cheeks are considered a delicacy by some. They are cut from the muscles on either side of the cheek bones and are coarsely textured, requiring long, slow cooking. They have a good, deep flavor and so benefit from being paired with other mild-tasting ingredients and properly seasoned before they are braised. This is the best—and many would say the only—way to cook them. They usually have to be special ordered and are typically packaged frozen.

GROUND BEEF

When you buy ground beef, please take our advice: Don't buy beef that is already ground and on display in a refrigerated cabinet. Ask the butcher to grind the meat for you as you wait. You never know exactly what is in the pre-ground mixture; it could contain any part of the animal, including trimmings that you would probably prefer not to eat. If you are dealing with a new butcher, the best way to get top-quality ground beef is to use the advice of a mother who sent her young daughter shopping. She told the girl to ask for "a pound of the top of the round." After it had been cut and weighed, she told her to say, "Ground, please."

Ground chuck is the classic choice for hamburgers and other ground meat dishes. Ground sirloin is sweet, lean, and tender and makes a good burger; and it is also recommended for steak tartare. Although most meat markets don't make flap (the tail of the porterhouse) available as ground meat, it has become one of our specialties. It's juicy and sweet-tasting and makes a truly delightful hamburger or meat loaf.

For the very best flavor and texture, we suggest that you buy two cuts of beef and have them ground together so that they are evenly mixed. This way, you will get enough fat and enough lean meat for great flavor, pleasing texture, and good moisture. The end result will be a fantastic burger, meatball, or meat loaf! In order of preference, our favorite combinations for ground-beef mixtures are: chuck and hanger steak, chuck and sirloin, chuck and flap. Top or bottom round alone makes a lean and tasty burger.

STEAK
Top Round
NDON BROIL
PRIME RIB
hâteaubriand
ank BRISKET
TENDERL

RECIPES

Steak Tartare

When you make steak tartare, it's crucial to buy meat from a reputable butcher you know. We recommend beef fillet (tenderloin) for this recipe, and partially freeze it so that it's easier to chop.

SERVES 4 TO 5 AS AN APPETIZER

1	pound beef fillet cut into 2 or 3 medallions wrapped individually and placed in the freezer for 30 to 45 minutes
1/3	cup minced yellow onion
	Scant 1 teaspoon minced garlic
3	tablespoons chopped cornichons (6 to 8; chopped into 1/8-inch dice)
1 1/2	tablespoons small capers, rinsed if packed in vinegar
1	large anchovy fillet, minced
2 1/2	tablespoons finely chopped fresh flat-leaf parsley
	Kosher salt
1/4	teaspoon freshly ground black pepper
1	tablespoon extra-virgin olive oil
1/3	cup homemade Mayonnaise (page 276)
2 1/2	tablespoons chili sauce or ketchup
1 1/2	tablespoons Dijon mustard
1/2	teaspoon Tabasco sauce
1	teaspoon Worcestershire sauce
1	large baguette, cut on a steep bias into slices and lightly toasted

1. Place the chilled beef medallions flat-side down on a clean work surface and, using a sharp knife, cut each into ¼-inch-thick slices. Stack a few of these slices and cut lengthwise into ¼-inch-wide strips. Turn the bundle 90 degrees and cut across the strips to make ¼-inch dice and transfer to a medium bowl. Repeat with the remaining beef, returning the bowl to the refrigerator between batches. If pieces are any larger than ¼ inch, return the diced beef to the work surface and coarsely chop to reduce the size. Cover tightly and chill for at least 15 minutes. Beef and other chopped ingredients can be prepared an hour or two ahead of time and kept separately, tightly covered in the refrigerator.

2. When ready to serve, gently combine the beef with the onion, garlic, cornichons, capers, anchovy, 2 tablespoons of the parsley, ½ teaspoon salt, the black pepper, and oil and return to the refrigerator, covered. In a small bowl, mix together the mayonnaise, chile sauce, mustard, Tabasco, Worcestershire, and ½ teaspoon salt, stirring to combine thoroughly. Remove the beef mixture from refrigerator and gently fold into it all but 1 tablespoon of the mayonnaise mixture until just combined. Taste and add salt and any or all of the remaining mayonnaise mixture to your taste. Place servings of steak tartare off-center on appetizer plates and sprinkle with the remaining parsley. Fan slices of toasted baguette alongside the beef and serve immediately.

True Texas Chili

This Texas classic doesn't include beans or tomatoes, only beef, homemade chile paste, and a few flavorings. It's what Texans call a "Bowl o' Red" and tastes intensely of its two main ingredients. Take care to cook the chili at the barest possible simmer to avoid evaporating the sauce before the beef is tender. Whatever combination of dried chiles you use, make sure they're as fresh as possible by buying from a store with good turnover. Dried chiles should be pliable (but not damp) and without signs of mold.

SERVES 4

2	ounces dried, whole New Mexico (California), guajillo, or pasilla chiles, or a combination (6 to 8 chiles)
1 1/2	teaspoons ground cumin seed
1/2	teaspoon freshly ground black pepper
	Kosher salt
5	tablespoons lard, vegetable oil, or rendered beef suet
2 1/2	pounds boneless beef chuck, well trimmed and cut into 3/4-inch cubes (to yield 2 pounds after trimming)
1/3	cup finely chopped onion
3	large cloves garlic, minced
2	cups Beef Stock (page 302), or canned low-sodium beef broth, plus more as needed
2 1/4	cups water, plus more as needed
2	tablespoons masa harina (corn tortilla flour)
1	tablespoon firmly packed dark brown sugar, plus more as needed
1 1/2	tablespoons distilled white vinegar, plus more as needed
	Sour cream
	Lime wedges

1. Place the chiles in a straight-sided large skillet over medium-low heat and gently toast until fragrant, 2 to 3 minutes per side. Don't let them burn or they'll turn bitter. Place the chiles in a bowl and cover them with very hot water and soak until soft, 15 to 45 minutes, turning once or twice.
2. Drain the chiles; split them and remove the stems and seeds (a brief rinse helps remove seeds, but don't wash away the flesh). Place the chiles in the bowl of a blender and add the cumin, black pepper, 1 tablespoon salt, and ¼ cup of the water. Purée the mixture, adding more water as needed (and occasionally scraping down the sides of the blender jar), until a smooth, slightly fluid paste forms (you want to eliminate all but the tiniest bits of skin). Set the chile paste aside.
3. Return the skillet to medium-high heat and melt 2 tablespoons of the lard. When it begins to smoke, swirl the skillet to coat and add half of the beef. Lightly brown on at least two sides, about 3 minutes per side, reducing the heat if the meat threatens to burn. Transfer to a bowl and repeat with 2 more tablespoons of lard and the remaining beef. Reserve.
4. Let the skillet cool slightly, and place it over medium-low heat. Melt the remaining 1 tablespoon of lard in the skillet; add the onion and garlic and cook gently for 3 to 4 minutes, stirring occasionally. Add the stock, the remaining 2 cups of water, and gradually whisk in the masa harina to avoid lumps. Stir in the reserved chile paste, scraping the bottom of the skillet with a spatula to loosen any browned bits. Add the reserved beef (and any juices in the bowl) and bring to a simmer over high heat. Reduce heat to maintain the barest possible simmer (just a few bubbles breaking the surface) and cook, stirring occasionally, until the meat is tender but still somewhat firm and 1½ to 2 cups of thickened but still liquid sauce surrounds the cubes of meat, about 2 hours.
5. Stir in the brown sugar and vinegar thoroughly and add more salt to taste; gently simmer for 10 minutes more. At this point, it may look like there is excess sauce. Turn off the heat and let the chili stand for at least 30 minutes, during which time the meat will absorb about half of the remaining sauce in the skillet, leaving the meat bathed in a thick, somewhat fluid sauce. Stir in additional broth or water if the mixture seems too dry. If the mixture seems a bit loose and wet, allow it to simmer a bit more (sometimes we like to partially crush the cubes of beef with the back of a spoon to let them absorb more sauce). Adjust the balance of flavors with a bit of additional salt, sugar, or vinegar, if you like.
6. Reheat gently and serve in individual bowls with a dollop of sour cream on top and a lime wedge on the side.

Corned Beef

Although corned beef takes five days to cure, it is otherwise very simple to make and more than worth the time. The result is a revelation to those familiar only with the stuff found in delis and diners, and if you've got leftovers, you can make the best Reuben Sandwiches (page 35) and Corned Beef Hash (page 33) you've ever had.

SERVES 8 TO 10

1 ½	cups kosher salt
½	cup brown sugar
4	large cloves garlic, crushed
2	sprigs fresh thyme
1	recipe Corned Beef Pickling Spice (page 298)
1	ounce pink curing salt, such as Insta-Cure #1 or Prague Powder #1 (see Note)
5	pounds fatty beef brisket (2nd cut if possible—called the "point cut"—but 1st cut works well, too)
1	medium onion, coarsely chopped
1	rib celery, coarsely chopped
1	large carrot, peeled and coarsely chopped

1. Put the kosher salt, sugar, garlic, thyme, pickling spice, and 1 quart water in a 6- to 8-quart pot. Bring to a boil over high heat, stirring to dissolve the salt and sugar. Remove from the heat and let the mixture steep for 5 minutes. Stir in the curing salt to dissolve, add 3 quarts of cool water, and transfer to the refrigerator to chill for at least 2 hours.
2. Put the brisket in a lidded, high-sided, food-grade plastic or metal container just large enough to contain the meat. Pour in the cooled curing liquid to cover the meat, weighting it with small plates, if necessary, to keep the beef submerged beneath the brine. Cover and refrigerate for 5 days, turning the meat over after 2 or 3 days.
3. Remove the meat from the liquid and place in a pot large enough to just contain it (reserve the curing liquid for now). Rinse the meat in two or three changes of water and drain. Strain the herbs, spices, and garlic from the curing liquid and discard the liquid. Add the spices to the pot with the meat and cover by 2 inches of water. Add the onion, celery, and carrot and bring just to a simmer over medium-high heat. Cover, reduce the heat to maintain the barest possible simmer, and cook until very tender but not yet falling apart (a carving fork should slide easily into the meat), 3 to 4 hours.
4. Carefully transfer the corned beef to a cutting board and, using a sharp knife, slice thinly across the grain. Serve each portion moistened with a few tablespoons of the cooking liquid (reserve enough cooking liquid to reheat any remaining beef).

NOTE: Curing salt helps protect curing meat from unsafe microorganisms and comes in several formulations for use in different circumstances. Here, we use one that contains just pure salt and 6.25% sodium nitrite (aka Insta-Cure #1). It is readily available online from butcher and sausage-making supply stores. Two that commonly sell to retail customers are: The Sausage Maker (sausagemaker.com; 716-824-5814) and Butcher & Packer (butcher-packer.com; 800-521-3188).

Corned Beef Hash

Although you can buy the corned beef for this dish at your local deli, there's no doubt that the best corned beef hash is made with a piece of our own homemade corned beef. When topped with a poached egg or two and served with thick slices of toast, this hash is the prince of leftovers.

SERVES 2

4	tablespoons unsalted butter
½	medium onion, finely chopped
½	green bell pepper, finely chopped
2	large cloves garlic, minced
1	teaspoon finely chopped fresh thyme
2	cups thickly sliced, coarsely shredded Corned Beef (facing page)
2	cups coarsely chopped cooked small red potatoes in their skins (about ½-inch pieces)
	Kosher salt
	Fresh, coarsely ground black pepper
¼	cup corned beef cooking liquid (facing page), Beef Stock (page 302), low-sodium broth, or water, plus more as needed.
2	teaspoons Worcestershire sauce
	Poached or fried eggs (optional)

1. Melt the butter in an 8- to 10-inch skillet (preferably well-seasoned cast iron) over medium-low heat. Add the onion and bell pepper and cook gently until the onion is translucent, about 5 minutes, stirring occasionally. Stir in the garlic and thyme and cook for 1 minute. Add the corned beef, potatoes, 1 teaspoon salt, and 8 to 10 generous grindings of black pepper, stirring to combine well.
2. Stir in the corned beef cooking liquid, ¼ cup water, and the Worcestershire sauce; spread the mixture evenly across the skillet, pressing on the hash with the back of a spatula to flatten the mixture so it makes thorough contact with the skillet. Raise the heat to medium and let the liquid evaporate. Continue cooking and pressing occasionally until the hash is browned in spots, 4 to 6 minutes, reducing the heat if it seems to be cooking too quickly. Scrape up the hash along with any browned bits; flip over and cook until the second side is browned like the first, another 4 to 5 minutes.
3. Break up the hash with the tip of your spatula, and repeat this pressing down, browning and flipping every few minutes until the hash has a mix of well-browned meat and potato pieces with lots of crisp edges, about 15 minutes more, adding a tablespoon or two of corned beef cooking liquid or water if the mixture seems a bit dry (don't rush the cooking; reduce the heat to medium-low if the hash seems to be cooking too fast). Add salt to taste. Serve each portion of hash topped with one or two poached or fried eggs, if you like.

Reuben Sandwich

Made with our own home-cured corned beef, our own Russian dressing, and topped with good-quality Swiss cheese, our Reuben Sandwich is a four-star eating experience. The only trick is to allow the cheese to melt completely by not rushing the browning of the sandwiches.

SERVES 2

- 1/2 pound thinly sliced Corned Beef (page 32), at room temperature
- 3 tablespoons Corned Beef cooking liquid (page 32) or water
- 4 pieces Jewish-style rye bread, such as Levy's
- 4 tablespoons Russian Dressing, plus more for serving (page 277)
- 3 ounces good-quality Swiss cheese, such as Emmentaler, thinly sliced, at room temperature
- 1 cup sauerkraut, drained and blotted dry, at room temperature
- 4 tablespoons unsalted butter

1. Preheat the oven or a toaster oven to 350°F. Place the corned beef on a large rectangle of foil and moisten with the cooking liquid. Fold up to form a tightly sealed, loose pouch and cook until the beef is heated through, about 15 minutes (to save time, this can also be done in a microwave with a heavy plastic container or on a plate covered with plastic wrap).
2. Smear one side of each bread slice with 1 tablespoon of the Russian Dressing. Divide the cheese between two of the slices. Neatly top each portion of cheese with half of the hot corned beef, followed by half of the sauerkraut, distributing them just to the edges of the bread. Top with the two remaining slices of dressed bread.
3. Melt 2 tablespoons of the butter in an 8- to 10-inch heavy skillet over medium-low heat. When the foam subsides, add the sandwiches, cheese-side down, and weight them evenly with a second skillet topped with a couple cans of food. (Alternatively, you can press regularly with the back of a spatula. In both cases, you want to compact the sandwiches somewhat without crushing them.) Cook gently until the first side is a rich golden brown, 4 to 6 minutes.
4. Remove the sandwiches to a plate and melt the remaining 2 tablespoons butter. Return the sandwiches to the skillet and cook the second side, without weighting them, until golden brown and the cheese has melted. (Flip the sandwich back and forth a few more times to completely melt the cheese without burning the toast, if necessary. This also crisps the first side, which can get soft.) Cut the sandwiches in half with the sharp stroke of a bread knife. Serve with more Russian Dressing on the side, if desired.

Beef Jerky

Our beef jerky is dried in a low oven and not in the open air as it was when it was a staple of pioneer life. We suspect this version is a lot tastier and more tender than the original. It makes a lovely snack or accompaniment to a glass of wine or beer. If you have a good-size oven, the recipe doubles easily.

MAKES ABOUT 3/4 POUND

- 2 pounds beef flank steak, trimmed of excess fat
- 2/3 cup Worcestershire sauce
- 2/3 cup soy sauce
- 1/2 teaspoon onion powder
- 1/2 teaspoon garlic powder
- 1/2 teaspoon crushed red pepper flakes
- 1 heaping teaspoon freshly ground black pepper
- 2 tablespoons molasses or brown sugar

1. Using a sharp chef's knife, cut the beef into strips between 1/8 and 1/4 inch thick and 5 to 10 inches long (this can be made easier by partially freezing the beef for 1 to 3 hours prior to cutting). Note: Cutting *with* the grain produces the classic, chewy texture of beef jerky; cutting *across* the grain yields a more tender texture. Try both, if you like, and see which you prefer.

2. Combine the remaining ingredients in a double-thick resealable plastic bag, shaking or stirring to dissolve the solid ingredients. Add the sliced beef, massaging the bag to coat all the pieces. Refrigerate for 3 to 6 hours, turning once to redistribute the marinade during this time.

3. Preheat the oven to 175°F (an oven thermometer is a help here if your oven setting doesn't go that low). Arrange baking or cookie racks over two large, foil-lined rimmed baking sheets. Drain the beef and lay the slices side by side on the baking racks (alternatively, if you don't have baking racks, the beef can be laid directly on the aluminum foil; you'll just have to turn the pieces over about halfway through the drying process). Place the beef in the oven and leave the door ajar about 5 inches by wedging a folded kitchen towel into it.

4. Dry the beef for 3 to 6 hours, depending on the thickness of the slices and your preferred level of chewiness (test as you go, keeping in mind that the jerky will continue to firm up as it cools). During drying, the oven should maintain a temperature of about 170°F; adjust heat as needed. Well-dried beef should last for a month or two (more tender, less dried beef, a few weeks) stored in an airtight container and kept in a cool, dry place.

Chicken-Fried Steak

This Texas classic has nothing to do with chicken but is all about beef and the creamy pan sauce that accompanies it. And for those who appreciate the savor of the original item, it's worth it to fry your steaks in pure lard.

SERVES 2

	All-purpose flour
	Kosher salt
1	teaspoon freshly ground black pepper
1	teaspoon ground cumin seed
1	egg
1 3/4	cups whole milk
1/4	cup heavy cream
	Tabasco sauce
1	generous cup lard or vegetable oil
Two	8-ounce pieces beef top round, each cut about 1/2-inch thick and pounded to 1/4 inch thickness
1/3	cup minced onion
	Worcestershire sauce for serving (optional)

1. Place 1 cup of flour in a wide rimmed dish or plate and mix well with 2 tablespoons salt, the black pepper, and cumin.
2. Whisk the egg with 1/4 cup of the milk, the heavy cream, and 3 or 4 generous dashes of Tabasco sauce in a small bowl. Pour the mixture into another wide-rimmed dish or plate.
3. Preheat the oven to 200°F. Place a rack large enough to hold the steaks over a rimmed baking sheet and set aside.
4. Heat the lard in a 12-inch heavy skillet over medium-high heat. Sprinkle the steak very lightly with salt on both sides. When the lard reaches 350°F to 365°F, working with one steak at a time, dredge the steak in the seasoned flour, shaking off any excess. Then, dip it into the egg mixture, allowing the excess to briefly run off. Dredge a second time in the seasoned flour, this time by piling the flour on the top of the steak and lightly pressing to help it adhere to the egg; shake off excess. Slip the steak into the hot lard and cook until rich golden brown on the outside and cooked to medium doneness within, turning once, about 2 minutes per side. Using a large spatula (to prevent damaging the crust) transfer the steak to the rack and baking sheet and keep warm in the oven. Repeat with the second piece of steak.
5. Discard all but 3 tablespoons of the fat in the skillet and let the skillet cool slightly. Return the skillet to medium-low heat and add the minced onion; cook gently for 1 minute, stirring. Whisk in 2 tablespoons of the flour and cook gently for 2 minutes, whisking regularly. Gradually whisk in the remaining 1½ cups milk and bring to a simmer over high heat, whisking regularly. Reduce the heat to medium-low and cook at a gentle simmer, stirring with a wood or rubber spatula and scraping down the sides of the skillet, until the sauce reaches a consistency just a bit thicker than heavy cream, 2 to 4 minutes more. Stir in any juices beneath the steaks and season with 1 teaspoon salt and a few drops of Tabasco or Worcestershire sauce, if you like.
6. Serve the steaks on large plates topped with the sauce, passing the Tabasco and Worcestershire at the table.

Flat Iron Steaks with Roasted Red Pepper Butter

This recipe makes more Roasted Red Pepper Butter than you'll use on the steaks. Store the remaining butter in the freezer; it's great as a delicious last-minute sauce for chicken, pork, lamb, fish, and vegetables.

SERVES 2

12	tablespoons unsalted butter (1½ sticks), 8 of the tablespoons well chilled and cut into pieces
2	tablespoons minced shallot
2	large cloves garlic, minced
½	teaspoon finely chopped fresh thyme
2	roasted red bell peppers (page 284)
1¼	teaspoons smoked sweet Spanish paprika, such as pimenton de la Vera "dolce," or regular sweet paprika
1¼	teaspoons kosher salt
	Freshly ground black pepper
Four	4-ounce chuck blade steaks (flat iron steaks), cut ¾ inch thick
2	tablespoons vegetable oil

1. Melt 4 tablespoons of the butter (not chilled) in a small skillet over medium-low heat. Add the shallot and garlic and cook until softened but not browned, about 3 minutes, stirring occasionally. Stir in the thyme; remove from the heat and let cool for 3 or 4 minutes.
2. Put the 8 tablespoons well-chilled butter, the roasted peppers, paprika, and salt in the bowl of a food processor. Scrape the contents of the skillet with the shallot-garlic butter into the processor and blend, pulsing at first, until smooth and well incorporated, scraping down the sides of the bowl as needed. Pack the flavored butter in a ramekin or roll it up in a large piece of plastic into a sausage shape. Refrigerate until firm. (Roasted Red Pepper Butter keeps in the refrigerator for a week or so and frozen for up to a few months.) Measure 2 to 3 tablespoons Roasted Red Pepper Butter for each 8-ounce serving of steak and let sit at room temperature while you prepare the steaks. Preheat dinner plates.
3. Generously salt and pepper the steaks. Preheat a large, heavy skillet over medium-high heat until almost smoking. Add the oil, swirling to coat the skillet. Add the steaks and reduce the heat to medium. Cook for 3½ to 4 minutes per side for medium-rare. Transfer the steaks to heated plates. Top each portion of steak with 2 to 3 tablespoons flavored butter and serve.

Seared Strip Steak with Black and Green Peppercorns

It's key to cook the steak in a preheated, heavy skillet over medium heat, but not much hotter. You don't want the peppercorns to burn and turn bitter. A lightly smoking skillet is fine; a violently smoking skillet isn't necessary here.

SERVES 2

2 1/2	cups Beef Stock (page 302), or canned low-sodium beef broth
1/2	small onion, chopped
1/2	small carrot, peeled and chopped
1/2	bay leaf
1	small sprig fresh thyme
1	teaspoon whole black peppercorns, plus 1 heaping tablespoon
1	heaping tablespoon dried green peppercorns (see Note)
2	boneless strip steaks cut 1 1/4 inch thick (12 to 16 ounces each), trimmed of excess fat (see Note)
	Kosher salt
	Vegetable oil
3	tablespoons unsalted butter, cut into pieces
1	heaping tablespoon finely chopped shallots
2	tablespoons cognac or similar brandy
1/4	cup dry white wine
1	tablespoon finely chopped fresh flat-leaf parsley

1. Put the stock, onion, carrot, bay leaf, thyme, and 1 teaspoon of the black peppercorns in a saucepan and bring to a boil over high heat. Lower the heat slightly and simmer until the broth is reduced in volume to ½ cup (including vegetables), 20 to 30 minutes. Pass the broth through a fine-mesh strainer into a small bowl, pressing on the vegetables to extract any liquid remaining. Discard solids and set the broth aside.

2. Meanwhile, place the remaining 1 heaping tablespoon of black peppercorns between two layers of a clean kitchen towel or inside a thick zip-lock plastic bag. Working with the underside of a small heavy skillet, a kitchen mallet, or a rolling pin, crush the peppercorns until cracked into coarse bits (they shouldn't become powder) by either sliding the tool while applying pressure or lightly pounding. Transfer the peppercorns to a dish large enough to hold the steaks. Repeat with the green peppercorns (they'll require less pressure than the black). Mix the peppercorns together in the dish. Firmly press the peppercorn mixture into the steaks, coating them evenly. Let the steaks rest at room temperature for at least 30 minutes. Preheat the oven to 200°F and warm the serving plates.

3. Preheat a heavy (preferably cast-iron) skillet just large enough to hold the steaks without crowding over medium heat for 3 minutes. Salt the steaks very generously on both sides. Cover the skillet with a thin film of oil; if the oil fails to smoke within 20 seconds or so, raise the heat slightly. When the oil begins to smoke, add the steaks, patting gently to help them make full contact with the skillet. Cook about 5 minutes per side for medium-rare and 1 to 3 minutes more per side for medium to well-done. Transfer the steaks to a dish and keep warm in the oven.

4. Let the skillet cool slightly and return to medium heat. Melt 1 tablespoon of the butter and cook the shallots gently for 1 minute, stirring occasionally. Add the cognac and wine and cook until reduced by half, about 2 minutes, scraping the bottom of the skillet to loosen any browned bits. Add the reserved beef broth and reduce by half again. Add any juices that have accumulated beneath the steaks and reduce the heat to low. Whisk in the remaining 2 tablespoons butter and the parsley and cook very gently, until the sauce thickens slightly, a minute or less. Salt to taste. Place the steaks on the warmed serving plates, spoon sauce over each steak, and serve.

NOTE: Green peppercorns are commonly available in two forms: pickled in brine or dried. If the dried type is unavailable, prepare the recipe with double the amount of black peppercorns. Some people don't like to eat an entire 3/4-pound or 1-pound slab of steak. You can instead serve smaller portions by simply cutting each steak in half crosswise and proceeding with the recipe.

Strip Steak with Oysters and Rockefeller Butter

Most familiar to late nineteenth and early twentieth–century diners, the pairing of beef and oysters is unusual but fabulously delicious. Ask your fishmonger if he's willing to shuck the oysters for you and reserve the oyster liquor. Try to have this done on the day you will be serving the dish; shucked oysters don't keep very well and the fresher they are, the better. This recipe makes more Rockefeller Butter than you'll need, but it's great as an instant sauce for chicken, fish, and vegetables. We call for strip steak or filet mignon here, but nearly any tender steak can be substituted.

SERVES 2

ROCKEFELLER BUTTER

- 12 tablespoons unsalted butter (1½ sticks), 8 of the tablespoons well chilled and cut into pieces
- ¼ cup finely chopped celery
- ¼ cup finely chopped fennel
- ⅓ cup thinly sliced scallion
- Half clove garlic, sliced
- ½ cup loosely packed chopped fresh flat-leaf parsley
- 1 cup loosely packed chopped watercress (tough stems removed)
- ½ teaspoon finely chopped fresh thyme
- Kosher salt
- 1 tablespoon Pernod, or similar anise-flavored spirit
- ¼ teaspoon Tabasco sauce
- 12 to 18 shucked oysters, stray shell bits removed, ¼ cup plus 1 tablespoon oyster liquor reserved
- Freshly ground black pepper
- One 1-inch-thick, 12- to 14-ounce boneless strip steak, trimmed and cut in two equal portions, or two 1-inch-thick tenderloin steaks (filet mignon), about 5 ounces each
- 2 tablespoons vegetable oil

1. To make the Rockefeller Butter, melt 4 tablespoons of the butter (not chilled) in a medium skillet over medium heat. When the foam subsides, add the celery, fennel, scallion, garlic, parsley, watercress, thyme, and ½ teaspoon salt. Cook gently without browning for 4 minutes, stirring regularly. Add the Pernod and ¼ cup oyster liquor and cook until evaporated.
2. Scrape the contents of the skillet into the bowl of a food processor and let cool slightly. Add the Tabasco and the 8 tablespoons chilled butter and process, pulsing at first, until smooth and well incorporated, scraping down the sides of the bowl as needed. Pack the flavored butter in a ramekin or roll it up in a large piece of plastic into a sausage shape. Refrigerate until firm.
3. Put 1 tablespoon of remaining oyster liquor and the oysters in a medium skillet along with 1 generous tablespoon of Rockefeller Butter. Set the skillet aside. Put 4 tablespoons of Rockefeller Butter, in 3 or 4 pieces, on a small plate and reserve in the refrigerator. Preheat dinner plates.
4. Generously salt and pepper the steaks. Preheat a small, heavy skillet over medium-high heat until almost smoking. Add the oil, swirling to coat the skillet. Add the steaks and reduce the heat to medium. Cook for about 4 minutes per side for medium-rare. Transfer the steaks to heated plates.
5. Place the skillet with the oysters over medium heat, swirling to distribute the butter. Cook until just heated through and the edges of the oysters curl, 2 to 4 minutes (depending on size), turning carefully with tongs or a soup spoon halfway through. Turn off the heat and add the chilled 4 tablespoons butter, swirling the skillet to melt and emulsify the butter. Spoon the butter and oysters over the steaks and serve.

Roasted Beef Fillet with Béarnaise Sauce

Although it may seem like a throwback to the 1960s, a roast beef fillet with béarnaise sauce is just so good that it doesn't hurt to bring it back now and again. It's especially delicious with steamed asparagus or green beans served alongside.

SERVES 6 TO 8

One	3-pound beef fillet, trimmed, about 3 1/2 to 4 inches in diameter, in one piece, tied for roasting
1	tablespoon unsalted butter, at room temperature
1	tablespoon olive oil
2 1/2	teaspoons kosher salt
2	teaspoons fresh, coarsely cracked black pepper
	Béarnaise Sauce (page 281)

1. Let the beef sit at room temperature for 1 hour or so before cooking.
2. Arrange an oven rack in the lower central part of the oven and preheat the oven to 550°F.
3. Place the beef in a rectangular glass or earthenware baking dish just large enough to contain it. Thoroughly rub or brush the butter and oil all over the beef. Evenly season on all sides with the salt and pepper.
4. Roast for 15 minutes. Turn the beef over and roast until a thermometer inserted in the center of the meat reads 130°F for medium-rare, 10 to 15 minutes more (to prevent the loss of internal juices, try to minimize poking the meat with the thermometer). Transfer the beef to a cutting board designed to catch the juices and let rest for 5 minutes. Cut into about ½-inch slices and serve with Béarnaise Sauce on the side.

Carbonade of Beef in Belgian Beer

Carbonade of beef is elemental, beefy, and delicious. Serve it with whatever Belgian beer you've put in the pot, along with a side dish of steamed or roasted small potatoes.

SERVES 6

3	tablespoons vegetable oil or lard
3	pounds trimmed beef chuck, cut into 2-inch pieces
4	tablespoons unsalted butter
6	medium onions, halved lengthwise and sliced
3	tablespoons all-purpose flour
3	cups Belgian beer or ale (see Note)
1	cup Beef Stock (page 302), or canned low-sodium beef broth
2	bay leaves
2	sprigs fresh thyme
	Kosher salt
½	teaspoon freshly ground black pepper
2	teaspoons tightly packed brown sugar

1. Heat the oil in a 10- to 12-quart heavy large pot over medium-high heat. When it is hot, add the beef, working in two batches, and cook until deeply browned on two sides, 5 to 7 minutes per side. Remove the beef to a plate.
2. Drain the fat from the pot and return it to high heat. Melt the butter and add the onions. Stir regularly for a minute or so and scrape up any browned bits stuck to the bottom of the pot with the help of the moisture given off by the onions. Cook, stirring regularly, until reduced in volume and beginning to brown, 6 to 8 minutes. Reduce the heat to low and cook gently until the onions are rich golden brown and almost creamy, about 30 minutes, stirring occasionally and reducing the heat if they threaten to burn.
3. Sprinkle the flour over the onions and cook, stirring almost continuously until the flour smells lightly toasty, 3 to 5 minutes. Stir in the beer, stock, bay leaves, thyme, 2 teaspoons salt, pepper, brown sugar, and the reserved beef and any juices on the plate. Bring to a simmer, scraping up any floury bits stuck to the bottom of the pot. Cover and cook at the barest possible simmer until the meat is very tender, 3 to 4 hours, stirring occasionally and checking to make sure pot is barely simmering.
4. Uncover and simmer gently until the liquid just lightly coats the back of a spoon, 10 to 20 minutes. Let the stew rest off the heat for 5 minutes; remove the bay leaves and thyme sprigs. Salt to taste and serve.

NOTE: Belgian beer styles vary greatly and, while any rich beer with good character can be used in this stew, there are a handful of unique, complex, and softly tart Belgian beers and ales that behave more like wine—both in the drinking and in the pot—and work a special kind of magic on this classic dish. Look for Liefmans *Goudenband* (a Flemish brown ale, which is beef carbonade's hometown brew), or any of the lambic-style beers called *gueuze*: Cantillon, Boon, and the more common Lindemans. Slightly sweet beers or ales will, of course, give a sweeter—but no less delicious—result. (If using a sweeter beer, reduce the brown sugar called for in the recipe, if you like.)

Provençal-Style Pot Roast

Flavored with orange peel, cinnamon, black olives, and lots of wine, this beloved southern French pot roast—or daube—becomes an outrageously satisfying feast when served over our mushroom-laced Provençal-style egg noodles.

SERVES 4 TO 5

- 2 tablespoons olive oil
- 4 ounces salt pork, cut into batons 1/4 inch thick and 1 inch long
- Kosher salt
- Freshly ground black pepper
- 3 pounds boneless beef chuck in one piece
- 2 medium onions, quartered lengthwise and peeled, root end attached
- 1/2 cup sliced shallots
- 2 medium carrots, peeled and sliced into rounds
- 12 large cloves garlic, lightly crushed and peeled
- 2 cups dry red wine
- One 15-ounce can crushed tomatoes in juice
- 2 sprigs fresh thyme, plus 2 teaspoons finely chopped fresh thyme leaves
- 1 bay leaf
- 1/8 teaspoon ground nutmeg
- One 1-inch-piece cinnamon stick
- 2 whole cloves
- Two 1-by-2-inch strips orange peel, white pith removed
- 1 pig's foot, split lengthwise by your butcher (about 1 pound)
- 1 cup small, mild-tasting black olives, such as Niçoise or Nyons
- 2 tablespoons finely chopped fresh flat-leaf parsley
- Egg Noodles for Provençal-Style Pot Roast (optional; facing page)

1. Put the oil and salt pork in a 10- to 12-quart ovenproof pot and set over medium heat. Cook until the salt pork is pale golden and crisp. Using a slotted spoon, transfer to a small plate.

2. Generously salt and pepper the beef on all sides. Raise the heat to medium-high and add the beef to the pot. Cook until deeply browned on all sides, 6 to 8 minutes per side, regulating the heat if it threatens to burn. During this time, add the onion quarters to the pot and cook until golden brown on both cut sides. Remove the meat and onions to a plate. Preheat the oven to 350°F.

3. Pour off all but 4 tablespoons of fat and return the pot to medium heat. Add the shallots, carrots, and garlic and cook, stirring occasionally, until pale gold at the edges, about 5 minutes. Add the wine and bring to a simmer. Simmer for 3 minutes, scraping up any browned bits stuck to the bottom of the pot. Add ½ cup water, the crushed tomatoes and their juices, thyme sprigs, bay leaf, nutmeg, and cinnamon. Stick the cloves into the orange peel and add to the pot.

4. Return the salt pork, beef, onions, and any juices on the plate to the pot. Add the split pig's foot to the pot and bring to a simmer. Cover tightly and transfer to the oven. Cook for 20 minutes. Reduce the oven temperature to 250° to 275°F to maintain the barest possible simmer in the covered pot. Cook until the meat is very tender, 3½ to 4 hours more, checking occasionally to make sure the pot is barely simmering (if, during cooking, the cinnamon or orange flavors come to dominate the other flavors, remove and discard one or both).

5. Remove the pot to the stovetop and let it rest, uncovered, for 5 minutes. Skim most of the fat from the surface and stir in the olives. Return to a gentle simmer and cook until the liquid has reduced by one-third and is richly flavored, about 1 hour more, occasionally basting the exposed surface of the beef. Remove the thyme sprigs, bay leaf, cinnamon stick, and orange peel, if you like.

6. Serve the beef smothered in its reduced braising liquid and garnished with the chopped parsley and thyme or with Egg Noodles for Provençal-Style Pot Roast.

Egg Noodles for Provençal-Style Pot Roast

SERVES 4

These noodles are richly flavored and satisfying, especially when served with our pot roast. This recipe is deliciously simple: egg noodles are tossed with sautéed mushrooms and some of the reduced pot roast braising liquid.

- 2 tablespoons extra-virgin olive oil
- 2 tablespoons unsalted butter
- 1/4 cup finely chopped shallots
- 10 ounces white mushrooms, quartered
- Kosher salt
- Freshly ground black pepper
- 3/4 pound ribbon egg noodles
- 1 1/2 cups Provençal-Style Pot Roast braising liquid (facing page), hot

1. Put the oil, butter, and shallots in a 10- to 12-inch skillet over medium-low heat. Cook gently for 3 minutes. Increase the heat to medium-high and add the mushrooms, tossing or stirring to coat. Cook until the mushrooms are just beginning to brown and are nearly tender, 4 to 5 minutes, tossing or stirring frequently. Reduce the heat to medium-low and cook until tender, a few minutes more. Stir in ½ teaspoon salt and a few grindings of black pepper. Remove from the heat and reserve. (The mushrooms can be prepared anytime during the preparation of Provençal-Style Pot Roast.)

2. When the pot roast has finished cooking (Step 5), cook the pasta in a large pot of well-salted water until tender but still a bit firm. Meanwhile, reheat the pot roast, if necessary. Drain the noodles and return to the pot. Scrape the contents of the skillet with the mushrooms into the noodles, stirring to coat. Stir in enough of the reduced pot-roast braising liquid to coat the noodles thoroughly. Divide the noodles among serving plates or wide, shallow bowls. Top with a portion of pot roast and a few spoonfuls of the reduced braising liquid. Garnish with the chopped parsley and thyme from the Provencal-Style Pot Roast and serve.

Neapolitan Long-Cooked Tomato-Meat Ragu

The grandma of all pasta sauces, this one takes all day to cook, but it's well worth it. We think the sauce is best enjoyed with just a bit of grated cheese on tube-shaped pasta or gnocchi. It is also used to flavor and partially moisten baked pasta specialties like lasagna or baked shells. The sauce can be added to sautéed wild mushrooms (especially porcini and black trumpets) to make a mushroom sauce, or combined with browned bits of pancetta or bacon to make it even meatier tasting. You can also toss in a handful of chopped fresh basil or parsley, or small amounts of finely chopped rosemary, sage, or thyme.

MAKES ABOUT 2 QUARTS

3	tablespoons extra-virgin olive oil, plus more as needed
3	pounds 1- to 2-inch thick pieces crosscut beef shank with marrowbones cut into 2- to 3-inch chunks
2	pounds pork hocks (or substitute split pig's feet)
1	medium onion, finely chopped
1	large head garlic, cloves peeled and crushed
2	cups red wine
Two	6-ounce cans tomato paste
Four	28-ounce cans whole tomatoes in juice, puréed with juices in a food processor or food mill
2	teaspoons kosher salt
1	teaspoon sugar, plus more as needed
1½	pounds fresh, unseasoned sweet pork sausage links

1. Heat the oil in a wide 12- to 14-quart pot over medium-high heat. When it is hot, add the beef and marrowbones and reduce the heat to medium. Cook until deeply browned on two sides, about 10 minutes per side (don't rush this; reduce the heat if browning too quickly). Transfer to a bowl and repeat with the pork hocks (these won't brown as darkly as the beef), adding more oil if needed.

2. Add the onion and garlic and cook gently until the garlic is just pale golden, 5 to 7 minutes, stirring occasionally. Add the wine; bring to a simmer and cook for 2 minutes, scraping up any browned bits stuck to the bottom of the pot. Reduce the heat to low and whisk in the tomato paste until dissolved. Let cook very slowly, with just a few bubbles breaking the surface, until the mixture is very concentrated, no longer fluid, and has darkened a few shades, 30 to 45 minutes, stirring regularly to prevent scorching. Each time you stir, scrape down the sides of the pot and then spread the paste across the bottom of the pot (don't rush this process; when done, the mixture should be at least as stiff as the tomato paste was when in the can).

3. Add the puréed tomatoes, salt, and sugar, whisking to incorporate. Add a bit more sugar if the tomatoes seem overly tart. Stir in the reserved beef, marrowbones, pork, and any juices in the bowl. Add the sausage to the pot and bring just to a simmer. Cover the pot, leaving the lid ajar a half inch. Reduce the heat so that no more than five or six bubbles break the surface at one time and cook for 5 hours, stirring well every hour or so.

4. After 5 hours, remove the meats and bones to a bowl with tongs or a slotted spoon, shaking or scraping any sauce clinging to them back into the pot. (It's fine if some very small bits of meat remain in the sauce; just sift through to make sure there are no stray pieces of bone. You can also pass the sauce through a colander or food mill with holes large enough to let the tomato sauce pass through while catching any stray meat bits.) Scrape out any marrow in the bones and add it to the pot along with any juices collected beneath the meats. Reserve the beef and sausages and discard the pork hocks.

5. Continue to cook the sauce, uncovered, at the same lazy rate as before—just a few bubbles breaking the surface at any one time—until the sauce falls from a spoon in fluid clumps and when a rubber spatula dragged across the bottom of the pot leaves a trail that slowly fills in behind the spatula, about 3 hours more. Stir regularly to prevent scorching.

NOTE: The sauce can be served on pasta—large, tubular shapes like rigatoni or ziti are best—using about 2 cups sauce for each pound of pasta. Cook the pasta in abundant salted water to al dente and reserve 2 cups of the cooking water. Reheat the sauce. Toss the drained pasta and sauce with about 1 cup of the reserved cooking water, stirring until sauce clings easily to the pasta but remains just slightly fluid (add more water as needed). Serve with freshly grated Parmigiano-Reggiano or pecorino romano cheese. The beef and sausage can be reheated in a small amount of sauce and either served atop the pasta or on the side. More commonly, they are served separately as part of a later meat course, perhaps with a green vegetable accompaniment. Let the sauce cool, and store covered in the refrigerator for 2 or 3 weeks or in the freezer for up to 6 months.

Stuffed Rolled Beef Fillet

This is an elegant restaurant dish from Parma, Italy, featuring that city's famous cured ham and aged cheese. These ingredients, along with a dose of garlic and herbs, flavor a fillet of beef topped with the seductively old-time flavors of Marsala, red wine, and cream. This dish is good with sautéed or steamed spinach. It can be assembled up to 1 day ahead. Store, covered, in refrigerator, and bring to room temperature before cooking.

SERVES 6

4	cloves garlic, peeled
	Kosher salt
1	tablespoon finely chopped fresh sage
1	tablespoon finely chopped fresh rosemary
½	teaspoon freshly ground black pepper
6	tablespoons extra-virgin olive oil
3	pounds beef fillet in one piece of even thickness, butterflied and pounded to ¾-inch thickness (see facing page)
1½	ounces finely grated Parmigiano-Reggiano, or similar cheese
¼	pound very thinly sliced prosciutto di Parma, or similar cured ham
⅔	cup dry Marsala wine, plus more as needed
⅔	cup red wine, such as a young, fruity Chianti
1	cup Beef Stock (page 302) or Chicken Stock (page 299), or canned low-sodium broth, plus more as needed
½	cup heavy cream, plus more as needed
1	tablespoon unsalted butter

1. Smash the garlic with the broad side of a chef's knife and sprinkle with ½ teaspoon salt. Roughly chop the garlic and then work the garlic and salt into a paste by repeatedly smearing it with the broad side of the knife against the work surface. Transfer the paste to a small bowl and add the sage, rosemary, black pepper, and oil, stirring to combine. Reserve.
2. Lay out the butterflied beef, cut-side up, with one of the lengthwise edges nearest you. Spread half of the reserved herb-garlic paste over the meat. Sprinkle with the cheese and lay out the ham in overlapping slices to just cover the entire surface. Starting with the edge nearest you, roll up the fillet, jelly-roll style, so it resumes its original shape. Tie up as for a roast using butcher's twine tied at 1- to 2-inch intervals.
3. Preheat the oven to 400°F.
4. Salt the meat generously on all sides and place, seam down, on a small roasting rack that just fits within an ovenproof skillet or small roasting pan. Set the meat and rack aside over a plate and heat the remaining 3 tablespoons oil in the skillet or roasting pan over medium-high heat. When the oil shimmers, add the meat and cook until nicely browned around its circumference, turning with kitchen tongs as you go, about 8 minutes total. Remove the meat to the roasting rack and reserve. Pour off all but 1 tablespoon of the fat in the skillet and return to the heat.
5. Add the Marsala and red wine to the skillet and bring to a boil. Cook until reduced by one-third, about 3 minutes, scraping up any browned bits stuck to the bottom of the skillet. Meanwhile, using a basting brush or a soup spoon, coat the outside of the roast with the remaining herb-garlic mixture. Add the stock to the reduced wine and bring to a simmer. Place the beef (on its rack) in the skillet, adding any juices and herbs accumulated on the plate. Transfer to the oven and roast to the desired doneness (125° to 130°F on an instant-read thermometer for medium-rare meat, 25 to 40 minutes, depending on the thickness of your roast; or 140°F for medium. We like this dish best when pulled from the oven between 130° and 135°F). Baste the meat twice during this time, adding a few tablespoons of stock or water if the liquid in the skillet evaporates (you want at least ¼ cup of liquid at the end of roasting).
6. Transfer the roast and rack to a cutting board and cover loosely with foil. Place the skillet over medium-high heat (carefully; the handle is hot) and add the cream. Simmer, stirring occasionally, until the sauce is thick enough to easily coat the back of a spoon, 3 to 5 minutes. The sauce should be deep brown

and richly flavored. Continue to reduce, if necessary, or add small amounts of additional cream and/or broth or a few drops of Marsala to adjust the flavor to your liking. Add salt to taste. Stir in the butter and any juices beneath the roast and keep the sauce warm over low heat. Cut the meat into 1-inch slices and arrange one or two slices attractively on each serving plate. Top each with a tablespoon or two of sauce and serve.

NOTE: Try to buy a roast from the "eye" of the fillet, which will have an even thickness throughout its entire length. This way, when the roast is butterflied, you'll have a more uniformly square (or rectangular) piece of meat with which to work. Ideally, you also want a fillet on the thicker side: at least 3 inches in diameter. The goal is to have a rectangle or square that's approximately 8 to 12 inches by 8 to 12 inches. You or your butcher can butterfly the meat by cutting an incision along the length of the fillet, parallel to the work surface, about 3/4 inch above where it meets the work surface. Continue working the knife, using shallow, lengthwise strokes while gradually "unrolling" or opening the meat up until it resembles the rectangle or square described above. The butterflied meat should be pounded to a thickness of 3/4 inch, if necessary, for use in this recipe. Don't worry if there's a hole or two in your butterflied meat, or if it's not a perfect square or rectangle. If the roast is stuffed, rolled, and tied neatly, the finished dish will be just as delicious.

Pampas-Style Stuffed, Rolled Flank Steak

Originally an Argentinian specialty, *matambre* is equally good served hot, warm, or cool. The rolled steak is cut open to reveal a brightly colored filling of egg, spinach, carrots, olives, and pimientos.

SERVES 4 TO 6

8 large cloves garlic, finely chopped
2 generous teaspoons finely chopped fresh thyme
1 ½ teaspoons ground cumin seed
¼ cup white wine vinegar
4 tablespoons olive oil
One 2-pound flank steak, butterflied and pounded to ¼- to ⅜-inch thickness, if necessary (you should have a 12-by-14-inch square or slightly rectangular shape) (see illustration)
6 slices bacon, cut into ½-inch pieces
1 onion, chopped
¼ teaspoon crushed red pepper flakes
Kosher salt
½ pound washed, trimmed, coarsely chopped spinach (about 6 loosely packed cups after trimming large stems)
Freshly ground black pepper
3 medium carrots, peeled and cooked in simmering salted water until just tender
3 hard-boiled eggs, peeled and halved
8 to 12 pimiento-stuffed green olives
3 tablespoons finely chopped fresh flat-leaf parsley
Chimichurri Sauce (page 288; optional)

1. Whisk together half of the garlic, all the thyme, 1 teaspoon of the cumin, the vinegar, and 3 tablespoons of the olive oil and reserve. Place the butterflied flank steak in a nonreactive baking dish just large enough to contain it when folded in half. Whisk the marinade again then pour over all surfaces of the steak, rubbing well to coat all sides. Fold the steak in half, cover, and let marinate in the refrigerator for 3 hours.
2. Meanwhile, place the remaining 1 tablespoon of oil and the bacon in a large skillet over medium heat. Cook, stirring and separating the pieces, until crisp-tender. Add the onion and cook, stirring occasionally, until softened, about 5 minutes. Stir in the remaining garlic, the red pepper flakes, the remaining ½ teaspoon cumin, and 1 teaspoon of salt, and cook for 1 minute more. Add the spinach in two or three batches, letting each batch wilt before adding the next (covering the skillet will speed the process). When the last batch has wilted, stir well to combine all the ingredients and transfer to a bowl to cool. Reserve.
3. Preheat the oven to 375°F. Lay the marinated meat opened up and in front of you on a large work surface, with the grain of the meat running from top to bottom. Sprinkle lightly with salt and generously with black pepper. Spread the cooled spinach mixture over the entire surface of the meat, leaving an empty 1-inch margin all around. Lay the carrots, horizontally, about 3 inches apart so their ends reach to the edges of the spinach (see the illustration) and lay the egg halves in two horizontal rows about 5 inches apart (parallel to the top and bottom carrots.) Nestle one row of olives among the carrots and eggs and sprinkle the parsley over all.

CONTINUED>

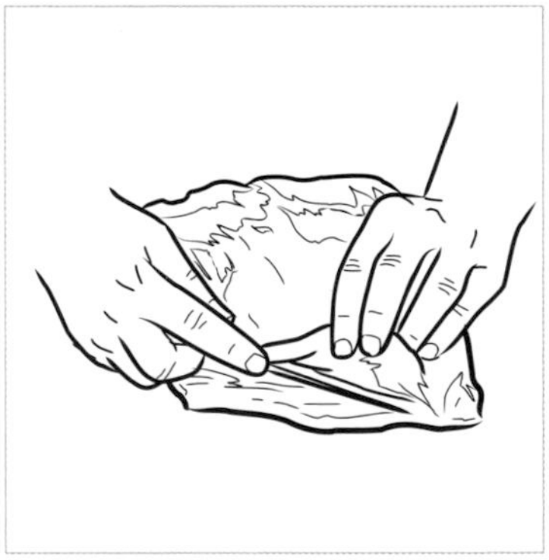

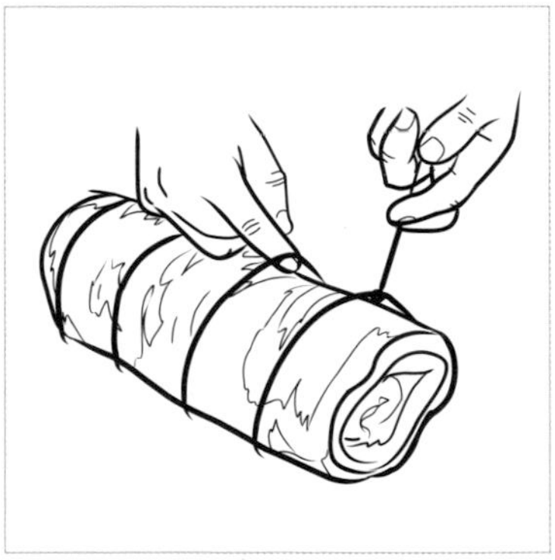

4. Starting with the edge nearest you, carefully roll up the steak, jelly-roll style (the roll should be compact but not so tight that the filling squeezes out—tuck in any filling that does), and tie it up as for a roast using butcher's twine tied at 1- to 2-inch intervals. Salt the meat on all sides and place, seam down, in a rectangular baking dish that comfortably contains it. (The dish can be assembled up to 1 day ahead. Store, covered, in refrigerator. Bring to room temperature before roasting.) Place in the middle of the oven and roast until a thermometer reads about 140°F in the center, about 50 minutes.

5. Remove from the oven and transfer to a cutting board. Loosely cover with foil and let the meat rest for 10 to 15 minutes to firm it up for easier slicing. Using a very sharp knife, cut the roll into 1-inch-thick slices, and carefully transfer to warmed serving plates, attractively overlapping slices so as to show off the brightly colored interior. Drizzle with a tablespoon or two of Chimichurri Sauce, if you like, and serve.

Rib Steaks with Cabrales Cheese Sauce

This delicious, savory specialty from the north of Spain is not for the fat-conscious, but it's an easily assembled treat that takes less than 15 minutes to prepare. Though we call for rib steak, this is great with almost any quick-cooking, tender cut. The steaks taste even better when grilled over a live wood fire instead of pan-fried. Typical Spanish accompaniments include roasted, peeled red bell peppers and baby potatoes—prepared any which way.

SERVES 2

- 3 tablespoons brandy or cognac
- 2 tablespoons unsalted butter
- 2 teaspoons all-purpose flour
- ½ cup heavy cream
- 2 ounces Cabrales, Picon, or similar strong-flavored Spanish blue cheese, or Roquefort

- Kosher salt
- Freshly ground black pepper
- 2 beef rib steaks, cut ¾ inch thick, at room temperature
- 1 generous tablespoon vegetable oil
- 1 tablespoon finely chopped fresh flat-leaf parsley

1. Heat the brandy in a medium skillet set over medium-low heat. Simmer until the liquid has reduced to a teaspoon or two. Swirl in the butter until just melted and sprinkle in the flour. Stir with a rubber spatula, breaking up any floury lumps and cook, stirring, for 2 minutes. Gradually add the cream and bring to a simmer. Add the cheese, and stir until the sauce is blended and smooth, about 30 seconds. Do not allow the sauce to boil or it will separate. Immediately remove from the heat and reserve.
2. Generously salt and pepper the steaks on both sides. Heat the oil over medium-high heat in a heavy skillet just large enough to contain the steaks. When it just begins to smoke, swirl the oil to evenly coat the skillet and add the steaks. Cook until nicely browned on both sides, 2½ to 3 minutes per side for medium-rare. Remove the steaks to warmed serving plates and reserve.
3. Gently reheat the sauce over medium-low heat while stirring. The sauce should easily coat the back of a spoon but be quite fluid. Stir in a bit of additional cream or milk to thin, if necessary. Spoon the sauce over the steaks, sprinkle with parsley, and serve.

Beef Picadillo Tacos with Chipotle Chiles

Stewed and shredded beef chuck makes a classic filling for soft corn tortillas, especially when tricked out with chipotle chiles, toasted almonds, and raisins. Arrange all garnishes and a salsa or two in bowls so that diners can outfit their tacos as they like. Serve tacos with a salad of oranges, avocado, and jicama.

MAKES ABOUT 4 CUPS AND FILLS 18 TO 22 TACOS

	Vegetable oil or lard
1½	pounds trimmed boneless beef chuck, cut into 1½-inch cubes
1	medium white onion, peeled and cut lengthwise into 4 wedges, plus ⅔ cup finely chopped white onion for garnish
6	large cloves garlic, peeled
2	bay leaves
	Kosher salt
8	medium canned tomatoes (about ¾ of a 28-ounce can)
½	cup slivered or coarsely crushed skinless almonds
3 to 4	medium chipotle chiles in adobo (from a 7-ounce can), stemmed and seeded (see Note)
½	teaspoon ground cinnamon
⅛	teaspoon ground cloves
¼	teaspoon freshly ground black pepper
½	cup raisins
	Soft corn tortillas, warmed (see Note)
	Tomatillo Salsa (page 287)
	Salsa Mexicana (page 286)
	Fresh cilantro leaves
	Lime wedges
2	ounces Cotija cheese (or similar aged Mexican cheese), or 1½ ounces Pecorino Romano, finely grated (about 6 tablespoons) (optional)

1. Heat 3 tablespoons of oil in a wide 10- to 12-quart pot over medium-high heat. When it begins to smoke, add the beef and brown very well on at least two sides, 4 to 6 minutes per side. Add 5 cups of water and scrape the bottom of the pot to loosen any browned bits. Add the onion wedges, garlic, bay leaves, and 2 teaspoons salt and bring just to a simmer. Skim the liquid and reduce the heat to medium-low and partially cover; gently simmer the mixture until tender, about 2 hours, stirring occasionally. Let the beef sit in its liquid, uncovered, until cool enough to handle.
2. Meanwhile, preheat the broiler. Lay the tomatoes on a rimmed baking sheet double-lined with foil. Drizzle with a few tablespoons of oil. Broil on both sides (drizzling second side with oil as well) until the tomatoes have concentrated and are blackened in spots, 4 to 8 minutes per side. Let cool and transfer along with any juices to the bowl of a blender.
3. Warm 2 teaspoons of oil in a small skillet over medium heat. Toast the almonds until pale golden, tossing and stirring regularly. Transfer to a plate to cool.
4. When the meat is cool enough to handle, remove it from the liquid and transfer to a bowl. Break the beef into small, bite-size pieces with your fingers and set aside. Discard the bay leaves from the cooking liquid and transfer ½ cup or so of the cooking liquid and half of the onion and garlic pieces from the pot to the jar of the blender. Add the chiles and a bit of the adobo sauce, the cinnamon, cloves, and black pepper. Process to form a nearly smooth thick paste, with no large bits of chile remaining, scraping the sides of the bowl and adding a bit more liquid as needed. Reserve 1 cup of the braising liquid (refrigerate the remaining liquid for another use).
5. Return the chile-tomato paste, beef, reserved 1 cup of braising liquid, and the raisins to the pot. Simmer the mixture over medium-low heat until the meat is coated in a thick, barely fluid sauce, 15 to 20 minutes, stirring occasionally. Stir in the reserved almonds and let the beef sit off the heat for a few minutes. Add salt to taste and serve in warm tortillas (2 to 3 tablespoons of filling per tortilla) with salsas, chopped white onion, cilantro, lime wedges, and Cotija cheese, if you like. The mixture can be made up to 2 days ahead and reheated on the stove top with a half cup or so of water, or partially covered in a microwave.

NOTE: Chipotle chiles (smoked jalapeño peppers) are available in a variety of forms: dried, packed in brine, and canned in adobo. Adobo chipotles are stewed in vinegar, tomatoes, garlic, and other seasonings. For use in this recipe, you can just pluck them from the can with a bit of their smoky sauce attached.

Corn tortillas can be wrapped in a towel and steamed in a vegetable steamer or Chinese bamboo steamer set over simmering water. They can also be steamed in a microwave in their plastic bags if the plastic is fairly thick: Remove and separate the tortillas, then poke a few holes in the plastic wrapper and return the tortillas to the bag. Hot tortillas can be wrapped in a towel and served in a basket. Two soft tortillas are often doubled up to enfold the fillings. If you want to serve the tacos like this (and we think they're better this way), make sure you purchase enough tortillas.

Chilean-Style Empanadas

There are as many kinds of empanadas as there are cooks. Our exceptional Chilean rendition is based on a recipe kindly shared with us by Leonor Olivares, a New Yorker originally from Valparaiso, Chile. Empanadas make a great snack or can be enjoyed as a full meal with a salad. The dough and filling can be made a few hours ahead of baking and kept at room temperature.

MAKES 14 EMPANADAS

DOUGH

8	cups all-purpose flour
1	tablespoon baking soda
1	tablespoon kosher salt
1 1/4	cups vegetable shortening
2	eggs, beaten
2	tablespoons white wine
1 1/2	cups whole milk

FILLING

1/4	cup olive oil
4	medium onions, very finely chopped by hand or pulsed in a food processor (about 3 1/2 cups)
1	pound fatty ground beef chuck
1	teaspoon dried oregano
1 1/2	teaspoons ground cumin seed
1 1/2	teaspoons sweet paprika
1 1/2	tablespoons kosher salt
	Fresh, coarsely ground black pepper
3/4	cup golden raisins, soaked in hot water until soft, and drained
1/4	cup toasted slivered almonds (optional)
1	tablespoon all-purpose flour
1/4 to 1/2	cup Beef Stock (page 302), or canned low-sodium beef broth
14	large pimiento-stuffed olives, cut in half crosswise, or 28 small olives, left whole
4	hard-boiled eggs, quartered lengthwise
1	egg, beaten with 1 tablespoon milk

1. To make the dough, combine the flour, baking soda, and salt in a large, wide mixing bowl and make a well in the center. Put the shortening, eggs, and wine in the well. Add the milk and, using your fingers and palms, work the ingredients until just incorporated and the dough looks like a rough, shaggy mass that just holds together in a ball. (This will be messy at first and will come together in a minute or so. Don't overwork dough.) Wrap in plastic and set aside while you make the filling.

2. To make the filling, heat the oil in a 10- to 12-inch skillet over medium-high heat. When it is hot, add the onions and cook, stirring regularly, until reduced in volume somewhat but without color, 5 to 7 minutes. Reduce the heat to medium-low and continue cooking and stirring regularly until the onions are soft and just the palest shade of gold, 10 to 12 minutes more, reducing the heat if the onions threaten to burn or brown.

3. Add the beef, mashing continually with the back of a large spoon or firm rubber spatula so it breaks up finely and is completely incorporated with the onion; let the meat cook until almost cooked through but still pink in places, about 2 minutes. Remove from the heat and add the oregano, cumin, paprika, salt, 6 to 8 generous grindings black pepper, raisins, almonds (if using), and flour, mixing well to combine. Stir in ¼ to ½ cup beef broth, just enough to moisten the mixture without making it runny. Let the filling cool. Preheat the oven to 375°F.

4. Measure ⅓ cup of dough and form into a puck or ball shape. On a well-floured work surface and with a rolling pin, roll out dough into an 8-inch circle ⅛ inch thick, rotating the dough and dusting with flour as you work. Cut a 7-inch circle of dough using an upturned bowl or cutting around a stencil or plate with a knife, discarding excess dough. Place ⅓ cup of the filling on the half of dough farthest from you and spread it out from 9 o'clock to 3 o'clock, leaving a ¾-inch margin to seal the dough. Center two olive halves (or two small olives) and one-quarter of a hard-boiled egg on top of the filling. Brush from 9 o'clock to 3 o'clock lightly with water and fold the dough over the filling to form a half moon, pressing lightly to seal. Working around the joined edge, press with a fork to seal completely (or make 8 or so overlapping folds around the edge to seal; this makes a more compact shape and is more traditional). Transfer the empanada to a greased or parchment-lined baking sheet and repeat with remaining dough and filling. (You'll need two baking sheets. Discard extra dough or reserve for another use.)

5. Brush tops of the empanadas lightly with the beaten egg mixture. Bake until pale golden on top and deep golden on the bottom, about 25 minutes, rotating the pan halfway through the cooking. Let cool for 5 minutes or so, and serve.

Skirt Steak with Venezuelan-Style Avocado Sauce

Like a tangy guacamole, the popular Venezuelan *salsa guasacaca* is ideal with grilled steak, but it is equally delicious alongside if the meat is simply pan-fried.

SERVES 4

- 1/4 cup red wine vinegar
- 1 teaspoon Tabasco sauce, plus more as needed
- 2 large cloves garlic, minced
- Kosher salt
- Freshly ground black pepper
- 3/4 cup finely chopped white onion
- 3/4 cup finely chopped tomato, with any juices
- 1/4 cup seeded and finely chopped green bell pepper or jalapeño pepper
- 1 hard-boiled egg, finely chopped
- 1 generous tablespoon finely chopped fresh flat-leaf parsley
- 1 generous tablespoon finely chopped fresh cilantro
- 2 ripe Hass avocados
- Scant 1/2 cup olive oil
- 2 1/2 pounds skirt steak, cut into 4 or 8 pieces

1. Combine the vinegar, Tabasco, garlic, 2 teaspoons salt, and a few generous grindings of black pepper in a large mixing bowl, stirring to dissolve the salt. Add the onion, tomato and any juices, bell pepper, egg, parsley, and cilantro.

2. Halve and pit the avocados. Remove the flesh from the avocado halves. Separate one-quarter of the flesh and cut into ½-inch pieces. Add these to the bowl with the other vegetables. Put the remaining avocado in a medium bowl with the oil and mash until smooth. Add the mashed avocado to the vegetable mixture and mix well. Add salt and more Tabasco to taste. The avocado sauce can be made up to 6 hours ahead and stored, covered, in the refrigerator. Bring partway to room temperature before serving. Makes 2½ to 3 cups.

3. Generously salt and pepper the steaks. Make a medium-hot charcoal fire or preheat a gas grill to medium-high heat. Clean and lightly oil the grates to prevent sticking. Grill the steaks 3 to 4 minutes per side for medium-rare and serve with avocado sauce on the side, about ½ cup per serving.

Jamaican Oxtail Stew

A rich, assertively flavored dish that tastes similar to a "jerked" beef stew. Serve the stew with a cool tropical fruit salad made with mango and papaya and a squeeze of lime. Note that after browning and seasoning the oxtails in the first three steps of the recipe, the meat is marinated for at least 8 hours.

SERVES 6

½	medium red onion, chopped
8	scallions, 6 chopped and 2 very thinly sliced for garnish
8	large cloves garlic, sliced
3	scotch bonnet or habañero peppers, halved, stemmed, and seeded
One	1½-inch knob fresh ginger, peeled and sliced
5	medium celery ribs, 1 chopped, 4 cut crosswise into ⅓-inch-thick pieces for finishing the dish
2	tablespoons ground allspice
2	teaspoons freshly ground black pepper
2	tablespoons fresh thyme leaves, plus 2 teaspoons for garnish
¼	cup soy sauce
	Kosher salt
	Vegetable oil
5	pounds oxtail, cut crosswise into 1-inch-thick pieces
	Cornstarch for dredging
4	ounces thick, country-style bacon, cut into ¼-inch pieces
2	medium yellow onions, chopped
3	medium carrots, peeled and cut into ¼-inch-thick rounds
3½ to 4	cups prepared lima beans, fava beans, or pigeon peas (1 pound dried beans cooked until tender but firm or two 15-ounce cans prepared beans, drained)
2	tablespoons unsalted butter, cut into pieces
	Freshly cooked white rice for serving
	Lime wedges for garnish

1. Combine the red onion, chopped scallions, garlic, peppers, ginger, the 1 rib chopped celery, allspice, black pepper, thyme, soy sauce, 1 tablespoon of salt, and 2 tablespoons of oil in the bowl of a food processor. Process to a coarse paste, 20 to 30 seconds, scraping the sides of the bowl as needed. Set aside.

2. Dredge the oxtail pieces in the cornstarch, shaking off any excess. Heat ¼ cup oil in a 10- to 12-quart heavy pot over medium-high heat. When it is hot, cook the oxtail, working in two batches, until deeply browned on both their flat sides and their rounded circumferences, 12 to 15 minutes per batch. As each batch finishes browning, transfer to a large bowl (if after browning the first batch, the bottom of the pot threatens to burn, drain and clean the pot; heat ¼ cup of fresh oil and continue browning the second batch).

3. Pour the reserved seasoning paste over the oxtail and toss well to coat. Cover tightly and let marinate overnight (or at least 8 hours) in the refrigerator.

4. Let the oxtail come to room temperature for 1 hour. Put the bacon and 2 tablespoons oil in a 10- to 12-quart pot over medium-low heat. Cook, stirring occasionally, until crisp-tender, 5 to 7 minutes. Raise the heat to medium and add the onions. Cook, stirring occasionally, until pale gold around the edges, 8 to 10 minutes. Add the oxtail and all of the marinade to the pot; stir in 6½ cups water and bring to a simmer over high heat, skimming any impurities that rise to the surface (try not to remove the spice paste). Reduce the heat to low, cover, and cook at the barest possible simmer until the meat is quite tender but not yet falling off the bone, about 3½ hours.

5. Turn off the heat and let the stew rest for 5 minutes, uncovered. Skim off some or all of the accumulated fat. Add the carrots and 4 ribs cut celery and return to a simmer over medium-low heat. Simmer uncovered for 1 hour.

6. Stir in the beans and continue simmering until the stew has thickened to a consistency somewhere between a soup and a stew, 15 to 30 minutes more (the stew will continue to thicken as it sits). Add the butter, shaking the pot or carefully stirring to distribute. Add salt to taste and let the stew sit off the heat for 5 to 10 minutes. Serve in wide, shallow bowls over rice, and garnish with thyme leaves, sliced scallions, and lime wedges on the side.

Beef and Spicy Tahini Casserole

Called *sinya* in Israel, this dish is a bit like a Middle Eastern shepherd's pie but with the potato on the bottom. The potato is topped with a spiced meat layer and then a lemony tahini sauce. Serve this simple, quick, and homey casserole with a chunky lettuce, tomato, and cucumber salad dressed with lemon juice and good olive oil. Braised carrots are also a great companion.

SERVES 4

- 3/4 pound non-starchy potatoes, such as Yukon gold
- Kosher salt
- 3/4 pound ground beef, lamb, or veal
- 1/4 cup finely chopped onion
- 3 tablespoons finely chopped fresh flat-leaf parsley
- 3 tablespoons Yemenite Hot Pepper–Cilantro Sauce (facing page)
- 2 tablespoons olive oil
- 1/2 cup tahini (sesame paste), plus more as needed
- 1/2 cup water plus more as needed
- 1/4 cup fresh lemon juice
- 1/2 teaspoon sugar
- 2 generous tablespoons pine nuts
- Fresh cilantro sprigs for garnish

1. Place the potatoes in a pot with 1 tablespoon of salt; cover with water by 1 inch and bring to a boil over high heat. Reduce the heat and simmer until tender, 20 to 30 minutes, depending on the size of the potatoes. Drain and very coarsely mash the potatoes with visible chunks remaining. Reserve.
2. Preheat the oven to 350°F.
3. While the potatoes cook, combine the beef, onion, parsley, hot sauce, ¾ teaspoon salt, and 1 tablespoon of the oil in a bowl. Mix well and reserve.
4. Grease an 8-by-8-inch baking dish with the remaining 1 tablespoon of oil. Completely and evenly cover the bottom of the dish with the mashed potatoes. Top the potatoes with the meat mixture, pressing to distribute it to the edges of the dish in an even thickness.
5. Whisk together the tahini, water, lemon juice, sugar, and ½ teaspoon salt in a bowl until well combined and about the consistency of a thin milk shake. Add a bit more water to thin or a bit of tahini to thicken, if necessary. Pour the tahini sauce evenly over the layer of meat and sprinkle with the pine nuts.
6. Bake until the meat layer is just cooked through (carefully check with a fork or knife), about 35 minutes. Remove from the oven and let the casserole rest for 5 minutes. Neatly scoop out individual servings, garnishing each with a few sprigs of cilantro. Serve with additional Yemenite hot sauce on the side, if you like.

Yemenite Hot Pepper–Cilantro Sauce

MAKES ABOUT 2/3 CUP

Called *zhoug* in much of the Middle East, this bright green spicy condiment is delicious with meat, fish, or eggs.

- 5 to 6 medium jalapeño peppers (about 1/3 pound), seeded and ribbed
- 2 1/2 to 3 cups loosely packed fresh cilantro leaves with thin stems, coarsely chopped
- 1 clove garlic, peeled and crushed
- 1 1/2 teaspoons ground coriander
- 1 teaspoon ground cumin
- 1/2 teaspoon ground cardamom
- 1/2 teaspoon freshly ground black pepper
- 3/4 teaspoon kosher salt
- 3/4 teaspoon crushed red pepper flakes (optional)
- 4 to 5 tablespoons extra-virgin olive oil

1. Place the peppers, cilantro, garlic, coriander, cumin, cardamom, black pepper, salt, and red pepper flakes (if using) in the bowl of a food processor and process until finely chopped and pesto-like, scraping down the sides of the bowl as needed.
2. With the motor running, add 2 tablespoons of the oil and process for 5 seconds more.
3. Transfer to a small bowl and stir in 2 more tablespoons of the oil by hand. Stir in additional olive oil or water to "loosen" the sauce, if necessary. The sauce should be thick but still somewhat pourable.
4. Store tightly covered.

Indonesian-Style Beef and Potato Croquettes

Called *perkedel* in Indonesia, these tasty croquettes are a great beginning to any Southeast Asian meal.

SERVES 3 TO 4 AS AN APPETIZER

½	pound Idaho or russet potatoes, peeled
1	medium onion, peeled
½	pound ground beef chuck
2	large cloves garlic, minced
2	teaspoons soy sauce
2	teaspoons fresh lime juice
1	teaspoon brown sugar
½	teaspoon (firmly packed) dried shrimp paste (*belecan*), roasted (see Note)
1	teaspoon Southeast Asian chile paste (*sambal oelek*)
1	tablespoon ground coriander seed
1	teaspoon freshly grated nutmeg
1½	teaspoons kosher salt
3	tablespoons finely chopped fresh cilantro
1	egg, beaten
	Peanut oil or vegetable oil
	All-purpose flour for dredging
	Fresh cilantro leaves for garnish
	Lime wedges for garnish
	Chile and Shallot Sambal (page 294) and/or Thai Chile-Herb Dipping Sauce (page 293)

1. Cook the potatoes in a pot of boiling water until tender, about 25 minutes. Drain, place on a double layer of paper towels to absorb excess moisture, and let cool for 20 minutes or so.

2. While the potatoes cook, grate the onion on the large (¼-inch) holes of a grater (finely chop any scraps) and lightly blot dry to absorb any excess juices. Put the onion, beef, and garlic in a mixing bowl. Combine the soy sauce, lime juice, sugar, and roasted shrimp paste in a small bowl, mixing to dissolve the solids. Add this mixture to the beef along with the chile paste, coriander, nutmeg, salt, cilantro, and egg.

3. When the potatoes have cooled somewhat, coarsely mash in a small bowl and add to the beef. Working with both hands, thoroughly combine all the ingredients; cover and refrigerate for 1 hour. (The mixture can be made up to 6 hours ahead of time.)

4. Heat 1½ to 2 inches of oil in a straight-sided skillet or wok to 375°F over high heat and preheat the oven to 200°F.

5. Shape the beef and potato mixture into 1½-inch balls and then flatten the balls into thick patties. Dredge the patties in flour and, working in two batches, slip them carefully into the oil and fry until deeply browned and cooked through, 3 to 5 minutes, turning them once about halfway through if the tops aren't browning like the bottoms. Remove with a wide, flat strainer or slotted spoon and drain on paper towels. Keep patties warm in the oven while you fry the second batch. Garnish with cilantro and lime wedges and serve with a small bowl of Chili and Shallot Sambal and/or Thai Chile–Herb Sauce on the side.

NOTE: *Belecan* is a powerfully aromatic, dark brown, barely moist cake (or brick) made from sun-dried shrimp paste that is essential to the cuisines of Indonesia and Malaysia. To mellow and enrich its flavor, it is usually roasted briefly before use. To roast: Enclose the measured amount of paste between two single thicknesses of aluminum foil sealed to make a 3- to 6-inch packet (depending on the amount of paste). On a firm work surface and pressing with your fingers, work the shrimp paste until it spreads out to an even thickness of about ¼ inch. The packet of paste can be roasted in one of three ways: **1)** hold the packet with kitchen tongs over the open flame of a burner set to medium; **2)** place the packet directly on a preheated electric burner set to medium-low; or **3)** place packet in a small, preheated skillet set over medium-low. In all cases, the paste is usually cooked until it is a few shades darker than its original color and when a roasted shrimpy aroma (and a steady wisp of smoke) has issued from the packet for 30 seconds or so per side. It should be lightly caramelized and richly browned, especially where the paste meets the foil. Total roasting time is from 1 to 2 minutes per side (if using a skillet, lightly press on the packet with a spatula to help it make contact with the surface). Let cool and use as needed.

Stir-Fried Beef with Chinese Black Beans and Ginger

We really like this simple Chinese classic, which has long been popular in the United States. The fermented black beans are easy to find in Asian markets and in the Asian foods section of many supermarkets, depending on where you live. Because the beef is cut thin and cooked quickly, both flank steak and sirloin are great here. Serve with white or brown rice.

SERVES 2 AS A MAIN COURSE; 4 AS PART OF A FAMILY-STYLE MEAL

- 2 generous tablespoons fermented black beans, rinsed two or three times
- 1 tablespoon soy sauce
- 1/4 cup Chicken Stock (page 299) or Beef Stock (page 302), or canned low-sodium broth
- 1 teaspoon kosher salt
- 1 teaspoon sugar
- 1 teaspoon Asian sesame oil
- One 1/2-inch-long (1-inch-thick) piece of fresh ginger with skin on, crushed, plus 2 teaspoons minced, peeled fresh ginger
- 3 tablespoons peanut oil
- 2 large cloves garlic, minced
- 1 pound well-trimmed beef flank steak or sirloin, sliced across the grain into pieces of equal thickness between 1/8 and 1/4 inch thick and about 2 inches long
- 3 scallions, thinly sliced crosswise
- 2 teaspoons cornstarch dissolved in 1 tablespoon cold water
- 10 to 15 whole fresh cilantro leaves for garnish (optional)

1. In a small mixing bowl, mash the black beans coarsely with the back of a fork. Add the soy sauce, stock, salt, and sugar, whisking to dissolve the solids. Whisk in the sesame oil and crushed ginger. Set aside for 30 minutes.

2. Heat a 14-inch wok over high heat. Have all ingredients close at hand. Add the peanut oil, using a Chinese spatula to coat the wok. When it just begins to smoke, add the minced ginger and the garlic. Cook, stirring, 5 to 10 seconds, until fragrant. Add the beef, spreading it out in a single layer, and cook undisturbed until lightly browned, 45 seconds to 1 minute. Add the scallions and turn the beef over. Remove the crushed ginger from the bean–ginger sauce, stirring well to combine. Stir in the dissolved cornstarch and continue to cook until the sauce has thickened but is still a bit fluid and the beef is just cooked through, 1 minute or so more, stirring regularly. Transfer to serving plates or a platter, garnish with the cilantro (if using), and serve.

NOTE: Many home cooks add red or green bell peppers, and you can do so here if you are so inclined. Cut the peppers into 2-inch-long slices and cook them in 2 tablespoons of the oil for 1 or 2 minutes before adding the beef in Step 2. Cook until softened but still somewhat crisp. Remove the peppers to a plate, leaving as much oil as possible in the wok. Add the remaining 1 tablespoon of oil and proceed with the recipe (browning the beef). Return the peppers to the wok when adding the black bean–ginger sauce.

Seared Beef Tataki with Ponzu Sauce

Neat rectangular slabs of sirloin steak are seared, chilled, and then very thinly sliced to reveal a deep pink sashimi-like center. The slices are moistened with a homemade soy and citrus ponzu sauce, which, when served with some or all of the suggested garnishes, makes a striking first course to any meal, Japanese or not. Although the ponzu sauce can be made just before preparing the beef (as outlined below), it's best to make it one day in advance, as the flavor improves with time.

SERVES 4 AS AN APPETIZER

	Grated zest of 1/2 lemon
	Grated zest of 1/2 lime
1/2	cup fresh lemon juice
1/4	cup fresh lime juice
1/2	cup mirin
3/4	cup dark Japanese soy sauce
1/4	cup unseasoned rice wine vinegar
1/2	ounce bonito flakes (about 2/3 cup)
One	3-inch square piece of kombu
1	pound beef sirloin steak in one uniform piece cut 1 1/2 to 2 inches thick (1 pound after thorough trimming)
1 1/2	teaspoons kosher salt
	Vegetable oil

GARNISHES

Grated fresh ginger; grated daikon radish; wasabi; thinly sliced scallion tops; thinly sliced cucumber

1. Combine the lemon and lime zests and lemon and lime juices in a small bowl. Set aside for 15 minutes. Strain and reserve the juice.
2. Meanwhile, bring the mirin to a boil in a small saucepan. Cook until reduced by half, to 1/4 cup, 2 to 3 minutes. Transfer to a mixing bowl and whisk in the soy sauce, vinegar, and bonito flakes. Add the kombu. Stir in the strained citrus juice and let the mixture sit for at least 8 hours but preferably a day or two. Using a fine-mesh strainer or cheesecloth, strain out and discard the bonito and konbu. *Makes about 2 cups and lasts for months in a tightly covered jar stored in the refrigerator.*
3. Bring the beef to room temperature; sprinkle with the salt on all sides and set aside for 30 minutes.
4. Preheat a small skillet, preferably cast iron, over medium heat for 5 minutes. Set up a bath of ice water in a medium bowl and keep near the stovetop. Increase the heat to high, and blot the beef dry. Turn on the vent hood. When the pan is smoking-hot, add a thin film of oil to the skillet, swirling to coat. Add the beef and sear all four sides until just beginning to form a brown crust, about 1 minute per surface (and supporting the beef with tongs if thin sides won't stand upright). Heat should penetrate no more than 1/8 to 1/4 inch all around. Immediately plunge the steak into the water bath for a minute or two to stop the cooking. Remove and blot dry. Wrap tightly in plastic wrap and place in the freezer until par-frozen (making it easier to cut into thin, uniform slices), 3 to 6 hours, depending on the thickness of the meat.
5. Using a sharp chef's knife or serrated knife, carefully slice the beef between 1/16 and 1/8 inch thick (see Note), discarding the two ends. Divide slices between serving plates, overlapping them slightly in an attractive pattern (either straight or circular). Place any garnishes directly on serving plates or on a designated garnish plate. Spoon about 2 tablespoons of the ponzu sauce over each portion of beef and serve.

NOTE: The beef is good sliced paper-thin (1/16 inch—very delicate), or a bit thicker (1/8 inch—more toothsome), but just as good. The beef soaks up ponzu sauce as it sits. If you cut the beef closer to 1/8 inch thick, saucing it 10 to 15 minutes before serving helps bind the flavor of meat and sauce together. Thinner slices are best sauced no more than 5 minutes before serving. You can completely freeze the meat and thaw it to a semi-frozen "cutting state," but some loss of juiciness will occur. If you want to sear meat earlier on the day of serving, it is better to sear it, let it cool, wrap, par-freeze, slice, and plate portions as directed. Tightly cover the beef with plastic wrap and store in the refrigerator for up to 6 hours before serving.

Thai Beef Salad

This salad is a classic Thai starter. Because the salad can be made with almost any tender steak, we suggest strip, sirloin, or tri-tip cuts. You can easily double the recipe if you want to serve more people.

SERVES 2

DRESSING

- 3 tablespoons fresh lime juice
- 3 tablespoons Thai or Vietnamese fish sauce (*nam pla* or *nuoc nam*)
- 1/2 teaspoon minced peeled fresh ginger
- 1/2 teaspoon sugar
- 1 1/2 teaspoons peanut oil

SALAD

- 1 heaping tablespoon jasmine or other long-grain rice
- 1/3 cup thinly sliced shallots
- 1/2 cup lightly packed fresh mint leaves
- 1/2 cup lightly packed fresh cilantro leaves with thin stems
- 2 tablespoons peanut oil
- Kosher salt
- 8 to 10 ounce strip, sirloin, or tri-tip steak, cut 3/4 inch thick, trimmed
- 1/2 teaspoon toasted sesame seeds

1. To make the dressing, in a small bowl, whisk together the lime juice, fish sauce, ginger, sugar, and peanut oil. Set aside.
2. To make the salad, place the rice in a small skillet over medium heat and cook, shaking and swirling the pan regularly, until toasted and pale golden brown, 3 to 5 minutes. Let cool on a small plate and transfer to a mortar or spice grinder and grind to the consistency of very fine cornmeal. Reserve.
3. Mix the shallots, mint, and cilantro together in a medium bowl. Set aside in the refrigerator.
4. Heat the 2 tablespoons oil in a heavy large skillet over medium-high heat until almost smoking. Generously salt the steak on both sides, add to the skillet, and cook for about 3 minutes per side for medium-rare, reducing the heat somewhat if it threatens to burn. Alternatively (and traditionally), the steak can be cooked on a grill, adding the flavor of live fire to the finished dish. (Be sure to oil the steaks before salting and grilling.) Transfer the steak to a cutting board designed to catch the juices and let rest for 10 to 15 minutes.
5. When ready to serve, slice the steak across the grain very thinly and then scatter the slices into the reserved bowl of herbs, adding any beef juices on the cutting board. Toss the reserved ground rice with the herbs and beef. Whisk the reserved dressing, add enough to coat the steak mixture, and toss gently with your hands. Divide the mixture between two wide shallow bowls, piling each serving attractively in the center. Pour any remaining dressing around each serving. Sprinkle with the sesame seeds and serve immediately.

Vietnamese-Style Beef Noodle Soup

This spectacular soup, known as *pho*, showcases our favorite meat in three delectable ways: it offers braised beef chuck *in* the soup; tender, thinly sliced raw beef *on* the soup that cooks briefly when it contacts the piping-hot broth (a fairly tender cut can substitute for the sirloin or filet we call for here); and the exotically aromatic broth itself, which is built on the savor of the meaty beef marrow bones. *Pho* garnishes vary from cook to cook: cilantro can take the place of the basil or mint; shallots, thinly sliced and quickly seared in a bit of oil, can stand in for the raw sliced onions; lemon wedges can even replace lime—feel free to improvise. The broth can be made up to 2 days ahead and refrigerated in a tightly covered container. Serve with chopsticks (or forks) and soup spoons.

SERVES 4

BROTH

6	pounds meaty beef marrowbones and knucklebones
2	onions, unpeeled but with loose skins removed
One	3-inch piece unpeeled fresh ginger
8	star anise pods
One	3-inch piece cinnamon stick
4	whole cloves
10	black peppercorns
½	pound beef chuck, cut into ½-inch slices
¼	cup Vietnamese or Thai fish sauce (*nuoc nam* or *nam pla*)
	Kosher salt
2	teaspoons sugar
10	ounces ⅛-inch-wide rice noodles (rice stick, Vietnamese *banh pho*, or Thai *sen lek*)
½	pound beef sirloin or filet mignon, partially frozen and sliced as thinly as possible
1	small onion, ends trimmed, halved lengthwise and cut into paper-thin lengthwise slices

1. To make the broth, place bones in a heavy stockpot (12 quarts or larger), cover with 2 inches of cold water, and bring to a boil over high heat. Skim any impurities that rise to the surface and boil vigorously for 5 minutes. Drain the bones in a colander and rinse thoroughly with cold water. Wipe out the pot, return the bones to it, and reserve.
2. Meanwhile, turn two or three burners on a gas stove or gas grill on medium heat and place the onions and ginger on grates over open flame. Turning with tongs, cook until well blackened on all sides, and softened somewhat, about 10 minutes (they can also be placed under a broiler). Remove from heat and let cool. Peel and rinse off some, but not all, of the blackened bits. Split the ginger in half lengthwise and crush slightly with the flat side of a large knife. Reserve.
3. Place the star anise, cinnamon, cloves, and peppercorns in a small skillet over medium heat and toast them, swirling the spices to prevent burning, until fragrant, 1 to 2 minutes. Reserve.
4. Fill the reserved pot of bones with 6 quarts of cold water and add the reserved onions and ginger and the beef chuck. Place over high heat, skimming thoroughly when the water comes to a simmer; add the reserved star anise, cinnamon, cloves, and peppercorns; reduce the heat to maintain a bare simmer and cook for 1½ hours, skimming occasionally (try not to remove the spices when skimming). Remove the slices of beef chuck (they should be tender but a bit firm; cook a while longer if necessary) and transfer to a small bowl to cool. Shred the meat and set aside. Continue cooking the broth at a bare simmer for 2 hours more, about 3½ hours total.
5. Pass the broth through a colander lined with cheesecloth or a fine-mesh strainer placed over a large bowl. Wipe out the pot. Return the strained broth to the pot (you should have 3 to 4 quarts). Add the fish sauce, 2 teaspoons salt, and the sugar. Set the pot over high heat and boil until reduced to 2½ quarts, 20 to 30 minutes. Broth should be light in texture but richly flavored and aromatic; continue reducing to 2 quarts, 5 to 10 minutes more, if you think it could be more concentrated. Turn off the heat, and salt to taste. After a few minutes, skim some, but not all, of the fat that rises to the top. Reserve the broth.
6. While the broth is reducing, bring a large pot of salted water to a boil; add the rice noodles and cook until tender but still quite firm, stirring occasionally, 5 to 10 minutes depending on the brand. Do not overcook (noodles will continue cooking in hot broth). Rinse under cold water to cool. Reserve. Refill the same pot with water and reserve on the stovetop.

1 generous cup mung bean sprouts, rinsed

5 tablespoons thinly sliced scallion tops (green parts only)

1 cup loosely packed Thai or other basil leaves (and/or mint leaves), torn if large

2 small hot red chiles, such as Thai bird or serrano peppers, thinly sliced into rings

4 lime wedges

7. When ready to serve, reheat the beef broth and bring the water in the reserved pot to a boil. Briefly plunge the noodles in the hot water in portions of 1 to 1½ cups and, using a long-handled strainer, place each drained portion at the bottom of four serving bowls. Divide the reserved shredded beef and the paper-thin onion slices among the bowls. Top each bowl with slightly overlapping slices of the raw sirloin (leaving a wide margin of noodles visible) and ladle about 2 cups of the hot broth over each. Center a small pile of bean sprouts in the bowls and garnish each with a scattering of scallion tops, basil, and chiles. Serve immediately, passing lime wedges at the table.

Korean-Style Barbecued Short Ribs

Korean beef is great simply marinated, grilled, and served alongside spicy napa cabbage kimchee or sautéed Asian leafy greens. In Korean homes and restaurants, these ribs get a more elaborate treatment: The grilled meat is cut into smaller pieces by each diner and rolled up in soft green or red leaf lettuce before being outfitted with steamed white rice, a smear of Korean chile and soybean pastes. It's also topped with sliced hot green chiles, raw or grilled garlic cloves, or sliced scallions marinated in equal parts soy sauce, rice wine vinegar, and sesame oil, which is spooned over each serving before rolling up and eating. The Korean way with short ribs, here grilled to just medium rare, will be a revelation to those who assume these cuts of meat are only enjoyable after hours of braising.

SERVES 4 TO 6

- ¾ cup soy sauce
- 3 tablespoons Korean rice wine (ch'ongju), semi-dry sake, or dry vermouth
- 2 tablespoons fresh lemon juice
- 3 tablespoons Asian sesame oil
- ½ cup lightly packed dark brown sugar
- 3 large scallions, thinly sliced, dark green slices reserved for garnish
- 3 large cloves garlic, thinly sliced
- 1 heaping tablespoon grated, peeled fresh ginger
- 2 star anise pods, broken into points
- ½ teaspoon freshly ground black pepper
- 6 pounds meaty English-style short ribs (about 12 ribs; each 3 inches in length), or 4 pounds flanken-style short ribs, cut ¼ inch thick (see Note)
- 2 teaspoons sesame seeds

1. Combine the soy sauce, rice wine, lemon juice, sesame oil, brown sugar, white and pale green scallion slices, garlic, ginger, star anise, and pepper in a 15-by-10-inch glass or ceramic baking dish, stirring to dissolve the sugar.
2. Nestle the short ribs in the marinade, coating both sides of each rib and spooning marinade over the tops of any exposed meat. Cover with plastic and marinate for 1 to 2 hours at room temperature, turning the meat once.
3. Make a medium-hot charcoal fire or preheat a gas grill to medium-high heat. Clean and lightly oil the grates to prevent sticking. Grill the short ribs for about 3 minutes per side for medium-rare. Transfer to serving plates and sprinkle with the reserved scallion slices and the sesame seeds.

NOTE: Either English-style or flanken-style short ribs may be used in this dish. Either one should be cut to a thickness of about ¼ inch, although because of their differing bone structures, the two cuts are handled differently. To prepare English-style short ribs for Korean barbecue, follow the diagram below (or show it to your butcher). For flanken-style ribs, simply ask your butcher to cut them ¼ inch thick on a band saw, which is one of the many ways that short ribs are offered at Korean markets.

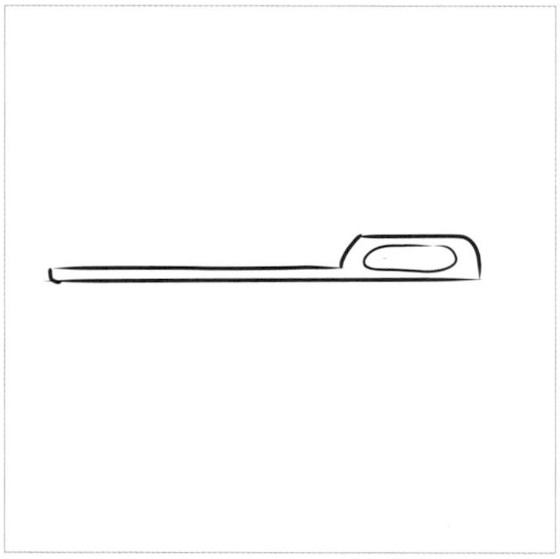

Korean-Style Noodles with Beef and Vegetables

This traditional, colorful, and celebratory Korean dish—called *chapch'ae* in its homeland—is served at room temperature. A fair amount of steps are involved in making it, but all except the final tossing together in Step 10 can be done well ahead of serving time. The ingredients listed should be available at any good Asian market.

SERVES 4 TO 6

- 2 ounces (6 to 8 medium) dried Korean p'yogo mushrooms (Japanese dried shiitake or Chinese black mushrooms)
- 1/2 cup plus 1 tablespoon soy sauce
- 2 tablespoons fresh lemon juice
- 2 tablespoons sugar
- 1/2 teaspoon kosher salt
- 1/4 teaspoon freshly ground black pepper
- 4 tablespoons Asian sesame oil
- 1 tablespoon finely grated peeled fresh ginger
- 5 scallions, white and pale green parts minced, green tops quartered lengthwise and cut into 2-inch strips
- 5 large cloves garlic, minced
- 3/4 pound well-trimmed boneless strip or rib-eye steak, cut 3/4 inch thick and prefrozen for one hour for easy slicing
- 1 pound baby spinach, or 1 1/2 to 2 pounds mature spinach, stemmed
- 10 ounces thin Korean-style noodles made with sweet potato starch (see Note)
- 5 tablespoons peanut oil or vegetable oil
- 2 eggs, lightly beaten
- 1 medium onion, halved and thinly sliced
- 1/2 large red bell pepper, stemmed, ribs removed, seeded and cut lengthwise in 1/8-inch-wide julienne strips
- 1 medium zucchini, cut into julienned strips, about 3 inches long by 1/8 inch wide

CONTINUED>

1. Nearly fill a 10- to 12-quart pot with water and bring to a boil. Place the mushrooms in a small bowl. Scoop out 2 to 3 cups of boiling water from the pot (reserve remaining water in pot) and pour over the mushrooms. Invert a small plate and place it over the mushrooms to submerge them. Soak until the mushrooms soften, about 30 minutes to 1 hour, turning them over periodically. Squeeze out excess water; remove and discard the stems and slice the caps about 1/8 inch thick.
2. Meanwhile, combine the soy sauce, lemon juice, sugar, and 1/4 teaspoon of the salt in a bowl, stirring until the sugar dissolves. Add the black pepper, 3 tablespoons of the sesame oil, the ginger, minced scallions, and garlic, stirring to combine. Toss the reserved mushrooms with 2 tablespoons of the soy-sesame sauce.
3. Lay the steak flat on work surface. Using a sharp knife and working parallel to the work surface, cut the steak in half to yield two thinner steaks, each about 3/8 inch thick. Slice each steak into strips about 1/8 inch thick and 3 inches long. Place the steak strips in a small bowl and toss thoroughly with 4 tablespoons of the soy-sesame sauce. Set aside.
4. Return the pot of water to a boil. Add the spinach and cook until just wilted, 20 to 30 seconds. Remove the spinach with a strainer and cool in ice water or under cold running water (don't drain the pot). Thoroughly squeeze dry and coarsely chop. Place the spinach in a small bowl and toss with 1 tablespoon of the soy-sesame sauce.
5. Add the noodles to the boiling water and cook, stirring occasionally, until tender but still a bit chewy, 4 to 6 minutes depending on the brand (don't overcook; test noodles early and often). Drain noodles (pouring off water) into a colander and rinse under cool running water. Grab a handful of noodles and snip them into roughly 6-inch lengths, letting them fall into a large bowl. Repeat with the remaining noodles. Toss well with the remaining 1 tablespoon sesame oil.
6. Heat 1 tablespoon of the peanut oil in a 12-inch skillet over medium heat. When it is hot, add the beaten eggs, tilting the skillet to distribute eggs evenly. Cook until the eggs are set but still very moist, less than 30 seconds and up to 1 minute. Fold the omelet in half with a spatula and continue cooking until the inside is nearly set, about 30 seconds more, flipping once or twice. The omelet should be bright yellow and tender. Transfer the omelet to a cutting board to cool. Cut crosswise into 1/3-inch-wide strips, 2 or 3 inches long.

2 medium carrots, peeled and cut into julienned strips about 3 inches long and 1/8 inch wide

2 long, medium-hot green Korean peppers, or 3 green jalapeño peppers, stemmed, seeded, and cut into julienne strips

1 tablespoon toasted sesame seeds

7. Wipe out the skillet, and return to medium heat with 2 tablespoons of the peanut oil. When hot, add the onion and cook, stirring occasionally, until softened but not browned, about 4 minutes. Add the scallion tops, red bell pepper, zucchini, carrots, and the remaining ¼ teaspoon salt, stirring regularly. Cook until crisp-tender, about 2 minutes more. Transfer to a bowl and toss with 2 tablespoons of the soy-sesame sauce.

8. Return the skillet to medium-high heat with 1 tablespoon of the peanut oil. When hot, add the reserved mushrooms and cook, stirring occasionally, until just golden at the edges, 3 to 4 minutes. Return them to their bowl.

9. Return the skillet to medium-high heat with the remaining 1 tablespoon of peanut oil. When hot, add the reserved beef and cook, separating the pieces into a single layer and turning once, until barely cooked through, 1 to 2 minutes (the beef need not brown). Transfer to the bowl with the mushrooms.

10. To serve, select a large, wide, low-sided serving bowl ample enough to easily hold all the noodles, vegetables, and meat. Place the reserved noodles in the bowl. Scatter the beef, mushrooms, spinach, and julienned vegetables over the top of the noodles and toss thoroughly with remaining soy-sesame sauce. Garnish with the egg strips, top with sesame seeds, and serve.

NOTE: Beautifully glassy to look at, Korean-style sweet potato noodles (actually, sweet potato starch noodles) add a pleasantly chewy, almost "springy" character to this classic Korean noodle dish. Though we much prefer sweet potato noodles to any other for this dish, medium-fine "bean thread," "mung bean thread," or other highly transparent "Chinese vermicelli" can be substituted. But take note: The labeling of Asian noodles is a world of confusion; what you want are transparent noodles (about the thickness of spaghetti) that retain a pleasingly toothsome, lightly rubbery "pull" when cooked. In addition to Korean sweet potato noodles, there are also a number of Chinese brands available.

Muslim-Style Beef Curry

A Muslin-style curry differs somewhat from what most of us usually associate with Thai curries: they are more markedly sweet-sour and are laced with warm spices like cinnamon and cardamom. They are said to have entered the former Kingdom of Siam by way of envoys from the sixteenth-century Persian court.

SERVES 4

- 1½ pounds beef flank steak or sirloin, trimmed and sliced against the grain into ⅜-inch-thick slices about 2 inches long
- 8 tablespoons Thai Massaman curry paste (see Note)
- 3 tablespoons peanut or vegetable oil
- 1 onion, peeled, halved lengthwise, and thinly sliced
- 4 large cloves garlic, minced
- 1½ tablespoons minced peeled fresh ginger
- 10 green cardamom pods
- 1 cinnamon stick
- ½ teaspoon ground cumin seed
- 2 bay leaves
- 1 tablespoon palm sugar (crushed if solid) or light brown sugar
- 1½ tablespoons tamarind concentrate (see Note)
- 2 tablespoons Thai or Vietnamese fish sauce (*nam pla* or *nuoc nam*)
- 4 cups Beef Stock (page 302), or canned low-sodium beef broth
- 2 Japanese eggplants (about ¾ pound) sliced ¼ inch thick (or other thin eggplant cut into 1½-inch pieces about ¼ inch thick)
- ¾ cup sliced canned bamboo shoots, drained, if canned (or cut into large bite-size pieces about ¼ inch thick if whole and packaged in Cryovac)
- 2 tablespoons fresh lime juice
- Kosher salt
- 4 cups freshly cooked white rice for serving
- ½ cup coarsely crushed unsalted peanuts
- 2 tablespoons finely chopped fresh cilantro

1. Combine the beef with 4 tablespoons of the curry paste in a medium mixing bowl, thoroughly coating the meat. Set aside at room temperature.
2. Heat the oil in a stockpot or large wok over medium heat and add the onion, garlic, and ginger. Cook gently, stirring occasionally, until slightly softened, about 5 minutes. Stir in the remaining curry paste, the cardamom, cinnamon, cumin, and bay leaves and cook, stirring regularly, for 2 minutes. Add the palm sugar, tamarind, fish sauce, and stock. Increase the heat to high and bring to a boil. Reduce to a simmer over medium heat and cook for 15 minutes to combine and concentrate the flavors.
3. Stir in the eggplant and cook until just tender, 10 to 15 minutes, stirring and turning the pieces occasionally. Add the bamboo shoots and the reserved beef, stirring well a few times to expose the beef to liquid on all sides. Cook, stirring occasionally, until the meat is just medium-rare in the center, 2 to 3 minutes. Stir in the lime juice, and salt to taste.
4. Spoon the curry next to or over a portion of rice. Sprinkle some of the peanuts and cilantro over each serving.

NOTE: A large range of Thai curry pastes are available at Asian markets or from online retailers. The popular Maesri brand comes in 4-ounce cans as well as resealable 14-ounce plastic containers. Tamarind concentrate, a ready-to-use product made from sieved and diluted tamarind paste, can also be found at Asian retailers. Any available brand is suitable for this dish. Occasionally it's labeled "sour soup base concentrate."

TENDERLOIN

RIB CHOPS

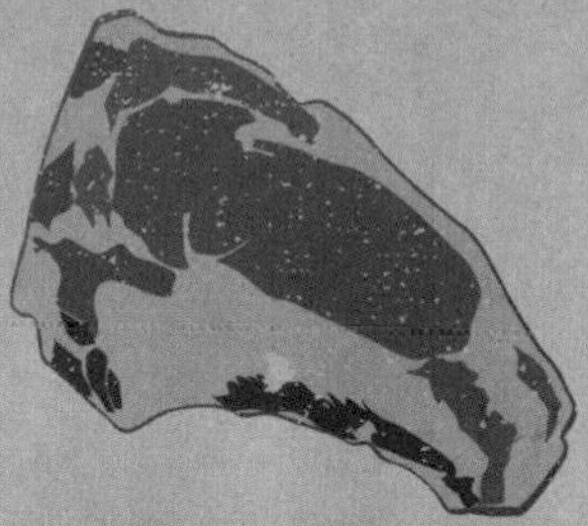

Top Round

ROUND STEAK

VEAL CHEEKS

VEAL

Rolled LOIN ROAST

BREA OF VE

RACK

VEAL
LONDON
BROIL

ST
AL

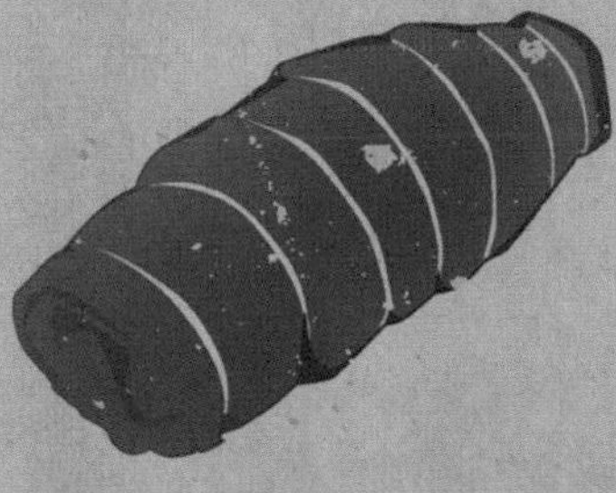

VEAL
Tails

OF VEAL

FORESHANK

WHOLE
FILET

CROWN
ROAST

Veal

FILET
MIGNON

SHOULDER and CHUCK
STEAK

VEAL LONDON BROIL
WHOLE FILET
ORESHANK
CROWN ROAST
Veal FILET MIGNON
VEAL
ails
VEAL
SHOULDER and CHUCK
STEA

CHAPTER TWO

Veal

Veal is one of our favorite meats, and happily, more and more people are discovering its tender, mild flavor and great versatility. For the most part, today's veal is humanely and carefully raised in open, well-ventilated, and lighted pens by growers who are working hard to please their customers with a superior product. If you have access to a butcher you trust, buy veal from him instead of the supermarket to ensure that you get excellent meat.

Buy veal that is white or pale pink and that looks moist and velvety. The bones should be soft and red (an indication of youth) and the thin layer of exterior fat should be white. Unlike beef, veal should not be marbled, as the animals do not grow large enough to develop much fat. This makes veal great for slow cooking and quick sautéing, although, with some exceptions, it is not the best meat for grilling.

Try to cook veal within a day or so of purchase—or freeze it for later use. Take the meat from the refrigerator about 30 minutes ahead of time so that it comes to cool room temperature before cooking or marinating. (Although we don't recommend leaving raw meat at room temperature for more than 30 minutes, large roasts may require more time to reach cool room temperature.) If the meat is too cold, the cooking time will be affected.

To understand how veal is butchered, it's helpful to look first at the hindsaddle of veal, which consists of the hindshank, top round, eye of round, bottom round, and top sirloin. The cuts taken from the hindsaddle have similar names to the corresponding cuts from a steer, although there are significant differences. For example, most of the veal round is used for veal roasts or, conversely, cut very thin for scaloppine (cutlets, scallops, and scaloppine are the same thing) and steaks. We prefer to oven-roast the top sirloin, eye of round, and bottom round. We like top round for scaloppine, and we like veal steaks cut from the round. We don't recommend veal round for stews or pot roasts because the meat is too lean and dries out. For stews and pot roasts, we use the chuck meat from the forequarter, which is also called the foresaddle.

STEAKS

VEAL CUTLET OR ROUND STEAK

Veal cutlets and steaks are cut from the top round of veal. It is the most tender part of the round and makes a good steak when it comes from the first cut.

When you use cutlets in recipes that call for them to be pounded until thin, put them between two pieces of plastic or wax paper and pound them gently until they are between ¼ and ⅛ of an inch thick.

VEAL SHOULDER AND CHUCK STEAK

The meat from the shoulder is what kosher butchers cut for scaloppine for those cooks who keep kosher. Bone-in veal chuck steaks, as well as boneless steaks, are also popular in kosher markets. They do well marinated and oven-roasted. When dealing with veal, steaks and chops are not differentiated. Both words mean the same thing.

VEAL FILET MIGNON

Just as beef filet mignon is cut from the tenderloin, so is veal filet mignon. Veal filet mignon is smaller, extremely tender, and requires very careful cooking to prevent it from becoming dry. It should always be pink in the middle, never cooked any further.

BONELESS VEAL RIB STEAK

A boneless veal rib steak is simply a boned veal chop. It's one of the most tender cuts of veal there is, with only filet mignon being more succulent. Veal rib steaks should be cooked only until pink in the middle. They have no graining, or marbling, so there is no fat to keep the meat moist.

VEAL SKIRT STEAK

A veal skirt steak is about one-third the size of a beef skirt steak but is just as tender, juicy, and flavorful. It is cut from the plate. The steak usually weighs about ¾ of a pound and is cut about ¼ of an inch thick. It is almost always the outside skirt and is great for broiling and grilling, although we also find it does well with light marinades. Like their beef counterparts, veal skirt steaks are used for fajitas, in which case, the inside veal skirt is sometimes used. Veal skirt steak may have to be special ordered.

VEAL LONDON BROIL

A London broil cut from veal can come from the top round or the shoulder, and is cut as a lean, flat steak. Like beef London broil, it does best when marinated and broiled or grilled and then sliced on the bias, or diagonal.

ROASTS

TOP ROUND

The top round roast of veal, cut from the leg, is an oblong piece of meat that will serve about eight people. To keep it moist during cooking, it needs some fat laid on it, such as beef or pork fat, which the butcher will provide if you ask. The fat does not have to be tied on but simply placed on top of the roast. Without it, the surface of the roast will crust over and be tough. When you roast beef, which has a lot of fat, the reverse is true: the outside crusts over and becomes tender. With the added fat, the veal will do the same thing.

BOTTOM ROUND

The bottom round roast is frequently attached to the eye of round, which in veal is very small and so rarely is removed. The bottom round can be roasted and while not as tender as the top round, still results in a very good roast. The preference is to cover the roast for the first half of the cooking time to keep it moist and then to finish it uncovered so that it browns.

LOIN OF VEAL ROAST

The loin section lies right next to the sirloin and is the final cut of the hindsaddle. We sometimes refer to this section as the porterhouse of veal. In a small calf it is only about eight inches wide and can be cut into small roasts or chops.

ROLLED LOIN ROAST

This is actually the same as loin roast above, but all the bones are removed. Before it is rolled, it can be stuffed with a flavorful mixture of bread crumbs, herbs, mushrooms, and similar ingredients. Once rolled, it should be tied for roasting.

WHOLE FILLET ROAST

The veal tenderloin is small when compared to the beef fillet, or tenderloin, and serves only three or four. As might be expected, the whole fillet is delectably tender and weighs from ¾ to 1½ pounds. Unlike the beef tenderloin, its head and tail are rarely trimmed and the whole fillet must be cooked with great care to avoid overcooking.

TENDERLOIN

This is another name for the whole fillet roast, opposite.

RIB OR RACK OF VEAL

This section is situated in front of the loin and comprises the first portion of the foresaddle. The first six bones are the most tender for either roasts or chops. The roast looks like a series of rib chops, which explains why it may be referred to as rack of veal. We usually crack the bones to make carving as easy as possible.

CROWN ROAST OF VEAL

This is made from two racks, each with five to six ribs. The butcher cracks between the rib bones and ties the racks from top to bottom in two places for a total of four ties. Cracking between the bones makes it very easy to serve the roast once it's brought to the table. As with a crown roast of lamb, the finished product resembles a crown that can be filled in the middle with a savory stuffing. A crown roast of veal serves up to ten people, with each person getting one chop.

The roast requires careful cooking because when the bones are cracked, a little meat is exposed. The rib chops are usually frenched, which means they are cleaned of meat, and for a very formal presentation might be dressed with paper frills. This cut may have to be special ordered.

BREAST OF VEAL

This is one of the most underrated veal roasts, which is a shame. Before you roast the breast, the butcher will need to crack the ribs. When the breast is correctly cooked, it's full of good flavor, due in part to the many bones in the meat and its tasty fat content. The breast requires long, slow roasting, but can be dry-roasted in the oven rather than braised. Many times, the butcher will cut a pocket in the breast that can be stuffed. It also can be boned and roasted without much diminishment of flavor. Boneless breast of veal is also available and is the cut we use in the recipe for Veal Breast with Sausage, Wild Mushroom, and Prune Stuffing (page 92).

This is an inexpensive cut and is surely a bone lover's delight. We particularly like it stuffed and slowly baked in the oven, but it can be cut into strips for slow roasting or into individual bones, and slow cooked, then grilled.

SHOULDER OF VEAL

The forward section of the foresaddle is not as tender as the leg section from the hindsaddle, but the shoulder has a lovely flavor when roasted. These roasts are sold bone-in or boned and the latter creates a pocket for stuffing. They can also be boned, rolled, and tied.

CHOPS

LOIN VEAL CHOPS

The loin veal chop is similar in appearance to a porterhouse beef steak and therefore is also called a porterhouse veal chop or porterhouse veal steak. The T-bone identifies the chops as loin chops, which also have a large eye and a tenderloin and generally are cut to be 1 to 1½ inches thick.

RIB VEAL CHOPS

Cut from the rib roast into individual chops, rib chops are often boned, butterflied, and flattened for dishes such as veal Milanese. On the other hand, many cooks cut a pocket in the side of the chops for stuffing. Both rib and loin chops are 1 to 1½ inches thick, and those that will be stuffed should be 1½ inches thick. Their bones can be frenched, which means the meat is removed, or not.

BLADE OR CHUCK SHOULDER CHOPS

These veal chops are cut from the chuck or the shoulder and have blade bones in the center. They can be a little tough and so do well roasted or baked, but when prepared carefully can be broiled or grilled, as we do in the recipe for Grilled Veal Shoulder Chop with Marinated Zucchini and Black Olive Salad on page 91. They are similar to shoulder lamb chops in appearance and uses. Because these chops are from the foresaddle, they are a kosher cut.

OTHER CUTS OF VEAL

HINDSHANK

This is the preferred cut of veal for making osso buco. It is meatier than the foreshank with a richer, larger piece of marrow in the marrowbone, which after you eat the meat can be eaten with a small fork—a bonus! Most of the time, the hindshank for osso buco or other braised dishes is cut from the whole shank into 2-inch-long pieces. Veal hindshank usually has to be special ordered.

FORESHANK

The foreshank can be used for osso buco just as easily as the hindshank and is a little less expensive, but it is not as flavorful as the hindshank and also has a tendency to fall apart during cooking. For this reason, ask the butcher to tie it with twine when you order it. It is often found in kosher butcher shops.

SHOULDER OF VEAL

When properly trimmed of veins and sinews and with the bone removed, veal shoulder can be cut into cubes for stewing. When left in one piece, it makes an excellent boneless roast, particularly when covered with a little fat. Because of all this trimming and boning, it is a relatively small roast and weighs from 2½ to 3 pounds.

NECK OF VEAL

The neck should be sold with the bone in for the best flavor, although you should ask the butcher to crack the bone at 1½ inch intervals. It's expensive and also a little tough, but makes a delicious pot roast. The neck meat can also be ground to make good burgers.

CUBED VEAL FOR STEW

We find that meat from the breast or the shoulder makes the best stew. Breast meat, with its high fat and collagen content, is moist and tender but it tends to fall apart and diners may have to separate the meat from the fat. Shoulder meat retains its shape and is nearly as tasty as breast meat. It has less fat, so there is less need to skim the stew as it cooks.

GROUND VEAL

When we grind veal, we like to grind it from the neck or chuck, which is common for most ground veal. It makes tender, lean burgers, but don't expect the same juiciness you would get from beef burgers. Mixed with other meats, such as ground chicken or turkey, ground veal provides stability and delicate flavor. It's also delicious combined with ground pork and beef for meat loaf and meatballs.

VEAL TAILS

Although veal tails are often sold as oxtails, they are not actually from oxen but from young cattle. They are extremely tender and flavorful and make excellent stews, soups, and pot roasts. Veal tails are not a common or popular cut and therefore are not easy to find in all but the most high-end butcher shops. You probably will have to special order them and even so may not be able to get them.

VEAL CHEEKS

Like beef cheeks, these are becoming more popular with home cooks, although they are still mainly served in restaurants. They need to be braised for optimal tenderness, but when well cooked, they are small, mouthwatering nuggets of rich, marbled meat. Veal cheeks usually have to be special ordered and are almost always sold frozen, which does not damage their texture or flavor.

VEAL
ONDON
ROIL

FORESHANK

WHOLE
FILET

CROWN
ROAST

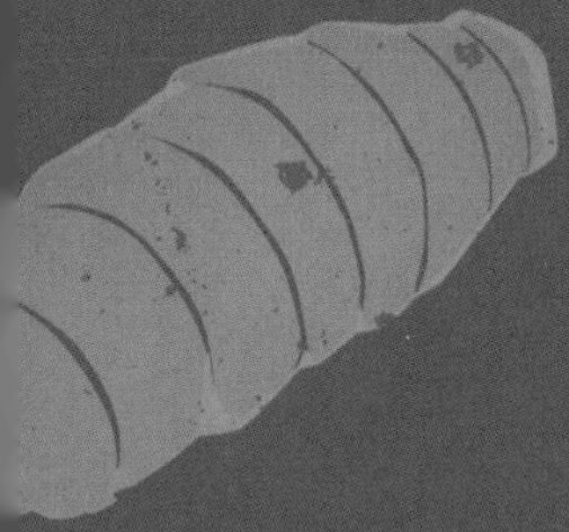

AL

ils

Veal

FILET
MIGNON

SHOULDER and CHUCK

Rolled
LOIN
ROAST
Round
ROUND
CHEEKS
OF
HINDSHANK
CUBED VEAL
for Stew

RECIPES

Veal, Onion, and Okra Stew

This is our twist on a traditional recipe from Egypt, where lamb and beef are more common than veal (and either of which can be substituted). An easy and appealing variation on the original, this is delicious served with white rice.

SERVES 4

3	tablespoons extra-virgin olive oil or vegetable oil
1 1/2	pounds trimmed veal shoulder, cut into 1-inch pieces
2	medium onions, chopped
4	large cloves garlic, crushed and peeled
2	tablespoons tomato paste
One	15-ounce can tomatoes, drained and coarsely chopped
1 1/2	teaspoons ground coriander seed
	Generous pinch of cayenne pepper
	Kosher salt
	Freshly ground black pepper
1 1/2	pounds fresh or frozen whole okra, tops trimmed
2	tablespoons fresh lemon juice

1. Heat the oil in a 10- to 12-quart pot over medium-high heat. When the oil is hot, cook the veal in batches until golden brown on just one side, 4 to 5 minutes. Transfer to a plate.
2. Reduce the heat to medium-low and add the onions and garlic, using the moisture of the vegetables to help scrape up any browned bits stuck to the bottom of the pot. Cook gently, stirring regularly, until the onions are soft and turning gold at the edges, about 10 minutes.
3. Dissolve the tomato paste in ½ cup warm water and add to the pot along with the tomatoes, coriander, cayenne, 1 tablespoon salt, a few generous grindings of black pepper, and 3 more cups of water. Return the veal to the pot along with any juices on the plate. Bring just to a simmer and cover the pot. Reduce the heat to maintain the barest possible simmer and cook until the veal is tender but still holding its shape, about 1½ hours, stirring occasionally.
4. Add the okra, making sure the pieces are immersed. Raise the heat slightly and simmer gently, uncovered, until the cooking liquid has reduced by about one-third and has concentrated to a thin, fluid, but flavorful tomato sauce, about 30 minutes more. Stir in the lemon juice and salt to taste. Let the stew sit off the heat for 5 minutes and serve.

Veal Shank Goulash with Paprika

Somewhere between a soup and a stew, this goulash contains green peppers, potatoes, and a relatively small amount of meat. Serve with egg noodles or dumplings (such as spaetzle) to soak up the abundant paprika-flavored broth.

SERVES 4

¼	cup vegetable oil
2½	pounds bone-in veal shank cut as for osso buco, then cut from the bone into 1-inch cubes (1½ pounds total meat; or substitute 1½ pounds boneless veal shoulder), any gristle and tendon removed, marrowbones reserved
2	medium onions, halved lengthwise and thinly sliced
4	garlic cloves, crushed
2	tablespoons best-quality, very fresh, Hungarian sweet paprika
¼	teaspoon cayenne pepper
¼	teaspoon ground caraway seed
1	cup dry white wine
2½	cups Beef Stock (page 302), or canned low-sodium beef broth
2½	cups water
	Kosher salt
½	pound russet potatoes, peeled and cut into ½-inch pieces
1	medium green bell pepper, seeded and cut into ½-inch pieces
	Prepared egg noodles, or spaetzle
2	teaspoons finely chopped fresh marjoram (optional)
4 to 6	tablespoons sour cream (optional)

1. Heat the oil in an 8- to 12-quart heavy, ovenproof pot over medium-high heat. When the oil is hot, cook the veal, working in batches, until deeply browned on two sides, about 5 minutes per side. Transfer to a plate and reserve. Preheat the oven to 350°F.

2. Reduce the heat to medium-low and add the onions and garlic. Cook until soft and pale gold at the edges, about 10 minutes, stirring occasionally. Stir in the paprika, cayenne, caraway, and wine. Bring to a simmer and cook for 3 minutes, scraping the bottom of the pot to loosen any browned bits. Add the stock, water, and 2 teaspoons salt. Return the meat, any juices on the plate, and the reserved marrowbones to the pot. Stir well and bring to a simmer. Cover pot, place in the oven, and cook for 20 minutes. Reduce heat to 275°F to maintain the slightest possible simmer. Cook until the meat is tender, about 1 hour and 40 minutes more, checking occasionally to ensure that the liquid is barely simmering.

3. Transfer the pot to the stovetop. Remove marrowbones and set aside until cool enough to handle. Meanwhile, skim off some or all of the fat and return to a gentle simmer. Stir in the potatoes and gently simmer, uncovered, until nearly tender, 15 to 20 minutes. Stir in the green peppers and simmer for 15 minutes more. When the marrowbones have cooled a bit, remove the marrow (if it hasn't dissolved) and mash it to a paste in a bowl; stir marrow paste into goulash. After cooking the peppers for 15 minutes, the goulash should be richly flavored but with a very loose consistency somewhere between a soup and stew; simmer briefly to reduce or add a bit of broth or water to thin, if necessary. Add salt to taste.

4. Ladle the goulash over noodles or dumplings. Sprinkle with marjoram and top with sour cream, if you like. Serve immediately.

Veal and Ricotta Meatballs

These meatballs are light, fluffy, and full of flavor. We like to serve them bathed in tomato sauce, but they're great on top of tomato-sauced pasta, too. To serve them with pasta, reheat a double-batch of our Quick Tomato Sauce and cook 1 pound of spaghetti or other pasta in well-salted water until al dente. Drain pasta, reserving a cup of the cooking water. Toss pasta with about three-quarters of the sauce, thinning it with a bit of cooking water if the pasta seems dry or too "tight." Divide the pasta between warmed serving bowls and spoon the remaining sauce over each. Top each portion with 2 or 3 meatballs and sprinkle with chopped fresh parsley. Serve the pasta with grated Parmesan on the side.

SERVES 4; MAKES ABOUT FOURTEEN 2½-INCH MEATBALLS

1	pound good-quality fresh ricotta cheese
1	pound ground veal (finely ground if possible; ask your butcher to pass it through the grinder an extra time—or better still, use a small gauge grinding disk)
1	cup coarse fresh bread crumbs soaked in milk and squeezed until nearly dry (to make coarse fresh bread crumbs, see Note, page 131)
2	eggs, beaten
2	ounces finely grated Parmigiano-Reggiano or similar cheese
2½	teaspoons kosher salt
½	teaspoon fresh coarsely ground black pepper
⅛	teaspoon freshly grated nutmeg
	All-purpose flour
	Olive oil for frying
	Double-batch Quick Tomato Sauce (page 280; optional)
2	tablespoons chopped fresh flat-leaf parsley for garnish (optional)

1. If the ricotta is excessively wet, place in a fine-mesh strainer set over a bowl or in cheesecloth suspended over a bowl and let drain, refrigerated, 2 or 3 hours or overnight.
2. Put the ricotta, veal, bread crumbs, eggs, cheese, salt, pepper, and nutmeg in a large bowl. Working with a rubber spatula or wooden spoon, stir the mixture briskly—nearly whipping the mixture—for 1 to 2 minutes to combine. Cover and chill for at least 2 hours.
3. Generously flour a baking dish or sheet pan large enough to comfortably hold 14 large meatballs. Have ready a cup or two of flour. Measure a level ⅓ cup of the chilled veal mixture and, using floured hands, gently shape it into a ball and place in the floured dish (if veal feels overly soft and squishy, dusting it lightly with more flour will help to firm it up, but don't overdo it). Repeat with the remaining veal mixture. Cover and chill for at least 1 hour. The meatballs can be made and kept tightly covered in the refrigerator up to a day ahead of cooking.
4. If serving with Quick Tomato Sauce, reheat it in a saucepan and keep hot over low heat. Warm serving plates in a low oven.
5. Pour ¾-inch of oil into a 10-to-14-inch straight-sided skillet or shallow pot and heat to 300°F on a deep-fry thermometer. Carefully place the meatballs in the hot oil and fry, working in two batches to avoid crowding, until golden brown on their immersed portions, 4 to 5 minutes. Turn and cook until the meatballs are golden all over and just cooked through, or when an instant-read thermometer inserted into the meatballs reads 150° to 160°F, 4 to 5 minutes more. Note: The chilled meatballs will lower the oil temperature to 275°F; this is the temperature you want to maintain throughout the frying.
6. Drain the meatballs on a paper towel–lined plate. If serving with tomato sauce, place ¼ to ⅓ cup of sauce for each meatball on warmed plates. Arrange one, two, or three meatballs on top of the sauce, depending on the number and size of the servings. Garnish with parsley (if desired) and serve.

Veal Scallops with Norwegian Goat Cheese Sauce

A deep caramel-colored Norwegian goat cheese called *Gjetost* lends its unique flavor to the sauce for this recipe. The whole thing comes together in minutes and is delicious when served with roasted root vegetables. Pound the veal to a thickness of ⅛ to ¼ inch to create thin, delicate veal scaloppine that are less apt to dry out during the brief cooking over fairly high heat.

SERVES 2

- 2 tablespoons unsalted butter
- 3 tablespoons vegetable oil
- 2 tablespoons finely chopped shallot
- 2 tablespoons finely chopped onion
- Kosher salt
- 1 pound veal scallops (6 to 8 pieces), pounded to thickness of ⅛ to ¼ inch
- ¼ cup Veal Stock (page 303) or Chicken Stock (page 299) or water
- ¾ cup sour cream
- ¼ teaspoon freshly ground black pepper
- 2 ounces *Gjetost* (Norwegian goat cheese) or another semi-firm goat cheese
- 1 tablespoon finely chopped fresh flat-leaf parsley

1. Preheat the oven to 200°F and put serving plates in the oven to warm.
2. Heat 1 tablespoon each of the butter and oil in a 12- to 14-inch skillet over medium-low heat. Cook the shallot and onion until softened but not browned, about 5 minutes, stirring occasionally. Using a rubber spatula, scrape the shallot and onion into a small bowl and reserve.
3. Salt the veal scallops on both sides and return the skillet to medium-high heat. When the skillet is very hot but not smoking, add the remaining 1 tablespoon butter and 1 tablespoon oil, swirling the skillet to coat. Working in batches, add the veal, briefly pressing on the pieces to help them make contact with the skillet, and cook until the edges are golden, about 1 minute on the first side; turn and cook for 45 seconds or so on the second side. Transfer veal to a baking dish and keep warm in the oven (meat should be slightly undercooked as it will continue to cook as it sits).
4. Scrape up and discard any blackened bits from the skillet and return to low heat. Add the reserved shallot and onion and the stock, scraping up any browned bits stuck to the bottom of the skillet and simmer until the liquid is reduced to 2 tablespoons. Increase the heat slightly and stir in the sour cream, black pepper, and ½ teaspoon of salt. When the sour cream is hot, stir in half of the cheese; when just melted, stir in the remaining cheese, stirring to incorporate and scraping down the sides of the skillet. The sauce should be hot but don't let it boil. Stir in any juices in the baking dish beneath the meat.
5. Return the veal briefly to the sauce to coat, then divide between warmed serving plates. Garnish with the parsley and serve.

Veal Scaloppine with Prosciutto and Sage

There are fewer veal dishes so easily prepared and so immensely satisfying to eat. Serve Saltimbocca alla Romana alongside a small mound of a sautéed leafy green vegetable like Swiss chard and accompany with a glass of light, cool, white wine.

SERVES 2 TO 3

1	pound veal scallops (6 to 8 pieces, pounded into similar shape about halfway between 1/8 and 1/4 of an inch thick (see Note)
6 to 8	large leaves fresh sage
6 to 10	paper-thin slices prosciutto di Parma, or similar cured ham
	Kosher salt
	Freshly ground black pepper
	All-purpose flour for dredging
3	tablespoons extra-virgin olive oil, plus more as needed
1/2	cup dry white wine
2/3	cup Chicken Stock (page 299), or canned low-sodium chicken broth

1. Preheat the oven to 200°F, and put a baking dish and serving plates in the oven to warm.
2. Rub one veal scallop on both sides with a sage leaf without tearing the leaf. Set the sage leaf aside. Trim a slice of prosciutto to fit more or less within the dimensions of the cutlet and press it into the meat to help it adhere. Center the reserved sage leaf on top of the prosciutto. Working lengthwise, weave a toothpick in and out of the veal to secure the prosciutto and sage, keeping the veal as flat as possible. Repeat with the remaining veal, prosciutto, and sage leaves.
3. Salt and pepper the veal (salt the prosciutto side of the veal more lightly than the opposite side). Set the veal scallops and a rimmed plate or baking dish filled with a cup or two of flour for dredging near the stovetop.
4. Heat the oil over medium-high heat in a skillet large enough to hold half the veal. While the oil is heating, dredge half the cutlets with flour, shaking off the excess.
5. When it begins to smoke, swirl the oil to coat the bottom of the skillet and cook the first batch, prosciutto-side down, 45 seconds to 1 minute (the heat should be high enough so that in this short time the edges of the veal brown nicely and the prosciutto gets a bit crispy; adjust the heat as needed). Turn and cook for 45 seconds or so (veal should be undercooked slightly as it will continue to cook as it sits). Transfer veal to the baking dish in the oven. Repeat with the second batch of veal, adding more oil to the skillet, if necessary. Transfer to the oven to keep warm.
6. Let the skillet cool for a few moments off the heat, then reduce the heat to medium, and return the skillet to the heat. Add the wine and simmer until reduced to 2 to 3 tablespoons, no more than 45 seconds. Add the broth and reduce to 1/3 cup, 35 to 45 seconds longer, scraping up any browned bits on the bottom of the skillet. Add any accumulated juices from the veal in the oven. If necessary, continue to simmer for a few seconds to concentrate the flavor of the sauce. Taste and season with salt, if needed.
7. Divide the veal scallops among the plates, attractively overlapping them in a shingle pattern. Drizzle the sauce over each and serve immediately.

NOTE: Whether you or the butcher pounds the meat, the cutlets should be of uniform thickness so that they cook evenly. Pounding them to a thickness between 1/8 and 1/4 of an inch creates thin, delicate veal scaloppine that are less likely to dry out when cooked quickly.

Stuffed Veal Chops with Fontina and Herb Butter

A rich, decadent treat, these stuffed veal chops—crisp with bread crumb crust and oozing Fontina cheese—can be assembled long before dinnertime and take less than 10 minutes to cook. Serve with simply prepared spinach or Swiss chard and sautéed mushrooms.

SERVES 2

4	paper-thin slices of bresaola, bunderfleisch, or similar air-dried beef (optional)
2	veal rib chops (about 3/4 pound and 1 1/2 inch thick), each with a pocket cut for stuffing and pounded to thickness of 3/4 inch (see diagram)
4	ounces Fontina Val d'Aosta, or similar semi-soft cheese, coarsely grated
	Kosher salt
	Fresh coarsely ground black pepper
	All-purpose flour for dredging
2	eggs, beaten
2/3	cup homemade dried bread crumbs
3	tablespoons extra-virgin olive oil or clarified unsalted butter
5	tablespoons unsalted butter, cut into pieces
2	tablespoons finely chopped fresh flat-leaf parsley
1	teaspoon finely chopped fresh sage
1/2	teaspoon finely chopped fresh rosemary
1/2	teaspoon finely grated lemon zest

1. Divide the bresaola (if using) between the pockets in each veal chop, laying the pieces as flat as possible. Divide the cheese between the chops, distributing it evenly. Preheat the oven to 175°F and put plates in the oven to warm.

2. Generously salt the veal chops on both sides, pressing the salt into the surface of the chops. Sprinkle chops with a generous grinding of black pepper. Place the flour, beaten eggs, and bread crumbs on separate wide-rimmed plates or bowls.

3. Dredge the chops in the flour, shaking off the excess. Dip both sides of the chops in the eggs, letting the excess run off, and transfer to the bowl of bread crumbs; thickly coat each side of the chops by firmly pushing the bread crumbs into the surfaces of each.

4. Heat the oil over medium-high heat in a skillet just large enough to contain the chops. When the oil is quite hot but not yet smoking, swirl it to evenly coat the skillet and add the chops. Reduce the heat to medium-low and cook until deep golden brown on both sides and the cheese has melted, about 4 minutes per side for medium. (If you're unsure as to the degree of doneness, you can make a small cut and peek inside a chop.) Divide the chops between warmed serving plates.

5. Wipe out the skillet and return to medium-low heat. Add the butter, parsley, sage, rosemary, and lemon zest, swirling the skillet until the butter is melted and frothy, 20 to 30 seconds. Pour over the veal chops and serve.

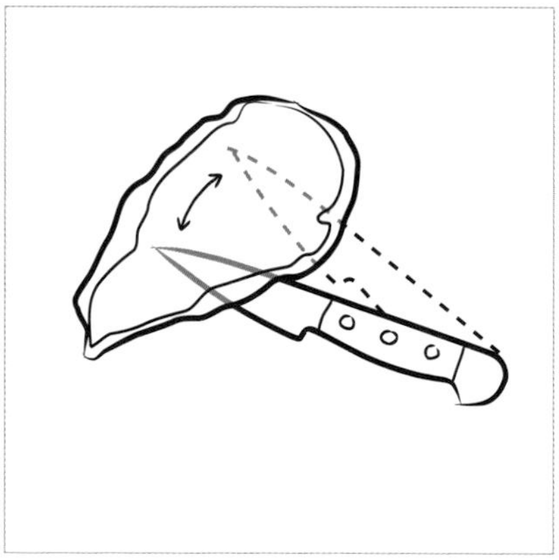

Grilled Veal Shoulder Chop with Marinated Zucchini and Black Olive Salad

What we like about this dish is that is showcases veal shoulder chops, an often overlooked but delicious and very affordable cut of veal. You can pan-fry the veal in a few tablespoons of olive oil instead of grilling it.

SERVES 2 TO 4

	Scant 1/2 cup extra-virgin olive oil
2	medium zucchini, cut in half lengthwise and sliced into 1/4-inch-thick half-moons
14 to 16	grape tomatoes, quartered lengthwise
1/2	cup chopped red onion
1/4	cup coarsely chopped pitted kalamata or similar black olives
2	large cloves garlic, crushed and peeled
	Kosher salt
	Fresh coarsely ground black pepper
1/2	teaspoon dried oregano
1/8	teaspoon crushed red pepper flakes
1/2	teaspoon sugar
1/3	cup white wine vinegar
One	1 1/2- to 2-pound veal blade shoulder chop (about 1 inch thick), cut into 2 to 4 pieces
1/3	cup finely crumbled feta cheese
2	tablespoons chopped fresh mint

1. Heat the oil in a 10- to 12-inch skillet over medium-high heat until almost smoking. Working in two or three batches, add the zucchini and spread it out in a single layer. Cook until mostly golden brown in spots on both sides and just tender, 2 to 3 minutes per side. Using a slotted spoon, transfer the zucchini to a glass or ceramic baking dish large enough to hold all the zucchini in a single layer.
2. Pour the oil from the skillet into a small bowl and reserve. Scatter the tomatoes, red onion, and olives over the zucchini.
3. Return the skillet to medium heat and add the garlic, ¾ teaspoon salt, ½ teaspoon black pepper, oregano, red pepper flakes, sugar, and vinegar. Bring to a simmer, swirling the skillet to dissolve the salt and sugar. Pour the hot vinegar mixture evenly over the zucchini, shaking the dish to help the zucchini soak up the vinegar. Pour the reserved cooking oil evenly over the zucchini, again shaking the dish to evenly distribute the ingredients. Set aside to marinate for at least 30 minutes and up to 3 hours.
4. Prepare a medium-hot charcoal fire and preheat an oiled grate (alternately, preheat a gas grill to medium-high). When the coals are covered in a light gray ash, salt and pepper the veal. Grill to desired doneness, about 5 minutes per side for medium. Transfer the veal to serving plates. Spoon a generous quantity of zucchini salad over the veal, as well as a few spoonfuls of the seasoned oil and vinegar mixture. Scatter the crumbled feta cheese and mint over each portion and serve.

Veal Breast with Sausage, Wild Mushroom, and Prune Stuffing

Leafy green vegetables like Swiss chard or spinach are delicious accompaniments to this dish. You can also serve it at room temperature with a salad or chilled raw or cooked vegetables tossed with vinaigrette.

SERVES 8

3	tablespoons unsalted butter
1/2	pound sweet Italian-style sausage
1	ounce dried porcini mushrooms soaked in 1 cup warm tap water until softened in a small bowl.
1	medium onion, finely chopped
2	ribs celery, finely chopped
3	large cloves garlic, finely chopped
5	cups very coarse, fresh bread crumbs (see Note on page 131)
1	apple, peeled, cored, and cut into 1/4-inch pieces
1/4	cup pine nuts
6	large fresh sage leaves, finely chopped
3	tablespoons chopped fresh flat-leaf parsley
	Kosher salt
	Fresh coarsely ground black pepper
1/4	pound pitted prunes, soaked in hot water for 30 minutes to soften
2	large eggs
One	3 1/2-pound piece boneless veal breast cut from the brisket end (about 1 1/2 inches thick), trimmed of excess fat and cut with a pocket for stuffing (see Note)
1	tablespoon olive oil
1 1/2	cups Veal Stock (page 303) or Chicken Stock (page 299), or canned low-sodium chicken broth

1. Melt the butter in a 10- to 12-inch skillet over medium heat. Remove the sausage from its casing and crumble it into the skillet. Cook until the sausage is lightly browned and just cooked through, about 4 minutes. As it cooks, break it up into small bits with a fork or wooden spoon. Using a slotted spoon, remove the sausage to a plate, leaving the fat in the skillet (if the sausage is still in large pieces, crumble by hand).

2. Remove the mushrooms from the soaking liquid, leaving any grit at the bottom of the bowl; squeeze most of the moisture from the mushrooms back into bowl and set the liquid aside. Add the mushrooms to the skillet and cook for 1 minute, stirring. Add the onion, celery, and garlic and cook until pale gold at the edges, 8 to 10 minutes, stirring occasionally.

3. Remove the skillet from the heat. Add the bread crumbs, apples, pine nuts, sage, parsley, the reserved sausage, ½ teaspoon salt, and a few generous grindings of black pepper. Chop the softened prunes into ½-inch pieces (discarding their liquid) and add to the mixture in the skillet. Thoroughly combine the ingredients (mixture can be transferred to a large bowl if more room is needed). Return the skillet and stuffing to medium heat. Stir for a couple of minutes to combine the flavors. Remove from the heat and let cool in the skillet. (The stuffing can be prepared up to this point 1 day ahead and stored, covered, in the refrigerator.)

4. Strain the mushroom soaking liquid through a fine-mesh strainer or paper towel to catch any grit. Measure ½ cup of the liquid and beat together with the eggs. Pour over the stuffing mixture. Mix well to coat all the ingredients with the egg mixture.

5. Preheat the oven to 325°F and arrange a rack in the middle of the oven.

6. Fill the pocket of the veal with the stuffing, spreading it evenly and into the corners. The veal will plump up considerably, but the top and bottom edges of the opening should still just close around the stuffing (depending on the dimensions of the veal, you may have up to a cup of stuffing left over). Secure by threading one or two heavy wooden skewers (or if you like, sew up the opening with a trussing needle and kitchen twine). Rub the outside of the veal with the oil and sprinkle generously with salt and a few generous grindings of black pepper.

7. Transfer veal, fat-side up, to a roasting pan or baking dish just large enough to contain it. Add the stock to the pan and cover tightly with foil. Roast for 2½ hours. Remove foil and baste the veal with cooking liquid. Continue to roast, uncovered, until golden brown, about 1 hour more, basting every 20 minutes.

8. Remove the pan to the stovetop and let the veal rest loosely covered with foil for 20 minutes to help firm the stuffing for easier slicing. Using a pair of spatulas, carefully transfer the veal to a cutting board and remove the skewers. Using a long serrated knife, cut into slices ¾ to 1 inch thick. Carefully transfer slices to serving plates (a long spatula is helpful for this). Spoon some cooking liquid over each portion and serve.

NOTE: A whole, bone-in veal breast (which is actually half a breast) weighs about 12 pounds. Once cut away from the bones, a flat, brisket-like piece weighing about 7 pounds remains. What you want is roughly the thickest half of this piece (around 1½ inches thick): a 3½-pound slab of veal with two sides about 15 inches long that connect a third side measuring about 10 inches long. Along its 15-inch length, the meat tapers to about 5 inches forming a shape that's irregular but easily outfitted with a pocket for stuffing. A butcher can make a pocket, but if you prefer to do it yourself, first trim most of the external fat from the meat and lay the meat on a work surface. Working with a sharp knife and with the thickest long edge of the meat facing you, insert a large knife horizontally into the center of this thick edge of the veal. Working in smooth strokes, gradually cut a pocket as evenly as possible, leaving a 1-inch border on three sides, taking care as you work near the edges and corners. If a few small holes occur, they can easily be patched—after stuffing—by inserting thin disks of veal cut from a thicker part of the breast. This will help prevent the stuffing from escaping.

If using wooden skewers, soak them in water for at least 30 minutes before threading them with the meat, and then wrap the long, exposed portion of wood with aluminum foil before putting them on the grill.

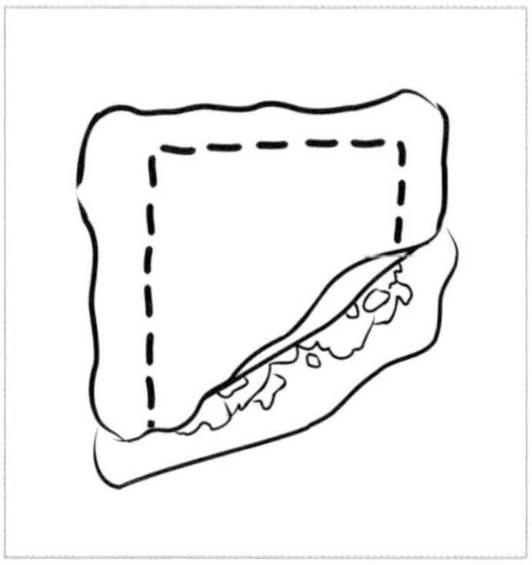

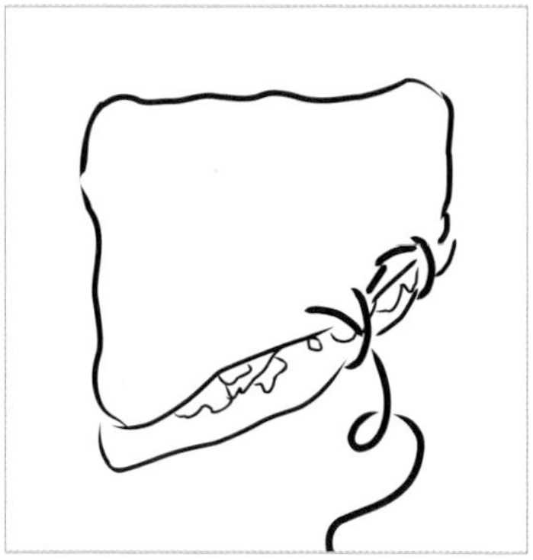

Poached Veal and Veal Tongue with Parsley Sauce

A simple variation of northern Italy's renown *bollito misto* or "mixed boil," this recipe is a great introduction to delicate veal tongue. Bring the meats to room temperature before poaching and use homemade chicken stock. Serve with forks, knives, and spoons—for sipping the tangy parsley-flavored broth. You can use a larger veal roast to feed more people without adjusting the recipe.

SERVES 4 TO 6

- 1 fresh veal tongue, 1 to 1½ pounds, rinsed, excess fat removed
- 1 medium yellow onion, quartered
- 2 bay leaves
- Kosher salt
- One 2-pound veal shoulder roast, tied
- 12 to 16 cups homemade Chicken Stock (page 299), or canned low-sodium chicken broth
- ½ pound end pieces (scrap) prosciutto di Parma or similar cured ham (optional—ask at your deli counter or butcher)
- 12 baby potatoes (about 1 pound), cut in half
- 3 to 4 large carrots, peeled and cut into 2-inch-long pieces
- 18 baby turnips, peeled, or 3 medium turnips, peeled and cut into 6 or 8 wedges
- 2 red onions, cut lengthwise into quarters (or sixths if large), stems attached, and peeled
- One small bundle of fresh herbs (tied together with kitchen string) consisting of: one large sprig thyme, one small sprig rosemary, four sage leaves
- 2 cups Piquant Parsley Sauce (page 290)
- 1½ tablespoons finely chopped fresh flat-leaf parsley

1. Place the veal tongue, yellow onion, bay leaves, and 1 tablespoon salt in a 6- to 8-quart pot with water to cover by 2 inches. Bring just to a boil; reduce the heat and simmer gently for 45 minutes, uncovered. Remove from the heat, keeping the tongue immersed in the cooking water until cool enough to handle. Using your fingers or a paring knife, peel the skin surrounding the tongue (it helps to first slip the knife point beneath an exposed edge of skin to free it from the flesh; continue peeling with your fingers). Cut away any remaining gristle and fat and return the tongue to the cooking liquid.

2. While the tongue is simmering, rub the veal shoulder with 1½ teaspoons salt and set aside. Bring 12 cups of the chicken broth, the ham (if using), and 2 teaspoons salt to a boil in an 8- to 10-quart pot. Add the veal shoulder and then enough additional stock to just cover the meat; cook at the barest possible simmer for 1 hour. Add the peeled veal tongue (discard its cooking liquid) to the pot; cover and continue cooking for 1½ hours, turning the tongue once during this time.

3. Preheat a large sauceboat in a low oven. Add the potatoes, carrots, turnips, red onions, and bundle of herbs to the stockpot; simmer, uncovered, until the vegetables are just tender, 20 to 30 minutes more, stirring occasionally. Remove and discard the ham and the herb bundle.

4. Fill the sauceboat with some of the cooking broth, a serving dish with parsley sauce, and a small dish with coarse salt to pass at the table. To serve, remove the strings on the veal shoulder and cut into ½-inch-thick slices. Cut the veal tongue on the bias, or diagonal, into ⅜-inch-thick slices. Place a few slices of each type of meat in warmed large, shallow serving bowls or deep plates. Place a piece or two of each vegetable in and around the meats. Moisten each serving with a small ladleful of cooking broth and sprinkle lightly with parsley. Cover and keep the remaining meat warm or return to warm broth. Serve immediately, with diners flavoring their meats with parsley sauce and salt at the table. Moisten meats with additional broth as needed.

Vitello Tonnato

Our version of vitello tonnato is not layered like a cake, as some are, with thick slices of braised veal separated by sauce and the entire assembly chilled overnight. Instead, we poach the veal until it is medium-rare, then chill it, slice it, and serve it more like beef carpaccio. It's at serving time that we add the sauce. Tightly wrapped, the meat and tuna sauce will keep for nearly a week in the refrigerator—so both can be made well ahead of serving. The sauce is also great on cold, poached chicken, turkey breast, or sautéed veal scallopine. Vitello tonnato is a great summer dish. It is best to begin preparing the veal 1 day in advance of serving so it can chill overnight. The sauce can be made a day ahead, too.

SERVES 4 AS A MAIN COURSE; 8 AS AN APPETIZER

- 2 tablespoons vegetable oil or extra-virgin olive oil
- Kosher salt
- 2 pounds veal sirloin, eye of round, or top round, cut from just one muscle and without any fat or gristle (see Note)
- 1 medium onion, coarsely chopped
- 1 small carrot, peeled and coarsely chopped
- 1 small rib celery, coarsely chopped
- 2 large cloves garlic, crushed
- 1 bay leaf
- 4 cups water
- 12 ounces (2 cans) high-quality, imported tuna in olive oil, drained
- 6 anchovy fillets
- 1 tablespoon capers, rinsed
- 2 tablespoons fresh lemon juice, plus additional as needed
- 2 cups homemade Mayonnaise (page 276)
- 2 tablespoons chopped fresh flat-leaf parsley
- Lemon wedges for garnish

1. Heat the oil in a 6-quart heavy pot over medium-high heat and generously salt the veal on all sides. When the oil is hot, add the veal and cook until pale golden on all sides, 6 to 10 minutes total, depending on the diameter of the veal. Remove to a plate and reserve.

2. Add the onion, carrot, celery, garlic, and bay leaf. Cook, stirring occasionally, for 2 minutes. Add the water and bring to a simmer, scraping the bottom of the pot to loosen any browned bits. Bring to a simmer and reduce the heat to low. Return the veal to the pot; cover and cook at the barest possible simmer, turning the meat once during cooking, until an instant-read thermometer registers 130°F when inserted in the center of the meat, 15 to 40 minutes, depending on the thickness of the meat (a 2½-inch-diameter eye of round will take 15 to 20 minutes to reach 130°F; a 3-inch piece, about 25 minutes; and a 4-inch piece, about 35 minutes). Try to gauge doneness without checking the temperature more than twice, so as not to excessively puncture the meat, which drains it of moisture.

3. When the veal reaches 130°F, remove it from the oven and place it on a baking rack set over a plate, and let cool to room temperature. Wrap the cooled meat tightly in a double layer of plastic and chill for at least 3 hours and preferably overnight.

4. Meanwhile, put the tuna, anchovies, capers, and lemon juice in the bowl of a food processor; process until very smooth, 2 to 3 minutes, pausing to scrape down the sides of the bowl as needed. Transfer to a mixing bowl.

5. Fold the mayonnaise into the tuna purée until well combined; add lemon juice and salt to taste, if you like. Chill for at least 2 hours or preferably overnight (the sauce will thicken and the flavors will meld).

6. Remove the veal from the refrigerator and, if tied, remove the butcher's twine. Using a very sharp knife, slice the veal across the grain between 1/16 and 1/8 inch thick, discarding the initial slice or two from the ends of the meat. Before plating, determine an attractive pattern in which to present the slices—the number of slices per serving depends on the diameter of the veal and whether these are first-course or main-course servings.

7. For smaller first-course servings, the slices of veal can be arranged in a flower-like pattern on large plates, the slices overlapping just barely or not at all, as beef carpaccio is often served. The tuna sauce can be attractively smeared over the slices, leaving a margin of the meat exposed. One first-course serving of sauce is between 4 and 6 tablespoons per plate.

8. For larger main-course servings, you'll have to overlap the slices, shingle style, in order to fit more slices on each plate. The amount of overlap and the overall pattern depend on the diameter of each slice. To serve, arrange one row of larger slices or two rows of smaller slices down the middle of a large serving plate. First, lay down a slice of veal, then smear some sauce over the slice—about ½ tablespoon for a smaller slice and around 1 tablespoon for a larger slice—leaving a small margin of meat exposed at the edges. Next, place a second slice of veal over the first, shingle style, and top with sauce. Repeat this process, layering meat and sauce on each of four plates. Figure on ½ to ⅔ cup sauce per main-course plate.

9. Scatter the parsley over each plate, garnish with a lemon wedge, and serve.

NOTE: Veal sirloin is expensive, but it's wonderful for this dish, yielding the silkiest texture. The usually less-expensive eye of round (the other cuts of round) is slightly chewier but tastes equally good. Whichever cut you buy, it's important to ask for a piece of meat composed of a single muscle, which will be without significant deposits of fat, veins of gristle, or connective tissue. This ensures that, once cooked, the veal will slice cleanly and, evenly, and be free of fat or gristle. The eye of round, for example, is a single, thin muscle, just 3 inches in diameter. Ask your butcher for a 2-pound piece of it. Whether narrow or wide in diameter, it should be as regular in shape as possible, appear roast-like in proportion, and, if shaped irregularly, tied like a roast.

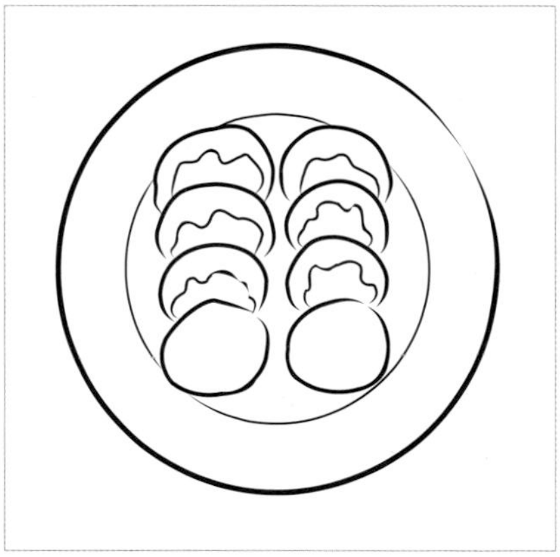

Sausage
Pork Belly
COUNTRY HAM
SALT PORK
WHOLE HAM
Tenderloin
PORK
AMERICAN-STYLE BACON
ST.

OUIS-STYLE RIBS

LARD

TON
TT

Baby Back
RIBS

ING

CENTER LOIN
PORK ROAST

SPECIAL
FATBACK

OSCIUTTO

apple

SLAB
BACON

PIG'S
FEET

M HOCKS

nk!"

Ham Shank

Pancetta

UIS-STYLE RIBS
LARD
Baby Back
RIBS
CENTER LOIN
PORK ROAST
OSCIUTTO
SPECIAL
FATBA
SLAB
BACON
ple
M HOCKS
PIG'S
FEET

CHAPTER THREE

Pork

Pork is a sweet, tender meat that has been eaten for more than 9,000 years. Hogs were domesticated long before sheep, goats, or cattle and so it is no small wonder that pork figures so prominently in most of the world's great cuisines. In this country, we eat pork chops and pork tenderloin in larger quantities than other cuts of pork from the butcher shop.

Pork is not graded as "prime" or "choice," as are beef and lamb, but instead as No.1, No. 2, or No. 3. The No. 1 grade, which is the grade of pork sold in retail markets, is the best. In the old days, the season for pork was late fall, when hogs were butchered during the first cold snap. Today's pork is good at any time but the best pork is available from May through October when the animals are most apt to have access to the most varied diet.

Look for pork with pinkish-gray, finely textured lean meat with streaks of firm, creamy white fat. The exterior fat should not be thick, but what there is should be a creamy white. The bones should have streaks of red running through them. Avoid deep red meat with a coarse texture, white bones, and yellowing or bright white fat.

Pork is bred so that it is lower in fat than in previous days, and according to the industry, is 31 percent lower in fat and cholesterol than it was 20 years ago. It is also very safe and does not need to be cooked until gray and overdone, as was the case several generations ago. It is at its best when cooked to a medium doneness. It's internal temperature should be 160°F, the temperature recommended by the U.S. Department of Agriculture. Use a meat thermometer to judge doneness. Remove large cuts of meat (such as pork tenderloins and loin roasts) from the oven when a meat or an instant-read thermometer registers 150°F and allow the meat to rest, during which time the internal temperature will rise by at least 5 degrees. Because pork is so safe, some chefs cook it to slightly lower temperatures. Follow the recommendations in the following individual recipes when it comes to internal temperatures.

If your butcher, supermarket, or gourmet shop carries heirloom or specialty pork, try it. Take our word for it—you will have a hard time going back to run-of-the-mill pork!

The flavor of heirloom pork is so satisfying that you will immediately understand why, in days gone by, the pork raised right there on the farm was so cherished and why the pigs were so carefully tended and well fed. We sell meat from pure- and cross-bred Tamworths, Gloucestershire Old Spots, and Large Black hogs, pasture-raised for us in Vermont, where they are fed a diet free of antibiotics and growth hormones. The result? Flavor so deep and rich it echoes the pork from that bygone era. The meat is gloriously juicy and tender—just the way pork should taste.

HIND SECTION

WHOLE HAM

Whole hams are the upper part of the leg, without the shank and foot. This thick, fleshy cut with its high ratio of lean meat to fat and bone, can be either fresh, or cured and smoked. Baking is the only way to cook these hams, and surely a baked ham is a favorite on many holiday tables. Cured and smoked hams and those sold in cans or otherwise labeled as "precooked" are ready to eat, although most people warm them in the oven. Whole hams can easily weigh as much as 20 pounds, although you can buy a small ham that weighs 14 or 15 pounds.

HAM BUTT

The butt, which is the rounder part of the whole ham, is the most desirable half because it has very little bone. It is sold either fresh or cured and smoked and has lots of good meat.

HAM SHANK

The end of the ham, the part farther down the leg, is rather bony and does not have as much solid meat as the butt. Consequently, the shank is not as popular, although because of its bone, it is extremely flavorful. Ham hocks come from the shank (see Ham Hocks, page 104). For the tastiest shanks, look for ones with a layer of skin and fat. Ham shanks need to be special ordered from most butchers; if you find that a minimum order is more than you need for a particular recipe, remember that these freeze very well.

PORK SHANK

Pork shank is another name for ham shank.

HAM STEAK

The ham steak is the center slice from a precooked, smoked ham, between the butt and the shank. It is oval, rimmed with white fat on one side, and has a round bone in the center. The meat is lean and fine-grained. Half-inch-thick cuts should be pan-broiled, while thicker steaks can be broiled, grilled, or baked.

PANCETTA

Pancetta is sometimes called Italian bacon and is used as a flavoring agent, in much the same way as bacon is. Cut from the belly of the hog, it is salt-cured ham that is not smoked. Pancetta tastes deliciously meaty and rich. It should be red and its fat white (never brown or dull) and there should be an almost equal distribution of both. Pancetta often is sold thinly sliced, although not as thinly sliced as prosciutto. Sometimes it is sold in chunks.

PROSCIUTTO

Authentic prosciutto is made in Parma, Italy, and is called Parma ham or *prosciutto di Parma*. To complicate the issue further, the word "prosciutto" means "ham" in Italian, which is why other Italian hams cured in a similar fashion are also called prosciutto. Prosciutto di Parma is cured very carefully for nearly a year with brine, sugar, and herbs. Prosciutto should be only slightly salty and its white fat should streak the pink meat. The ham should be sliced very thinly as close to serving time as possible. Paper-thin slices of prosciutto are featured on antipasti platters, wrapped around melon and figs, and sometimes served in sandwiches and pasta dishes.

COUNTRY HAM

Country ham is salted, hung, tied, smoked, and allowed to age for months—some for up to a year—so that its meat is very dry and intensely flavored. Some consider it an acquired taste. These hams also are called Virginia hams or, perhaps more famously, Smithfield hams for the Virginia town where many of them are cured. Other southern states are well known for curing great hams, but because they do not get as cold as Virginia does, the curing methods are different (they usually are salt-brined and not smoked).

Country hams are sold cured but not already cooked. Most aficionados recommend cooking them by means of a time-consuming process requiring soaking and simmering over a period of several days. But once they are cooked, the meat lasts for a long time and most people only eat a little at a time.

CENTER CUTS

CENTER SECTION OF THE HOG

This large portion of the animal is divided lengthwise into two sections that are completely different in character and use. The top section is the loin, which is full of tender, juicy, lean meat, usually sold as fresh pork for roasts and chops. The meat in the section below the loin, which is the belly, is interspersed with fat and bones and very often cured and smoked. It's all good: the fat is bacon and the bones are ribs!

WHOLE LOIN OF PORK
The whole loin consists of the loin and the chops between the shoulder and the leg. Characteristically, it is divided into different cuts of roasts and chops.

SIRLOIN PORK ROAST
Right in front of the butt is the sirloin. The roast is tasty and tender with a small round bone and is always sold fresh. It is also called the sirloin end roast.

SIRLOIN PORK CHOPS
These very flavorful chops are cut from the front part of the sirloin roast. They require slow cooking in the oven, and unless they are marinated do not do well if broiled or grilled. In some markets, they are boned and sold as pork steaks.

CENTER LOIN PORK ROAST
This is called a rib roast by some butchers and home cooks because of the T-bone and rib bones involved. The front part has a tenderloin. This is one of the more popular pork roasts we sell in our shop.

ROLLED LOIN PORK ROAST
The only difference between this and the center loin pork roast is that the bones are removed. It is rolled and tied so that it's very easy to slice. We like to take the bones off in one piece and then tie them back on the roll in such a way that they can be used as a rack for the roast to rest on during cooking. When the roast is done, the strings are cut and removed and the bones are discarded before the meat is sliced.

TENDERLOIN OF PORK
The tenderloin, or fillet, lies beneath the ribs. Similar to beef tenderloin but much smaller, it is tender and lean and requires cautious cooking so that it does not dry out. Pork tenderloin is fantastically popular these days for grilling, but needs to be watched carefully and taken off the heat while still pink in the middle. Like the beef tenderloin, the pork tenderloin can be cut into medallions.

LOIN PORK CHOPS
These chops are cut from the front of the center loin. They have a nice little nugget of tenderloin next to the T-bone and are juicy and flavorful.

RIB PORK CHOPS
The meat from a rib pork chop is similar to that of the loin chop, but there is a longer rib bone and no tenderloin. The meat is incredibly tasty, and if you like the flavor of spareribs, you will love these. When we have a choice, we choose these over loin chops simply because of their glorious flavor.

BLADE PORK CHOPS
These chops are cut from the blade section of the pork loin and are husky, meaty chops with good girth, thickness, and flavor. They need to be cooked a little longer than loin or rib chops.

PORK RIBS

SPARERIBS
When it comes to ribs, pork spareribs are the gold standard. Although "spareribs" is a term that applies to any pork or beef ribs, true pork spareribs are the breast and rib bones and the tender, juicy, lean meat between them. They come from the lower part of the hog's center section and may be either fresh or smoked. They do well rubbed with a spice mixture, precooked, and then grilled.

ST. LOUIS–STYLE RIBS
Cut from spareribs and trimmed to be shorter and neater, St. Louis–style ribs are meaty and not as bony as spareribs. Our customers like them because they are the choicest part (center cut) of the sparerib.

COUNTRY-STYLE RIBS
Country-style ribs are split blade pork chops and are available boned or with the bone in. Bone-in country-style ribs are sold mostly for grilling. They are meatier than spareribs or baby back ribs. Boneless ribs also can be grilled or cooked slowly after being seasoned with a dry rub and then served with or without a barbecue sauce.

BABY BACK RIBS

Baby back ribs are the back ribs of the pork loin and are sold in racks, which have up to 13 bones. When cooked slowly, they are as tender as can be. They also grill well, although many cooks, including us, like to parcook them (by braising) before putting them on the grill.

SHOULDER

FORELEG OR SHOULDER OF PORK

Like the leg, the foreleg section of the hog can be purchased whole or divided into various cuts. It, too, may be fresh or smoked.

BOSTON BUTT

The Boston butt is almost always sold fresh. It's the fatty, bony, upper part of the shoulder and yet is juicy and flavorful. It has a high proportion of lean, tender meat with a uniform covering of clean, white fat. We recommend it for roasting and for pork stews. If you have a smoker, it's great for that, too, and is commonly used for pulled pork.

PICNIC SHOULDER ROAST

This roast, also called an arm roast, is cut from the arm and foreleg. Usually available as a half piece—the upper arm or the lower foreleg—the preferred piece is the meatier arm, which is usually sold bone-in. Both pieces are sold with skin. This is a tasty, economical pork roast.

BLADE PORK STEAKS

When the Boston butt is not sold as a whole roast, it is cut into individual steaks called blade pork steaks or pork steaks. These are similar in texture and shape to lamb shoulder chops and make an excellent stew that is so full of flavor, it's unlike any other stew you have ever tasted.

OTHER CUTS OF PORK

SUCKLING PIG

A whole suckling pig is a young hog that usually weighs around 25 pounds. If you can find a smaller pig, one that weighs about 15 pounds, the meat will be even more tender and delicious. Smaller pigs can be grilled on a large grill or roasted in the oven, while larger ones—those weighing as much as 25 pounds—need to be roasted in a pit. You may have to find a specialty butcher if you want to order a suckling pig. In any event, they need to be ordered well in advance. They are usually sold cleaned and frozen.

HAM HOCKS

Hocks come from the lower part of the ham shanks or the forelegs. They can be fresh or smoked and make an excellent addition to soups and stews, adding full, bold flavor. They contain good-size nuggets of flavorful, lean meat.

PIG'S FEET

These come from both the hindlegs and the forelegs. Typically, pig's feet are pickled in vinegar or smoked. If you find them fresh, simmer them until tender and serve them cold in their own jelly.

SLAB BACON

Most people buy bacon pre-sliced and packaged, but until you buy a complete slab you haven't given your taste buds a chance to appreciate true bacon flavor. We like to cut slab bacon so that the strips are nearly ¼ inch thick. All bacon has been previously cured and smoked; slabs are cut from the side meat, from which the spareribs have been removed. If you are not up to carving a slab at home, you can special order a slab from the butcher and ask him to slice it to the thickness you desire—keep in mind that slices that are cut thicker than you are accustomed to are truly mouthwatering. Some butchers and specialty stores sell presliced slab bacon, which is worth trying, too.

AMERICAN-STYLE BACON

You probably just call this "bacon." Everyone knows the familiar thinly sliced strips of smoked pork fat and meat sold in half-pound and one-pound packages in every supermarket in the country.

CANADIAN BACON

Canadian bacon is the eye of the pork chop and as such is more like ham than American-style bacon. In the United Kingdom, a similar (but not exactly the same) product is called Irish bacon, and American-style bacon is called streaky bacon.

PORK BELLY

When pork belly is cured, it's called bacon. It can also be sold unsmoked, with or without a rind. It can be salted, in which case it's called salt pork and often is used to cover the outside of a roast to provide extra moisture and flavor. In days gone by, it was commonly used to bard meat, which means it was inserted into the meat with barding needles to give the roast more fat and flavor.

FATBACK

Fatback comes from the pork belly. It is the strip of fat on top of the belly and contains no meat, just firm, white pork fat. Fatback is rarely smoked and is used to flavor stews, pot roasts, and braised or wilted greens. Lardons, which may be nothing more than cubed pieces of fat, are cut from fatback and are used to provide extra fat to a lean cut with a technique called "larding." Other lardons, often used in salads and similar dishes, have streaks of meat running through them and are cut from the belly.

HAM FAT

If a recipe calls for ham fat, ask the butcher or a good deli owner to cut a few pieces of rind from a cured ham. These pieces will have a layer of fat attached to them that is easy to remove with a knife. Butt ends of the hams are often sold cheaply and you can remove the fat from them, too.

LARD

Lard is rendered fatback that is allowed to solidify and then is sold in blocks and labeled "lard." Lard can also be made from any piece of fat from the pig that cannot otherwise be used. The process is the same: It is rendered, left to solidify, and then called lard. Lard does not have intense flavor, but quality lard has good flavor and adds good texture and body to any number of pork dishes. Lard is also prized by bakers, as it makes an especially tender and flaky pie crust.

SALT PORK

Salt pork is nothing more exotic than pork belly that is cured with a dry salt or brine cure. Because it's cut from the belly, it contains both meat and fat, although there is more fat than meat. Small pieces are used to flavor stews, braises, cabbage dishes, and wilted greens. Classic American fare such as Boston baked beans and New England clam chowder would not taste authentic without salt pork!

SAUSAGE

Pork sausage is a mixture of ground pork meat and pork fat that is flavored with various spices, herbs, and other ingredients. It is sold as plain sausage meat or, perhaps more commonly, stuffed into casings to make links. These casings used to be made from sheep entrails; these days, edible synthetic casings are more commonly used. Nearly every ethnic group has its own style of sausage, which can be made with other meats, too, such as beef, turkey, veal, and chicken. Pork is the meat of choice for most traditional sausages, although as the times change, this is changing as well. Purchasing sausage from a butcher or specialty shop that makes its own usually is a good bet, but you can also make it yourself.

SCRAPPLE

Scrapple is a Pennsylvania Dutch specialty, and as such has roots in both American and German culinary traditions. It is a mixture of sausage meat, meat from the head of the pork (head meat), and cornmeal that is usually sliced and fried, much like sausage patties.

Sausage
Belly
TRY HAM
T PORK
HOLE HAM
derloin
RK
MERICAN-STYLE BAC
ST. LO
BOST
BUT
SUCKL
PIG
PR
Scr
HA

RECIPES

Pork, Hominy, and Vegetable Stew with Green Chiles and Pumpkin Seeds

This dish, called *pozole verde* in Mexico, features bits of braised pork, chicken, and hominy lolling in a thick, flavorful broth of puréed chile, tomatillo, onion, garlic, and ground pumpkin seeds and is garnished with a raft of good things including chunks of avocado, sliced radishes, cilantro, and crisp tortilla chips. Pozole is both the Mexican name for hominy as well as the name for this ancient family of stew-like soups that feature the vegetable. With all its delicious variation of taste, texture, and nutrition, it is very much a meal in itself.

SERVES 4

3	pounds meaty pork neck bones (or 1½ pounds pork neck bones and 1½ pounds fresh pork hocks)
1	pound chicken wings
1	large white onion, quartered lengthwise, peeled with stem intact plus ½ large white onion, finely chopped and soaked in a few changes of water, 5 to 10 minutes each, drained
3	large cloves garlic, 2 crushed, 1 left whole in its skin
	Kosher salt
16	cups cold water
½	pound tomatillos (about 6 medium), husked and washed
¾	cup raw hulled pumpkin seeds (pepitas)
2	green serrano chiles, or 2 small jalapeños
1	large poblano chile
2	teaspoons ground coriander
1	teaspoon ground cumin
1	generous tablespoon lard or vegetable oil
Two	15-ounce cans white or yellow hominy (see Note), rinsed and drained

CONTINUED>

1. Place the pork bones, chicken wings, two of the onion quarters, the crushed garlic, and ½ teaspoon salt in a heavy 12- to 16-quart stockpot and cover with the water. Bring just to a simmer and skim off any impurities that rise to the top. Reduce the heat to maintain the barest possible simmer and cook for 2½ hours, checking occasionally to make sure that only a few bubbles break the surface as it cooks. Strain through cheesecloth or a fine-mesh strainer placed over a bowl, reserving pork and chicken. When meats are cool enough to handle, pick the flesh from the bones (discarding bones and connective tissue). Shred the meat fairly fine, and if you have more than 3 cups, reserve remainder for another use. Wipe out the pot and measure the broth; you should have about 6 cups. Add water or stock or simmer broth to reduce volume, if necessary.) and pour it into the pot.
2. Meanwhile, bring a medium pot of water to a boil over high heat and add the tomatillos. Reduce the heat and simmer until tomatillos are soft but not falling apart, about 10 minutes. Drain and reserve.
3. Place the pumpkin seeds in a large skillet over medium-low heat. Toast the seeds, stirring and tossing regularly, until about half have turned a pale nut brown color, 5 to 10 minutes. Do not burn. Transfer to a small bowl and reserve.
4. If using an electric stove, preheat the broiler.
5. Return the skillet to medium heat and add the 2 remaining onion quarters, cut-side down, and the remaining clove of garlic in its skin. Cook, until the onion is lightly blackened on the two cut sides, 5 to 10 minutes, pushing on them to help them make contact with the skillet. Transfer to an enclosed paper or plastic bag or covered bowl to steam and reserve.
6. If using a gas stove, place the serrano and poblano peppers on one of the gas burners over a medium-high flame. Roast until blackened and blistered all over, 4 to 8 minutes, turning every few minutes to expose all surfaces to the flame. If using the broiler, place the peppers about 4 inches from the heat and handle as above (take care with smaller thin-skinned chiles so the flesh beneath doesn't incinerate). Place blackened peppers in the bag with the onions and garlic and let them steam until cool enough to handle.
7. Peel the peppers to remove most of the blackened bits of skin but don't wash them. Seed, stem, and coarsely chop the peppers and place in the bowl of a blender. Peel the reserved garlic clove and coarsely chop along with the reserved blackened onion and add to the blender. Add reserved pumpkin seeds, tomatillos, coriander, and cumin to the blender; first pulse and then process the mixture, adding a few tablespoons

- 2 cups shredded green cabbage
- 1/2 cup loosely packed fresh cilantro leaves
- 1 ripe Hass avocado, cut into 1/2-inch pieces and tossed with the juice of one-half lime
- 3 to 4 radishes, thinly sliced
- 2 small limes, cut into 8 wedges
- 1/2 cup crema or sour cream
- Best-quality corn tortilla chips (see Note)

of the reserved meat broth as needed, until a thick paste forms and the pumpkin seeds are almost entirely smooth and incorporated into the paste.

8. Heat the lard in a skillet over medium-high heat until just smoking. Carefully add the chile–pumpkin seed paste (it will splatter initially if excessively wet) and cook, stirring and scraping it up with a spatula almost constantly, until the paste smells rich and is no longer raw, is somewhat darkened in color, and no longer fluid, 5 to 10 minutes, scraping the sides of the skillet as necessary and reduce the heat if the mixture is splattering. Do not burn. Stir the thickened paste, the hominy, and 1 tablespoon salt into the reserved pot of broth. Bring to a simmer and cook at a bare simmer for 30 minutes, stirring occasionally to prevent sticking to the bottom of the pot and again, scraping the sides of the pot where solids accumulate.

9. Add the reserved pork and chicken meat. The stew should be thick and rich with hominy and meat but should still be surrounded by abundant, slightly thickened broth—still soup-like. If too thin, continue to simmer uncovered for 15 to 30 minutes more (note that the stew will thicken as it cools). If the thickness seems right, cover the pot during this last period of simmering. Add salt to taste.

10. Ladle the stew into heated bowls. Place a small handful of shredded cabbage in the center of each bowl and nestle a small cluster of cilantro leaves against the cabbage. Scatter about 4 tablespoons chopped onion, 1/4 of the avocado, and a few slices of radish around the bowl. Drizzle a few tablespoons of crema or thinned sour cream (if using) around the bowl. Repeat with the remaining bowls. Serve posole with lime wedges, tortilla chips, and any garnishes that remain, arranging the items on small plates or in bowls for diners to help themselves.

NOTE: While purchased tortilla chips are acceptable, there's no substitute for freshly fried corn tortillas: Stack 10 to 12 fresh corn tortillas and cut them into quarters. Fry the tortillas in two or three batches in an inch or two of lard or vegetable oil heated to 360° to 375°F until pale golden brown. Drain on paper towels and sprinkle with a bit of salt while still warm.

What we call hominy, Mexicans call pozole. It is made from a starchy and not-at-all sweet sort of field corn whose preparation—which involves a soak in a calcium hydroxide solution to dissolve the outer husk—takes a good bit of time to cook even after initial preparation. Here we've substituted canned, prepared, and fully cooked hominy (Goya sell a decent version) which is admittedly far less tasty than dried hominy prepared from scratch. If you'd like to use dried hominy instead of canned, you can look for two other Goya products called Mote Blanco Pelado (whole kernels) or Maiz Trillado Blanco (coarsely ground hominy) available in 1 pound bags at many Latin American markets. Cook following package directions and add about 2 1/2 cups in place of the canned hominy called for here.

Alsatian Pork-and-Potato Casserole

This is a brothy, yet full-bodied casserole that, along with a salad, makes a full meal. The pork should be marinated overnight before cooking.

SERVES 4 TO 5

2	cups dry Alsatian Gewürztraminer wine or other dry white Alsatian wine
1/4	cup finely chopped shallots
1	small rib celery, thinly sliced
1	carrot, peeled and thinly sliced
2	large cloves garlic, finely chopped
2	bay leaves
2	sprigs fresh thyme
3/4	teaspoon ground coriander seed
2	whole cloves
2	juniper berries, lightly crushed
	Freshly ground black pepper
2	teaspoons sugar
1 1/2	pounds boneless pork shoulder, cut into 1 1/4-inch pieces
1/2	cup duck fat, goose fat, or rendered lard warmed until fluid (see Note on page 134)
2	pounds large waxy potatoes (such as Yukon gold), peeled and sliced crosswise 1/8-inch thick (see Note)
	Kosher salt
1	medium onion, chopped
1	large leek (white and pale green parts only), chopped
2	cups Pork Stock (page 301), or Chicken Stock (page 299), or canned low-sodium canned chicken broth
1/2	pound thick-sliced bacon

1. Simmer the wine in a small saucepan over medium heat until reduced by half to 1 cup, 10 to 15 minutes. Meanwhile, place the shallots, celery, carrot, garlic, bay leaves, thyme, coriander, cloves, juniper berries, 6 or 8 generous grindings of black pepper, and the sugar in a deep mixing bowl. Pour the hot wine over the vegetables and herbs. Let cool to room temperature and stir in the pork. Mix well, cover and marinate in the refrigerator overnight, stirring once or twice if the pork is not entirely submerged.

2. Preheat the oven to 375°F. Grease the bottom and sides of a 4-quart heavy lidded ovenproof pot (see note) with 1 tablespoon of the fat. Lay one-third of the potatoes in an overlapping, circular fashion, completely covering the bottom. Sprinkle with salt. Distribute half of the onion and leek over the potatoes. Remove half of the marinated meat, vegetables, and flavorings from the marinade and distribute evenly over the onion and leek. Drizzle with one-third of the remaining fat and sprinkle with saltmore generously than before. Arrange another one-third of the potatoes on top of the meats and sprinkle generously with salt. Follow with a layer of the remaining onion and leek and then another layer of the remaining meat and vegetables. Pour the marinade and the stock over all. Drizzle with another one-third of the fat and sprinkle generously with salt. Arrange the last third of the potatoes in an attractive circular pattern on top, pressing with both hands to level the mass of meat and potatoes if necessary. Drizzle with the remaining fat and sprinkle again with salt. Cover the casserole tightly (if the lid doesn't fit snugly, lay a sheet of foil between the lid and the pot to help seal it).

3. Place the pot in the oven and cook for 45 minutes. Reduce the heat to 225° to 275°F to maintain the barest possible simmer and cook for 3 ½ hours, basting the top layer once or twice. Remove from the oven and let the casserole rest for 15 to 30 minutes. While the casserole cooks, cut the bacon crosswise into batons about ½ inch thick and cook until crisp. Drain and reserve. Divide the casserole among shallow bowls and place a large ladleful of the broth in each. Garnish with the reserved bacon and serve immediately with forks and spoons.

NOTE: A 3 1/2- to 4 1/2-quart pot will work fine if it is not too tall and narrow. We use a 4-quart pot that is 8 inches across and 4 inches deep which is just the right size to accommodate the layers of meat and potatoes and the cooking liquids. A mandoline or Japanese vegetable slicer makes quick work of slicing the potatoes thinly and evenly.

Pork Chops with Peppers, Vinegar, and Black Olives

Smothered with sweet red peppers, tangy vinegar, and earthy black olives, this dish offers a satisfying intensity of flavors that nearly jumps off the plate, yet it's a dish that's simple to prepare. Halved and roasted baby potatoes make a great accompaniment.

SERVES 4

4	rib pork chops, cut 1 1/4 to 1 1/2 inches thick, lightly scored around fatty edges
1/2	recipe Brine for Pork (page 304; optional)
	Kosher salt
	Fresh coarsely ground black pepper
3	tablespoons extra-virgin olive oil, plus more for drizzling
	All-purpose flour for dredging
2	large red bell peppers, seeds, stems and ribs removed, cut into 1/4-inch-thick strips
1	small red onion, peeled and cut into 1/4-inch-thick rings
1/4	teaspoon crushed red pepper flakes
3/4	cup dry white wine
1/4	cup good-quality white wine vinegar
2	large anchovy fillets, chopped and then mashed to a paste, or 2 teaspoons anchovy paste
1/3	cup coarsely chopped black olives, such as gaeta or kalamata

1. If brining the chops, place them in a large bowl and immerse in the brine. Transfer to the refrigerator to brine for 2 to 3 hours. (See page page 304 for brining tips.) Remove from the brine, pat dry, and bring to room temperature before cooking. Warm plates in low oven.
2. If using brined chops, lightly salt the chops on both sides. If using unbrined chops, generously salt them on both sides. Sprinkle chops generously with black pepper.
3. Heat the oil in a 12-inch skillet over medium-high heat. Dredge the chops in the flour, knocking off any excess. When the oil begins to smoke, add the chops, pushing on them to help them make contact with the skillet, and cook until deep golden brown on both sides, but still somewhat raw in the center, 5 to 6 minutes on the first side and 3 to 4 minutes on the second. Transfer to a plate and reserve.
4. Add the peppers, onion, red pepper flakes, and 1 teaspoon salt to the skillet and toss thoroughly to coat with the oil. Cook until the peppers begin to color at the edges, 3 to 5 minutes, stirring occasionally. Add the wine, vinegar, anchovies, and ¼ cup water; bring to a simmer and cook for 2 minutes, scraping up any browned bits on the bottom of the skillet. Reduce the heat to medium-low and stir in the olives. Return the pork chops to the skillet, laying them on top of the peppers and adding any juices on the plate. Cover the skillet, leaving the lid slightly ajar, and simmer gently until an instant-read thermometer inserted in the center of the chops registers 135°F, for 4 to 8 minutes more.
5. Transfer chops to warmed serving plates. Increase the heat and simmer the liquid in the skillet stirring often until just ¼ to ½ cup of flavorful sauce remains, 2 to 3 minutes. Add salt to taste and divide the peppers and sauce among the plates, placing them over and around the chops. Drizzle each with a tablespoon or so of olive oil and serve.

Pork Chops with Chorizo Vinaigrette

The chorizo vinaigrette is less of a dressing and more of a dense, flavorful sauce. It makes a great companion for pork, beef, and even fish. It's also delicious with potatoes and bitter greens of all kinds, exactly what ought to be served alongside these chops.

SERVES 4

- 4 rib pork chops, cut 1¼ to 1½ inches thick, lightly scored around the fatty edges
- ½ recipe Brine for Pork, (page 304; optional)
- 2 cups Chicken Stock (page 299), or canned low-sodium chicken broth
- 1 sprig fresh thyme
- ½ bay leaf
- Extra-virgin olive oil
- ¼ cup thinly sliced shallots
- 4 large cloves garlic, sliced
- 2 ounces cured Spanish chorizo sausage, cut into ¼-inch pieces
- ⅓ cup chopped canned tomatoes, drained
- ½ teaspoon sweet paprika
- ⅛ teaspoon crushed red pepper flakes
- 1 tablespoon red wine vinegar
- Kosher salt
- Fresh coarsely ground black pepper
- 2 tablespoons chopped green olives (optional)
- 2 tablespoons finely chopped fresh flat-leaf parsley for garnish

1. If brining the chops, place them in a large bowl and immerse in the brine. Place in the refrigerator to brine for 2 or 3 hours (see page page 304 for brining tips.) Remove the chops from the brine, pat dry, and bring to room temperature before cooking.
2. Meanwhile, put the chicken stock, thyme, and bay leaf in a small saucepan; bring to a simmer and cook until reduced by half to 1 cup. Set aside. Heat 2 tablespoons oil in a small skillet over medium-low heat. Add the shallots and garlic and cook without coloring for 3 minutes, stirring occasionally. Add half of the chorizo and cook for 1 minute. Stir in the tomatoes, paprika, and crushed red pepper and cook gently for 5 minutes, stirring occasionally. Remove the bay leaf and thyme from the stock and discard; place the stock and the chorizo-tomato mixture in the jar of a blender. Blend on high until the mixture is smooth and no bits of chorizo remain, 30 seconds to 1 minute. Add the vinegar, ½ teaspoon salt, and ¼ cup of olive oil and blend for a few seconds more. Transfer the vinaigrette to a small bowl and stir in a few generous grindings of coarse black pepper, the remaining chorizo, and the green olives, (if using). If necessary, add more salt and vinegar to taste. The vinaigrette can be made a few days ahead and stored in the refrigerator. Bring to room temperature before serving.
3. Heat 3 tablespoons oil in a 12-inch skillet over medium-high heat. When the oil just begins to smoke, reduce the heat to medium and add the chops, pushing on them with a spatula to help them make contact with the skillet. Cook until deep golden brown on both sides, 5 to 6 minutes per side for medium (135°F to 140°F on an instant-read thermometer). Transfer the chops to a serving plate and spoon about ⅓ cup of the vinaigrette over them. Garnish with the parsley and serve.

Marinated Pork with White Wine, Garlic, and Oranges

The marbled texture of blade chops makes them perfect for braising, and the citrus acidity of this sauce is the perfect counterpoint to their rich flavor. Note that the meat needs to marinate overnight.

SERVES 4

	Kosher salt
	Freshly ground black pepper
2	pounds boneless blade pork chops (also called country-style pork chops), cut into 8 pieces, each about 4 inches long by 2 inches wide by 1 inch thick
	All-purpose flour
6	tablespoons extra-virgin olive oil, plus more as needed
12	large cloves garlic, peeled and sliced
2 ½	cups dry white Muscat wine or other dry white wine
3	bay leaves
3	whole cloves
¾	cup Pork Stock (page 301), Chicken Stock (page 299), canned low-sodium chicken broth, or water
1	tablespoon fresh orange juice
1	teaspoon white wine vinegar
3	small or 2 large oranges, peeled and sectioned (32 to 40 sections)
	One bunch watercress (about 4 loosely packed cups), washed and dried

1. Generously salt and pepper the pork on both sides. Coat one side of the pork pieces with flour and shake off the excess.
2. In a very large skillet, heat 4 tablespoons of the oil over medium-high heat. When hot, add the pork and cook the unfloured side until rich golden brown, about 5 minutes. Reduce the heat to medium, turn the pork pieces over, and cook the floured side until rich golden brown, about 3 minutes more, regulating the heat if the meat threatens to burn. As the pork finishes browning, transfer to a medium bowl and reserve.
3. Scrape or blot up any burned bits in the skillet. Add enough oil to the fat in the pan to equal 4 tablespoons. Reduce the heat to medium-low, add the garlic and cook, stirring occasionally, until pale gold at the edges, 1 to 3 minutes. Add the wine, bay leaves, and cloves. Simmer gently, scraping the bottom of the skillet to loosen any browned bits, until reduced by half (to about 1¾ cup including the solids), 10 to 12 minutes. Pour over the reserved pork, cool slightly, cover, and refrigerate for at least 6 hours or overnight, turning the meat once during this time, if the meat isn't submerged beneath the marinade.
4. Preheat the oven to 350°F.
5. Transfer the meat and marinade to a 6-quart casserole, cover, and let it come to room temperature (or, if you don't have time, slowly heat it over very low heat).
6. Add the stock and ½ teaspoon of salt to the casserole. Cover, transfer to the oven, and cook for 20 minutes. Reduce the temperature to 250°F and cook at a bare simmer, until pork is very tender, 2 to 2½ hours. Adjust the oven temperature to maintain a bare simmer.
7. The liquid surrounding the pork should resemble a very fluid sauce that is flavorful and only slightly thickened. Simmer for 1 to 2 minutes to concentrate or add small amounts of broth or water to thin. Cover the casserole and set aside.
8. In a large bowl, whisk together the orange juice, vinegar, and a generous pinch of salt. Slowly whisk in the remaining 2 tablespoons olive oil and set the dressing aside.
9. Divide the pork among serving plates, placing it just off center. Spoon the sauce and garlic slices over the pork. Scatter 8 to 10 orange slices around each plate.
10. Toss the watercress with the reserved dressing and divide among the plates, nestling each bunch attractively alongside the pork, and serve.

Rolled Roast Loin of Pork

Ask your butcher to butterfly the roast or do it yourself (see illustration). The butterflied meat is smeared with a garlic-and-herb paste, rolled back up, and tied in its original shape before being roasted. Serve the pork on bed of white beans.

SERVES 4 TO 6

One	4-pound bone-in center cut or blade-end pork loin roast, some external fat remaining, butterflied for stuffing
1	recipe Brine for Pork (page 304; optional)
4	large cloves garlic
5	large fresh sage leaves
	Needles from 4-inch sprig fresh rosemary, plus needles from one 1-inch sprig
1	teaspoon fennel seed, finely ground with a mortar and pestle or in a spice mill or clean coffee grinder
½	teaspoon fresh coarsely ground black pepper
½	teaspoon crushed red pepper flakes
	Kosher salt
2	tablespoons extra-virgin olive oil, plus more for serving
3 ½	cups Pork Stock (page 301)
1	generous tablespoon chopped fresh flat-leaf parsley for serving

1. If brining the pork, place the unrolled, butterflied loin in a nonreactive dish large enough to contain it. Pour the brine over the pork, lifting the meat to let the liquid flow beneath it. Brine for 2 to 3 hours in the refrigerator, turning once or twice (see page page 304 for brining tips). Remove the pork from the brine, blot dry, and bring to room temperature before roasting.
2. Put 3 garlic cloves, 4 sage leaves, and the rosemary on a cutting board and chop together until minced. Put in a small bowl with the ground fennel seed, black pepper, crushed red pepper, and ½ teaspoon salt. Stir in the oil to make a paste. Lay the butterflied pork, cut-interior-side up, on a work surface. Spread the herb paste so that it evenly coats this exposed side all the way to the edges. Tightly roll up the pork, jelly-roll style. Using kitchen twine, tie between the bones as for a roast (having an extra pair of hands to help hold the roll tight while tying the twine is helpful, though not necessary). Rub any escaped spice paste on the exterior of the roast.
3. Preheat the oven to 450°F. Salt the pork loin generously all over. Place pork, fat-side up, on a roasting rack set in a roasting pan. Roast for 30 minutes. Lower the heat to 300°F and continue roasting until an instant-read thermometer registers 135°F when inserted in the center of the roast, 20 to 25 minutes more. Transfer the roast to a cutting board designed to catch the juices and let it rest for 10 to 15 minutes loosely covered with foil. Set the roasting pan aside.
4. While the pork is roasting, put the pork stock in a saucepan and bring to a boil over medium-high heat. Reduce the heat to medium and add the remaining clove of garlic, 1 sage leaf, and the rosemary sprig. Simmer until reduced to 1½ cups. Discard the garlic and herbs and set the reduced stock aside.
5. While the roast rests, place the roasting pan over low heat and add the reduced pork stock. Using a spatula, scrape up any browned bits on the bottom of the pan. Keep warm.
6. Snip the strings from the roast. Slice between the bones into chops and carefully transfer to serving plates. Spoon about ¼ cup of reduced pork stock over and around each chop; drizzle with a bit of olive oil, sprinkle with the parsley, and serve.

Pork Tenderloin Kababs with Herbs and Bacon

We like to serve these kababs atop of a bed of white beans or French lentils: Purée a third of the cooked beans or lentils with some of their cooking liquid and a bit of cream, then fold this mixture back in with the whole beans or lentils. The kababs are also delicious with sautéed apple slices.

SERVES 4

1	tablespoon finely chopped fresh parsley
1	tablespoon finely chopped fresh sage
1	tablespoon finely chopped fresh rosemary
1	tablespoon finely chopped fresh thyme
1 3/4	pounds trimmed pork tenderloin, cut crosswise into twelve 1-inch-thick medallions (see Note)
12	slices bacon
	Olive oil
	Kosher salt
	Freshly ground black pepper

1. Spread the chopped herbs on a plate and roll the edges of the pork medallions in the herbs, coating each around its circumference. Trim the bacon slices to match the 1-inch thickness of the pork medallions and wrap each medallion with a bacon slice around its circumference so it fits snugly, with the ends of the bacon overlapping an inch or so; trim off any excess length of bacon.

2. On a work surface, lay 3 pork medallions, large-sides down, side by side. To keep the bacon securely wrapped, arrange the medallions so that each of the seams formed where the bacon overlaps presses against the place where the medallions touch one another. Thread a skewer evenly through the center of the 3 medallions (it will resemble a triple-decker lollipop). Repeat with the remaining pork and skewers.

3. Preheat a grill or grill pan over medium-high heat. Brush each pork kabab with olive oil to lightly coat. Generously salt and pepper both sides of the kababs. Place the kababs on the grill and cook to the desired doneness, about 4 minutes per side for medium (140°F on an instant-read thermometer is our preference) and serve.

NOTE: You will have to purchase two whole pork tenderloins—usually 2 1/4 to 2 1/2 pounds—and cut them from the thickest three-quarters of the tenderloin's length to yield the 12 roughly equal-size pork medallions called for in the recipe. The remaining tapering "thin end" of each tenderloin can be cut up and used for a stir-fry or similar dish.

If using wooden skewers, soak them in water for at least 30 minutes before threading them with the meat, and then wrap the long, exposed portion of wood with aluminum foil before putting them on the grill.

Twice-Cooked Pork with Cabbage

If Americans eat pork belly at all (aside from bacon), it's usually braised for a few hours until meltingly tender. This classic Szechuan Chinese dish treats pork belly differently. First, it is simmered until just cooked through. Once cool, it's sliced (like short, thick-cut pieces of bacon) and tossed in a very hot wok to crisp slightly before being finished with the other ingredients. The result is a bit chewy, a bit tender, and a bit crisp. When making any stir-fry, it's best to have all your ingredients prepared and close at hand before beginning to cook. Also, read through the recipe at least once before you start. You can make this in a large skillet if you do not have a wok—you'll just have to be more vigilant about turning the pork pieces so that both sides turn pale golden before adding the other ingredients. If you have a 14-inch wok, it's easy to double the recipe. Chile bean paste (*dou ban jiang*), Szechuan sweet bean paste (*tim min jiang*), and dark soy sauce can be found at good Asian markets. Serve with white rice.

SERVES 2

3/4	pound pork belly with skin (see Note)
One	2-inch piece fresh ginger, peeled
10	scallions, 8 cut into 2-inch lengths
2	tablespoons chile bean paste
1	tablespoon sweet bean paste
1 1/2	teaspoons dark soy sauce
1 1/2	teaspoons unseasoned rice wine vinegar
1	tablespoon fermented black beans, rinsed
1	teaspoon sugar
10	ounces green cabbage, cored and cut into 1 1/2-inch squares, leaves separated (about 2 cups)
1	generous tablespoon peanut oil
1	teaspoon minced peeled fresh ginger
1 1/2	tablespoons Shaoxing wine (Chinese rice wine)

1. Put the pork in a medium pot and cover with cold water by 1 inch. Remove the pork from the pot and set aside. Add the piece of ginger and 2 whole scallions to the pot and bring to a boil, covered. Add the reserved pork and reduce heat to a bare simmer; cook uncovered for 20 minutes, or until pork registers about 125°F on an instant-read thermometer. Turn off the heat and let the pork rest in the cooking liquid until cool enough to handle. Scoop out a cup or so of the cooking liquid and reserve. (Pork can be cooked up to 1 day ahead and stored, in its liquid, in the refrigerator. Bring to room temp before proceeding.)
2. Working from the end of the slab of pork, slice across the layers of fat, lean meat, and skin into 3/16-inch-thick pieces 1½ to 2 inches in size and set aside.
3. Combine the chile bean paste, sweet bean paste, soy sauce, vinegar, black beans, and sugar in a small bowl and reserve. Combine the cut scallions and the cabbage in another small bowl and reserve.
4. Preheat a wok over high heat and add the oil, swirling to coat the wok. When the oil begins to smoke, add the reserved pork slices and cook, stirring regularly, until pale gold on both sides, a bit crisp at the edges, and some of the fat has rendered, 2 to 3 minutes (spread the pork slices around the wok to help them brown). Add the minced ginger and cook for 15 seconds, stirring. Add the wine and cook for 15 seconds more. Add the reserved scallions and cabbage, tossing thoroughly with the pork. Stir in the reserved chile-bean mixture and ⅓ cup of the reserved cooking liquid, tossing all the ingredients in the wok to combine well. Reduce the heat to medium and cook, stirring regularly, until the sauce clings lightly to the ingredients, the vegetables are crisp-tender, and just a small amount of liquid remains, about 2 minutes more. Cook additionally to thicken and concentrate the sauce or add a bit more cooking liquid to thin and lighten it. Serve immediately.

NOTE: Pork belly is typically cut in a long rectangular piece and looks like slab bacon (which, minus the curing process, is exactly what it is). It usually comes with the skin attached; as the pork is prepared here, the slivers of skin on each piece get pleasantly crispy, adding another texture to the dish. If you prefer, you can slice the skin off after cooking in Step 1. Cutting the pork into 3/16-inch-thick slices, as we instruct in Step 2, may seem an odd choice, but thinner slices tend to dry out when stir-fried; thicker slices can be too chewy.

Kansas City–Style Baby Back Ribs

To imitate the flavor of real pit barbecue, we season the ribs with a generous quantity of dry rub and cook them in sealed foil pouches with a bit of liquid smoke and water to perfume the meat. This bit of successful trickery would make a purist wince, but it's a method that nevertheless makes a great-tasting batch of ribs, with or without our indulgent barbecue sauce. Serve with barbecue beans, coleslaw, or perhaps a side of cooked collards or kale. The spice mix makes enough for four 2-pound racks of baby back ribs, so you can easily double the recipe or cut the spice mixture in half, if you like. This recipe also works on full-size pork spare-ribs or center-cut "St. Louis–Style" ribs. It is best to let the ribs sit overnight with the dry rub.

SERVES 2 TO 4

- 1/4 cup tightly packed brown sugar
- 1 tablespoon kosher salt
- 2 tablespoons Old Bay Seasoning
- 1 tablespoon chili powder
- 3 tablespoons sweet paprika
- 1/2 teaspoon cayenne pepper
- 1 tablespoon freshly ground coarse black pepper
- 1 tablespoon garlic powder
- 1 tablespoon onion powder
- 1 tablespoon ground celery seed
- 1 teaspoon powdered thyme
- 1 teaspoon rubbed (crumbled) sage
- 2 racks baby back pork ribs (about 2 pounds each)
- 1/2 cup Liquid Smoke or similar smoke-flavored concentrate
- 1/4 cup water
- Sweet-and-Sour Barbecue Sauce (recipe on facing page; optional)

1. In a small bowl, combine the brown sugar, salt, Old Bay seasoning, chili powder, paprika, cayenne, black pepper, garlic powder, onion powder, celery seed, thyme, and sage, breaking up any lumps of brown sugar.

2. Lightly rub 4 to 6 tablespoons of the spice mixture into each of the racks of ribs (work over a large sheet pan to help with clean up), coating the meaty top sides with a bit more of the rub. (Note: Use a bit more or less spice mix if your ribs are much larger or smaller than 2 pounds.) Wrap each rack in plastic and let sit for at least 2 hours but preferably 24 hours in the refrigerator. Bring to room temperature before cooking. Preheat the oven to 325°F.

3. Lay two double-thick pieces of aluminum foil—one for each rack of ribs and each piece of foil a bit more than twice the length of one rack—on a work surface. (The foil should be able to comfortably envelop each rack of ribs with room to spare.) Remove the ribs from the plastic wrap and center each rack of ribs lengthwise, meaty-side up, on each piece of foil. Pour 1/4 cup of Liquid Smoke and 2 tablespoons of water around (not on) each rack of ribs, folding in the edges of the foil slightly to contain the liquids. Fold the foil around each rack of ribs to form a loose-fitting but airtight package, using more foil if necessary. Transfer the ribs to a large baking sheet and cook for 2 3/4 hours, rotating the pan once during the cooking.

4. Remove from the oven and let the ribs rest in the foil for 20 to 30 minutes. The ribs can be served at this point, or grilled. To grill, prepare a medium charcoal fire or set a gas grill to medium. Cook until lightly browned and crusted in spots, but do not let them dry out too much. Cut between individual ribs and serve with barbecue sauce, if you like. (Note: If the smoky-flavored cooking juices within the foil pouches aren't too bitter, these can be spooned over the ribs.)

Sweet-and-Sour Barbecue Sauce

MAKES ABOUT 1½ CUPS

1	teaspoon sweet paprika
1	teaspoon chili powder
1	teaspoon ground dry mustard
1	teaspoon freshly ground black pepper
¼	teaspoon ground cinnamon
¼	teaspoon freshly grated nutmeg
¼	teaspoon ground allspice
¼	cup distilled white vinegar
¼	cup dark molasses
¾	cup chili sauce or ketchup
½	teaspoon Tabasco sauce

Stir together the paprika, chili powder, mustard, black pepper, cinnamon, nutmeg, and allspice in a mixing bowl. Using a whisk, stir in the vinegar to dissolve the mustard. Stir in the molasses, chili sauce, and Tabasco, mixing well to combine. Keeps tightly covered in the refrigerator for 1 month or more.

Korean-Style Spicy Pork Ribs with Vegetables

This is our take on a Korean homestyle standard, loosely modeled on the delicious version found in Hi Soo Shin Hepinstall's *Growing Up in a Korean Kitchen*. Eat these powerfully flavored riblets with your fingers, if you like, but be sure to put out forks or chopsticks to enjoy the pieces of braised radish, potato, cabbage, mushroom, and chestnut that enrich the dish. Serve with white rice and a bowl to catch the discarded rib bones.

SERVES 4 TO 6

- 2 ounces (6 to 8 medium) dried Korean p'yogo mushrooms (Japanese dried shiitake or Chinese black mushrooms)
- Peanut oil or vegetable oil
- 3½ pounds pork spare ribs, cut by your butcher across the bone into 2½-inch "racks," each rack cut between the bone into individual riblets (see illustration on page 124)
- 2 tablespoons soy sauce
- 3 tablespoons Asian rice wine, such as Korean chongju or Chinese Shaoxing wine
- 1 tablespoon sugar
- ¼ cup Korean hot pepper paste (*kochujang*), plus 1 tablespoon to finish dish
- 2 tablespoons Korean hot pepper powder (*kochukaru*), or more to taste
- 1½ tablespoons minced garlic
- 1½ tablespoons finely grated peeled fresh ginger root
- ½ cup minced scallion, plus 2 scallions thinly sliced for garnish
- ½ teaspoon freshly ground black pepper
- 2 tablespoons corn syrup
- 2 tablespoons Asian sesame oil
- 2 tablespoons toasted sesame seeds
- ½ pound daikon (giant white) radish, peeled and cut into ¾-inch cubes

1. Put the mushrooms in a small bowl and cover with boiling water, inverting a small plate and placing it over the mushrooms to submerge them. Soak until softened, about 1 hour, turning mushrooms periodically. Squeeze out excess water, reserving 1 cup of the soaking liquid; remove and discard the stems, and slice the caps about ¼-inch thick.

2. Meanwhile, heat 3 tablespoons of peanut oil in a wide, 12-quart pot over medium-high heat. When the oil is hot, and working in batches, cook the riblets on all sides—including the thin meaty edges—until deep golden brown, about10 minutes. Transfer to a large mixing bowl.

3. While the ribs brown, combine the soy sauce, rice wine, and sugar in a mixing bowl, stirring to dissolve the sugar. Add the pepper paste, pepper powder, garlic, ginger, ¼ cup of the minced scallions, black pepper, corn syrup, 1 tablespoon of the sesame oil, and 1 tablespoon of the sesame seeds, stirring until well mixed. After transferring the ribs to the mixing bowl, add the soy–hot pepper marinade to the ribs while they are still warm, tossing well to combine. Let the ribs marinate for 1 to 2 hours at room temperature, tossing once or twice.

4. Wipe out the pot (leaving the browned bits in the pot) and return it to medium-high heat with 3 tablespoons of peanut oil. When the oil is hot, add the reserved mushrooms and cook, stirring occasionally, until pale gold at the edges, about 4 minutes. Add the reserved mushroom soaking liquid, scraping up any browned bits stuck to the bottom of the pot, and cook until the liquid is nearly evaporated. Add the daikon, potatoes, cabbage, and 1 teaspoon salt and cook, stirring occasionally, until the cabbage is somewhat wilted, about 5 minutes. Transfer the vegetables to a bowl and combine with the chestnuts.

5. Put the ribs with the marinade in the pot; stir in the 2 cups stock and 1 teaspoon salt, pushing to submerge the ribs. Bring to a simmer over medium-high heat. Cover the pot, reduce the heat to low, and cook at a bare simmer, stirring occasionally, until the ribs are tender but not yet falling from the bone, 1¼ to 1½ hours.

- ½ pound waxy potato, such as Yukon gold, peeled and cut into ½-inch cubes
- ¾ pound napa cabbage cut into strips 1 inch long by 1½ inches wide (about 5 cups)
- 6 ounces prepared, peeled chestnuts, broken into about ½-inch pieces (see Note)
- 2 cups Pork Stock (page 301), Chicken Stock (page 299), or canned low-sodium chicken broth, plus ½ cup to finish dish
- 1½ tablespoons cornstarch

6. Add the reserved vegetables, shaking the pot to distribute them, and making sure the daikon and potatoes are submerged. Cover the pot and continue cooking at a bare simmer until the potatoes are just tender, about 20 minutes. Dissolve the cornstarch in the remaining ½ cup of stock and whisk in the remaining tablespoon of Korean hot pepper paste and the remaining tablespoon of sesame oil; add this mixture to the pot, again shaking to distribute it throughout the pot and/or carefully stirring so as not to break up the meat and vegetables. Simmer uncovered until the stew thickens somewhat, about 2 minutes more. Let the stew rest off the heat for about 5 minutes and serve, garnished with the remaining sesame seeds and the thinly sliced scallion.

NOTE: Korean ingredients can be found at any of the growing number of Korean supermarkets in many metro areas throughout the country—H-mart (Han Au Rheum) and 99 Ranch are the best known. Koamart.com and Kgrocer.com are good online sources.

Dry-packed bottled or vacuum-sealed peeled, precooked whole chestnuts are convenient, readily available, and work well in most dishes. But if you can find fresh whole chestnuts in the shell, mostly available in the fall and winter, the extra effort of peeling them is worth it. To peel fresh, raw chestnuts, you have to blanch them first. Working with one nut at a time, firmly hold the chestnut in a kitchen towel; using the tip of a sharp paring knife, make an X incision on the flat face, cutting through only the shell and the skin beneath. Simmer the nuts in a saucepan of lightly salted boiling water for 5 minutes. Remove from the heat and use a slotted spoon to lift the chestnuts from the water one at a time. Carefully peel them, using the knife to help pry off the shells.

Marinated Thai-Style Pork Spareribs

These addictive and deeply flavored ribs make a great starter as part of a larger Thai meal, or they can be served as a main course accompanied by jasmine rice and a sautéed or braised leafy or bitter green vegetable. On the other hand, they make a terrific snack to go along with a cold beer.

SERVES 4 AS A MAIN COURSE; 8 AS AN APPETIZER

1	cup sliced shallots
10	scallions, coarsely chopped
One	3-inch piece fresh ginger, sliced
8	large cloves garlic, peeled
1	cup coarsely chopped fresh cilantro including thin stems (and roots, if possible)
6	tablespoons soy sauce
2	tablespoons Thai or Vietnamese fish sauce (*nam pla* or *nuoc nam*)
1	teaspoon kosher salt
1	teaspoon fresh coarsely ground black pepper
2	tablespoons sugar
4	pounds pork spare ribs, cut by your butcher across the bone into 2- to 3-inch "racks," each rack cut between the bones into individual 2- to 3-inch-long riblets
	Thai Chile–Herb Dipping Sauce (page 293)

1. Put the shallots, scallions, ginger, garlic, cilantro, soy sauce, fish sauce, salt, pepper, and sugar in the bowl of a food processor. Process to a loose, finely chopped paste, scraping down the sides of the bowl once or twice.
2. Place the ribs in a large bowl or two heavy resealable plastic bags. Thoroughly coat the ribs with the marinade, massaging the paste into the flesh for a minute or so. Cover and let marinate at room temperature for 2 hours or up to 5 hours in the refrigerator, tossing the ribs once or twice during this time.
3. Preheat the oven to 350°F. Spread the ribs out, bone-side down, on two large, parchment-lined baking sheets and bake until the ribs are deeply colored and very tender but not yet falling from the bone, about 1½ hours, occasionally rotating the pans to encourage even cooking. Remove from the oven and serve with small bowls of Thai Chile–Herb Dipping Sauce.

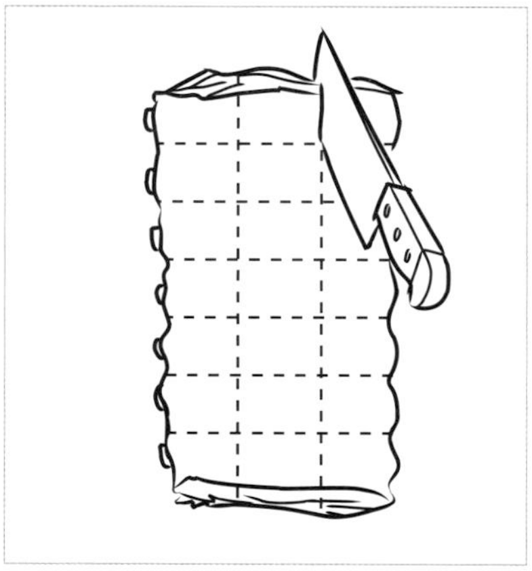

Pork Satay with Thai Cucumber Salad

This dish is an example of classic Thai street food. It is also excellent if the pork is replaced with boneless chicken breasts or a tender cut of beef.

SERVES 4 AS AN APPETIZER

- 1/2 cup coarsely chopped shallot
- 2 tablespoons chopped lemongrass (tough outer sheaths and upper stalk removed; use just the pale lower core)
- 1/2 teaspoon cumin seed, toasted in a dry skillet until fragrant, coarsely ground in a mortar, or ground cumin
- 1 teaspoon coriander seed, toasted in a dry skillet until fragrant, coarsely ground in a mortar, or ground coriander.
- 1 teaspoon ground turmeric
- 1 teaspoon kosher salt
- 1 teaspoon sugar
- 2 tablespoons Thai or Vietnamese fish sauce (*nam pla* or *nuoc nam*)
- 1/4 cup peanut oil or vegetable oil
- Generous 3/4-pound pork loin or tenderloin cut into strips about 2 inches long by 1 inch wide by 3/8 inch thick (see Note)

Satay Sauce (facing page)
Thai Cucumber Salad (facing page)

1. Combine the shallot, lemongrass, cumin, coriander, turmeric, salt, sugar, fish sauce, and oil in the bowl of a food processor. Process until a nearly smooth paste forms, 15 to 25 seconds, pausing to scrape down the sides of the bowl as needed. Combine the pork and the spice paste in a bowl, working the mixture into the pork with your fingers. Marinate at room temperature for 1 hour or in the refrigerator for up to 3 hours.

2. Thread two or three pieces of the pork onto each skewer, positioning the meat along the 5 inches nearest the sharp end of the skewer, nestling each piece so it just touches its neighbor (the pieces will look a bit "wavy" on the skewer but they shouldn't be too much so). Let the pork come to almost room temperature before grilling.

3. Grill over a medium-hot charcoal fire, or on an indoor griddle over medium-high heat, until just cooked through, 1½ to 2 minutes per side (placing aluminum foil over the surface of the grill above which the exposed end of the skewers will rest is a good way to prevent them from burning, or simply wrap exposed ends in foil). Serve skewers alongside a shallow dish of Satay Sauce for dipping and a dish of Cucumber Salad.

NOTE: Any tender cut works well for this dish. If you purchase meat with a fair amount of fat or gristle or buy chops on the bone, plan on purchasing a pound or so more than called for, so that after trimming and cutting into strips, you will have the 3/4 pound required. If you use a nearly gristle- and fat-free cut, such as tenderloin, a generous 3/4 pound is all you'll need from the butcher.

Satay Sauce

MAKES ABOUT 1¼ CUPS

Jars of Thai red curry paste are available in the Asian food sections of many supermarkets.

- ¾ cup canned coconut milk, shaken thoroughly before use
- 2 tablespoons chunky, unsweetened, natural peanut butter
- 1 tablespoon Thai red curry paste (see Note on page 73)
- 3 tablespoons tamarind concentrate or homemade tamarind "water"(see Note on page 212)
- 2 tablespoons Thai or Vietnamese fish sauce (*nam pla* or *nuoc nam*)
- 1 tablespoon sugar

1. Place coconut milk in a small saucepan and warm over medium-low heat just shy of a simmer. Add the peanut butter, stirring until dissolved. Stir in the curry paste, tamarind, fish sauce, and sugar and bring just to a simmer, stirring to dissolve the sugar. Remove from the heat. Adjust flavors to taste, adding small amounts of some or all of these ingredients.
2. Let cool to room temperature (it will thicken somewhat as it cools but should remain quite fluid and sauce-like; add water or coconut milk to thin and peanut butter to thicken, if necessary). Serve the sauce in shallow dishes for dipping alongside the pork satay.

Thai Cucumber Salad

MAKES ABOUT 4 CUPS

This salad is best if assembled within an hour or two of serving.

- 1 cup unseasoned rice wine vinegar
- ½ cup water
- 3 tablespoons sugar
- ½ teaspoon kosher salt
- 2 cucumbers, peeled, quartered lengthwise, and sliced ⅛ inch thick (about 4 cups)
- ½ cup very thinly sliced shallots
- 1-inch cube fresh ginger, peeled and cut into paper-thin julienne
- ¼ cup coarsely chopped fresh cilantro leaves, loosely packed
- One 2- to 3-inch fresh red Thai "bird" chile or other hot red chile, thinly sliced into rings, or seeds removed before slicing (optional)

1. Bring the vinegar, water, sugar, and salt to a boil in a small saucepan over high heat, stirring to dissolve the solids. Let cool to room temperature.
2. Put the cucumbers, shallots, ginger, cilantro, and chile, if using, into a bowl and pour the vinegar mixture over the vegetables, pushing to submerge them beneath the level of the liquid, if necessary.
3. Serve at room temperature or refrigerate until cool, tossing occasionally. Serve in small dishes alongside the pork satay.

Burmese Pork Curry

This is a mellow and satisfying curry. It is our adaptation of a recipe first encountered in Charmaine Solomon's *The Complete Asian Cookbook*, which, since the mid-1970s, has helped bring Asian cooking into Western kitchens. Serve it with white rice and a delicious Burmese garnish of gently fried slices of crisp garlic, drained and scattered over the finished curry.

SERVES 4

3	medium onions, coarsely chopped (about 4 cups)
1	large head of garlic cloves, crushed and peeled
One	4-inch by 1-inch piece fresh ginger, unpeeled and sliced into coins
	Kosher salt
2	teaspoons brown sugar
1½	tablespoons rice wine vinegar
1	tablespoon Thai or Vietnamese fish sauce (*nam pla* or *nuoc nam*)
2	pounds trimmed pork shoulder cut into 1-inch cubes (see Note)
1	teaspoon ground turmeric
1	teaspoon sweet paprika
⅛	teaspoon cayenne pepper
3	tablespoons peanut or vegetable oil
1	teaspoon Asian sesame oil
2	tablespoons chopped fresh cilantro

1. Put the onions, garlic, and ginger in the bowl of a food processor. Process to a smooth, slushy purée, about 1 minute, scraping down the sides of the bowl as needed. Transfer the purée to a fine-mesh strainer (or a colander lined with cheesecloth) set over a bowl. Working with a large spoon or rubber spatula, repeatedly press the purée to extract nearly all the liquid from it (the solids should remain slightly damp). Place the sieve with the solids over another bowl and set aside.

2. Pour the extracted onion-ginger liquid into a 10- to 12-quart pot and add 2½ teaspoons salt, the brown sugar, vinegar, and fish sauce, stirring to dissolve the salt and sugar. Add the pork, stirring to coat and distributing it evenly in the pot. Bring just to a simmer over medium-high heat. Reduce the heat to very low; cover and cook at the barest possible simmer until tender, 1½ hours to 2 hours, stirring one or twice.

3. Meanwhile, stir the turmeric, paprika, and cayenne into the bowl beneath the reserved onion-ginger purée solids in the sieve; add the purée and stir to combine. Heat the peanut oil in a 6- to 8-inch skillet over medium-low heat until very hot. Swirl the oil to coat the skillet and carefully add the purée, spreading it out across the entire surface of the skillet. Cook for 2 minutes and then scrape the purée up, stir it around, and spread it out again. If the purée sticks to the skillet, add about a tablespoon of water to help scrape up the stuck bits before spreading the mixture out again (a small amount of browning is fine). Repeat this process of scraping (adding water if needed), stirring and spreading every few minutes until the purée concentrates and becomes a few shades darker and takes on a warm, roasted smell, 20 to 25 minutes. Don't rush this process; reduce the heat if the purée seems to be cooking too quickly or threatens to burn (and keep a glass of water by the stove for use in scraping up the stuck bits of purée). When the purée has finished cooking, remove from the heat, stir in the sesame oil and set aside.

4. When the meat is tender, thoroughly stir in the onion-ginger paste. If the pork isn't yet falling apart and seems a bit "cube-like," use the back of a fork or spoon to partially crush the cubes of meat to help them absorb the cooking liquid. Continue to simmer, uncovered, until the cooking liquid becomes thickened and flavorful but still a bit fluid, 10 to 15 minutes more (thin with stock or water if it seems a bit dry). Add salt to taste and serve, garnished with cilantro.

NOTE: If a few meaty pork bones are available from your butcher, toss them into the pot for extra flavor. Discard before serving, if you like.

Sardinian-Style Pork, Fennel, and Fava Bean Stew

If you like split-pea soup, you will love this traditional Sardinian dish, which, in an exotic way, it resembles. Four kinds of pork—pancetta, sausage, fresh pork, and smoked pork hock—make it especially delicious. The richness of the fava beans adds to the stew's heartiness and full flavor. Serve it with soup spoons.

SERVES 4

1	large smoked prepared pork hock (about 1/2 pound)
1/4	cup extra-virgin olive oil
1/3	pound pancetta, sliced 1/8 inch thick and chopped into 1/4-inch pieces
1	medium onion, finely chopped
1	medium fennel bulb, cored and finely chopped, fronds reserved and chopped to yield about 3/4 cup
5	cloves garlic, chopped
3	tablespoons finely chopped fresh flat-leaf parsley
1/2	teaspoon ground fennel seed
1/8	teaspoon crushed red pepper flakes
2	tablespoons tomato paste
1/2	pound sweet pork sausage (without added flavorings), removed from casings
1/2	pound boneless pork loin, preferably from the rib or loin ends, cut into 1/2-inch pieces
1	pound dried large skin-on fava beans (3 to 3 1/4 cups), soaked in abundant water overnight, skins peeled and soaking water reserved (see Note)
	Kosher salt
	Fresh coarsely ground black pepper
	Country-style bread, sliced and toasted

1. Put the pork hock in a 4- to 6-quart pot over high heat and cover with cold water by 2 inches. Bring to a boil; reduce the heat to maintain a simmer and cook for 15 minutes. Drain and set aside.

2. Meanwhile, heat the oil in a 10- to 12-quart pot over medium heat. Add the pancetta and cook until just crisp at the edges but still tender, about 5 minutes, stirring occasionally. Add the onion, fennel, fennel fronds, garlic, parsley, fennel seed, and crushed red pepper; cook gently until the vegetables are softened but without color, 10 to 12 minutes, stirring occasionally.

3. Add the tomato paste, mashing it with the back of a wooden spoon or rubber spatula to incorporate with the vegetables. Stir in the sausage, breaking it up into small pieces with the wooden spoon and cooking until it is no longer raw, 2 to 3 minutes. Add the pork loin and the fava beans, stirring to coat. Add 6 cups of the reserved bean soaking liquid (strain it first and add water, if necessary); increase the heat to high and bring to a simmer. Cover and reduce heat to maintain the barest possible simmer and cook, stirring occasionally, until the beans are nearly tender but still somewhat firm, 35 to 45 minutes.

4. Uncover the pot and stir in 2 teaspoons salt and 5 or 6 generous grindings of black pepper. Cook at a simmer, uncovered, until the stew has thickened somewhat and the meats and beans are surrounded by (but not swimming in) the cooking liquid, 10 to 20 minutes. The consistency should be midway between a soup and a stew; simmer longer if needed.

5. Turn off the heat and let the stew rest, uncovered, for about 10 minutes. Meanwhile, remove the pork hock and rinse under running water to cool. Shred the meat, discarding the gristle and bone, and stir the meat into the pot. Season with salt to taste. Ladle the stew into wide, shallow bowls and serve with toast.

NOTE: Although it takes an extra 20 minutes or so, we peel our fava beans after soaking them because the taste and texture of the dish is improved—though you can leave the skins on, if you like (some Middle Eastern markets sell pre-peeled dried fava beans; go ahead and use them, just reduce the soaking time or follow package instructions). The age and quality of the beans will cause cooking times to vary; your beans may (or may not) begin falling apart before the cooking time has elapsed. Broken beans cause the stew to thicken more readily and make it less chunky because the beans are no longer whole. Bear this in mind when simmering and thickening the stew in Step 4. Ideally, you want some beans to break apart and thicken the stew, and others to remain whole (or nearly so), for texture. However, the dish is delicious no matter what becomes of your fava beans, so don't fret over it.

Spaghetti with Italian-Style Bacon, Onion, and Tomato

Better known as *pasta all'amatriciana*, this dish features *guanciale*, which is cured, unsmoked pork jowl—a popular ingredient in central Italy. Happily, guanciale is increasingly available in this country. If you can't find it, you can substitute fatty pancetta instead. In addition to spaghetti, bucatini (a thick, hollow spaghetti), is commonly paired with the sauce.

SERVES 4 AS AN APPETIZER; 2 AS A MAIN COURSE

- 2/3 pound *guanciale* (Italian-style cured pork jowl; see Note) or fatty pancetta, sliced like thick bacon (about 3/8-inch thick)
- 2 tablespoons extra-virgin olive oil
- 1/2 medium onion, finely chopped (about 1/2 cup)
- 3 large cloves garlic, minced
- 1/4 teaspoon crushed red pepper flakes
- One 28-ounce can tomatoes (in juice, not purée), 1/3 cup tomato juices reserved, tomatoes drained and chopped
- 1/4 cup dry white wine
- Kosher salt
- 2/3 pound spaghetti or bucatini
- 1/2 cup pecorino romano or similar cheese, finely grated
- 2 tablespoons finely chopped fresh flat-leaf parsley

1. Stack 3 or 4 slices of guanciale and cut across the slices to form short matchsticks about 3/8 inch thick. Repeat with the remaining guanciale. Place in a 12- to 14-inch skillet along with the oil over medium-low heat and cook very gently in a single layer until much of the fat has rendered and the guanciale is somewhat crisp but still tender, 10 to 20 minutes, stirring occasionally and separating any pieces bunched together (do not rush this; rendering the fat takes time and forms the base for the sauce). Remove guanciale with a slotted spoon, leaving the fat in the skillet, and transfer to a paper towel–lined plate.
2. Remove all but a generous 1/3 cup of rendered fat in the skillet (reserve the rest for another use) and return the skillet to medium-low heat. Add the onion and cook until very soft but without much color, about 8 minutes, stirring occasionally. Add the garlic and crushed red pepper and cook for 2 minutes, stirring. Stir in the tomatoes and reserved tomato juice, wine, and 1/4 teaspoon salt. Bring to a simmer over medium-high heat; reduce the heat to maintain a gentle simmer and cook until thickened considerably but still slightly fluid, about 30 minutes, stirring occasionally.
3. Cook the pasta in well-salted water until tender but still quite firm (al dente) and reserve 1 cup of the cooking water. Reheat the sauce, if necessary. Drain the pasta and return to the pot over very low heat. Add the tomato sauce, 1/2 cup of reserved cooking water, all but a few tablespoons of the reserved guanciale, 2 tablespoons of the cheese and the chopped parsley. Stir well to coat the pasta, 30 seconds to 1 minute, adding a bit more cooking water if the pasta seems dry or too "tight" (it should be damp and somewhat saucy; note that it will continue to thicken once served). Add salt to taste. Divide pasta and sauce among warmed serving bowls. Sprinkle each with the remaining guanciale and serve immediately, passing the remaining cheese at the table.

NOTE: Three sources for guanciale are: laquercia.us; Salumicuredmeats.com; and buonitalia.com.

Italian-Style Meat Loaf Stuffed with Egg and Spinach

This Italian version of an American classic is richly flavored but easy to make. It shows off a brightly colored interior of yellow, white, and green when sliced, which makes for a dramatic presentation. It's great when served on a bed of almost any wilted or braised greens, such as spinach, chard, or escarole.

SERVES 4

1/2	pound stemless spinach leaves
3/4	pound ground pork
3/4	pound ground beef chuck
1/4	pound thinly sliced mortadella, very finely chopped
1 1/2	cups coarse fresh bread crumbs (see Note)
1 1/2	ounces Pecorino Romano or Parmesan cheese, finely grated
1	medium onion, finely chopped
2	large cloves garlic, finely chopped
1	teaspoon finely chopped fresh rosemary
	Freshly ground black pepper
1/4	teaspoon freshly grated nutmeg
	Kosher salt
2	large eggs, lightly beaten, plus 2 large hard-boiled eggs
	Extra-virgin olive oil
1/2	cup dry white wine

1. Bring a large pot of salted water to a boil. Immerse the spinach and cook, stirring, until just wilted, 10 to 20 seconds. Transfer to a bowl of ice water to cool. Drain the spinach, squeezing firmly to remove water, and coarsely chop if the leaves are large. Reserve.
2. Preheat the oven to 400°F.
3. In a large bowl, combine the pork, beef, mortadella, bread crumbs, cheese, onion, garlic, rosemary, 1 teaspoon black pepper, nutmeg, 2 teaspoons of salt, and the lightly beaten eggs. Mix the ingredients gently but thoroughly. Lay a 1½-foot-long sheet of parchment or wax paper on a work surface; divide the meat mixture in half and transfer half to the parchment. Shape meat on the parchment into a 9-by-5-inch rectangle (2 or 2½ inches thick). Lay half of the reserved spinach lengthwise in a 2-inch strip down the center.
4. Place the hard-boiled eggs, end to end, on top of the spinach, nestling the eggs ¼ inch down into the surface of the meat. Lay the remaining spinach on top and tucked in and around the eggs. Roughly shape the remaining meat into a 9-inch-long rectangle and lay it over the meat, spinach, and eggs; gently shape the whole into a neat loaf, sealing the eggs and spinach within so no air pockets remain around them and thoroughly pinching the seams together where the upper and lower rectangles of meat come together.
5. Pick up the meat loaf on the parchment and transfer to a 9-by - 15-inch glass or ceramic baking dish, carefully sliding the loaf off the paper, right-side up. Brush the top of the loaf with 1 tablespoon or so of the oil. Place in the oven and cook for 30 minutes; add the wine and ¾ cup water to the baking dish and cook until an instant-read thermometer inserted in the middle of the loaf registers 155°F, about 30 minutes more.
6. Remove from the oven and let the meat rest for 10 minutes. Turn the meat loaf out onto a cutting board. Season the liquid in the baking dish with salt and pepper, and strain it, if you like. Cut the meat loaf into thick slices with a serrated or sharp chef's knife and arrange the slices on warmed serving plates, overlapping them. Moisten each serving with a bit of the cooking liquid; drizzle each with a little olive oil and serve.

NOTE: To make fresh bread crumbs for this dish, trim the crusts from 2 or 3 thick slices of fresh or day-old French, Italian, or other good-quality white bread (it shouldn't be dried out). Tear bread into chunks and pulse in a food processor to make coarse, fluffy, large crumbs (at least four or five times larger than ordinary fine bread crumbs). The size and softness of these crumbs will lighten the texture of the meat loaf.

French-Style Potted Pork Spread

This is a classic French rillettes, a staple of nearly every French butcher that begins with seasoned pork cooked in fat until the meat falls from the bone. The pork is then shredded and bound with some of the cooking fat. The spread is delicious smeared on toasted country bread as an appetizer or as the centerpiece of a picnic. Serve it with cornichon pickles, as the French do. A jar of rillettes makes a great gift.

SERVES 16 TO 20 AS AN APPETIZER

- 1/4 cup kosher salt
- 2 tablespoons sugar
- 2 teaspoons freshly ground black pepper
- 1/8 teaspoon ground cloves
- 1/4 teaspoon freshly grated nutmeg
- 1/4 teaspoon ground allspice
- 1/4 teaspoon ground cinnamon
- 4 bay leaves, each broken into 3 to 4 pieces
- 2 heads garlic, the cloves of one peeled and crushed, the other head halved crosswise
- 3 pounds thoroughly trimmed boneless pork shoulder, cut into 2-inch chunks
- 2 1/2 to 3 pounds rendered duck fat, goose fat, and/or lard (see Note)
- 2 large sprigs fresh thyme
- 3 teaspoons Armagnac, Cognac, or similar brandy

1. Thoroughly combine the salt, sugar, pepper, cloves, nutmeg, allspice, cinnamon, bay leaves, and crushed garlic in a large mixing bowl. Add the pork and toss to coat, pressing and rubbing all the spices onto every surface of the meat, so the mixture adheres to the pork. Cover tightly with a double layer of plastic wrap, pressing the first layer directly on top of the pork. Refrigerate for 12 to 24 hours.
2. Bring the pork to room temperature. Arrange a rack in the lower middle portion of the oven and preheat the oven to 250°F.
3. Begin melting the duck fat in a 5- to 7-quart heavy ovenproof casserole or pot over medium-low heat. Brush the garlic and bay leaves off the pork; reserve half of the bay leaves. When the fat is almost liquefied, but not yet very hot, slip the pork into the casserole (leaving any liquid in the marinade bowl behind) so that it is completely submerged, adding a bit more fat if needed. Add the halved head of garlic, the thyme sprigs, and reserved bay leaves. When the fat just begins to send up tiny bubbles, after 10 or 20 minutes, cover the casserole and place in the oven; cook until pork is very tender and easily falls apart when pinched, 3 to 4 hours. Check the casserole after 45 minutes to ensure that the fat is just gently bubbling. Adjust the oven temperature as needed.
4. Remove the casserole from the oven and let sit for 30 minutes. Using a slotted spoon or tongs, transfer the meat to a large bowl. Meanwhile, pass the fat through a fine-mesh strainer or cheesecloth into a bowl, leaving behind any dark meat juices in the casserole. Set aside a generous 2½ cups of fat to finish the dish; cool the remaining fat and store in the refrigerator for another use for up to 6 months.
5. When it is cool enough to handle, finely shred the meat in the bowl, discarding any fatty or gristly bits. Add 2 cups of the reserved fat to the shredded pork, stirring vigorously with a wooden spoon or rubber spatula to incorporate.
6. Moisten the insides of six 10-ounce preserve jars with ½ teaspoon each of Armagnac (cover and shake the jar to coat); stir the pork to incorporate the fat once more, and then divide the pork mixture among the jars, packing the mixture fairly firmly and rapping it on the counter a few times to eliminate air pockets. Spoon a few tablespoons of the remaining fat over the pork to cover it completely (if giving these as gifts, you may like to set a whole bay leaf in the fat; for an attractive presentation). Seal the jars and store in the refrigerator for at least 24 hours—preferably a week or so—before serving with toasted country-style bread (let rillettes come partway

CONTINUED>

French
Potted
Pork

to room temperature before serving). Rillettes will last three or more months when covered completely with a layer of fat and refrigerated.

NOTE: We prefer duck fat for making these rillettes, though goose and good-quality rendered pork fat (lard) are nearly as good. Duck and goose fat are available at many fine food shops; and duck fat is available by mail order from D'Artagnan in 7-ounce containers (www.dartagnan.com). (You will need five or six of these containers to make this recipe.) Use leftover fat for frying meat, poultry, and most especially, potatoes.

Apple and Riesling Sauerkraut with Grilled Sausages

In Germany's Pfalz region, cooks prepare sauerkraut by braising it with onion, sweet apple, herbs, spices, and the local Riesling wine until the taste of pickled cabbage is replaced by a milder flavor than most Americans are accustomed to. Buy the best-quality sausages you can find, and, if you're really hungry, accompany the dish with baby potatoes boiled in their skins.

SERVES 4

2	tablespoons vegetable oil
5	ounces salt pork or fatty unsmoked bacon, such as pancetta, sliced thinly and cut into ½-inch pieces
2	medium onions, chopped
1	large sweet apple, peeled and cut into ½-inch pieces
4	bay leaves
12	juniper berries
½	teaspoon, coarsely ground fresh black pepper
	Kosher salt
½	teaspoon sugar
1½	cups off-dry Riesling wine, such as a German QbA or Kabinett
2	pounds sauerkraut in brine, thoroughly rinsed and drained
1	cup Pork Stock (page 301), Chicken Stock (page 299), canned low-sodium chicken broth, or water
8	German-style sausages, such as Bratwurst and/or Bockwurst
	German-style mustard (optional)

1. Put the oil and salt pork in a 5- to 8-quart heavy pot set over medium-low heat. Cook, stirring occasionally, until most of the fat has rendered and pieces are crisp, about 10 minutes. Remove the solids with a slotted spoon and save for another use. Add the onions to the fat in the pot and cook without browning them, stirring occasionally, until very soft, about 20 minutes.
2. Increase the heat to medium-high and stir in the apple, bay leaves, juniper berries, black pepper, 1 teaspoon salt, the sugar, and wine. Bring to a simmer and cook for 3 minutes. Add the sauerkraut, stirring to coat. Stir in the stock, cover the pot, and cook at a bare simmer over low heat for 45 minutes.
3. Uncover the pot and raise the heat to medium. Simmer until the liquid has nearly evaporated, stirring regularly, 5 to 10 minutes more. Add salt to taste. (The sauerkraut can be made up to one week ahead.)
4. Grill or pan-fry the sausages according to package instructions. Reheat the sauerkraut if necessary and divide among serving plates. Top each with two sausages and serve with mustard, if you like.

Spanish-Style Meatballs with Romesco Sauce

The reason these meatballs are so delicious is they are enriched with Serrano ham and chicken livers. As a main course, serve them with Swiss chard or spinach and steamed or roasted potatoes. They can also be served as an appetizer or as part of a tapas assortment.

SERVES 3 TO 4 AS A MAIN COURSE; 8 TO 10 AS AN APPETIZER (MAKES 26 TO 30 ONE-INCH MEATBALLS)

- 2 ounces Serrano ham or similar cured ham, very thinly sliced
- 4 ounces chicken livers (about 2 pairs), trimmed of connective tissue
- 1 pound ground pork
- 1 cup coarse fresh bread crumbs (see Note)
- 3 tablespoons minced onion
- 2 teaspoons minced garlic
- 1/4 cup finely chopped fresh flat-leaf parsley
- Kosher salt
- 1/2 teaspoon fresh coarsely ground black pepper
- 1 large egg, beaten
- 6 tablespoons extra-virgin olive oil
- 1 1/4 cups Romesco Sauce (page 285)
- 3/4 cup Chicken Stock (page 299), canned low-sodium chicken broth, or water, plus more as needed
- 2 tablespoons finely chopped fresh flat-leaf parsley (optional)

1. Stack the slices of Serrano ham and cut crosswise into very thin (about 1/8 inch wide) julienne strips. Arrange the strips in a bundle and cut these crosswise into very tiny bits (1/8 inch or less); chop additionally as needed. Transfer to a large mixing bowl.
2. Mince the chicken livers by working the knife repeatedly over them at varying angles until nearly a paste. Transfer to the mixing bowl.
3. Add the pork, bread crumbs, onion, garlic, parsley, 1½ teaspoons salt, pepper, and beaten egg to the mixing bowl and gently but thoroughly combine. Working with damp hands, shape the pork mixture into 1-inch round meatballs and place on a parchment– or wax paper–lined rimmed baking sheet. Refrigerate for 1 to 3 hours.
4. Divide the oil between two 12- to 14-inch skillets placed over medium-low heat. When the oil slides easily in the skillets, add the meatballs and cook until golden brown on all sides and just cooked through, about 10 minutes, turning every few minutes with kitchen tongs.
5. While the meatballs are browning, put the Romesco Sauce into a small saucepan and stir in the stock. Heat gently over medium-low heat, stirring occasionally, until warmed through. The sauce should be slightly fluid but still thick; simmer additionally to thicken, or add small amounts of additional stock or water to thin, if needed. Add salt to taste and keep warm.
6. When the meatballs are almost cooked through, divide the sauce among warmed serving plates, spreading sauce to cover the bottoms of the plates (a scant ½ cup of thinned sauce is plenty for 7 to 10 meatballs (one main-course serving). Remove the cooked meatballs, one at a time, from the skillet and place attractively over the Romesco Sauce. Garnish with the parsley (if using), and serve.

NOTE: To make fresh bread crumbs for use in this dish, trim the crusts from 2 or 3 thick slices of fresh or day-old French, Italian, or other good-quality white bread (it shouldn't be dried out). Tear bread into chunks and pulse in a food processor to make coarse, fluffy large crumbs (at least 4 or 5 times larger than ordinary fine bread crumbs). The size and softness of these crumbs lightens the texture of the meatballs.

Braised Pork Tacos with Ancho Chiles

In this dish, the warm spicy flavor of an easily made ancho chile paste bathes tender pieces of braised pork, which makes an ideal filling for soft corn tortillas. Serve the various garnishes and salsas in separate bowls so that diners can help themselves when assembling their tacos.

MAKES ABOUT 3 CUPS TO FILL 14 TO 18 TACOS

3	tablespoons vegetable oil or lard
1 1/2	pounds trimmed boneless pork shoulder or boneless county-style ribs, cut into 1 1/2-inch cubes
1	medium white onion, peeled and cut lengthwise into four wedges, plus 2/3 cup finely chopped white onion for garnish
6	large cloves garlic, peeled
2	bay leaves
	Kosher salt
1 1/2	ounces ancho chiles, about 3 medium
1/2	teaspoon ground cumin seed
1	teaspoon ground coriander seed
	Soft corn tortillas (see Note)
	Tomatillo Salsa (page 287)
	Salsa Mexicana (page 286)
	Fresh cilantro leaves
2	ounces Cotija cheese (or similar aged Mexican cheese) or Pecorino Romano, finely grated (optional)
	Lime wedges

1. Heat the oil in a wide 10- to 12-quart pot over medium-high heat. When it begins to smoke, add pork and brown very well on at least two sides, 4 to 6 minutes per side. Stir in 5 cups of water, scraping the bottom of the pot to loosen any browned bits. Add the onion wedges, garlic, bay leaves, and 2 teaspoons salt and bring just to a simmer. Skim the liquid, reduce the heat to medium-low, and partially cover. Cook at a slight simmer until tender, about 1½ hours, stirring occasionally. Remove from the heat and let the pork sit in its liquid, uncovered, until cool enough to handle.

2. Meanwhile, preheat a skillet over medium heat and briefly toast the chiles by pressing them lightly with a spatula until fragrant, no more than 1 minute per side. Transfer the chiles to a bowl, cover with hot water, and soak until well softened, about 30 minutes. Stem and seed the chiles, chop coarsely, and set aside.

3. Remove the cooled meat from its liquid and transfer it to a bowl. Shred the pork into small, bite-size pieces with your fingers and set aside. Discard the bay leaves from the cooking liquid and transfer ½ cup or so of the liquid, and the onion and garlic pieces from the pot to the jar of a blender. Add the reserved chiles, the cumin, and coriander and process to form a thick, nearly smooth paste, with no large bits of chile remaining, scraping down the sides of the bowl and adding a bit more liquid as needed.

4. Return the chile paste and the pork to the pot. Simmer the mixture over medium-low heat until the meat is coated in a thick, barely fluid sauce, about 20 minutes, stirring occasionally. Let the pork sit off the heat for a few minutes. Add salt to taste, and serve in warm tortillas (about 2 to 3 tablespoons per tortilla) with the salsas, chopped white onion, cilantro, Cotija cheese, and lime wedges, if you like. (The mixture can be made up to 2 days ahead and reheated on the stovetop with ½ cup or so of water, or partially covered in a microwave.)

NOTE: Corn tortillas can be wrapped in a kitchen towel and steamed in a vegetable steamer or Chinese bamboo steamer set over simmering water. They can also be steamed in a microwave in their plastic packaging if the plastic is fairly thick: remove and separate the tortillas, poke a few holes in the plastic wrapper, and return the tortillas to the plastic bag. Hot tortillas can be wrapped in a towel and served in a basket. Two soft tortillas are often used to enfold the filling, if you want to eat them like this (and we think they're better this way), make sure you purchase enough.

Cuban-Style Roast Pork

As it cooks, this Cuban favorite fills the house with tempting aromas of roasting pork and garlic. It's cheap, easy, and very satisfying, especially when smothered in citrusy mojo sauce. Serve with coarsely mashed potatoes or, as the Cubans do, with boiled yuca. Note that the meat needs to marinate overnight.

SERVES 6 TO 8

1	heaping tablespoon annatto seeds (achiote), optional, available in Latin American shops and some supermarkets
½	cup olive oil
1	large head of garlic, cloves peeled and sliced
1	teaspoon dried oregano
1	teaspoon dried thyme
2	heaping teaspoons ground cumin seed
1	teaspoon freshly ground black pepper
5	bay leaves, ground or finely crumbled in a spice grinder or mortar
	Finely grated zest of 1 orange
	Finely grated zest of 1 lime
1½	tablespoons kosher salt
	6- to 8-pound bone-in, skin-on pork picnic shoulder (upper arm roast)
	Cuban-Style Citrus-Garlic Sauce (page 291)

1. If using annatto, combine with the oil in a small saucepan, bring to a very gentle simmer, and cook for 5 minutes. Remove the pan from the heat and let it sit for 10 minutes, allowing the annatto to color the oil. Meanwhile, combine the garlic, oregano, thyme, cumin, black pepper, bay leaves, orange and lime zests, and salt in a mixing bowl. Strain the warm oil into the mixing bowl, stirring to combine (if omitting annatto, just heat the oil and pour over the other marinade ingredients). Discard the annatto seeds and let the mixture cool. Transfer to the bowl of a food processor and process to a loose paste, about 30 seconds.

2. Using a sharp knife, score through the pork's skin, fat, and about ¼ inch of the flesh diagonally at 1½-inch intervals, forming a diamond-like crisscross pattern, covering the entire surface of the skin side. Rub all over with the marinade mixture making sure it gets into the slits in the meat. Place the pork in a dish just large enough to hold it and cover with foil, or place it in a double-lined resealable plastic bag. Marinate in the refrigerator overnight. Bring to room temperature before roasting.

3. Preheat the oven to 325°F. Place the pork, skin-side down, on a rack set within a roasting pan and roast for 3 hours, basting every so often. Turn the pork skin-side up and roast for 1½ to 2½ hours more, or until an instant-read thermometer inserted in the center of pork registers 190°F (cover with foil if skin seems to be browning too much). Transfer to a cutting board and let rest for 45 minutes to 1 hour. Slice the pork (or tear into chunks), making sure that each diner gets both meat and crisp skin (if crisp fat is difficult to cut through, remove large sections of the skin from the meat first and cut it into pieces). Serve doused with citrus-garlic sauce, passing additional sauce at the table.

RIBLETS

BUTTERFLIED LEG OF LAM

Lamb Neck

LAMB KEBABS

BREAST OF LAM

Baby Lamb

RIB LAMB CHOPS

CROW ROAS of Lamb

English LAMB CHOPS

LAMB

LA

LOIN LAMB CHOPS

Ground Lamb

French Rib Lamb Chops

LEG OF LAMB

LAMB SHOULDER

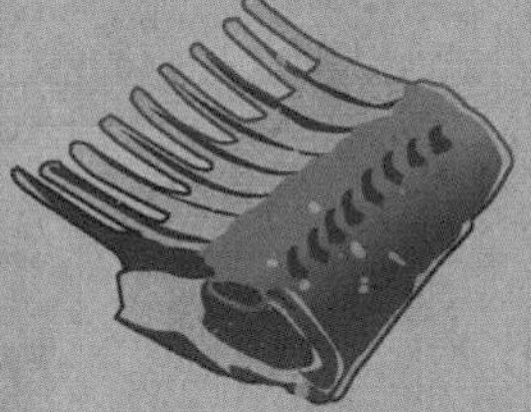

RACK OF LAMB

Shank Half of Leg

B SHANK

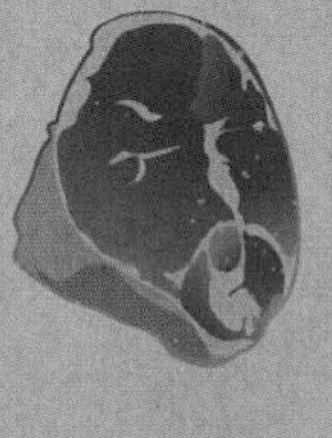

Ground Lamb

French R

Lamb Ch

LEG OF LAM

LAMB SHOULD

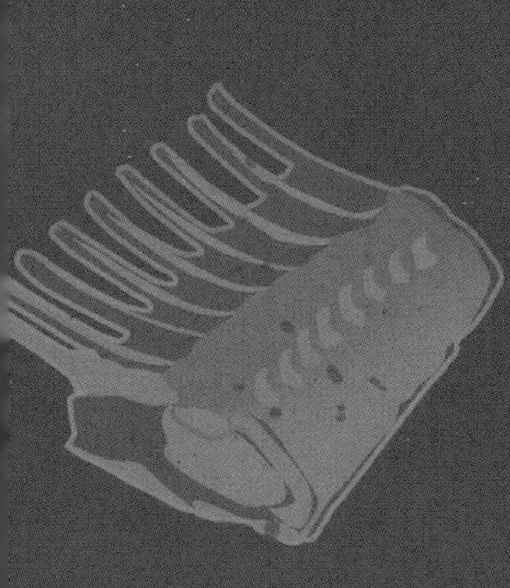

RACK OF LAM

Shank Half of

CHAPTER FOUR

Lamb

Lamb's full flavor is more assertive than pork's, and yet its sweetness makes it a brilliant match for any number of vegetables, fruit, and grains. Its distinctive flavor also makes it more of an acquired taste than other meats, but for those who love lamb, there is no better red meat. Still, as a nation we do not eat nearly as much lamb as we do other meats. In fact, only about 20 percent of Americans have even tried lamb—and it represents only about one percent of all meat consumption in the nation.

We hope this will change because lamb is a superb meat, whether it's grilled, roasted, or braised. To qualify as lamb, a sheep must be less than a year old and the meat is graded prime and choice, although these grades are rarely used as selling points for the consumer.

Look for meat that is pink, firm, and lean. The external fat should be firm and white, and not too thick. The bones should be moist with red coloration. Stay away from lamb with deep red meat, yellowish fat, and pure white bones. These indications mean the animal is too old for lamb and so will be tough and taste like the mutton it most likely is.

Not everyone agrees with us, but we find lamb is best when bought in season, from April through October. This is particularly true for lamb that is pasture raised, as it is during the warm months that the animals graze on the sweetest grass and if you are fortunate enough to buy pasture-raised lamb from a local farmer, this certainly will be true. Expect the sweetest, most tender meat during these months. But don't avoid lamb at other times of year—it will be very good, particularly the cuts that need long, slow cooking.

Farms around the country are raising heritage lamb, just as they are raising heritage beef and pork. If you are able to find it, try it. The meat will be succulent and mildly flavored. Katahdin sheep, named for a mountain peak in Maine, are bred mainly for meat as their wool is not really long enough for shearing. An old North American breed is Tunis lamb, which is as prized for its wool as well as its meat. Tunis lamb has suffered a decline in numbers but dedicated breeders are working hard to bring it back. Another heritage lamb that is being reintroduced to the public is the Navajo-Churro, which originally came from Spain but was quickly adopted by Native Americans.

Besides domestic lamb, very good lamb is imported from New Zealand and Australia, countries that produce top-quality lamb all year long. As good as this lamb is, it is no better than American lamb, so we recommend that you buy what is best at the time of purchase.

LEG

LEG OF LAMB

Leg of lamb, which is so often the centerpiece of Easter dinners and dinner parties, is cut from the hind leg and includes both the top and the lower parts of the leg, which are called, respectively, the sirloin (or butt) and the shank. Leg of lamb is considered a treat by most lamb lovers. It's an expensive cut but is absolutely delicious.

Most people buy the whole leg, but if you have a small family, you might want to buy a half leg. On the other hand, you could buy a whole leg, have the butcher cut it into two roasts, and freeze one half. Or, if a whole leg is just slightly too big for your needs, the butcher can slice a few steaks from the sirloin end, which could be served at a later meal.

SIRLOIN (BUTT) HALF OF LEG

The top part of the leg, this is a very tender, meaty roast with wonderful flavor. We like it for small gatherings, as it serves only four or five. It can be cut into chops, which are sometimes called lamb steaks.

SHANK HALF OF LEG

The shank roast is small and therefore attractive for small families. It is not as tender as the butt end, so does best when cooked slowly.

BONED AND ROLLED LEG OF LAMB

When a customer asks for a boned leg of lamb for rolling, we cut the tip end from the shank and then bone the leg of lamb so that it can be rolled and tied. The home cook can unroll the meat and fill it with a savory stuffing made up of herbed bread crumbs, dried fruit, vegetables, and other ingredients, and then roll it up and tie it again.

When you buy a trimmed leg of lamb, it will weigh about 1½ pounds. If you plan to trim your own boned leg of lamb, it will weigh 2 to 2½ pounds before the fat and silverskin are cut away.

BUTTERFLIED LEG OF LAMB

This is a boned leg of lamb (see Boned and Rolled Leg of Lamb, above) that is opened and flattened and used most often for grilling. It's impossible to flatten the leg meat evenly, which means this is a lumpy cut that will not cook evenly as will a beef or veal steak. Lamb lovers do not object to this at all and instead claim that this makes the butterflied leg of lamb perfect for a group: the thicker and thinner parts of the meat cook to different degrees of doneness, so everyone's tastes are accommodated.

LEG LAMB CHOPS

Generally, these chops are quite large and therefore are cut about 1¼ inches thick and often are referred to as lamb steaks rather than chops. They are characterized by a small marrowbone in the center. In the springtime, when lamb is at its best, these are especially tasty.

LAMB KABABS

Cubes of meat appropriate for threading on skewers and grilling or broiling can be cut from other parts of the lamb but we feel the best kababs come from the leg. It's most important to be sure all sinews and veins are cut out, which is a task for the butcher unless the home cook feels confident he or she can handle this. If you buy precut cubes of lamb meat for kababs, take a good look at the meat to make sure it is correctly cleaned and cut. If the meat is cut from the leg, it will be extremely tender and flavorful and therefore does not need marinating, although many home cooks like to bathe them in a lively mixture to add extra flavor.

GROUND LAMB

Leg meat makes the leanest ground lamb, but because it's lean, it may be a little dry. For juicier ground lamb, choose fattier lamb shoulder meat. See Lamb Shoulder, page 146.

LOIN OF LAMB

SADDLE OF LAMB

The two loins connected by the backbone are called the saddle, for obvious reasons. The cut is also referred to as the full loin of lamb, and when trimmed weighs upward of 6 pounds. This is not commonly sold as a retail cut and because of its configuration, it is always roasted and then sliced lengthwise. It can be tricky to slice, so we don't recommend that our customers who want to serve a saddle at a dinner party do so without first practicing and gaining a little experience.

There also is a hindsaddle of lamb, which consists of the two hindlegs and the short loin. This is rarely seen nowadays, but an Old World dish called baron of lamb is made using the hindsaddle.

LOIN OF LAMB

The loin is one half of a saddle; its location on the lamb corresponds to where the porterhouse is on a steer. It contains the tenderloin (fillet) and a small T-bone that separates the tenderloin from the eye. The meat is exceptionally tender and requires careful cooking. The loin can be cut into chops but makes a lovely roast when left whole. Ask the butcher to leave a respectable coating of fat on the loin for roasting. The lamb loin is a great party dish.

BONED AND ROLLED LOIN OF LAMB ROAST

When the entire saddle or just half of the saddle (a single loin) is boned, flattened, and rolled, it can be filled with a light stuffing and rolled back up and tied for roasting. The meat is first trimmed of excess fat, then the tail is removed; what is left is the eye and fillet. Sometimes the lamb kidneys are inserted before the meat is tied up. The boned saddle weighs about four pounds and serves four to six. This is very easy to slice, and so is a party favorite.

LOIN LAMB CHOPS

Loin lamb chops are small and tender with small T-bones that separate the tenderloin from the eye (the nugget of meat). Some also have a kidney neatly inserted below the tenderloin and then the tail is curved around it and secured with a skewer.

ENGLISH LAMB CHOPS

English lamb chops are double chops cut from the saddle with the tails tucked around them to form almost a circle of meat. The double chops have two T-bones, two tenderloins, and two eyes. These double chops are considered a delicacy and usually have to be special ordered.

RACK OF LAMB

RACK OR RIB ROAST OF LAMB

The rack is next to the loin and is characterized by long rib bones, but no tenderloin. The meat, or eye, is delicious and tender, and the rack can be cut into individual chops or left whole and roasted. When it comes to flavor, texture, and tenderness, we prefer this meat to the loin. The rack is actually a series of rib chops; when you buy a rack of lamb, purchase one with eight or nine ribs. If the rack has ten ribs, the last one is cut from the shoulder and will not be as tender as the others. The rib bones should have visible streaks of red running through them, any fat should be creamy and white, and the meat should be pink with flecks of graining, or fat. The butcher will remove the chine bone and crack between the rib bones, which makes it easy to carve the roast into individual chops before serving.

CROWN ROAST OF LAMB

The crown roast is made from two racks of lamb that are attached to make a circle of rib chops. The bones are frenched—stripped of meat—so that they resemble a crown; we recommend wrapping the exposed bones with aluminum foil to prevent them from becoming brittle and cracking in the oven. The butcher will crack the bones slightly and then curve and tie the racks into the circle. The center of the crown is usually filled with stuffing before the lamb is roasted.

RIB LAMB CHOPS

These chops are cut from the rack of lamb. They can be cut into single, double, or even triple chops. They have no tenderloin, but nonetheless are absolutely delicious. Single chops, trimmed of excess fat, sometimes are sandwiched between sheets of wax paper and flattened with a mallet or cleaver. They are then breaded and pan-fried.

FRENCH RIB LAMB CHOPS

What dainty and delectable little chops! The fat is well trimmed and the end of the bone is exposed. It might be considered old-fashioned, but it's classic to top the frenched bones with paper frills, which makes the chops easy to pick up if they are passed as individual chops.

BREAST OF LAMB

The breast is the meat that extends from the ribs and tends to be fatty, without as much meat as other cuts of lamb. It can be trimmed with a pocket for stuffing and will weigh only 2 to 3½ pounds. When it is trimmed and sold this way, with a pocket cut into it, it's actually a half-breast. The breast can be cut into riblets, which are great for grilling. The ribs in the breast should be cracked by the butcher to make it easy to cut. This is an unfamiliar cut today, although even 50 years ago it was quite popular, mainly because it was the only cut immigrants seeking lamb could afford. While this is not an expensive cut, the breast sometimes needs to be special ordered.

LAMB SHOULDER

LAMB SHOULDER

The shoulder has generous amounts of moist meat as well as bone. In the springtime, when lamb is at its best, shoulder chops are excellent for grilling, and the meat is good for kababs. Shoulder meat is also our favorite for braises and lamb stew. It has more graining (which is what we call marbling in lamb and refers to the amount of thin streaks of fat running through the meat) and flavor than other lamb meat and is more reasonably priced.

Any lamb chop labeled "bone-in lamb shoulder chop," "blade chop," "flat-bone chop," or "round-bone chop" works in any recipe that calls for shoulder meat, although the ratio of bone to meat differs somewhat from chop to chop. Round bone chops are easier to cut into chunks than blade chops; blade chop meat should be separated from the bone by a butcher.

BLADE LAMB CHOPS

These chops are located in the shoulder, right next to the rack. We find them to be the most flavorful of the shoulder chops; they're also more familiar and easy-to-find than other shoulder chops. Because the muscles running through the chops differ in terms of texture, these do nicely when marinated and cooked slowly, as in the recipe for Lamb Tagine with Two Squashes, Apricots, and Almonds on page 168. They are especially tender in the springtime.

ARM LAMB CHOPS

Arm lamb chops are cut from the lower part of the shoulder, near the shank, and have a small round bone. While tasty, they tend to be a little drier than blade lamb chops.

LAMB SHANK

Lamb shanks can be cut from the shoulder or the hind section. When the hindshank is removed from the hind leg, it is called a lamb shank, but when a shank is cut from the shoulder, it is labeled the foreshank. The foreshank is best when braised or otherwise slowly cooked. The meat makes great stew and also can be ground to make delicious lamb burgers.

OTHER CUTS

RIBLETS

See Breast of Lamb, page 145.

LAMB NECK

At the bottom of the neck is a long line of bones; the meat from this section is sweet and tender when cooked slowly. Although neck meat is usually used for lamb stew, it can also be boned and then ground. In this case, we like to grind it with meat from the foreshank—the combination of the two makes for a great lamb burger!

LAMB STEW MEAT

We recommend boned shoulder meat for lamb stew. Because of the amount of bone in the shoulder, the meat is sweet, flavorful, and juicy.

GROUND LAMB

For the juiciest, most flavorful lamb burgers, use the meat from the shoulder. Leg meat makes leaner, drier burgers.

BABY LAMB

Baby lamb, which is also called hothouse lamb, usually is 6 to 8 weeks old, although we have sold it when it is only 1 or 2 weeks old. It has been fed entirely on ewe's milk, which means it's incredibly tender and pale colored. The lamb is never more than 10 to 12 pounds and when the meat is cooked, it can practically be cut with a fork. For large parties, we supply a whole lamb, but for smaller gatherings, we halve or quarter the lamb.

The bones are sometimes cracked before the lamb is cooked, although they are so soft they can be cut with a good, sharp knife. The leg and shoulder areas may fall apart during cooking and the meat will fall off the bone. Baby lamb has a delicate flavor and is a popular choice for holiday dinners. Baby lamb has to be special ordered.

F LAMB
OIN
LAMB CHOP
Ground Lamb
Neck
LEG
LAMB
AST
LAMB
R
ROWN
OAST
Shank

LAMB KEBABS
Baby Lamb
RIB LAMB CHOPS
English
LAMB CHOPS

RECIPES

ound
amb
French Rib
Lamb Chops
EG OF LAMB
MB SHOULDE
RACK OF LAMB

Scotch Broth

This is a great one-pot meal halfway between a soup and a stew. You can substitute small amounts of any vegetable of your choice for all but the leeks in this recipe. Other choices include kale, potatoes, and celery, all of which are nice alternatives as long as the total quantities of vegetables in the recipe remain the same.

SERVES 4

2	pounds bone-in blade lamb chops and/or meaty chunks of lamb neck
5	quarts cold water
1	bay leaf
	Kosher salt
1/2	cup yellow or green split peas
1/2	cup pearl barley, rinsed
1	small onion, chopped (about 1/2 cup)
2	large leeks, white and pale green parts only, chopped (about 1 1/2 cups)
2	carrots, peeled and cut into 1/2-inch dice (about 1 cup)
1	small turnip, peeled and cut into 1/2-inch dice (about 1 cup)
1/3	of a very small head of green cabbage, cored and chopped into 1/2-inch pieces (about 1 1/2 cups)
	Freshly ground black pepper
3	generous tablespoons chopped fresh flat-leaf parsley

1. Place the lamb, water, bay leaf, and 1 tablespoon salt in a heavy 12-quart pot over high heat, skimming off any impurities as it comes to a boil. Reduce the heat to maintain the slightest possible simmer and stir in the split peas and barley; cook, skimming occasionally, for 1 hour. Stir in the onion, leeks, carrots, turnip, and cabbage; return to a bare simmer and cook for 1 hour more.

2. Turn off the heat and remove the lamb to a bowl or plate until cool enough to handle. Shred the meat fairly finely with your fingers, discarding bones and excess fat. If the lamb pieces are still large, chop into small, bite-size pieces (you should have about 2 cups). Return the lamb to the pot, increase the heat to high, and bring to a boil. Reduce the heat and cook at a brisk simmer until the broth thickens to a point midway between a soup and porridge, stirring occasionally to prevent sticking, 5 to 20 minutes (note that it will continue to thicken off the heat).

3. Stir in at least another 1 or 2 teaspoons of salt or more to taste and a generous grinding of black pepper. Ladle into bowls, garnish generously with the chopped parsley, and serve. The broth can be made a day or two ahead. When reheating, thin it with broth or water to the consistency described in Step 2.

NOTE: Bone-in blade lamb chops are widely available; we chose them for this recipe because the bone helps flavor the broth. Lamb neck makes a more flavorful broth still, so if you can find it, include a piece or two along with the meatier blade chops. Although lamb neck meat takes longer than blade meat to reach tenderness (a little longer than the two hours we call for here), in this dish, it hardly matters if the neck meat retains a bit of chew, because the meat is shredded into such small pieces that when returned to the broth, you don't notice the slight difference in texture. But the neck bone addition does give the broth a flavor boost, as it does for all lamb broths.

Lamb Chops with Parmesan-Bread Crumb Crust

This recipe is based on a favorite from Marcella Hazan's very first book, *The Classic Italian Cookbook*, published in 1973. The lamb chops should cook with a lively—but not violent—bubbling at the edges, to prevent the coating from getting too dark before the chops are cooked through. The heat should be reduced if the coating appears to be coloring too fast. This recipe is delicious when paired with zucchini or eggplant flavored with basil and garlic.

SERVES 2

1½	ounces Parmigiano-Reggiano or similar cheese, grated on the smallest holes of a grater (about ½ cup)
2	large eggs
1	tablespoon whole milk
¾	cup good-quality dried fine bread crumbs
8	single-rib lamb chops (about 1½ pounds), each trimmed and pounded to a thickness of ½ inch (see Note), at room temperature
	Kosher salt
	Fresh coarsely ground black pepper
	Vegetable oil for frying

1. Place the grated cheese on a dinner plate. Beat the eggs with the milk in a wide shallow bowl. Spread the bread crumbs on a second plate. Place a small baking rack over a third plate to hold the coated lamb chops.

2. Generously salt and pepper the lamb chops on both sides, and, working with one chop at a time, dip the chop in the grated cheese, pressing to coat all surfaces, including the edges. Tap the chop to shake off any excess. Pass both sides of the chop through the beaten egg to coat, letting the excess drip back into the bowl. Dip the chop in the bread crumbs, pressing lightly to coat all surfaces; shake off any excess. Put the chop on the baking rack and repeat with the remaining chops. Reserve. You can prepare up to this point 1 or 2 hours ahead; store them uncovered on the rack in the refrigerator. Bring to room temperature before cooking.

3. In a heavy skillet large enough to hold the chops comfortably in a single layer, heat ¼ inch of oil over medium heat to 300°F. Fry the chops until golden in color and cooked to your liking, about 2½ minutes per side for medium-rare, reducing the heat if the coating on the chops appears to be coloring too quickly. Briefly transfer the chops to a paper towel–lined plate to drain before serving.

NOTE: It's easier to trim the silverskin and fat from these chops when you start with a rack of lamb (because it's in one large piece) and then slice the rack into individual chops. The butcher can do this for you. Enclose the chops in a resealable plastic bag and pound to a uniform thickness of ½ inch. Thin chops are important because the meat needs to cook through in the same amount of time it takes to brown the coating. Don't bother frenching the chops; the cheesy, fried rib edges are great to gnaw on.

Charcoal-Grilled Lamb Chops with Garlic and Marjoram

A simple and savory centerpiece to an outdoor meal—Greek or otherwise. Thinly pounded rib lamb chops marinate for a few hours in garlic, fresh marjoram, and olive oil and are then grilled quickly over a live fire to medium doneness—which is a preference for many Greeks. Serve with Greek lemon-roasted potatoes and sautéed spinach—which can be prepared prior to grilling the lamb and served at warm room temperature.

SERVES 2

One	8-rib rack of lamb (1 1/2 to 2 pounds)
3	large cloves garlic, peeled and minced
2	tablespoons finely chopped fresh marjoram or oregano, or 2 teaspoons dried
1/3	cup extra-virgin olive oil
	Kosher salt

1. Using a sharp knife, separate the rack into 8 chops. With a meat mallet or the bottom of a small, heavy skillet, gently pound each chop to a thickness of about ½ inch. (You can ask the butcher to prepare the chops for you.)
2. Combine the garlic, marjoram, and oil in a small bowl and let stand for at least 5 minutes. Transfer the marinade to a baking dish just large enough to hold the chops in a single layer. Dip each lamb chop in the marinade, massaging each with the mixture and making sure that each chop is coated with at least a few bits of garlic. Cover and let marinate at room temperature for 2 to 3 hours or refrigerate for 6 to 8 hours. Turn and rub the marinade into the chops occasionally. Bring to room temperature before grilling.
3. Prepare a medium-hot charcoal fire and preheat the grate. When the coals are covered in a light gray ash, spread them out and grill the lamb chops—sprinkling each side generously with salt as you go—until they're cooked through, 3 to 4 minutes per side for medium doneness.

Loin Lamb Chops with Eggplant Caponata

This sweet-and-sour eggplant caponata is packed with vegetables and flavored with capers, raisins, pine nuts, and orange. This recipe makes more than you'll need for four servings of lamb chops, but you'll like having it around to enliven a selection of antipasti or a cheese tray, or to spoon alongside other meats and fish. The flavors are most distinct when freshly made, but caponata keeps well for a week or more.

SERVES 4

2 cups Eggplant Caponata (facing page) at room temperature
Kosher salt
Fresh coarsely ground black pepper
2 tablespoons olive oil
8 trimmed loin lamb chops, cut 1 inch thick

Spoon about ½ cup caponata onto each of four serving plates and set aside. Salt and pepper the lamb generously on both sides. Heat the oil in a skillet large enough to hold the lamb chops (or use two skillets) over medium-high heat. When the oil is hot, add the lamb and cook until nicely browned on both sides and cooked to your liking, about 3½ minutes per side for medium-rare. Transfer the lamb to plates with the caponata and serve.

NOTE: Loin, rib, and shoulder blade chops, as well as butterflied leg of lamb, all taste fabulous with our eggplant caponata. The match may even be better when the lamb is cooked over a wood fire on a grill—so don't hesitate to fire it up. And because the caponata is served at room temperature, any extra work or focus that outdoor cooking might require is kept to a minimum.

Eggplant Caponata

MAKES ABOUT 6 CUPS

- 3 large very fresh eggplants (3 to 3½ pounds)
- ⅔ cup plus 3 tablespoons extra-virgin olive oil
- Kosher salt
- Fresh coarsely ground black pepper
- ¼ cup tomato paste
- 1 large onion, cut into ½-inch pieces (about 2 cups)
- 3 ribs celery cut into ½-inch pieces (about 1½ cups)
- 1 small head fennel, cut into ¼-inch pieces (about 1¼ cups)
- 3 large cloves garlic, finely chopped
- ½ teaspoon finely grated orange zest
- ⅓ cup fresh orange juice, plus more to taste
- ⅓ cup red wine vinegar, plus more to taste
- 2 tablespoons sugar
- 2 roasted red bell peppers (recipe page 284, or from a jar), cut into ½-inch pieces (about 1 cup)
- 1 heaping tablespoon capers, chopped if large
- 1 heaping tablespoon toasted pine nuts
- ¼ cup golden raisins, soaked in hot water until plump

1. Preheat the oven to 425°F. Peel about two-thirds of the skin from each eggplant by running a vegetable peeler the length of it, leaving alternate bands of skin and peeled areas (this just adds a bit of color and texture to the finished dish). Remove stems and cut the partially peeled eggplants into ¾-inch cubes.

2. Put half of the cubed eggplant into a large mixing bowl and gradually drizzle in ⅓ cup olive oil, tossing to coat. Gradually sprinkle in 1 teaspoon salt and a few generous grindings of black pepper, while tossing to evenly distribute the seasonings. Spread out the eggplant in one layer on a large metal baking sheet (lined with parchment or wax paper, if you like), keeping the pieces from crowding. Repeat the process with the remaining eggplant. Roast until just tender and golden-brown on the undersides, about 30 minutes, rotating the pans after 15 minutes to encourage even cooking.

3. While the eggplant roasts, dissolve the tomato paste in ¼ cup water and set aside. Heat 3 tablespoons olive oil in a 10- to 12-inch skillet over medium-high heat. When the oil just begins to smoke, add the onion and celery and cook until the vegetables just begin coloring at the edges, but are still crisp, about 3 minutes, stirring regularly. Stir in the fennel and garlic and cook for 2 minutes. Reduce the heat to medium and cook until the fennel is tender but still a bit firm, 8 to 10 minutes, stirring occasionally (the vegetables should brown only slightly at the edges and each should retain its shape and some firmness). Stir in the dissolved tomato paste and 1 teaspoon salt and cook for minutes, stirring regularly. Transfer the vegetable mixture to a large mixing bowl.

4. When the eggplant is tender, remove from the oven and let cool for at least 10 minutes. Meanwhile, put the orange zest, orange juice, vinegar, and sugar in a small saucepan. Bring to a simmer over medium heat, stirring to dissolve the sugar. Simmer until reduced in volume by one-third, 2 to 3 minutes. Remove from the heat.

5. Using a thin metal spatula, scrape up the eggplant on the pans to inspect the undersides of the pieces. Discarding any that have deeply burned (though some blackened bits are fine), put the roasted eggplant into the bowl with the vegetable mixture. Add the roasted red peppers, capers, pine nuts, and plumped raisins, folding gently with a large rubber spatula to combine (try not to mash the eggplant). Gradually drizzle in the warm orange-vinegar mixture while continuing to fold until everything is well combined. Add salt to taste and, if necessary, additional vinegar and orange juice to taste. The caponata should be pleasingly sweet and sour but not excessively sharp. Serve at room temperature or slightly cool.

Stuffed Lamb Breast

Because lamb breast is relatively flat and doesn't have a lot of meat, it is an ideal cut to stuff. This Italian-inflected recipe is great as we present it here, but it would also be delicious covered in a simple tomato sauce or sitting atop a pile of braised white beans. It is good served warm or cool; a salad on the side completes the meal.

SERVES 3 TO 4

3	tablespoons extra-virgin olive oil, plus more as needed
1	small onion, finely chopped (about 1/2 cup)
4	large cloves garlic, finely chopped, plus 8 cloves garlic, unpeeled
4	ounces thinly sliced pancetta, finely chopped
1/2	pound ground lamb
1/2	cup fresh or frozen green peas
	Kosher salt
One	slice of crustless country-style bread, 3 by 3 by 1 inch thick
2	teaspoons finely chopped fresh marjoram, oregano, or rosemary, plus 2 fresh sprigs
2	tablespoons finely chopped fresh flat-leaf parsley
3/4	ounce finely grated Parmesan or similar cheese
1	large egg, beaten
1	bone-in breast of lamb (about 3 pounds after trimming), trimmed of most external fat and opened up by your butcher to create a pocket the entire length of the breast (see Note and illustration)
	Freshly ground black pepper
1	cup dry white wine
	Quick Tomato Sauce (page 280; optional)

1. Heat the oil in a medium skillet over medium-high heat. Add the onion, chopped garlic, and pancetta. Cook until the onion is translucent, about 5 minutes, stirring occasionally. Add the ground lamb and cook until the meat is lightly browned, 3 to 5 minutes, breaking it up with a wooden spoon as it cooks. Add the peas, ¼ teaspoon salt, a few tablespoons of water, and cook for 1 minute more, scraping the skillet to loosen any browned bits. Transfer the mixture to a large bowl and let cool slightly. Soak the bread in water or milk to cover until soft. Break up to form a coarse paste. Drain excess liquid and crumble the bread into the bowl with the meat. Add the chopped marjoram, parsley, cheese, and egg and combine thoroughly. Preheat the oven to 450°F.

2. Fill the lamb breast with the stuffing, spreading it evenly and into the corners (it should plump up nicely but don't pack too firmly). To help hold the filling in its pocket, use kitchen string to tie 5 or 6 individual loops along the length of the meat—between the bone—as you would for a roast (see photograph). You can also sew the opening shut using kitchen string and a trussing needle. In either case, the seal doesn't need to be particularly tight because the stuffing will continue to firm up shortly after the roast is put in the oven.

CONTINUED>

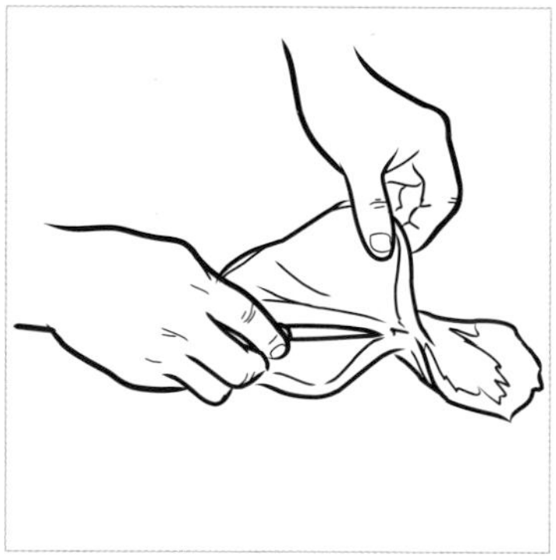

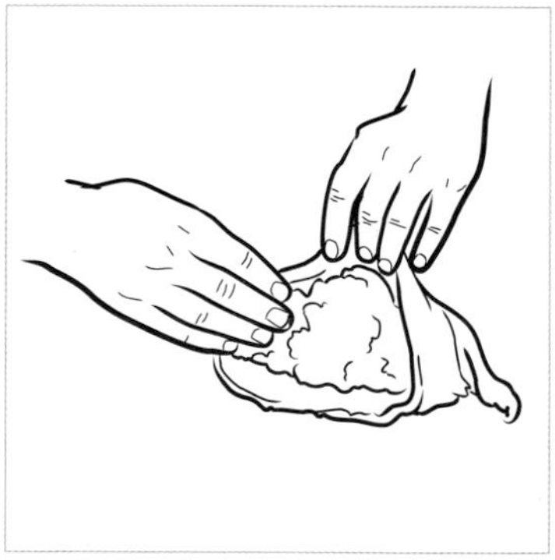

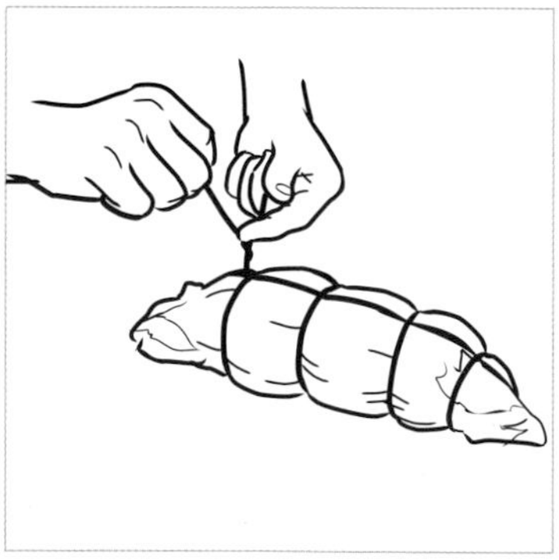

3. Generously salt and pepper the lamb breast and place bone-side down on a roasting rack set in a roasting pan or baking dish just large enough to contain it (there should be space enough to fit a basting spoon between the rack and the pan). Drizzle the top with a tablespoon or so of oil and roast for 20 minutes. Reduce the heat to 350°F and roast for 45 minutes. Carefully pour off the fat from the roasting pan and add the whole garlic cloves, marjoram sprigs, and wine. Cook for 1 hour and 15 minutes more, basting the lamb breast every 20 minutes or so. Remove from the oven and let rest for 15 to 30 minutes to firm up filling before slicing.

4. Place the lamb on a cutting board. Snip and discard the strings and, using a sharp, heavy knife, cut the breast into slices between the ribs, carefully cutting through the filling and then pressing firmly to cut through the breastbone. If breastbone won't easily separate into ribs, the meat and filling can be lifted off the bones instead—either in one whole piece or in portions. With the meat and filling removed, it's easy to cut the remaining breast bones into individual ribs. Serve these alongside the meat and filling. If serving with tomato sauce, spoon warmed sauce over each portion.

NOTE: One length of lamb breast (a half breast), trimmed, weighs between 2 and 4 pounds. If you can't find a single piece that weighs about 3 pounds after trimming, as called for, you can make this dish with two 1½- or 2-pound pieces, have a pocket cut in each, and divide the stuffing between them. Your butcher can cut the pockets for you, if you like (see illustration, page 156).

Roast Lamb with Romesco Sauce

Lamb with Romensco is a Spanish favorite. Serve it with a combination of roasted or grilled vegetables, such as small potatoes, zucchini, and leeks. Simmer potatoes or leeks in salted water until almost tender before grilling them. The Romesco Sauce and reduced lamb broth can be prepared up to 2 days ahead, if you like.

SERVES 6

- 4 cups Lamb Stock (page 300)
- Kosher salt
- 1 large sprig fresh thyme
- Freshly ground black pepper
- 4 pounds boneless leg of lamb (preferably from the sirloin end) with an exposed layer of fat, rolled and tied as for a roast
- 2 cups Romesco Sauce (page 285)

1. Bring the stock to a boil in a medium saucepan; reduce the heat to maintain a brisk simmer and reduce by half, to 2 cups, about 30 minutes. Remove from the heat and salt to taste. While still hot, add the thyme and let it steep in the broth for 5 minutes. Remove and discard the thyme and reserve the broth.

2. Preheat the oven to 375°F. Turn the roast fat-side up. Working with a sharp knife, score the lamb fat in a ½-inch crosshatch pattern without cutting into the flesh beneath. Generously salt and pepper the lamb. Place the lamb, fat-side up, on a wire roasting rack set in a roasting pan. Roast the lamb, basting once or twice, until an instant-read thermometer inserted into the center of the roast reads 130°F for medium lamb, 1½ to 2 hours. Remove from the oven and let the lamb rest for about 20 minutes (internal temperature will increase as it rests). Reheat the reduced lamb stock. Cut the lamb into ½-inch slices and serve, surrounding each serving with a ladle or two of the reduced lamb stock and a dollop of Romesco Sauce. Pass the remaining sauce at the table.

Skillet Lamb with Artichokes, Peas, Egg, and Lemon

This recipe features a classic combination of springtime flavors and ingredients. It's great with fried or roasted potatoes.

SERVES 4

5	tablespoons extra-virgin olive oil
4	large cloves garlic, crushed
4	large artichokes (or 5 medium, or 10 to 12 baby artichokes), cleaned with some stem intact, each cut into lengthwise wedges 3/8 inches thick at the widest point (see Note)
3/4	cup dry white wine
1 1/4	cups Lamb Stock (page 300), Chicken Stock (page 299), canned low-sodium chicken broth, or water
	Kosher salt
3/4	teaspoon finely chopped fresh rosemary
1	extra-large egg
2	tablespoons fresh lemon juice
	Fresh coarsely ground black pepper
1 1/2	pounds well-trimmed leg of lamb, cut into 1-inch cubes
3/4	cup fresh or frozen green peas

1. Put 3 tablespoons of the oil and 2 cloves of the garlic in a 10- to 12-inch skillet over medium-low heat. Cook until the garlic is pale golden on both sides, about 8 minutes. Discard the garlic and add the artichokes, tossing or stirring to coat. Add the wine and simmer for 2 minutes. Add ¾ cup stock, 1 teaspoon salt, and ½ teaspoon of the rosemary; stir well. Cover tightly and bring to a simmer. Reduce the heat to maintain a gentle simmer and cook until the artichokes are tender when pierced with the tip of a knife, 15 to 30 minutes (depending on the age and type of artichoke), stirring well two or three times. If, when they're tender, less than ½ cup of liquid remains in the skillet, add stock or water to measure ½ cup. *Artichokes can be made up to 6 hours ahead of time.* Keep covered over very low heat.
2. Beat the egg, lemon juice, 8 to 10 generous grindings of coarse black pepper, and the remaining ¼ teaspoon rosemary together in a small bowl and set aside. Heat the remaining 2 tablespoons oil and 2 cloves garlic in a 10- to 12-inch skillet over medium-low heat. Cook until the garlic is pale golden on both sides, about 8 minutes. Discard the garlic. Increase the heat to medium-high. When the oil is just smoking, add the lamb in a single layer and cook until deep golden brown on the first side and nearly two-thirds cooked through, 5 to 7 minutes. Sprinkle with 1½ teaspoons salt and add the peas and the remaining ½ cup stock, scraping up the lamb and any browned bits stuck to the bottom of the skillet.
3. Stir the hot artichoke mixture into the lamb and reduce the heat to medium-low. Whisk a few spoonfuls of the hot cooking liquid into the reserved egg-lemon mixture. Drizzle the mixture into the pot in a thin stream, stirring and shaking the skillet to thoroughly distribute. Cook very gently, frequently stirring and shaking the pot to coat the meat and vegetables, until the cooking liquid has thickened somewhat and the lamb is cooked as you like it, 1 to 3 minutes more for medium. Do not let the sauce boil. Add salt to taste. Spoon the lamb, vegetables, and sauce into wide, shallow bowls and serve.

NOTE: Both small and large artichokes are cleaned in much the same way, with the hairy choke removed. Baby artichokes, which can be as small as a walnut and don't have fuzzy chokes, can be eaten nearly whole with minimal trimming.

When you work with artichokes, it's a good idea to dip them in acidulated water, which is simply plain water mixed with the juice of one or two lemons, to prevent browning. Once they are trimmed, they can be held in this water for up to two days. Drain and pat dry before using.

TO CLEAN A LARGE ARTICHOKE, pull off the hard outer leaves to expose the pale green leaves beneath. Trim off any tough or browned stem and, using a vegetable peeler or paring knife, remove a thin layer of the peel surrounding the stem and the underside of the artichoke bottom. Peel any traces of dark green that remain, mostly where the leaves previously met the bottom. Slice off the tops of the leaves to remove the thorny tips (you could use kitchen shears or a serrated knife). If not cooking immediately, submerge in acidulated water,.

TO CLEAN A SMALL ARTICHOKE, trim and discard the top of the leaves (about one-half to three-quarter inches from the tips). Pluck off any dark green leaves (there are far less of these on a small artichoke than on a large one), and scrape or peel any dark green skin from the stem. Submerge in acidulated water.

TO REMOVE THE CHOKES FROM THE TRIMMED ARTICHOKES, quarter them and cut out the hairy choke by holding the artichoke quarter and a paring knife in the classic manner (best understood if you imagine the peeling of potatoes in the old-fashioned way) and then sliding an inch or so of the knife's end just beneath the place where the choke meets the flesh of the artichoke heart; beginning at the pointed end of the artichoke quarter, draw the blade beneath the choke to free it. Use the artichoke as instructed in the recipe. To remove the choke from whole artichokes (without quartering), use a thin-edged spoon (a grapefruit spoon works well) to reach down into the center of the artichoke with the spoon and repeatedly scrape just beneath the place where the choke meets the flesh of the heart, removing the choke in small tufts until no choke remains. Submerge artichokes in acidulated water until ready to use.

Rack of Lamb with Fresh Fava Beans

Lamb partners well with any kind of bean, fresh or dried. Here's a great way to show off the earthy-green flavor of fava beans, a springtime specialty. Fresh beans are best, but the frozen ones that have already been shelled and peeled are nearly as good and available year round.

SERVES 4

5	cups shelled fresh fava beans (from about 4 pounds fresh pods)
1	teaspoon minced garlic
	Kosher salt
	Fresh coarsely ground black pepper
3/4	cup extra-virgin olive oil for fava beans, plus 3 tablespoons for browning lamb
1	tablespoon plus 1 teaspoon fresh lemon juice
1	generous tablespoon finely grated pecorino romano cheese
1/3	cup chopped fresh mint leaves, loosely packed, plus 1 tablespoon for garnish
3	cups homemade Lamb Stock (page 300)
1	small sprig fresh rosemary
Two	8-rib racks of lamb (1 1/4 to 1 1/2 pounds each), trimmed of excess fat and silverskin
	Lemon wedges for garnish

1. Bring a large pot of generously salted water to a boil over high heat. Add the fava beans and cook until crisp-tender but still bright green, 3 to 6 minutes (depending on the size and age of the beans), stirring occasionally. Using a skimmer, remove beans and plunge them into a large bowl of ice water to cool. Drain, and slip the fava beans from their skins.

2. Place the fava beans, garlic, 1 teaspoon salt, a few generous grindings of black pepper, the ¾ cup oil, and the lemon juice in the bowl of a food processor. Pulse until the favas are chopped into about ¼-inch pieces, and the ingredients are blended, scraping down the sides of the bowl once or twice. The beans should remain somewhat coarse and chunky; do not purée. Transfer to a mixing bowl and stir in the cheese and ⅓ cup mint. The mixture should be stiff but not dry; stir in a few teaspoons more of olive oil and/or lemon juice to moisten, if necessary. (The fava beans can be prepared, without cheese and mint, up to 24 hours ahead and kept in the refrigerator. Let come to room temperature and stir in the cheese and mint before serving.)

3. Bring the stock to a boil in a small saucepan. Reduce the heat to maintain a brisk simmer and reduce by half, to 1½ cups, about 20 minutes. Remove from the heat. While still hot, add the rosemary and let it steep in the broth for 5 minutes. Remove and discard the rosemary and reserve the broth.

4. Preheat the oven to 375°F. Generously salt and pepper the racks of lamb.

5. Heat the remaining 3 tablespoons oil in a 12-inch ovenproof skillet over medium-high heat until almost smoking. Cook the lamb around the convex, fatty side of the rack until golden brown in places, 3 to 4 minutes. Cook until just lightly browned around the eye of the meat, maneuvering the racks and propping them against the sides of the skillet (or against one another) as needed, 3 to 4 minutes more. Arrange the racks fat-side up with the rib ends supported by the edge of the skillet and roast in the oven to desired doneness, or until instant-read thermometer inserted in the center of the lamb registers 130°F for medium-rare, about 15 minutes more.

6. Transfer the lamb to a cutting board and let rest for 5 minutes. Reheat the reduced lamb stock and add a pinch or two of salt to taste. Stir the fava beans and place one-quarter of the mixture in a mound just off-center on each plate. Cut the lamb between the ribs into single or double chops and arrange chops attractively against or next to the fava beans. Spoon reduced stock around the lamb and serve garnished with the remaining tablespoon chopped mint and lemon wedges.

Grilled Ground-Lamb Skewers

These skewers are fantastically tasty on their own, but they are perked up with any number of accompaniments. Some of our favorites are Arabic-style flat bread or pita bread; chopped or sliced tomato; lettuce leaves; chopped scallion; chopped parsley; lemon wedges; and onion slices, either raw or marinated in vinegar and sprinkled with ground sumac. Other possibilities include prepared hummus, tahini sauce, or hot pepper sauce. Roll the grilled lamb in the bread with any combination of these garnishes and eat it like a sandwich or wrap. The skewered lamb is also wonderful served over a bed of chopped and dressed salad—say, tomato, lettuce, cucumber, bell pepper, and onion—or a Middle Eastern specialty like tabbouleh. Another great accompaniment is the Green Olive, Walnut, and Pomegranate Relish on page 283.

SERVES 4

2	cups coarsely chopped yellow onions (2 to 3 small onions)
2	cups tightly packed fresh flat-leaf parsley leaves (small stems can be included)
3	pounds bone-in lamb shoulder blade chops, each with a sizable layer of external fat, cut from the bone, trimmed of connective tissue and silverskin to yield 1½ pounds trimmed meat; cut into 1- to 2-inch pieces
4 to 6	ounces of pure lamb fat cut into smaller pieces (see Note)
2	tablespoons kosher salt
	One batch Kafta Spice Mix (page 295)
	Olive oil for brushing

1. Put the onions in the bowl of a food processor and pulse until finely minced, but not puréed, scraping down the sides of the bowl once or twice as needed. Transfer to a large bowl and set aside. Put the parsley in the bowl of the food processor and pulse until finely chopped, but not puréed, and add to the bowl with the onions (no need to clean the processor bowl between additions). Add half of the lamb and half of the lamb fat to the food processor and process, scraping down the sides of the bowl once or twice as needed, until the meat is finely ground and resembles a dense paste, 20 to 30 seconds (the meat will lighten in color and begin pulling away from the sides of the bowl toward the end of processing). Transfer to the bowl with the onions and repeat with the remaining lamb and fat.
2. Add the salt and the spice mix to the bowl and combine the ingredients with your hands and then knead thoroughly for 2 to 3 minutes. Wrap tightly and refrigerate for at least 1 hour and up to 8 hours.
3. Divide the mixture into 8 equal portions. If using flat skewers (see Note), work one portion of lamb around the skewer to form either a roughly rectangular shape 5 to 6 inches long and ½ to ¾ inches thick or a torpedo shape of about 1 to 1½ inches in thickness, leaving an inch or so of the pointed end of the skewer exposed. If cooking the lamb without skewers or in a skillet, roll each of the 8 portions into a ball and then into either of the shapes described above (though not traditional, you could also form them into burgers).
4. Brush the lamb with a bit of olive oil and grill over a medium charcoal fire (or in a large skillet with a few tablespoons of olive oil over medium heat), turning every minute or so, until medium to medium-well done, 4 to 8 minutes total cooking time, depending on the thickness of the meat. Slip the meat from the skewers (if using) and serve immediately with suggested accompaniments.

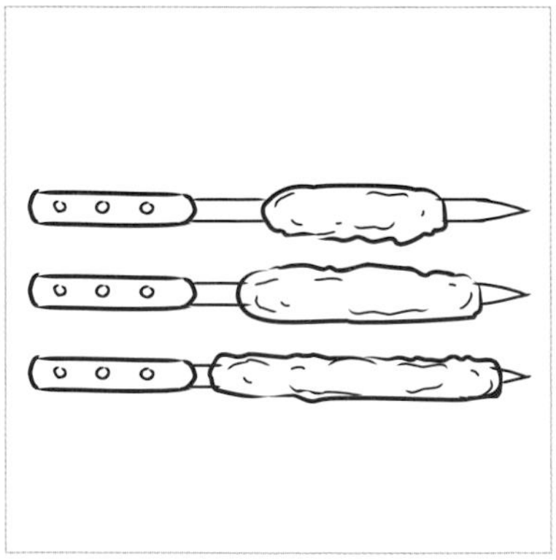

NOTE: These lamb skewers rely on an additional quantity of fat included in the mix to self-baste the meat during cooking (though much of this fat is rendered as it cooks). To accomplish this, look or ask for lamb blade chops that have a thick band (up to 1/2 inch) of fat around much of the chop. If fatty chops are hard to find, you can substitute boneless, precut shoulder meat and gather the quantity of fat required by asking for the fat that covers the racks of lamb, which is fat that is often discarded by the butcher when trimming and/or frenching these racks before sale. What you want is fat that is as firm, pale, and clean as possible. Also, what's important for the recipe—in addition to having the quantities of meat and fat listed above—is that as much of the silver-skin, sinew, and connective tissue as possible is removed before use so that these unpleasantly chewy bits don't make it into the finished dish.

The traditional flat skewers for kafta are available at Middle Eastern markets and specialty stores. It is very difficult to use the more conventional thin skewers to accommodate ground meat because the mixture tends to rotate on the skewer—making them nearly impossible to turn while cooking—and sometimes even slides right off it. The greater surface area of the flat, sword-like skewers eliminates these problems, allowing the meat mixture to cling completely. If you can't find flat skewers, you can either thread each portion with two regular skewers inserted parallel to one another, or you can mold each portion into the traditional kafta shape (or almost any shape) and grill without skewers as you would a hamburger.

Andalusian-Style Lamb Kababs

Spain meets North Africa in these lamb kababs, which are a popular tapa in Spain. The kababs are sometimes made with pork as well as lamb and are spiced with a heady mix of seasonings, including paprika, coriander seed, cumin, black pepper, and saffron. Serve these over white rice with a green vegetable, such as spinach or green beans, on the side. Or, if you like, accompany these with the Green Olive, Walnut, and Pomegranate Relish (page 283)—it's fabulous with grilled lamb. The kababs are also good with a salad of lettuces, tomato, and red onion served with Arabic-style bread. Note that kebabs need to marinate 6 hours or overnight.

SERVES 2 AS A MAIN COURSE; 4 AS AN APPETIZER

3	tablespoons extra-virgin olive oil
2	tablespoons finely chopped onion
1	teaspoon paprika
1	teaspoon ground coriander seed
1/2	teaspoon freshly ground cumin seed
1/2	teaspoon ground black pepper
1/4	teaspoon cayenne pepper
30	saffron threads (about 1/5 gram)
1	large clove garlic, minced
1	teaspoon finely chopped fresh thyme leaves
1	tablespoon finely chopped fresh flat-leaf parsley
1	tablespoon fresh lemon juice
1 1/2	pounds leg of lamb, trimmed of all fat and silverskin, cut into 1-inch cubes (to yield 1 pound cubed meat after trimming; see Note)
1 1/2	teaspoons kosher salt
	Lemon wedges for garnish

1. Place the oil, onion, paprika, coriander, cumin, black pepper, and cayenne in a small skillet. Crumble the saffron threads into the skillet and place it over medium-low heat. Cook, stirring occasionally, until the onion softens somewhat, about 3 minutes. Let cool.

2. Stir the garlic, thyme, parsley, and lemon juice into the skillet of spiced oil. Place the lamb in a bowl and, using a rubber spatula, scrape the spiced oil over the lamb and toss the meat very well to coat with the spices. Cover tightly and marinate in the refrigerator for at least 6 hours or overnight, tossing once or twice. Let the meat come to room temperature before grilling.

3. In the bowl, sprinkle the lamb with the salt and toss very well to distribute evenly. To make four appetizer portions, thread three lamb cubes on each of eight skewers, snuggling the cubes next to one another about ½ inch from the point of the skewer. For two main-course servings, thread four lamb cubes on six skewers in the same fashion (see Note). Divide any remaining lamb between the skewers or thread them on an additional skewer.

4. Light a medium-hot charcoal fire or preheat a gas grill to medium-high and grill the kababs on all four sides, about 2 minutes per side (8 minutes total) for medium lamb (the way we like these kababs). Serve immediately with lemon wedges for garnish.

NOTE: If you're using meat from the leg for kababs, as we do here, look carefully at the meat in the butcher's case: Cuts of meat from different portions of the leg have different amounts of the chewy connective tissue that you'll want to remove before cutting your leg of lamb into cubes for this recipe. The lower portion of the leg has much more connective tissue and silverskin—though the meat is perfectly delicious—than meat cut from the upper part of the leg, where the muscles are larger. Thus, if using meat from the lower leg, you'll need 1 1/2 pounds or slightly more to give you the 1 pound of gristle-free cubes needed for this recipe. If using meat from the upper part of the leg, 1 1/4 pounds should be enough.

After trimming, make a point of cutting the cubes as evenly as possible and threading them carefully on their skewers, so that when grilled, all the cubes of meat will touch the grill's surface, which will ensure that they cook properly (meat that does not make contact with the grill will simply steam). Another tip: If you find yourself with smaller or irregular pieces of lamb, these "scraps" can be combined to approximate a 1-inch cube or folded over on themselves before skewering to approximate the shape of the properly cut cubes.

If using wooden skewers, soak them in water for at least 30 minutes before threading them with the meat, and then wrap the long, exposed portion of wood with aluminum foil before putting them on the grill.

Greek-Style Meatballs with Lemon-Egg Sauce

Bathed in a smooth, lemony, pale yellow sauce, these herb-filled lamb meatballs taste and look great alongside asparagus, zucchini, artichokes, or fresh fava beans, alone or in combination. A side of roasted potatoes doesn't hurt, either!

SERVES 4

- 1 1/2 pounds ground lamb
- 1 cup fresh bread crumbs (see Note, page 131), briefly soaked in milk and squeezed dry
- 1/4 cup long-grain white rice
- 1/2 cup finely chopped onion
- 1/4 cup finely chopped celery
- 3 tablespoons finely chopped fresh flat-leaf parsley
- 3 tablespoons finely chopped fresh mint
- 1 teaspoon dried oregano
- 3/4 teaspoon finely grated orange zest
- Kosher salt
- Fresh coarsely ground black pepper
- 1 large egg, beaten, plus 3 large eggs
- 2 quarts Chicken Stock (page 299), or canned low-sodium chicken broth
- All-purpose flour for dredging
- 1 tablespoon cornstarch dissolved in 3 tablespoons water
- 1/3 cup fresh lemon juice

1. Place the lamb, soaked bread crumbs, white rice, onion, celery, parsley, mint, oregano, orange zest, 2 teaspoons salt, a few generous grindings of black pepper, and 1 beaten egg in a mixing bowl and combine thoroughly, gently kneading the mixture to incorporate. Form into 1½-inch balls by rolling a small amount of the mixture between your moistened palms, and set them aside on a plate.

2. Bring the stock and 2 teaspoons salt to a gentle simmer in a covered 10- to 12-quart pot.

3. Put the flour in a wide bowl or plate and dredge the meatballs, knocking off any excess. Drop the meatballs in the stock (the stock should just cover the meatballs; add more stock or water as needed). Cover and return to a bare simmer. Cook until the meatballs are cooked through and the rice is just tender, about 20 minutes, checking after a few minutes that the stock is gently simmering.

4. A minute or two before the meatballs are finished cooking, whisk the 3 remaining eggs in a mixing bowl until very frothy. Whisk in the dissolved cornstarch and then the lemon juice.

5. When the meatballs are done, turn off the heat and scoop out 2½ cups of the stock. Gradually add the hot stock to the lemon-egg mixture while gently beating with the whisk. Carefully transfer the meatballs and the remaining stock to a large bowl and reserve.

6. Return the empty pot to low heat and add the lemon-egg mixture. Cook, stirring with the whisk in a zig-zag pattern almost continuously, until the mixture thickens and easily coats the back of a spoon, 3 to 5 minutes. Keep the sauce hot but don't let the mixture come to a simmer or boil. Add salt to taste.

7. If serving the meatballs without vegetable accompaniments, remove them from the stock using a slotted spoon (reserve the stock for another use) and divide between plates or wide, shallow bowls. Spoon about ⅔ cup of the lemon-egg sauce over each portion and serve. If serving with vegetables, first ladle the lemon-egg sauce onto the plates. Place the meatballs on one side of the plate, place the vegetables opposite the meatballs, and serve.

Lamb Tagine with Two Squashes, Apricots, and Almonds

More than perhaps any other meat, lamb seems tailor-made to complement and be complemented by the rich sweetness of both dried fruits and nuts as here in this Moroccan favorite. A warm dish of couscous is a good accompaniment.

SERVES 4

4	tablespoons vegetable oil
3	pounds bone-in lamb blade chops cut about 3/4 inch thick, trimmed of excess fat and cut again into about 2-inch bone-in pieces (see Note on page 151) (Bone-in chops can be cut into pieces by your butcher or you can do it yourself with a heavy cleaver)
6	tablespoons unsalted butter
2	medium yellow onion, chopped
50	saffron threads (about 2 large pinches)
3/4	teaspoon ground cinnamon
3/4	teaspoon fresh coarsely ground black pepper
3/4	teaspoon ground turmeric
1/8	teaspoon cayenne pepper
1	generous tablespoon grated peeled fresh ginger root
	Kosher salt
4	cups water
5	sprigs fresh cilantro, tied in a bundle, plus 1/2 cup coarsely chopped fresh cilantro for garnish
1 1/4	pounds butternut squash, peeled and cut into 1/2-inch-thick half-moons or crescents (see Note)
3	tablespoons honey
2	medium zucchini, quartered lengthwise and cut into 2- to 3-inch lengths
1/2	cup blanched, roasted almonds
16	dried apricots, cut into quarters (see Note)
	Freshly cooked couscous (optional)

1. Heat 2 tablespoons of the oil in a 10- to 12-quart heavy ovenproof pot with a lid over medium-high heat. When the oil begins to smoke, add half of the lamb and lightly brown the meat on two sides, 3 to 4 minutes per side, reducing the heat if the meat threatens to burn. Transfer the meat to a plate or bowl and set aside. Repeat with the remaining lamb and reserve. Preheat the oven to 350°F.

2. Discard the oil from the pot. Let the pot cool slightly and return it to medium-low heat. Melt 4 tablespoons of the butter and add the onion, saffron, cinnamon, black pepper, turmeric, cayenne, and ginger, using the moisture from the onions to help loosen any browned bits stuck to the bottom of the pot. Cook gently for 10 minutes.

3. Add the reserved lamb and any accumulated juices along with 2 teaspoons salt, stirring to coat the lamb with the spice mixture. Stir in the water, increase the heat to high, and bring just to a simmer, again scraping up any browned bits on the bottom of the pot. Add the bundle of cilantro; cover and transfer to the oven and cook for 20 minutes. Reduce the heat to 225°F to 275°F to maintain the lightest possible simmer, cook for 1 hour and 20 minutes.

4. Meanwhile, prepare the squash: Heat the remaining 2 tablespoons of oil in a large skillet over medium-high heat. When the oil is hot, and working in batches if necessary, sauté the butternut squash on both sides, lightly salting each side as you go, until golden brown on both sides and nearly tender, about 5 minutes per side, reducing the heat if it threatens to burn. Toward the end of cooking (and combining the batches, if necessary), add the remaining 2 tablespoons of butter and drizzle the honey over the squash. Swirl the pan to blend the ingredients and gently toss the squash to coat. Turn off the heat and reserve in the skillet.

5. After the stew has cooked for 1 hour and 40 minutes total, transfer the pot to the stovetop and skim some of the fat from the surface. Return to a simmer over medium-low heat and add the zucchini, almonds, and apricots, nestling them between the pieces of lamb and under the liquid. Simmer uncovered until the zucchini is almost tender and cooked through, 20 to 30 minutes. Add the reserved squash and simmer for 5 to 15 minutes more, or until all the vegetables are tender. Taste the braising liquid and simmer for a few minutes longer to concentrate if necessary; it should be fairly thin but flavorful, and there should be enough to moisten four servings with ¼ to ½ cup of the liquid. Add salt to taste. Let rest off the heat for 5 to 10 minutes.

6. If serving with couscous, mound couscous in the center of each plate and make a well. Spoon the lamb mixture and a good amount of the juices in the center of the well. Garnish with the chopped cilantro and serve, passing any remaining braising liquid in a sauceboat at the table.

NOTE: Dried apricots vary from brand to brand. Some are dried whole, usually producing a moister result than those that are first cut in half before drying, which tend to be chewier. If your apricots are chewy, soak them for 15 to 30 minutes in very hot water to soften them before adding them to the stew. And if your apricots are "halves," use a few more than the recipe calls for.

For this recipe, you need only the seedless neck of a medium to large butternut squash, which should weigh-in pretty close to the 1¼ pounds called for here. Peel and halve the neck lengthwise, then cut it into ½-inch-thick half-moons as called for and reserve the remaining squash for another use.

Braised Persian-Style Lamb Shanks with Quince

This is an exotic but subtly flavored *koresh*, a Persian or Iranian stew, that is thickened with a handful of yellow split peas. The peas are a common ingredient and adding them is a traditional technique that brings a soothing, nutty dimension to the rich, sweet and sour flavors of the dish. Quince is in season in the fall, the time of year when this hearty stew would be most savored. Serve with rice pilaf or buttered rice on the side.

SERVES 4

- 3 to 3½ pounds lamb shank, cut crosswise into 1½-inch-thick pieces, as for osso buco (see Note)
- Kosher salt
- 3 tablespoons olive oil or vegetable oil
- 2 medium onions, ends removed, halved and thinly sliced lengthwise
- ¼ teaspoon freshly ground black pepper
- ¼ teaspoon ground cinnamon
- ¼ teaspoon ground cardamom
- ¼ teaspoon ground turmeric
- 3 cups water
- 3 tablespoons unsalted butter
- 2 medium quinces, peeled, cored, and cut into wedges about ½ inch thick at the widest point
- ¼ cup lightly packed dark brown sugar
- ¼ cup fresh lime juice
- 50 saffron threads (2 generous pinches), crumbled and dissolved in 2 tablespoons warm water
- ⅓ cup yellow split peas, rinsed
- Lime wedges for garnish (optional)

1. Preheat the oven to 375°F.
2. Sprinkle the lamb on all sides with a scant tablespoon of salt. Heat the oil in a wide, heavy 10- to 14-quart ovenproof pot with a tight-fitting lid over medium-high heat until just smoking. Add the lamb (in batches if necessary) and cook until golden brown on the two flat sides, 5 to 6 minutes per side, reducing the heat if they threaten to burn. Transfer to a plate and reserve.
3. Add the onions to the pot and cook, stirring occasionally, until pale gold at the edges, 6 to 8 minutes. Stir in the black pepper, cinnamon, cardamom, turmeric, 1 teaspoon salt, and the water, scraping to loosen any browned bits stuck to the bottom of the pot.
4. Return the lamb shanks and any juices on the plate to the pot and bring to a simmer. Cover and transfer to the oven and cook for 20 minutes. Reduce the heat to 225° to 275°F to maintain a slight simmer and continue to cook for another 1 hour and 10 minutes.
5. Meanwhile, heat the butter in a large skillet over medium heat. When the foam subsides, add the quince, tossing to coat with butter, and cook until lightly browned on both sides, about 10 minutes total, reducing the heat if they threaten to burn. Transfer to a small bowl and reserve.
6. After the lamb has cooked for 1½ hours total, transfer the pot to the stovetop and skim most of the fat from the surface. In a small bowl, dissolve the brown sugar in the lime juice and stir into the lamb. Stir in the saffron water, the reserved quince, and the split peas, making sure the peas are submerged. Return the liquid to a simmer, then cover and return to the oven and cook at a slight simmer until the split peas are just tender but still a bit firm and holding their shape, 40 to 60 minutes, depending on the age and type of peas.
7. Transfer the pot to the stovetop and let the stew rest, uncovered, for 15 minutes. The stew should be quite fluid but lightly thickened from the peas; it should be richly flavored and mildly sweet and sour. If necessary, simmer for up to 10 minutes more to concentrate the flavors. Skim again and add salt to taste, if needed, by shaking the pot to and fro to distribute it, taking care not to break up the meat and pieces of fruit. Divide the lamb, quince, and sauce among serving bowls and serve garnished with lime wedges, if you like.

NOTE: Lamb shank is usually used whole, but here we cut it crosswise as it would be for osso buco (your butcher can do this on a bandsaw). Before cutting, your butcher should trim the shank of most or all of its fat, but not remove the thin skin or membrane next to the meat itself: it helps to retain the circular shape of the crosscut shanks during cooking. Two front and two rear lamb shanks should give you the 3 to 3½ pounds needed for this recipe.

Sultan's Delight: Stewed Lamb with Creamy Eggplant

Here is a Turkish classic that features an aromatic lamb stew surrounded by a smooth, smoky eggplant purée. For best results, use very fresh, firm eggplants. The eggplant purée and the lamb stew can be made ahead if necessary and then reheated before serving. If you make the purée ahead of time and it becomes too solid, simply thin the purée with a few tablespoons of milk. Likewise, the stew, when reheated, can be thinned with a few tablespoons of water to achieve the desired consistency.

SERVES 4

- 3 medium eggplants (about 3 1/2 pounds)
- 1 tablespoon fresh lemon juice
- Kosher salt
- 3 tablespoons olive oil
- 3 to 3 1/2 pounds bone-in lamb shoulder blade chops (about six 3/4-inch chops), trimmed of fat and silverskin cut from the bone, meat cut into 3/4-inch cubes (to yield 1 1/2 pounds trimmed meat), bones reserved (see Note)
- 5 tablespoons unsalted butter
- 2 medium yellow onions, chopped
- 3 large cloves garlic, minced
- One 15-ounce can tomatoes, drained and chopped
- 1/2 teaspoon ground allspice
- 1/2 teaspoon fresh coarsely ground black pepper
- 1/4 teaspoon ground cinnamon
- 2 bay leaves
- 3 tablespoons all-purpose flour
- 1 1/2 cups whole milk
- 1 1/2 ounces young, tender Manchego, kasseri, or Kashkaval cheese, grated
- 3 tablespoons pine nuts for garnish
- 2 tablespoons finely chopped fresh cilantro for garnish

1. Using the tip of a small knife, poke 6 or 8 small holes all over each eggplant. Put each eggplant on a gas burner over a medium-high flame. Cook until blackened, semi-collapsed, and tender within, turning every few minutes to expose entire surface to the flames, 10 to 20 minutes. To aid in cleanup, it may be helpful to line your stovetop with a layer of aluminum foil before roasting the eggplant.
2. Using a spatula, transfer the eggplants to a large resealable plastic bag; snip off two of the corners (to allow the bitter juices to run out) and let drain in the sink until cool enough to handle (see Note). Peel the blackened skin from the eggplants and, with the help of a thin stream of tap water, brush away most of the remaining small bits stuck to the flesh. Dry well with paper towels, cut off the stems, and transfer to the bowl of a food processor. Add the lemon juice and 1/4 teaspoon of salt and purée until very smooth. Reserve.
3. Preheat the oven to 350°F.
4. In a wide, heavy 12-quart ovenproof pot, heat the oil over medium-high heat until just smoking. Cook the lamb in batches, if necessary, until golden brown on at least two sides, 8 to 10 minutes, reducing the heat if it threatens to burn.
5. Reduce the heat to medium and melt 2 tablespoons of the butter; add the onions and cook, stirring occasionally, until they are pale gold at the edges, 8 to 10 minutes. Stir in the garlic and cook for 2 minutes more. Stir in the tomatoes, allspice, black pepper, cinnamon, bay leaves, 2 cups water, and 2 teaspoons salt. Scrape up any browned bits stuck to the bottom of the pot; add the reserved lamb bones and bring to a simmer. Cover the pot and transfer to the oven; cook for 20 minutes. Reduce the heat to 250°F, and continue cooking until the meat is fairly tender, about 45 minutes more.
6. Meanwhile, melt the remaining 3 tablespoons butter in a large skillet over medium-low heat. When the foam subsides, sprinkle in the flour, whisking to avoid lumps. Whisking almost continuously, cook until pale brown and nutty smelling, 3 to 4 minutes. Add the milk in a slow stream, whisking to smoothly incorporate into the flour. Whisk in 1 teaspoon salt; increase the heat and bring to a simmer, then reduce the heat to a bare simmer, and cook until the béchamel achieves the consistency of a thin milk shake, occasionally scraping down the sides of the skillet, 4 to 6 minutes. Gradually whisk in the cheese until smooth. Fold in the reserved eggplant mixture until well combined (don't add more salt; the creamy eggplant purée should taste only slightly salty to offset the more intense and saltier lamb stew). Remove from the heat and reserve.

7. Once the lamb has cooked for about 65 minutes total, return the pot to the top of the stove. Uncover, and over medium heat, simmer to reduce the sauce until it begins to cling to the meat and 1 to 1½ cups remain, 5 to 10 minutes. The liquid should be concentrated and very flavorful; cook a little longer if necessary and salt to taste. Let the stew sit off the heat for 5 minutes. Pluck out and discard the lamb bones and bay leaves, adding back any meat clinging to the bones, if you like.

8. Reheat the eggplant purée over medium heat, stirring. Divide among warmed serving plates, spreading the purée out to the edges of each plate and creating a well in the center to accommodate the lamb. Divide the lamb and sauce among plates and garnish with pine nuts and cilantro. Serve immediately.

NOTE: Blade shoulder chops (which we suggest for this dish) have a smaller meat-to-bone ratio than the other kind of commonly seen lamb shoulder chop (those called "round bone shoulder chops"—which can also be used in this dish). This means that you will need 3 to 3½ pounds of the blade chops to yield the 1½ pounds of trimmed meat called for in the dish. In spite of this low yield, the succulent meat combined with all those bones add flavor to the finished dish that is unmatched by round bone chops.

One of the attractions of this dish is the smoky taste of the purée, which is achieved in Step 1 by cooking the eggplant over the direct flame of a gas burner (cover the stovetop with aluminum foil to help with cleanup). Traditionally, the eggplants were charred over a charcoal fire, which produces the most distinctively smoky flavor. You can also char the eggplants under a broiler, or roast them in the oven, but they won't taste as smoky as when cooked over a live flame. Roast the eggplants in a 500°F oven for 20 or 30 minutes, turning occasionally, until softened and partially collapsed. Proceed with Step 2 of the recipe.

Indian-Style Fritters with Lamb

This is a famous Indian snack and appetizer called *pakora* that has many variations. Though most of these habit-forming small bites are vegetarian, there are some delectable meaty versions, too. This one features highly-seasoned lamb encased in a crisp, puffy turmeric-flavored crust. You can find chickpea flour at Indian and Middle Eastern markets and at health food stores.

SERVES 4 TO 6 AS AN APPETIZER

3	scallions, coarsely chopped
One	1-inch long by 1-inch wide piece of fresh ginger, peeled and sliced crosswise
1	large clove garlic
1	green serrano chile, seeded, or 1 small jalapeño
½	cup tightly packed fresh cilantro (including thin stems)
1	teaspoon Garam Masala Spice Blend (page 296)
1	teaspoon ground coriander seed
½	teaspoon ground cumin seed
2	teaspoons kosher salt
1	pound ground lamb
1	cup coarse, fresh bread crumbs, soaked in water and squeezed dry (see Note, page 131)
	Peanut oil or vegetable oil for frying
	Pakora Batter (page 297)
	Coarse salt (optional)
	One recipe Cilantro-Lime Chutney (page 289)

1. Put the scallions, ginger, garlic, serrano pepper, cilantro, garam masala, coriander, cumin, and salt in the bowl of a food processor. Process until all ingredients are very finely chopped (but not puréed), pausing a few times to scrape down the sides of the bowl as needed. Transfer to a mixing bowl and, using your hands, combine well with the lamb and the soaked bread crumbs.

2. Form the lamb mixture into ½- or 1-inch balls (see Note); press the balls into patties a bit less than ¼ inch thick (patties don't have to be perfectly round; when fried, they actually look better if their shapes are irregular). Place patties on plates or a baking sheet until ready to fry (place in refrigerator if not frying right away). (The patties can be made up to a day ahead and kept covered in the refrigerator on a greased baking sheet.)

3. Preheat the oven to 200°F. Heat 2 inches of oil to 375°F in a large skillet or wok. Arrange the lamb, Pakota Batter, and a paper towel–lined baking dish or baking sheet near the deep-fry setup. To test, dip a lamb patty in the batter, letting the excess drip back into the bowl. Carefully slip the patty into the oil and fry until rich golden brown, puffy, and cooked through, about 2 minutes, turning the fritter 2 or 3 times with a Chinese strainer or slotted spoon. Drain on a paper towel–lined dish. If the batter has not formed a crisp but tender, puffy shell around the lamb, thin with a bit of water or thicken with a bit of chickpea flour.

4. Working in small batches and without crowding, repeat with the remaining patties. As each batch finishes cooking, drain and keep warm in the oven. Transfer finished fritters to individual plates or a platter, sprinkle with coarse salt and serve with Cilantro-Lime Chutney.

NOTE: Forming the meat mixture into 1-inch balls makes a patty that is 2 or more inches in diameter when thinly pressed; this yields about 25 pieces. Forming the meat into ½-inch balls yields about 50 patties that are 1 inch in diameter. The difference? The larger patties, because there are fewer of them, take less work to make. But because of their size—they're kind of floppy when pressed into a thin disk—they are more difficult to handle, especially in the batter (chilling makes them easier to handle). The smaller patties take more work in the forming and the frying, but are easier to manipulate in and around the batter. It's your call.

CHICKEN LEGS

Whole Fryer

TURKEY SAUSAGE

TURKEY CUTLETS

POULTRY AND RABBIT

GROUND CHICKEN

TURDUCKEN

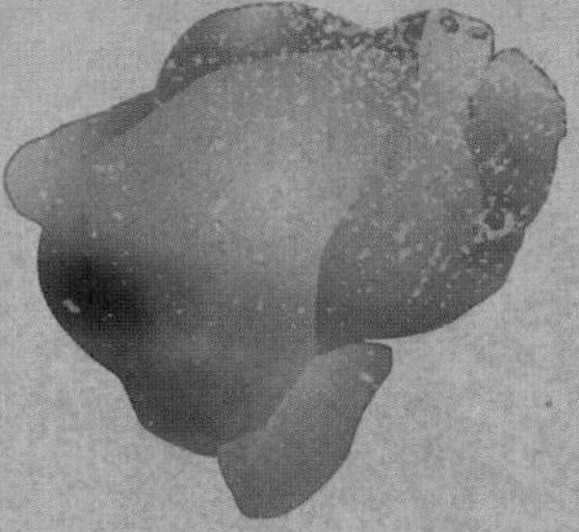

DUCK

TURKEY BREAST

Capons

GOBBLE GOBBLE!

Poussin

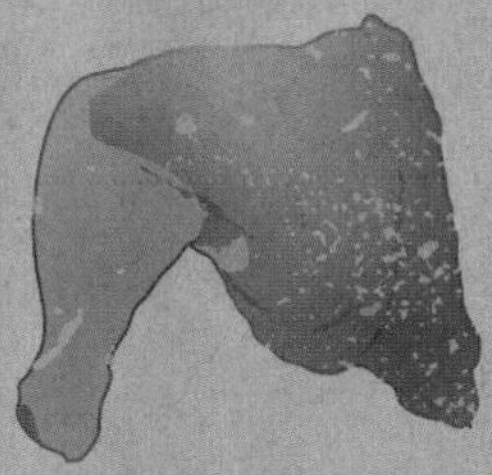

GUINEA HEN

Moulard

ROCK CORNISH GAME HEN

CHICKEN LEGS
BONELESS
CHICKEN
BREASTS
TURKEY
CUTLETS

CHAPTER FIVE

Poultry & Rabbit

Poultry is always best fresh. Since much supermarket chicken has been either completely or partially frozen, it pays to buy chickens from a reputable butcher or specialty market. If you buy chickens labeled "free-range," "organic," "pasture-raised," or "raised responsibly," rather than factory-raised birds, you will notice a marked difference in taste and texture: The birds will be leaner, more fully flavored, and more tender.

Pasture-raised chickens, turkeys, and other fowl have lately entered the market with some fanfare. The term is more specific than the catch-all "free range" and refers to birds raised in the open (in pastures) in floorless pens that the farmer can move around a fairly large area. These birds are usually fed supplemental grain, but the theory is that they eat naturally growing vegetation and dig up grubs and insects so that their diet is rich and varied. They also exercise quite a lot, which means their meat is firmer, less fatty, and more full flavored. Look for pasture-raised poultry at farmer's markets, green markets, and specialty butchers.

Regardless of your opportunities to buy free-range, organic, or pasture-raised birds, always look for chickens and other poultry with labels that state "no antibiotics administered" or "no animal by-products in feed," or both.

Light-colored meat and skin is preferable to yellow, which indicates a lot of fat. Look for plump, well-developed breasts and rounded thighs, indications of firm meat and just the right amount of fat. There should be no visible marks or bruises near the leg or wing bones.

Because it's so easy to cut up a chicken, we recommend buying whole birds. We also understand that most home cooks prefer to buy their chickens already cut up, so our next best recommendation is to ask the butcher to cut up the whole birds for you.

If you buy prepackaged chicken, open the package at purchase and sniff the contents; if it smells even slightly off, don't buy it, even if the expiration date on the label is still valid. Those expiration dates are not required by the government and are not always reliable for poultry. If you can't open the package in the store, check the meat the minute you get home; if it smells off, take it right back. A sure sign of improper handling—so common with pre-wrapped chicken—is liquid puddling inside the package. This means the bird was flash frozen, defrosted (often unintentionally), and then refrozen. These birds will have dry, tasteless meat.

Turkey is fast becoming a year-round favorite. Whole turkeys should have rounded breasts and thighs and their skin may have a bluish cast. When you buy a turkey breast, look for a rounded breast, not one that is pointy or oval.

Ground turkey should be ground from breast meat; this way you know it will be low in fat. If you buy packaged ground turkey that is not specified as breast meat, you won't know what you are getting. If you grind your own and you prefer dark meat, grind it with some breast meat.

Store all poultry in the refrigerator soon after purchase, in its original packaging. If it's leaking, overwrap it with plastic wrap, waxed paper, or aluminum foil and put it on a plate. Never leave uncooked poultry at room temperature, unless you are almost ready to cook it. If you plan to freeze poultry for later use, do so soon after you get home.

While it's a good practice to leave thawed but still chilled chicken (or other small birds) on the counter to reach room temperature before cooking, never leave it out for longer than 30 minutes. In hot and humid weather, never leave it out for longer than 20 minutes. A thawed, chilled turkey can sit at room temperature for an hour or so.

Wash all work surfaces and utensils that have come into contact with raw poultry with hot, soapy water, and keep other foods away from the uncooked birds and their juices to avoid cross-contamination. Be sure to wash your hands before moving on to the next task—a good habit regardless of what you preparing.

We include rabbit in this chapter because it's the most logical place to put it. Rabbit is more like chicken than anything else in terms of size, cooking methods, and flavor.

CHICKEN

Most chickens that are sold whole are either broilers or roasters, and both can be roasted. Whole chickens were always identified as "broilers," "fryers," or "roasters" in days gone by, but nowadays, they are usually sold as nothing more specific than "whole chickens." The weight of the bird determines the most successful cooking method.

Whole broiler/fryer chickens vary in weight from 2½ to 4 pounds. For broiling, they should be cut into halves or quarters so that they can lie relatively flat. Roasting chickens weigh 4½ pounds and up. Large roasting chickens, which can weigh 6 or 7 pounds, can be halved or quartered for slow roasting, or what we call baking. Grilling is a good and very popular way to cook halved, quartered, or even whole chickens as long as the bird is carefully tended and not allowed to overcook and dry out. To avoid this, it's important to turn the chicken pieces often during grilling to encourage even cooking. Some home cooks parcook the chicken in the oven or microwave and finish it on the grill.

Many of our customers prefer to buy chicken parts, and indeed that's the way most people buy chicken in supermarkets. Look for fresh chicken parts; most are slaughtered at least three days before they are available for sale. If you can smell the chicken at all, pass it by. You can buy white or dark meat or a combination. When you buy chicken parts, the price per pound increases and you won't get the breast halves or legs from the same bird. Look for a good formation: The leg and thigh should be attached with no apparent broken bones; any visible bone in the thigh should be white with a rosy tinge; the breast should not be flat and the breast bone should be clear and white; if it's brown, the chicken breast is old—don't buy it, or if you discover this when you get home, take it back and ask for an exchange. The skin should not be torn and there should not be any red or dark marks in the skin or the meat. We suggest that you buy the largest pieces you can find: attached leg and thigh pieces and whole breasts, for instance. But we urge home cooks to buy whole chickens and cut them up themselves. This is where a good pair of poultry shears somes in handy. Or ask the butcher to cut up the chicken for you. It's a lot easier to judge the freshness of a whole chicken than its parts, which are smaller and often stacked on top of one another.

Cook chicken within 48 hours of purchasing. Our preference is to get the chicken home, wash it, salt it lightly with kosher salt and perhaps a sprinkling of mixed herbs to retain its freshness, and cook it that day or the next. If you season the bird and refrigerate it for 12 to 24 hours, it will pick up good flavor. If you don't have time for this, leave it in its wrapper and put it at the back—or in the coldest—section of the refrigerator. Chicken does well in the freezer. It does not have a thick covering of fat and so should never be left in the freezer for more than 3 months in the winter or six weeks in the summer. Leave the chicken in the store packaging and wrap well in plastic wrap.

Chicken is generally recognized as a high-quality protein that is not especially caloric. It has high vitamin and low fat contents and what fat there is mostly seeps off during cooking. A normal portion of skinless chicken has about one gram of fat.

BONELESS CHICKEN BREASTS

Boneless chicken breasts, usually sold as breast halves, are extremely popular because they cook so quickly. To ensure that you are buying them as fresh as possible, make sure the meat looks wet—not dry—and has a slightly rosy hue. The moisture can often evaporate in plastic packaging; Cryovac keeps chicken fresher longer.

Chicken breast halves can be pounded gently to flatten; they can then be stuffed and rolled. They are best cooked gently in a sauté pan and then blanketed with sauce, and are not recommended for grilling unless carefully watched to prevent them from drying out.

Chicken cutlet is another name for a boneless chicken breast half. Chicken tenders are breast meat cut into strips.

CHICKEN LEGS AND THIGHS

Chicken legs and thighs, the so-called dark meat from the bird, are far tastier than the white meat, despite the popularity of the latter. These parts are more muscled than breasts, which gives them more flavor. Very often, legs and thighs (also called the second joint by some people) are sold attached. If you can, buy them this way and detach them at home using a good boning knife if you want them in two pieces. Many chicken purveyors sell legs and thighs separately, putting 4 or 8 thighs in one package and 4 or 8 legs in another. Buy them from a reputable butcher and look for evenly colored skin and light-colored bones. Dark bones or any indication of blood around them, indicate that the bird is not young or that it may have been injured. Neither means you can't eat the chicken, but a young and fresh bird will taste better.

GROUND CHICKEN

Ground chicken is not as popular or as readily available as other ground meats, partly because it's so wet that it's hard to work with. You can stabilize it by mixing it with another ground meat, such as ground veal. When you work with ground chicken, we suggest chilling it very well, or even partially freezing it, and using moistened hands to prevent sticking. Cook chicken burgers on a lightly oiled pan or grill.

CHICKEN SAUSAGE

Chicken sausage is a mixture of white and dark chicken meat and is lower in fat than most other sausages (and while it is not as popular as turkey sausage, it is not uncommon). Like all sausages, it can be flavored with any number of seasonings. Cook and serve it like any other sausage. Chicken sausages are best bought fresh, not frozen.

CAPONS

Capons are roosters that are castrated at four weeks old; as they grow, they develop into large, full-breasted birds ideal for roasting and stuffing. At seven months, a typical capon—which has led a tranquil life for a rooster—weighs from seven to ten pounds with meat that has the texture and exceptionally mild flavor of a broiler. As deliciously juicy as they are, capons are not as common as they once were and so may have to be ordered from a good, well-stocked butcher.

POUSSIN

These are small, immature chickens that weigh about a pound. They are popular in France and lately have gained a foothold in this country because of their delicate, tender meat. You may have to special order them. If you cannot find poussin, substitute Rock Cornish game hens.

ROCK CORNISH GAME HEN

These delectable little birds were the brainchild of a printer of exceptional engravings who also had a taste for fine art and gourmet food. Jacques Makowsky and his wife, Therese, came to America via Russia and France. After living in New York City for eight years, where Makowsky worked at his printing craft, they retired to a farm in Pomfret Center, Connecticut. The wild beauty of the surroundings—plus his idleness—inspired Makowsky to call his farm Idle Wild, and to fill his time, he raised specialty poultry. He first raised guinea hens, but later he and his wife, after much experimenting, came up with a crossbreed of Cornish game cocks and Plymouth Rock hens in 1950. The result was a plump little bird with all-white meat, large enough for a single serving.

TURKEY

Evidence indicates that the Aztec, Maya, and Incas had domesticated turkeys well before Europeans arrived in the New World. Clearly, the tradition of serving turkey at a feast started long before the first Thanksgiving gathering in 1621. Turkey has played an important culinary role in our history; indeed, Ben Franklin was so admiring of the large bird that he wanted it—instead of the bald eagle—to appear in the Great Seal of the United States. In a letter to his daughter, he wrote: "I wish the bald eagle had not been chosen as the representative of our country; he is a bird of bad moral character; like those among men who live by sharping and robbing, he is generally poor and often lousy . . . the turkey is a much more respectable bird, and withal a true original native of America."

Today, turkey is an all-season favorite, with Americans eating nearly twice as much of it as they did just a decade or so ago. The modern turkey is plumper, meatier, and more compact, with a larger proportion of breast meat, than turkeys of even a few generations ago. They have a low fat content, are high in B vitamins, and head the list of lean meats with low cholesterol counts.

Turkeys are usually white, even faintly blue. They should be plump and rounded over the breast bone. For a ready-to-cook turkey, called a dressed turkey, that weighs 12 pounds or less, figure ¾ to 1 pound per person. If the bird weighs more than 12 pounds, estimate ½ to ¾ pound per person. Because everyone likes leftover turkey, our rule of thumb is to select a turkey that weighs twice that of the number of people it will serve. For six, we suggest 10 to 12 pounds; and for people, a 20-pound bird.

Turkeys are usually raised for 18 to 21 weeks; hens weigh 8 to 16 pounds, while toms can weigh as much as 32 pounds. Even with weight variations, the hens and the toms of comparable ages are almost equal in tenderness, although the hen is slightly more tender. The younger the bird, the more tender it will be. But unfortunately, it's nearly impossible to know the age of the turkey unless you purchase it from a local farmer, or your butcher does. Tenderness is also affected by the cooking method you choose—we find the slower, the better. If you buy a free-range or pasture-raised turkey, it will cook more quickly than others, so it's important to know what you are buying and to rely on traditional tests for doneness, such as meat thermometers and checking to see when the thigh juices run clear. Before you buy, take stock of your kitchen equipment: A large turkey can be clumsy to cook and requires a spacious oven and a large roasting pan. You may want to roast two smaller turkeys instead.

Nearly 90 percent of the whole turkeys and turkey breasts sold are "fresh-frozen." These are available from butchers and also can be found in supermarket freezers. Frozen turkeys should be carefully thawed, which take three or four days in the refrigerator. While thawing the turkey in the refrigerator (left in its wrapper) is the preferred way, you can also do a quick thaw in a sink filled with cool tap water. Make sure the bird is completely submerged and change the water as often as you can. This can take up to 10 hours. Do not let the turkey thaw on the countertop or in the microwave.

TURKEY BREAST

Turkey breasts can weigh from 4 to 15 pounds, or sometimes even more. They have a breast bone and can be roasted. Boned turkey breasts can be stuffed and rolled. A roasted turkey breast is a good supplement to the Thanksgiving turkey when one whole bird is not enough and two are too many.

Turkey cutlets are pieces of breast meat cut to about the size of a boneless chicken breast half. Turkey tenders are simply breast meat cut into strips.

GROUND TURKEY

While ground turkey breast is very good, it can be dry. If you mix it with ground dark meat, the flavor improves. If you want a very lean burger or meat loaf, stick with ground turkey breast. If possible, avoid packaged ground turkey. Instead, ask the butcher to grind it for you, which we think is important for the best taste and optimal shelf life.

TURKEY WINGS, THIGHS, AND LEGS

Turkey wings are great when seasoned with salt and pepper and paprika, slowly roasted, and served with barbecue sauce. If you are a wing person, you will find these meaty and delicious.

Turkey thighs have richly flavored, moist meat. Roast them slowly. Depending on the size of the thigh, this can take up to 2½ hours. Cover them with aluminum foil during the first half of cooking, then remove it during the second half.

Turkey legs are meaty and full of flavor. Often the meat is used for ground turkey. You (or the butcher) can cut turkey legs into short, cylindrical pieces and cook them like osso buco. We find that fresh turkey legs are more tender than those that have been frozen and defrosted.

TURKEY SAUSAGE

Turkey sausage is a mixture of white and dark turkey meat. Like all sausages, it can be flavored with any number of seasonings, but is far lower in fat than pork sausage, for instance. Serve and cook it like any other sausage. Turkey sausages are best bought fresh, rather than frozen.

TURDUCKEN

This novelty meat is popular in Louisiana's Cajun country and has captured the imagination of home cooks elsewhere in the country. It's a holiday dish composed of a boned duck stuffed inside a boned chicken inside a semi-boneless turkey. A layer of dressing is placed between each bird. Turduckens require long, slow cooking. You can order turducken from Cajun butchers and some local butchers will prepare one for you.

DUCK

Until fairly recently, Long Island, New York, was the center for duck production in the United States, but now more ducks are raised in the Midwest. The ducks raised on farms in both locales are White Pekin, but sometimes are referred to as Long Island duckling. Domestic ducks are marketed when they are between two and four months old. These are actually young enough to be called duckling.

Muscovy is another kind of duck often available to the home cook. It reaches market when it is slightly older than White Pekin and consequently, its breast meat is more flavorful. Muscovy ducks are sometimes raised for foie gras.

Moulard duck is a hybrid cross of White Pekin and Muscovy. It's a large duck with full-flavored meat and is well worth trying. Moulard are favored for foie gras and when they are, their breasts, called magrets, are gorgeously full bodied and tender. Some aficionados think these are the best duck breasts available anywhere.

Mallard ducks are far smaller and leaner than the others and are available from October through February. They taste as close to wild duck as a domesticated bird can and very often have to be special ordered.

Duck skin is almost white, not yellowish like chicken skin. Many cooks prepare only duck breasts, which is a shame because the whole duck has great flavor. As you might expect, we think duck breasts cooked with the bone in are more flavorful than boneless duck breasts although boneless duck meat is extremely tender. Some people think duck on the bone is chewy, which might explain why it is often served with a sauce.

All ducks have a lot of fat, which should be drained during cooking to leave the duck skin crisp and golden. For this reason, many recipes call for pricking the fat covering the duck breasts or whole duck to enable the fat to drain easily.

More than half of the ducks sold are frozen, but if you can find fresh duck, buy it for its superior flavor. Frozen duck should be thawed in the refrigerator for one or two days and then, once thawed, should be permitted to reach room temperature, wiped dry with a paper towel, and then cooked.

You can often buy duck breasts at the supermarket, but whole ducks will require special ordering. If you are fortunate enough to examine a whole duck before purchasing it, look for a soft, pliable beak, smooth legs, and soft webbing between the toes.

GOOSE

Fresh geese are available during the holidays, from Thanksgiving through New Year's Day; during the rest of the year they must be special ordered. The fresh geese not sold during the holidays are frozen for sale later in the year. Geese can weigh from 8 to 20 pounds; because so much fat is lost during cooking, allow about 1½ pounds per person.

There is a clear difference in tenderness and flavor when the goose is fresh rather than frozen. The meat is darker and fattier than either turkey or duck, with a gamy flavor that appeals to many and which pairs nicely with fruit and fruit sauces.

Our preference is to cook goose very slowly and then turn up the oven temperature during the last 30 minutes of roasting to crisp the skin. Because of the high fat content, a goose must be cooked on a rack; otherwise it will swim in its own fat and the skin will be soft, not crispy.

GUINEA HEN

Wild guinea fowl were introduced to Europe in the sixteenth century from Africa by way of Turkey. Today, domestically raised guinea hens are popular game birds. They have dark gray feathers with a lavender tinge and dots of a pearl white color. There are also white African guineas. All guinea fowl have a slight, pleasantly full flavor—one that could be described as "rich chicken." The meat is usually white but slightly drier than that of other birds, so it's important not to overcook it. They do beautifully roasted or baked in clay pots, which retain moisture in the oven. The hen is much more tender than the cock, which is why recipes nearly always call for guinea hens. These usually have to be special ordered.

RABBIT

The rabbits we sell usually weigh 2 to 3 pounds. Small rabbits can be broiled, oven-roasted, or braised. Although rabbit meat is almost white, it takes on a dark color when marinated and cooked. Rabbit is usually cut into pieces by the butcher, but you can do it yourself because it's as easy to cut up as a chicken. You might prefer to ask the butcher to do it for you.

We recommend buying rabbit fresh whenever possible. Its delicate flavor and texture can suffer in the freezer and when it's fresh, it's more likely to include the liver, heart, and kidneys, which we find to be delicious. You may have to order it in advance but it's worth the effort to plan ahead.

HOW TO CUT A CHICKEN INTO PARTS

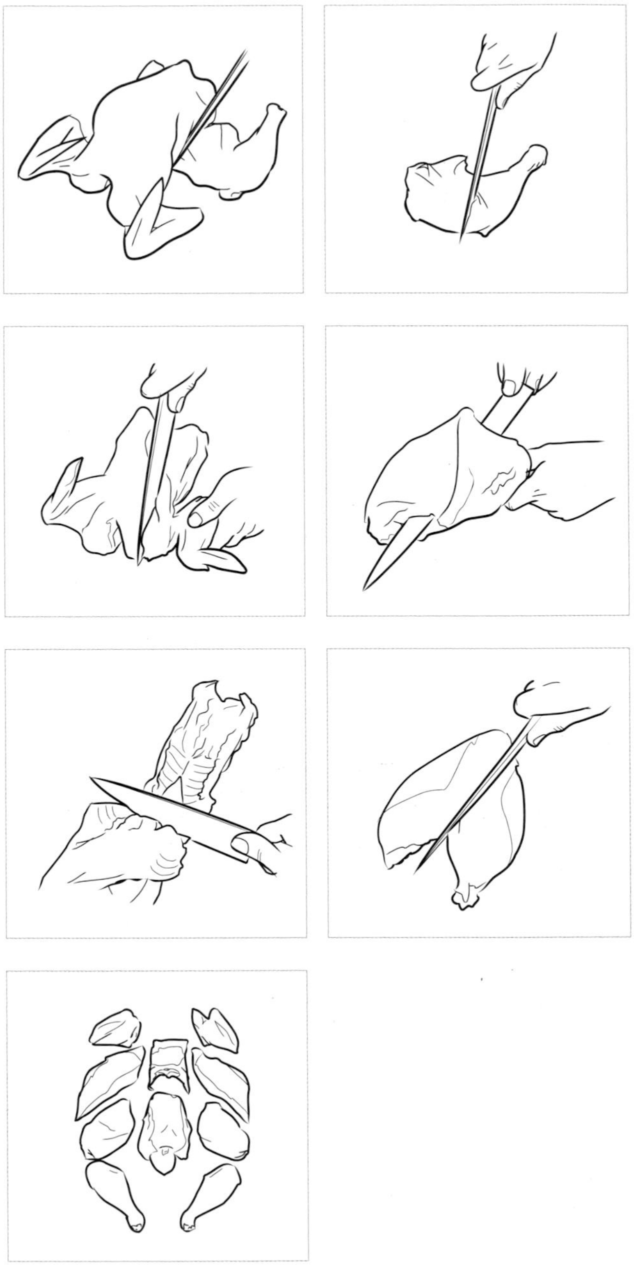

TURKEY SAUSAGE
GOOSE
CKEN WINGS
TRY
BBIT

OUND CHICKEN
DUCKEN
RKEY
EAST
BBLE
BBLE!
Capons
DUCK
Poussin
GUINEA HEN

RECIPES

Buffalo Wings

Buffalo chicken wings are something of an American classic nowadays, although it wasn't too long ago that no one had heard of them. They were first served at the Anchor Bar in Buffalo, New York, as a bar snack, in 1964. The owners of the bar good-naturedly dispute the details of their invention, but they agree that they decided to put blue cheese dressing and celery alongside the wings because that was what they had on hand. Instant success! Most of the buffalo wings you get today are over-seasoned, without much meat, and frankly, not worth bothering with. Not so for these; they're the real thing, and they hit the spot whether you are watching football or just want a good, messy snack for a casual get-together.

SERVES 2

2 1/2 pounds chicken wings (12 to 15 whole), cut in two (wings and drumettes), wing tips discarded (24 to 30 pieces total)

Peanut oil or canola oil for frying

3/4 cup cayenne pepper sauce, preferably Frank's RedHot Cayenne Pepper Sauce or similar (*not* Tabasco)

1/2 cup margarine or unsalted butter

Blue Cheese Dressing for Buffalo Wings (facing page)

Celery sticks

1. Spread the chicken wings out on a baking sheet and blot dry. Set aside, uncovered, to air dry further and to warm to room temperature for 15 minutes or so.
2. Preheat the oven to 200°F.
3. Heat 2 inches of oil in a large, heavy pot to 375°F. Use a deep-fat thermometer to measure the oil temperature.
4. Meanwhile, combine the pepper sauce and margarine in a very large skillet and bring to a simmer over medium-high heat. Cook until slightly thickened and reduced in volume by one-quarter, 3 to 4 minutes. Turn off the heat and reserve the sauce in skillet.
5. Deep-fry the chicken in the oil, working in two batches until deep golden brown and cooked through, 10 to 14 minutes per batch, depending on the size of the pieces (drumettes may take a bit longer than wings). Drain the first batch of chicken on a baking rack set over a baking sheet and keep warm in the oven while frying the second batch.
6. When all the chicken is fried, reheat the reserved pepper sauce over medium heat and add the chicken to the skillet, turning the pieces over in the sauce until well coated, about 1 minute. Transfer the chicken to plates (leaving excess sauce in the skillet) and serve immediately with blue cheese dressing and celery sticks.

Blue Cheese Dressing for Buffalo Wings

MAKES ABOUT 3/4 CUP

1/2 cup homemade Mayonnaise (see page 276)

1/4 cup sour cream

1 tablespoon minced shallot

1/2 teaspoon minced garlic

1/4 teaspoon kosher salt

1/2 teaspoon freshly ground black pepper

1 teaspoon fresh lemon juice

2 ounces good-quality blue cheese, crumbled (about 1/2 cup)

1 to 2 tablespoons milk, as needed

1. Place the mayonnaise, sour cream, shallot, garlic, salt, pepper, and lemon juice in the bowl of a food processor and pulse to combine, scraping down the sides of the bowl as needed. Add the blue cheese and pulse until well combined but with bits of blue cheese still noticeable.
2. Chill and serve in ramekins alongside Buffalo Wings (if dressing appears too thick, thin it with a bit of milk before serving). The dressing can be made up to a day or two ahead and stored, covered, in the refrigerator.

Baby Chickens with Apple Cream

An authentic rendition of this specialty from the French region of Normandy requires the best-quality butter, cream, apples, and cider you can find. For cooks who want to save some time, the apple cream in Steps 3 and 4 can be prepared later while the birds are in the oven. Serve with roasted or steamed potatoes or root vegetables.

SERVES 4

4	poussin (baby chickens), each about 1 pound
	Kosher salt
	Freshly ground black pepper
4	large sprigs fresh thyme, plus ½ teaspoon finely chopped fresh thyme leaves
4	tablespoons unsalted butter, plus 4 tablespoons unsalted butter at room temperature
¼	cup chopped shallots
1	large sweet-tart apple, peeled, cored, and cut into wedges ⅛ inch thick
¾	cup best-quality heavy cream
25	fresh, peeled, or frozen (thawed) pearl onions
⅓	cup apple cider
½	cup Calvados or similar dry apple brandy

1. Generously salt and pepper the cavities of each bird and insert a sprig of thyme in each. Working with one bird at a time, truss the legs by crossing the bird's ankles and then tying the legs together with twine so the legs and thighs fit snugly against the sides of the breasts.
2. Preheat the oven to 425°F.
3. Melt 4 tablespoons butter in an 8-inch skillet over medium-low heat. Add the shallots and cook, stirring occasionally, until translucent but without color, about 3 minutes. Stir in the apple and ¼ teaspoon salt, tossing to coat. Reduce the heat to low; cover and stew the apples gently, stirring once or twice, until very tender but not falling apart, about 15 minutes (add a few teaspoons of water and lower the heat if the apples or shallots threaten to brown).
4. Using a rubber spatula, scrape the contents of skillet into the bowl of a blender. Add the cream and process until the mixture is very smooth, 20 to 30 seconds. Transfer to a bowl and reserve.
5. Rub the birds all over with the softened butter, generously coating the breasts. Generously salt and lightly pepper the birds all over. Tuck the wings beneath the back so they don't hang loose and place the birds in a 10-by-15-inch earthenware or glass baking dish with space between them.
6. Scatter the pearl onions around the birds and place the dish in the middle of the oven; roast for 15 minutes. Baste or brush the birds with a bit of the melted butter in the baking dish and stir the onions to coat. Continue to roast for 15 minutes. Add the cider to the baking dish and cook until the juices run clear when a thigh is pricked, about 15 minutes more.
7. Remove and discard the strings from the birds and transfer to warmed serving plates. Pour the Calvados into the hot baking dish, scraping to dislodge any browned bits stuck to the bottom. Transfer the contents of the dish to a 6- to 8-inch skillet and bring to a simmer over medium heat. Carefully ignite the skillet with a kitchen match; let the flames die while shaking the skillet and then simmer until liquid has reduced by half, about 2 minutes. Increase the heat slightly and stir in the reserved apple cream and ½ teaspoon thyme leaves and bring to a simmer. The sauce should easily coat the back of a spoon but still be quite fluid. If not, continue simmering for 1 to 3 minutes, but don't over thicken. Add salt to taste. Spoon the sauce and onions around the birds and serve.

Classic Chicken in Cream Sauce

This is a rich and hearty French classic. The dish is even better when fresh wild mushrooms (especially morels) replace cultivated ones. To substitute, simply sauté the wild mushrooms first with a bit of butter and salt and stir them into the dish about halfway through cooking.

SERVES 3 TO 4

5	tablespoons unsalted butter
40 to 45	fresh or frozen pearl onions (about 1/2 pound), peeled
One	3 1/2- to 4-pound chicken, cut into 8 pieces: 2 legs, 2 thighs, 2 boneless breast pieces with first wing joint attached, each breast halved crosswise
	Kosher salt
3	tablespoons finely chopped shallots
12	ounces small white button mushrooms, quartered if large, stems trimmed
2	tablespoons all-purpose flour
3	tablespoons cognac or similar brandy
1 1/4	cups off-dry white wine, such as demi-sec Vouvray
1 1/4	cups Chicken Stock (page 299), or canned low-sodium chicken broth
1	herb bundle tied in cheesecloth, composed of 2 sprigs fresh flat-leaf parsley, 2 sprigs fresh thyme, 1 sprig fresh tarragon (optional), 1 bay leaf, 1 crushed peeled garlic clove, 5 black peppercorns
1/2	cup crème fraîche
1	tablespoon finely chopped fresh flat-leaf parsley

1. Melt 2 tablespoons of the butter in an 8- to 10-inch skillet over medium heat. Add the pearl onions and cook, stirring regularly, until light golden all over, 6 to 8 minutes. Remove and reserve the onions. Generously salt the chicken on all sides. Melt the remaining 3 tablespoons butter over medium heat in a wide 10- to 12-quart pot. Add the chicken, in batches if necessary, and cook gently, without coloring, to "seal" both sides, about 3 minutes per side. Remove the chicken to a plate.

2. Add the shallots to the pot and cook for 2 minutes without coloring. Add the mushrooms and cook for 2 minutes, stirring. Sprinkle the flour over the mushrooms and cook for 1 minute more, stirring. Add the cognac and let it evaporate. Add the wine, bring to a simmer, and cook for 3 minutes, scraping the bottom of the pot to loosen any browned bits. Add the stock, herb bundle, 1 teaspoon salt, and the reserved pearl onions. Return the chicken and any juices on the plate to the pot.

3. Reduce the heat to low, cover the pot, and bring to a bare simmer; simmer until the breast pieces are nearly cooked through, about 10 minutes (breasts should be very warm but not hot at the center—remove thinner pieces first); remove the breast pieces to a plate and cover with foil. Continue to gently simmer the remaining chicken, covered, until quite tender, about 50 minutes more. Remove to the plate and cover with foil.

4. Increase the heat to high and cook until the liquid is reduced by a bit more than half, or until it has thickened somewhat and easily coats the back of a spoon, 10 to 12 minutes. Reduce the heat to low and stir in the crème fraîche. Add salt to taste. Return the chicken and any juices on the plate and cook, uncovered, at a bare simmer until the breasts are just cooked through and the sauce easily coats the chicken, 4 to 6 minutes more. Divide the chicken among plates; top with the sauce and vegetables, sprinkle with the parsley, and serve.

Roast Chicken with Lemon-Herb Stuffing

This recipe for slow-roasted chicken filled with a lemony, herb-packed stuffing is homey and flavorful. It's great served with nearly any green vegetable.

SERVES 3 TO 4

4	tablespoons unsalted butter
1/4	pound thinly sliced pancetta, or similar unsmoked bacon, finely chopped
1	small onion, finely chopped
1	rib celery, finely chopped
1	large clove garlic, peeled and finely chopped
3	cups very coarse, fresh bread crumbs (see Note, page 131)
1	apple, peeled and cut into 1/4-inch pieces
1/3	cup finely chopped fresh tarragon
1/3	cup finely chopped fresh basil
1/3	cup finely chopped fresh chives
1/3	cup finely chopped fresh flat-leaf parsley
	Kosher salt
	Fresh coarsely ground black pepper
	Finely grated zest of 1 lemon (about 1 1/2 teaspoons)
1	tablespoon fresh lemon juice
1	extra-large egg, beaten
2	tablespoons extra-virgin olive oil
One	5-pound chicken, rinsed and patted dry
1	cup Chicken Stock (page 299), or canned low sodium chicken broth

1. Heat 2 tablespoons of the butter in a 10- to 12-inch skillet over medium heat. Add the pancetta and cook until it begins to brown, 3 to 4 minutes. Add the onion, celery, and garlic and cook until the onions are translucent, about 5 minutes, stirring regularly.
2. Remove the skillet from the heat and add the bread crumbs, apple, tarragon, basil, chives, parsley, ½ teaspoon salt, a few generous grindings of black pepper, and the lemon zest. Mix well to combine. Return the skillet to medium heat and stir for 2 minutes to further combine the flavors. Remove from the heat and let the stuffing cool in the skillet. *Stuffing can be made up to this point a day ahead and stored in the refrigerator.* Beat the lemon juice with the egg and pour over the bread crumbs. Mix very well to coat all the ingredients with the egg.
3. Preheat the oven to 350°F. Melt the remaining 2 tablespoons butter and combine with the olive oil in a small dish.
4. Fill the chicken with the stuffing, packing it fairly firmly (there may be a small amount left over). Cross the legs and tie with kitchen twine to help contain stuffing. Brush the chicken generously all over with the butter-oil mixture and salt and pepper the bird generously on all sides.
5. Transfer the chicken to a rack set in a roasting pan and roast in the center of the oven for 1¾ hours. After 30 minutes, brush the top and sides of the chicken with the butter-oil mixture. For the remainder of the cooking, brush the bird every 20 minutes or so with the fat accumulated at the bottom of the roasting pan once the butter-oil mixture runs out.
6. Remove the roasting pan to the stove top and transfer the bird to a cutting board designed to catch the juices. Let the chicken rest for 10 minutes.
7. Meanwhile, spoon off some of the fat from the roasting pan. Set the pan over medium heat. Add the stock and simmer until the liquid is reduced by one-third, about 5 minutes, scraping up any browned bits stuck to the bottom of the pan. Carve the chicken and divide the stuffing and chicken among warmed serving plates. Pour any juices on the cutting board into the roasting pan to combine. Spoon pan juices around each portion and serve.

Chicken with Sausage and Sweet and Pickled Peppers

Here's our version of the flavor-packed Italian-American classic, chicken scarpariello, which translates to "shoemaker's chicken." The pungent pickled peppers offer lively contrast to the richness of the chicken and sausage. Serve with a side of roasted potatoes.

SERVES 3 TO 4

One	4-pound chicken, backbone and wing tips removed and discarded, chicken cut into 14 roughly equal-size bone-in pieces: 6 breast, 4 thigh, 4 leg, 2 wing pieces
	Kosher salt
	Freshly ground black pepper
3	tablespoons olive oil
3/4	pound sweet Italian-style sausage, cut into 1-inch sections
	All-purpose flour for dredging
1	medium onion, halved lengthwise and sliced 1/4 inch thick
1	large red bell pepper, stemmed, seeded, and sliced into 1/4-inch-thick strips about 2 inches long
4	large cloves garlic, thinly sliced
1/4	cup seeded and finely chopped hot pickled cherry peppers (3 to 6 peppers), or more to taste
1/2	teaspoon finely chopped fresh rosemary
1	cup dry white wine
1	cup Chicken Stock (page 299), or canned low-sodium canned broth
1/3	cup good-quality red wine vinegar
2	tablespoons chopped fresh flat-leaf parsley

1. Generously salt and pepper the chicken pieces on all sides and set aside.
2. Heat the oil in a 12- to 14-inch skillet over medium-high heat. When the oil is hot, cook the sausage pieces until golden brown on two sides, but still raw inside, about 5 minutes. Transfer to a plate with a slotted spoon.
3. Dredge the chicken pieces in the flour, shaking off any excess. Cook the chicken, in batches if necessary, until rich golden brown on both sides, 4 to 5 minutes per side, reducing the heat if they threaten to burn. Transfer to a plate, keeping the breast pieces separate from the legs, thighs, and wings.
4. Stir in the onion, bell pepper, and garlic, and cook until pale gold at the edges, about 5 minutes. Stir in the cherry peppers, rosemary, and wine and let the mixture simmer for 1 minute, scraping up any browned bits stuck to the skillet. Add the stock, vinegar, ½ teaspoon salt, and a few grindings of black pepper. Place the thigh, leg, and wing pieces in the skillet and bring to a simmer. Cover and reduce the heat to maintain a bare simmer and cook for 30 minutes. Warm serving plates in a low oven.
5. Add the breast pieces to the skillet along with any juices on the plate. Distribute the sausage pieces around the chicken; cover and continue to cook at a bare simmer until the breast pieces are nearly cooked through, 12 to 15 minutes (remove any smaller breast pieces to a plate if they finish cooking before the others). Uncover and simmer until the sauce has thickened somewhat and concentrated in flavor but is still very fluid, for 1 to 2 minutes.
6. Using tongs or a slotted spoon, divide the chicken and sausage among warmed plates. Taste the sauce and simmer for another minute or so if necessary to concentrate the flavor. Salt to taste and pour the vegetables and sauce over the chicken. Sprinkle with parsley and serve.

Chicken and Sausage Jambalaya

With goodly amounts of Spanish, French, Creole, and Cajun in its DNA, jambalaya is a delectably hybrid Louisiana rice dish and one of the most satisfying one-pot meals around. Serve with a simple green salad and pass the hot sauce.

SERVES 4

4	tablespoons vegetable oil
6	large cloves garlic, 4 crushed, 2 finely chopped
½	teaspoon cayenne pepper
1	teaspoon paprika
2 ½ to 3	pounds chicken thighs (about 8 pieces), trimmed of excess fat
	Kosher salt
¾	pound andouille sausage or similar smoked sausage, sliced ¼ inch thick
2	onions, chopped
½	large green bell pepper, seeds and ribs removed, chopped
2	large bay leaves
1 ½	teaspoons finely chopped fresh thyme
1 ½	cups long-grain rice
3	cups Chicken Stock (page 299), or canned low-sodium chicken broth
½	teaspoon freshly ground black pepper
3	scallions, thinly sliced into rounds
1 ½	tablespoons finely chopped fresh flat-leaf parsley
	Louisiana-style hot sauce for passing at the table

1. Combine 2 tablespoons of the oil with the crushed garlic, cayenne, and paprika in a large bowl and toss well with the chicken pieces to coat. Cover and set aside to marinate for 15 minutes or up to 2 hours at room temperature or overnight in the refrigerator, tossing once or twice during this time. Bring to room temperature before cooking.
2. Spread the chicken out on a plate (discarding the garlic) and salt generously on both sides. Reserve.
3. Heat the remaining 2 tablespoons oil over medium-high heat in a 10- to 12-quart heavy pot. When the oil shimmers, add the sausage and cook until lightly browned on both sides, 2 to 3 minutes. Using a slotted spoon, remove to a small bowl, leaving the fat in the pot.
4. Working in batches, if necessary, add the chicken skin-side down, and cook for 2 minutes. Reduce the heat to medium and continue cooking until deep golden brown on the first side, 8 to 10 minutes. Turn and cook until lightly browned on the second side, about 6 minutes more. Transfer the chicken to a plate and reserve.
5. Spoon off all but 4 tablespoons of fat in the pot and add the onions, green pepper, and bay leaves. Using a spatula and the moisture given off by the vegetables, scrape up any browned bits stuck to the bottom of the pot. Cook, stirring occasionally, until the vegetables are very soft and golden at the edges, 15 to 20 minutes. Reduce the heat if they threaten to burn. Stir in the chopped garlic and the thyme and cook for 2 minutes more. Increase the heat to medium-high and stir in the rice. Cook, stirring regularly until the rice is lightly toasted, about 3 minutes. Add the stock, black pepper, and 1 teaspoon salt (a bit more if your broth is unsalted) and again scrape up any browned bits on the bottom of the pot. Add the reserved chicken and any liquid on the plate and arrange the reserved sausage between the chicken pieces. Bring to a simmer, cover tightly, and reduce the heat so the broth is gently simmering. Cook until the broth is almost completely absorbed and the rice is just tender, about 25 minutes.
6. Let the jambalaya stand off the heat, covered, for 5 to 10 minutes and then gently stir in the scallions and parsley. Serve, passing hot sauce at the table.

Chicken Paella with Shellfish and Vegetables

This recipe offers the perfect excuse to get yourself a real paella pan, though a very large skillet works well, too.

SERVES 4

18	small littleneck clams, or 24 mussels
	Kosher salt
4 ½	cups Chicken Stock (page 299), or canned low-sodium chicken broth
50	saffron threads (2 large pinches)
6	bone-in chicken thighs (about 2 pounds), each cut into 3 pieces (for each thigh, cut off one boneless piece and then hack through the bone to make two more pieces; this can be done by your butcher)
5	tablespoons extra-virgin olive oil
3	ounces cured Spanish chorizo sausage, skinned, quartered lengthwise, and cut into ¼-inch-thick pieces
1	medium onion, finely chopped
½	red bell pepper, stemmed, seeded, ribs removed, and cut into strips 2-inches long and ¼-inch wide
2	large globe artichokes, cleaned (see page 160) and cut into wedges ½ inch thick at the widest point (about 24 wedges)
3	ounces green beans, trimmed and cut into 2-inch lengths
2	cloves garlic, minced
3	medium canned tomatoes, drained and finely chopped (about ⅓ cup)
2	cups paella rice, such as Spanish *bomba* rice (see Note on following page)
	Lemon wedges for serving

1. Scrub the clams or mussels under running water and rinse in repeated changes of water until the water runs clear. Dissolve 1 tablespoon salt in a large bowl filled with water and submerge the clams for an hour or so to help purge any sand (mussels don't require this step). Drain clams or mussels and reserve.

2. Bring the stock just to a simmer and add the saffron and ¾ teaspoon salt. Reduce heat to very low; cover and keep hot at a very bare simmer. Generously salt the chicken on both sides and reserve.

3. Set the oven rack in the lower part of the oven and preheat the oven to 500°F.

4. Heat the oil in a 13-inch paella pan or ovenproof skillet over medium-high heat. When the oil is hot, add the chorizo and cook, stirring regularly, until slightly crisp but still tender, 30 seconds to 1 minute. Remove with a slotted spoon to a small bowl and reserve. Add the chicken, skin-side down, and cook until golden on both sides and nearly cooked through, 4 to 5 minutes per side. Remove to a plate and reserve.

5. Let the pan cool somewhat and return it to medium heat. Add the onion and bell pepper and cook until the onion is softened but without color, about 5 minutes, stirring occasionally and using the moisture of the vegetables to scrape up any browned bits stuck to the bottom of the pan. Add the artichokes and green beans and cook for 5 minutes, stirring regularly. Stir in the garlic, tomatoes, and ½ teaspoon salt and cook, stirring, for 2 minutes more.

6. Add the rice and cook for 1 minute, stirring to coat the grains. Add the hot stock and distribute the chicken, skin-side up, around the pan; add any juices remaining on the plate. Distribute the clams and/or mussels around the pan and scatter the reserved chorizo over all. Shake the pan once or twice to ensure that the rice is submerged and evenly distributed. Using 2 burners and/or rotating the pan to heat up its entire bottom surface (this cooks the rice and other items more evenly), bring to a simmer over medium heat. Simmer for 5 minutes, still rotating the pan regularly to maintain even heat, but do not stir.

7. Transfer to the oven and cook just until the liquid evaporates, 13 to 15 minutes (chicken will be cooked through and the shellfish should be opened). Remove from the oven and cover pan tightly with a lid wrapped in a clean kitchen towel to absorb moisture; let paella rest for 6 to 8 minutes before serving with lemon wedges.

CONTINUED>

NOTE: Most rice used for paella and other Spanish rice dishes comes from a variety of short- or medium-grain rices grown in a handful of recognized Spanish locales. These rices excel in absorbing quantities of flavorful stock while remaining firm but still tender to the bite (like the rice in a good risotto minus the fluid, creamy quality). A number of these rices are increasingly available in this country. Two words seen on Spanish rice packages here include *bomba*, the name of a well-known variety of Spanish rice; the other, *Calasparra*, is not a variety of rice, but a geographical designation that generally indicates excellent quality. Any true short- or medium- grain rice from Spain is a good candidate for paella. Short-grain Japanese rice and Italian risotto make only fair substitutes.

Stuffed Chicken Legs with Vegetable Sauce

This is an old central Italian dish that is both tasty and appealing to a wide range of people. The bones are removed from each leg and replaced by a ground meat-and-cheese stuffing. The legs are browned and then braised in a vegetable sauce. Stuffing each leg takes a bit of finessing, consisting of about 20 minutes of patience, but it can be done well ahead of the cooking. The rest is easy and the result is simple and elegant in equal parts, perfect for informal entertaining.

SERVES 4

4	large whole chicken legs (about 3 pounds; leg and thigh attached), boned (see Note)
	Kosher salt
1/4	pound ground chicken
1/4	pound ground pork
1	ounce Parmigiano-Reggiano or Pecorino Romano cheese, finely grated
1/4	cup heavy cream
1/4	cup fresh ricotta cheese
1	egg, beaten
2	tablespoons finely chopped fresh flat-leaf parsley
1/4	teaspoon freshly grated nutmeg
	Salt
	Freshly ground black pepper
4	tablespoons extra-virgin olive oil, plus more for drizzling
	All-purpose flour for dredging
1	medium onion, finely chopped
1/2	medium carrot, finely chopped
1	medium celery rib, finely chopped
3	large cloves garlic, minced
1	cup dry white wine
Generous	1/4 teaspoon finely chopped fresh rosemary
	Pinch of crushed red pepper flakes
One	15-ounce can whole tomatoes, well chopped or passed through a food mill with a few tablespoons of their liquid

1. Remove the bones from the chicken legs per the illustration. Lightly salt the insides of the boned legs. In a large mixing bowl, combine the ground chicken, pork, cheese, cream, ricotta, egg, parsley, nutmeg, ½ teaspoon salt, and pepper. Divide the mixture between the boned chicken legs and roll and tie the leg as outlined in the sidebar. Depending on the size of your chicken legs you may not use all the stuffing.

2. Heat the oil in a large skillet over medium-high heat. Salt the stuffed chicken legs on all sides; dredge them in the flour and add them to the hot oil, seam-side up. Cook until a rich golden brown on at least 3 sides, turning the pieces gently and regulating the heat if they threaten to burn, 10 to 12 minutes. (If the filling leaks a bit, don't bother browning the seam side.) Remove to a plate.

3. Pour off all but 4 tablespoons of fat in the skillet and reduce the heat to medium. Add the onion, carrot, celery, and garlic. Cook for 5 minutes, stirring occasionally. Add the wine and simmer until reduced by two-thirds. Stir in the rosemary, crushed red pepper, tomatoes, and ¼ teaspoon salt. Return the chicken legs to the skillet along with any liquid on the plate. Bring to a bare simmer, basting with the vegetable sauce. Cover loosely with aluminum foil and simmer gently until the chicken and stuffing are cooked through, or an instant-read thermometer registers 160°F when inserted in the center of a leg, about 25 minutes. Turn and baste the chicken once during this time.

4. Remove the chicken from the skillet to a cutting board. Snip the kitchen string and discard. Using a serrated knife, slice each leg into 5 or 6 pieces and divide among serving plates. Simmer the sauce to concentrate the flavor, if necessary. Top the chicken with the sauce, drizzle with a bit of olive oil, and serve.

NOTE: To bone and stuff a chicken leg, remove the thigh and two-thirds of the leg bone. This way, nearly all of the interior of the rolled leg can accommodate a maximum amount of the stuffing. Because the last inch or so of the leg bone remains intact, the leg retains much of its shape.

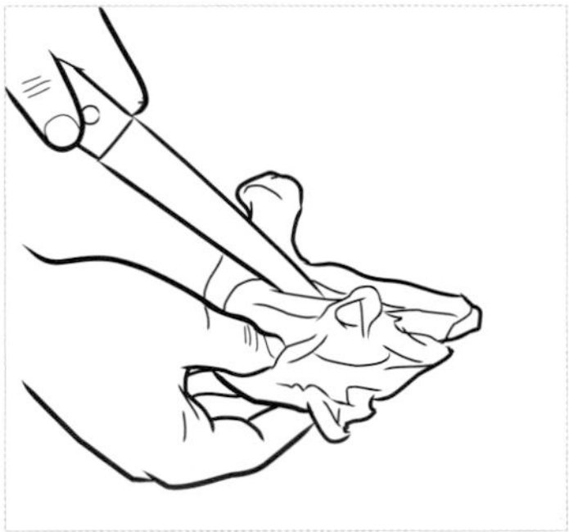

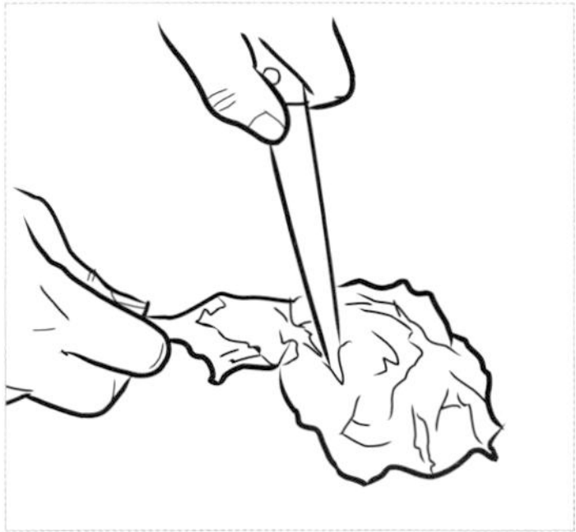

Oven-Baked Chicken with Spanish Peppers

Called *pollo a la chilidron* in Spain, the deliciousness of this dish relies on the flavor of that country's much-loved roasted piquillo peppers (now widely available in the United States in jars or tins at most gourmet food shops and online at www.tienda.com and www.spanishtable.com), which are used in abundance to flavor small, bone-in pieces of chicken baked in a casserole with white wine, saffron, and garlic. Small roasted potatoes make a great side dish.

SERVES 4

50	saffron threads (about 2 large pinches)
5	tablespoons extra-virgin olive oil
1	slice of crustless country-style bread, 3 by 5 by 3/4 inches thick
3 to 3 1/2	pounds chicken thighs, each thigh cut in half across the bone to yield 16 to 20 pieces
	Kosher salt
1	medium onion, finely chopped
3/4	cup dry white wine
10	ounces jarred roasted piquillo pepper, drained, 8 ounces quartered into lengthwise strips
3	large cloves garlic, sliced
1	teaspoon sweet paprika
1 1/2	cups Chicken Stock (page 299), or canned low-sodium chicken broth
3	tablespoons finely chopped fresh flat-leaf parsley
2	bay leaves

1. Place the saffron in a small dry skillet over medium heat. Toast for about 1 minute, shaking pan to avoid burning. Remove and let cool. Crumble the saffron threads with dry fingertips back into the pan; add ¼cup warm water and set aside.
2. Warm the oil in a large, heavy pot or straight-sided skillet over medium-low heat. Add the bread and cook gently until toasted and colored a rich golden brown on both sides, 4 to 6 minutes. Remove from the pot and reserve.
3. Salt the chicken generously on both sides. Add enough oil to equal 3 tablespoons, if needed, and increase the heat to medium-high. Cook the chicken in two batches until golden brown on both sides, 4 to 6 minutes per side. Transfer to a 9-by-12-inch ceramic or glass baking dish, skin-side up, and reserve. Preheat the oven to 325°F.
4. Pour off all but 3 tablespoons fat in the pot and return it to medium-low heat. Add the onion and cook until soft but not browned, stirring occasionally, about 5 minutes. Add the wine and simmer gently for 3 minutes, scraping up any browned bits stuck to the bottom of the pot. Turn off the heat and reserve the pot.
5. Dip both sides of the reserved toast into the wine in the pot until softened. Place the toast in the bowl of a food processor, breaking it into chunks. Add the 2 ounces whole piquillo peppers and the garlic to the food processor and process to a coarse paste, 10 to 20 seconds, pausing midway to scrape down the sides of the bowl. Add the paprika, the reserved saffron water, and the chicken stock. Process briefly to incorporate.
6. Stir the pepper-broth mixture into the onions in the pot. Stir in 2 tablespoons of the parsley, the bay leaves, and 1 teaspoon salt. Bring to a simmer and pour the mixture evenly over and around the chicken. Cover tightly with aluminum foil and place in the oven for 45 minutes. Uncover the baking dish and cook for 1 hour more, basting the exposed meat every so often.
7. Remove the casserole from the oven and distribute the piquillo pepper strips all over the casserole, tucking them in between the chicken and partly below the surface of the liquid. Return to the oven and bake for 10 to 20 minutes more, or until the liquid has thickened somewhat and reduced to at least halfway down the sides of the chicken pieces. Cook additionally, if necessary. Turn off the oven and let the chicken rest in the oven, uncovered, for 15 minutes, allowing the sauce to thicken further. Sprinkle with the remaining parsley. Divide the chicken and peppers among plates, spooning sauce over each serving.

Stewed Chicken with Spicy Tomato-Peanut Sauce and Okra

Variations of this fall-off-the-bones stew are popular all over West Africa. Although other parts of the chicken could work, the thighs produce the most delectable result. Serve this with white rice to soak up the thick, abundant sauce.

SERVES 4

3	to 3 1/2 pounds chicken thighs (about 10 pieces), trimmed of excess fat
	Kosher salt
2	tablespoons peanut oil or vegetable oil
1	large onion, chopped
3	carrots, peeled and cut into 3/4-inch pieces
4	large cloves garlic, peeled and crushed with the broad side of a chef's knife
One	2-by-1-inch piece fresh ginger, peeled and crushed with the broad side of a chef's knife
One	15-ounce can tomatoes, drained and coarsely chopped
3	cups Chicken Stock (page 299), or canned low-sodium chicken broth
3	cups water
1	habañero pepper, pricked 8 or 10 times with a toothpick
2	large sprigs fresh thyme
	Freshly ground black pepper
1/2	cup smooth natural peanut butter (with no added sugar or salt)
2	tablespoons tomato paste
1	pound fresh or frozen okra, cut into 3/4-inch lengths (about 4 cups)
1/3	cup unsalted roasted peanuts, coarsely chopped for garnish (optional)

1. Salt the chicken pieces generously on all sides. Heat the oil in a large, heavy pot over medium-high heat. When the oil is hot, cook the chicken in two batches until rich golden brown on both sides, 10 to 12 minutes per batch, reducing the heat if it threatens to burn. Transfer each batch to a plate and set aside.

2. Reduce the heat to medium and add the onion; cook until softened and translucent, about 5 minutes, stirring occasionally. Stir in the carrots, garlic, and ginger and cook for 1 to 2 minutes. Add the tomatoes, stock, water, habañero, thyme, 2 generous teaspoons salt, and ½ teaspoon black pepper and bring to a boil over high heat.

3. Reduce the heat to a simmer and ladle 2 cups of hot broth into a small bowl. Dissolve the peanut butter in the hot broth, mashing and whisking it with a fork. Stir this mixture into the pot. Repeat, dissolving the tomato paste in 1 cup of the hot broth and return the mixture to the pot. Return the reserved chicken and any juices on the plate to the pot and return to a simmer. Reduce the heat and cook at the slightest possible simmer for 2 hours, stirring occasionally. Taste periodically, and when the stew is as spicy from the habañero as you'd like, remove the pepper and reserve (it can be chopped up later and passed to those diners who'd like to spice up their servings).

4. After 2 hours, stir in the okra; increase the heat slightly and cook at a brisk simmer until the okra is cooked and the stew has thickened somewhat, 20 to 30 minutes. The finished stew should be abundantly saucy but flavorful: thick enough to lightly coat the back of a spoon but still quite fluid. Simmer a few minutes more to concentrate or thin with a bit of broth, if necessary. Add salt to taste and let the stew rest off the heat for 5 minutes before serving (stew will continue to thicken once served). Remove and discard the ginger and thyme sprigs. Divide the chicken among large shallow bowls alongside a pile of white rice. Top the chicken with abundant sauce, garnish with chopped peanuts, if using, and serve.

Jerked Chicken

With this recipe, you can make a fantastic jerked chicken without building a fire—unless you want to (a hardwood fire adds even more great flavor). Serve the chicken alongside a pile of white rice. Take special care when handling Scotch bonnet or habañero peppers, which are very hot and can burn your skin, especially if you have even the tiniest cut. Wear rubber gloves or wash your hands thoroughly after handling the peppers and rubbing the chicken with the marinade. Note that the chicken needs to marinate at least one day and up to three.

SERVES 4 TO 6

1/2	medium red onion, coarsely chopped
6	scallions, coarsely chopped
2	Scotch bonnet or habañero chiles, halved, stemmed, and seeded
One	1-inch piece fresh ginger, peeled and chopped
3	large cloves garlic, sliced
2	tablespoons ground allspice
2	teaspoons fresh coarsely ground black pepper
1	teaspoon ground nutmeg
1	teaspoon ground cinnamon
1	tablespoon dried thyme, finely crumbled with fingers
2	teaspoons kosher salt
1/3	cup soy sauce
1/4	cup fresh lime juice
1/4	cup vegetable oil
12	bone-in chicken thighs (about 4 1/2 pounds), trimmed of excess fat

1. Put the onion, scallions, chiles, ginger, garlic, allspice, black pepper, nutmeg, cinnamon, thyme, and salt in the bowl of a food processor; pulse 15 to 20 times or until finely chopped, scraping down the sides of the bowl once or twice as needed. Combine the soy sauce, lime juice, and oil in a small bowl; with the motor running, pour the mixture through the feed tube of the processor and process to a fluid paste with just the tiniest bits of vegetable still visible, 20 to 30 seconds.

2. Place the chicken in a nonreactive dish large enough to hold it in a single layer. Sliding your fingers between the skin and flesh, loosen the skins of the chicken thighs without separating the skin completely. Pour the reserved jerk seasoning paste over the chicken and, working with your fingers, thoroughly rub generous amounts of the paste under the skin and all over the remaining surfaces of the chicken, taking care not to completely separate the skin from the meat. Cover tightly with plastic wrap and let marinate in the refrigerator for at least 12 and up to 36 hours.

3. Let the chicken sit at room temperature an hour or so before cooking. Preheat the oven to 350°F. Place the chicken pieces, skin-side up and without touching one another, on an oiled, aluminum foil–lined rimmed baking sheet. Reserve the marinade remaining in the dish. Bake the chicken for 30 minutes; remove from the oven and smear each piece with a teaspoon or two of the reserved marinade to coat tops. Rotate the pan and return the chicken to the oven. Bake until the chicken is very tender and the skins have darkened and are somewhat crisp, about 45 minutes more. Remove from the oven and let the chicken rest for about 5 minutes before serving (if any juices remain on the sheet pan, spoon these over each portion).

Puerto Rican Soupy Rice with Chicken, Summer Vegetables, and Lime

This brightly colored and exotically flavored chicken and rice soup—called *asopao* in Puerto Rico—is made especially vibrant thanks to the addition of green olives, cilantro, jalapeno, and lime. *Asopao* is rich and varied enough to serve as a one-pot, one-dish meal.

SERVES 4

10 to 15	good-quality green olives, pitted and chopped into 1/4-inch pieces
2	teaspoons finely chopped fresh oregano
3	tablespoons finely chopped fresh cilantro
	Finely grated zest of 1 lime, plus 4 lime wedges for serving
3	large cloves garlic, 1 mashed to a paste with 2 teaspoons of kosher salt using the broad side of a chef's knife, 2 cloves minced
	Freshly ground black pepper
6	tablespoons extra-virgin olive oil
1 1/4	pounds boneless chicken thighs or breasts (or a combination), cut into small bite-size pieces about 1/4 inch thick by 3/4 inch long
1	red bell pepper
1	medium onion, finely chopped
2	jalapeño peppers, seeded and minced
2	ounces thinly sliced smoked ham (such as Black Forest), cut into 1/4-inch pieces
One	15-ounce can tomatoes, drained and chopped
6	cups Chicken Stock (page 299), or canned low-sodium chicken broth
2/3	cup long-grain white rice (not instant), repeatedly rinsed in changes of cold water until it runs clear, drained
	Kosher salt
3/8	pound butternut squash, peeled and cut into 1/2-inch cubes (about 1 1/4 cup)
1/4	pound green beans, ends trimmed, cut into 1/3-inch lengths (about 2/3 cup)

1. In a medium bowl, combine the olives, oregano, cilantro, lime zest, the garlic-salt paste, a few grindings of black pepper, and 3 tablespoons of the oil. Add the chicken, tossing it thoroughly with the mixture. Cover and set aside at room temperature.

2. Place the red pepper on the burner of a gas range over medium-high heat. Char and blacken one face of the pepper, rotating it when the exposed side just begins to look ashen. Repeat until blackened all over; 10 to 15 minutes. (Alternatively, you can roast the pepper in a 450°F oven for about 40 minutes, turning once; just place it in the oven before you begin Step 1 of the recipe.) Enclose the pepper in a paper or plastic bag and allow the pepper to steam for at least 15 minutes. Peel off the blackened skin and remove the ribs and seeds. Cut the pepper into strips about 1/4 inch thick by 1 inch long and set aside.

3. Meanwhile, add the remaining 3 tablespoons oil to a large stockpot over medium-high heat. When the oil is hot, add the onion, minced garlic, and jalapeños and cook, stirring occasionally, until softened but not browned, about 5 minutes. Reduce the heat if the mixture threatens to burn. Add the ham and cook for 1 minute. Add the tomatoes and cook for 3 minutes more. Add the stock and bring to a boil.

4. Stir in the rice and 1 teaspoon of salt; gently simmer for 2 minutes, stirring occasionally. Stir in the squash and beans and continue to simmer, stirring occasionally, until the rice is still a bit firm but almost cooked through, 10 to 15 minutes. Add the chicken, scraping all of the marinade ingredients into the pot and cook, stirring occasionally, until the meat is just cooked through and the vegetables are tender but firm, about 3 minutes more. Add salt, if necessary. Stir in the reserved red pepper strips and ladle into wide bowls (including the broth). Serve with spoons, passing the lime wedges at the table.

Nonya-Style Spiced Curry Noodle Soup with Chicken

This is our take on chicken curry *laksa*, which is just one of the countless spicy noodle soups popular in Malaysia and Singapore that are called *laksa*. The vibrant yellow-gold bowl of spicy chicken broth, chicken, rice noodles, and bright green herbs is based on a broth enriched with a homemade spice paste that features shallots, ginger, lemongrass, and a lashing of homemade hot Malaysian pepper sauce.

SERVES 4

6	cups Chicken Stock (page 299), or canned low-sodium chicken broth
3/4	pound skinless boneless whole chicken breast
1/2	cup Chile and Shallot Sambal (page 294)
2	tablespoons plus 1/4 cup Thai or Vietnamese fish sauce (*nam pla* or *nuoc nam*)
1	cup plus 3/4 cup thinly sliced shallots
4	large cloves garlic, sliced
One	1-inch piece (1 inch thick) fresh ginger, unpeeled, thickly sliced
2	generous tablespoons thinly sliced fresh lemongrass (cut from the lower 3 to 5 inches of peeled stalk)
1/4	cup (about 1 ounce) unsalted roasted candlenuts (available at Malaysian ond Indonesian markets) or macadamia nuts
1	tablespoon ground coriander seed
2	teaspoons ground turmeric
	Peanut oil or vegetable oil
One	14-ounce can unsweetened coconut milk (shaken before use)
2	tablespoons fresh lime juice
1	pound medium-wide (about 1/8-inch) rice noodles (rice stick, Vietnamese *banh pho*, or *Thai sen lek*)
4	cups mung bean sprouts
2	large kaffir lime leaves, cut into thinnest possible filaments (available fresh or frozen at many Asian markets)

CONTINUED>

1. Bring the stock to a bare simmer in a 5- to 6-quart heavy pot. Add the chicken and cover, leaving the lid slightly ajar, and gently poach the chicken until just cooked through, 12 to 15 minutes. Let cool on a plate. Shred the meat into fairly thin, ropy strands and set aside. Leave the stock, covered, on the stovetop.

2. Meanwhile, put the Chile-Shrimp Sambal, 2 tablespoons fish sauce, 1 cup sliced shallots, garlic, ginger, lemongrass, nuts, coriander, and turmeric in the bowl of a food processor. Process to a nearly smooth paste, 2 to 3 minutes, scraping down the sides of the bowl as needed (add a few teaspoons of water to help the process along, if necessary).

3. Heat 3 tablespoons of oil in a 6- to 8-inch skillet over medium heat. When the oil is very hot, carefully add the puréed spice paste (it may sputter), spreading it out across the surface of the skillet with a spatula. After a minute or two of cooking, scrape up the paste, stir well, and spread it out again. If the purée sticks to the skillet, add about a tablespoon of water to help scrape up the stuck bits before spreading the mixture out again (a small amount of browning is fine). Repeat this cooking and spreading process until the paste is a few shades darker, much of the moisture has evaporated, and the raw taste of the vegetables is gone, 10 to 12 minutes. Don't rush this process; reduce the heat if the paste threatens to burn or brown excessively.

4. Add the coconut milk, whisking to incorporate thoroughly. Reduce the heat and cook at a bare simmer, stirring occasionally, until thickened somewhat but still quite fluid, about 10 minutes. Stir in the lime juice and the remaining 1/4 cup of fish sauce. Transfer this mixture to the pot with the chicken stock, stirring well to combine. Taste and simmer the soup base for 5 minutes or so to concentrate the flavor, if necessary.

5. Heat 2/3 cup oil in another 6- to 8-inch skillet over medium-high heat. When the oil is hot, add the remaining 3/4 cup shallots and cook for 2 minutes, separating the rings with tongs or a spatula. Reduce the heat to low and cook, stirring regularly, until the shallots are deep brown-gold (they will crisp when removed from the oil), about 15 minutes more. Using a slotted spoon, transfer the shallots to a paper towel–lined plate to cool (reserve the oil for another use).

6. Bring 2 to 3 quarts of water to a boil in a large pot. Put the noodles in a large bowl and cover with abundant boiling water. Let noodles soften until tender but still a bit firmer than you'd want to eat them (quite a bit firmer than al dente), stirring occasionally, 5 to 10 minutes depending on the brand (don't overcook; test noodles early and often). Immediately rinse

25 to 30 whole cilantro leaves (an equal amount of Vietnamese coriander (aka *laksa* or *rao ram*), coarsely chopped if large

25 to 30 whole fresh mint leaves, coarsely chopped if large

3 to 4 small hot red chiles, such as Thai bird or serrano, very thinly sliced into rings

Lime wedges

under cold running water to cool. Drain in a large strainer with a handle and set aside in strainer. Refill the same pot with water and reserve on the stovetop for reheating the noodles when finishing the dish.

7. When ready to serve, reheat the soup base and bring the water in the reserved pot to a boil. Add the reserved shredded chicken to the soup and simmer for 2 minutes. Meanwhile, plunge the strainer with the noodles in the boiling water until just heated through, 20 to 30 seconds. Drain the noodles; using tongs, divide the noodles among large, deep bowls and ladle the soup and chicken over the noodles. Place 1 cup of bean sprouts in a pile in the center of each bowl. Scatter the lime leaves, cilantro, mint, chiles, and reserved fried shallots over each. Serve with soup spoons, chopsticks, and lime wedges on the side.

NOTE: The soup base (Steps 1 through 4) can be made up to a half day ahead. Store the chicken and cooled soup base tightly covered separately in the refrigerator. The fried shallots in Step 5 can also be made half a day ahead and stored in a dry place. The noodles can be cooked and stored in the refrigerator and moistened with cold water if they stick together.

Also note that candlenuts—commonly used in Malaysia and Indonesia as a thickener in dishes like this one—should not be eaten raw due to the presence of a very mild toxin that disappears when cooked.

Senegalese-Style Grilled Chicken with Lemon and Onions

A Senegalese classic, lemon-lashed chicken yassa is an onion-lover's dish. The chicken can be broiled instead of grilled if necessary, but the results are not anywhere near as good—or traditional. Note that the chicken should marinate overnight. This dish is best when simply served with white rice.

SERVES 3 TO 4

One	4-pound chicken, back removed and reserved for another use, chicken cut into 6 pieces: 2 whole legs, 2 bone-in breast halves with drumettes attached, and 2 wings
1 1/2	tablespoons finely grated peeled fresh ginger
	Kosher salt
	Freshly ground black pepper
5	medium onions (about 2 1/2 pounds), halved lengthwise and sliced (about 10 cups)
1	fresh habañero chile, halved lengthwise, seeds and ribs removed (use gloves to prevent getting any caustic oils on your hands or in your eyes)
2	large bay leaves
1	cup fresh lemon juice
6	tablespoons peanut oil
1/2	cup Chicken Stock (page 299), or canned low-sodium chicken broth
1	teaspoon sugar

1. Rub the chicken parts thoroughly with the ginger. Salt the pieces on both sides with 1 generous tablespoon salt and season both sides generously with black pepper. Place one-quarter of the onions in a double-lined large resealable bag and top with one-half of the chicken pieces. Add one habañero half and a bay leaf and top with another one-quarter of the onions. Pour half of the lemon juice and 2 tablespoons of the oil into the bag. Seal the bag and then gently shake to distribute the lemon and oil, keeping the chicken buried in the onions. Repeat with another double-lined resealable plastic bag and the remaining ingredients. Marinate the chicken overnight in the refrigerator.
2. Remove the chicken from the marinade and let come to room temperature, covered. Remove and reserve the habañero halves. Meanwhile, empty the marinade ingredients into a large colander set over a large bowl, pressing on the onions to release excess liquid, and set aside.
3. Build a moderately hot charcoal fire, or preheat a gas grill to medium, and blot the chicken dry; sprinkle the chicken lightly with salt. Grill the chicken until deep golden brown and charred in spots, 4 to 6 minutes per side (the goal is to brown the chicken and impart the smoky taste of the grill; the meat should remain mostly raw inside). Remove the chicken to a plate and reserve, loosely covered with aluminum foil.
4. Heat the remaining 2 tablespoons oil in a large, heavy pot over high heat. When the oil begins to smoke, carefully add the drained onions and bay leaves in the colander (they'll sizzle and steam), reserving the marinade. Cook, stirring occasionally, until excess moisture evaporates and some of the onions begin to turn golden at the edges, 10 to 15 minutes, reducing the heat if they threaten to burn (don't let them brown or soften too much; they should be wilted somewhat but still crisp).

CONTINUED>

5. Reduce the heat to medium-low and stir in the stock, sugar, 2 teaspoons salt, the reserved marinade, and the reserved habañero halves. When the onions are as spicy as you like, remove the chiles and reserve; they can be chopped up by those diners who'd like to spice up their servings. Stir in any juices beneath the reserved chicken and nestle the chicken legs and wings into the onions. Cover, and bring just to a simmer, and cook for 15 minutes. Add the chicken breasts (and any juices) to the pot; cover and simmer until the breasts are just cooked through (about 150°F internally), 15 to 25 minutes more.

6. Remove the chicken to a cutting board designed to catch the juices and tent loosely with foil. Boil the onion mixture for up to 10 minutes to concentrate its flavors, adding any juices on the cutting board (the cooking liquid should be rich and lemony with a consistency somewhere between a broth and sauce). Meanwhile, cut the chicken into serving-size pieces and divide among warmed serving plates. Spoon a generous amount of onions and sauce over each and serve, garnished with chopped habañero pieces, if you like.

Thai-Style Barbecue Chicken

The trick to this Thai specialty is to complete the interior cooking of the butterflied bird at the same time that you've achieved a crisp, flavorful and deeply colored exterior. It isn't difficult to master, but two things should be mentioned: One, you'll need enough of a wood or charcoal fire to generate fairly consistent heat for the entire roughly 45 minutes of cooking; and two, because the chicken cooks fairly slowly next to (and not over) a live fire for that length of time, the dish requires you to use your instinct throughout the process (more, anyway, than a steak or a chop demands). You'll probably need to slow down or speed up the cooking of the interior at some time and encourage or discourage the browning of the exterior; both achieved by moving the bird to a cooler or hotter part of the grill whenever your instinct tells you to. When it all comes together, though, the results are really special. And although we prefer to slow "grill-roast" this chicken next to a wood and/or charcoal fire, a gas grill can also be used. Serve with a green Asian vegetable and jasmine rice.

SERVES 2 TO 3

12	large cloves garlic, sliced
½	cup thinly sliced shallots
½	cup cilantro roots and stems (if roots are unavailable, substitute stems), chopped
One	2-inch-piece fresh ginger
3	tablespoons soy sauce
	Kosher salt
One	2½- to 3-pound chicken, butterflied through the breast
⅓	cup peanut oil or vegetable oil
1	tablespoon jasmine rice or other long-grain rice
6 to 8	dried whole Thai, or other hot, dry chiles (each about 2 inches long)
1	heaping tablespoon finely chopped scallion
2	tablespoons finely chopped fresh mint

1. Combine 6 of the sliced garlic cloves, the shallots, cilantro, ginger, soy sauce, and ½ teaspoon of salt in the bowl of a food processor and process until a loose, finely chopped paste forms, scraping down the sides of the bowl once or twice. Reserve the marinade.
2. Place the chicken, skin-side down, in a glass or ceramic baking dish and coat with the marinade, massaging the herb paste into the flesh for a minute or so. Cover and marinate at room temperature for 1 to 2 hours, massaging again with the herb paste once during this time.
3. Put the oil with the remaining 6 sliced garlic cloves in a small saucepan and cook over medium heat until the garlic is pale golden. Strain into a small bowl and reserve (discard the garlic or reserve and fold into a cooked vegetable accompaniment).
4. Put the rice in a small skillet over medium heat and cook, shaking the pan, until fragrant and lightly toasted, less than 1 minute. Transfer to a spice or coffee grinder and let the rice cool. Process until almost powdered; transfer to a small bowl and reserve. Place the chiles in the same skillet and cook over medium heat until lightly toasted, 30 to 45 seconds, shaking the skillet to avoid burning. Transfer to a spice or coffee grinder and let the chiles cool. Pulse the grinder until coarsely chopped and transfer the chiles to the bowl with the rice (the rice and the chiles can also be ground separately with a mortar and pestle). Add the scallion, mint, cilantro leaves, sugar, fish sauce, and lime juice to the bowl, stirring to dissolve the sugar. Cover and reserve the chile-herb sauce (it can be made a few hours ahead.)
5. Open the top and bottom vents on the grill kettle. Build a medium-hot indirect charcoal fire with enough charcoal-free area to accommodate the chicken. Remove the chicken from the marinade and blot dry. Brush generously with the reserved garlic oil and salt generously on both sides. When the flames have settled down somewhat, but before the wood or briquettes have turned completely to coal, place the chicken on the grill (over the charcoal-free side), cut side down and legs toward the heat. Place a foil-wrapped brick over the breast and cover the grill (the intensity of the fire will drop to medium-low when covered, which is where you want it). Cook the chicken for 25 minutes, checking once or twice to ensure that the chicken isn't browning too quickly; if it is, move it to a cooler part of the grill and/or close the grill's vents to reduce the temperature. Carefully flip the chicken. Return the brick to the breast; cover the grill and cook the second side for about 20 minutes, or until the juices of the thigh run clear

2 tablespoons finely chopped fresh cilantro leaves
2 teaspoons sugar
3 tablespoons Thai or Vietnamese fish sauce (*nam pla* or *nuoc nam*)
⅓ cup fresh lime juice

when pricked and skin is golden. Let the chicken rest for a few minutes before cutting into serving-size pieces. Accompany with the reserved chile-herb sauce.

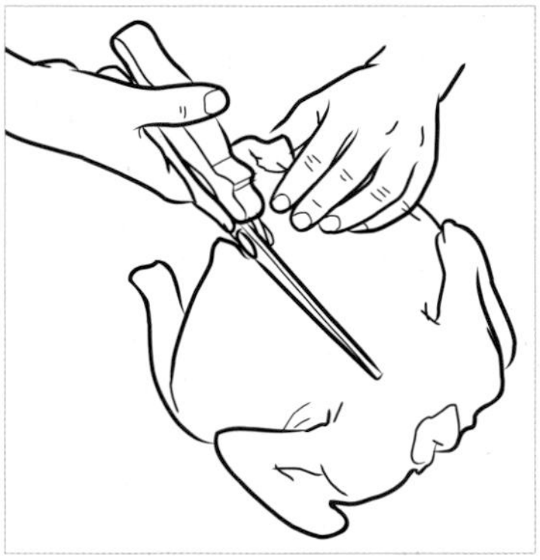

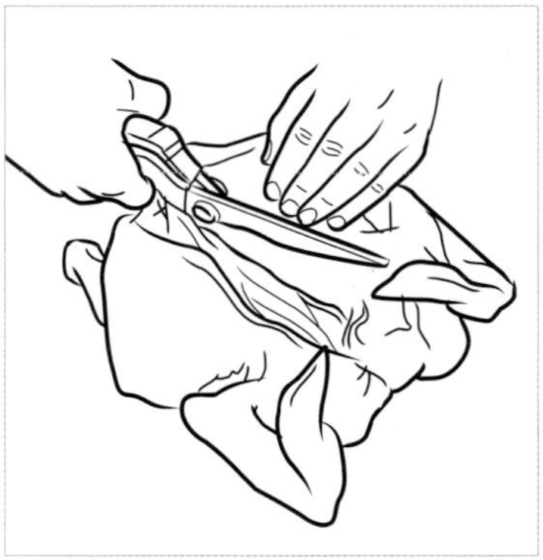

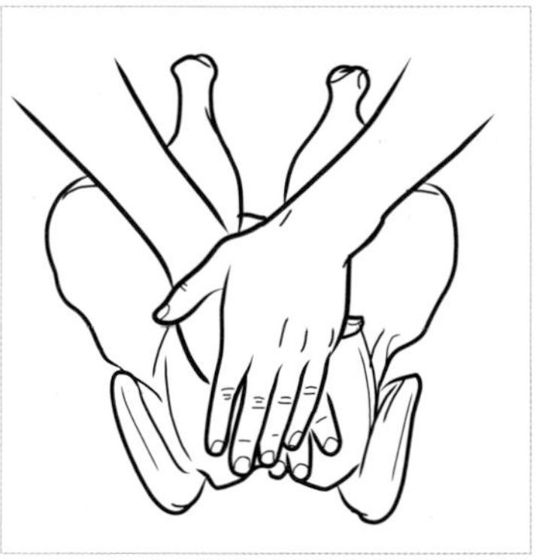

Chicken Pad Thai

We think our version of pad thai dish is much better than what is commonly served in Thai restaurants. The key to making this dish is to have all the ingredients prepped and close at hand before cooking (to keep the wok hot throughout, bring all ingredients to room temperature first). Also, pay attention to the rice noodles when soaking: The goal is to make them pliable, nearly tender, but still a little firmer than al dente. Otherwise, they turn to mush in the hot wok. If you prefer pad thai with shrimp, substitute half a pound of peeled, deveined medium shrimp for the chicken.

SERVES 2

- 6 ounces Thai or Vietnamese medium-width flat rice noodles (*sen lek* or *banh pho*)
- 1/4 cup Thai or Vietnamese fish sauce (*nam pla* or *nuoc nam*)
- 1/4 cup tamarind concentrate or homemade tamarind water (see Note)
- 2 tablespoons palm sugar, or 1 1/2 tablespoons brown sugar
- 1 teaspoon Asian chile paste, such as *sambal oelek*, plus more for serving
- 4 tablespoons vegetable oil
- 1/4 cup coarsely chopped shallots
- 3 ounces pressed tofu, cut into 3/8-inch cubes or batons that measure 1/4 inch thick by 1 inch long
- 2 teaspoons finely chopped preserved radish (*hua chay poa*, aka preserved turnip), rinsed (optional)
- 2 tablespoons dried baby shrimp, softened in hot water for 5 to 20 minutes if hard, (optional)
- 6 ounces boneless chicken breast, thinly sliced into pieces 1 to 2 inches in length
- 2 eggs
- 3 tablespoons crushed unsalted roasted peanuts, plus more for garnish
- 1 1/2 cups mung bean sprouts, plus more for garnish
- 1 small handful Chinese chives or green onion tops cut into 3/4-inch lengths (about 1/2 cup)
- Lime wedges for garnish

1. Bring 2 to 3 quarts of water to a boil in a large pot. Put the noodles in a large bowl and cover with abundant boiling water. Let the noodles soften until tender but still a bit firmer than you'd want to eat them, stirring occasionally, 5 to 10 minutes depending on the brand (don't overcook; test noodles early and often). Immediately drain in a colander and rinse thoroughly under cold running water. Set aside.
2. Put the fish sauce, tamarind, sugar, and 2 tablespoons water in a small saucepan and bring to a simmer, stirring to dissolve the sugar. Let simmer for 1 minute. Remove from the heat and taste the mixture: it should be salty, sour, and just slightly sweet; adjust with small amounts of each ingredient as needed. Stir in the chile paste and transfer the sauce to a small bowl and reserve. The dish can be made up to this point a few hours ahead. Before beginning to cook, have all the ingredients prepared, at room temperature, and close at hand.
3. Heat a 14- to 16-inch wok over medium-high heat for 2 to 3 minutes. Add the oil, swirling to coat the wok. Add the shallots and cook, stirring, until beginning to brown, for a few seconds. Add the tofu (and radish and shrimp, if using) and cook, stirring frequently, until tofu begins to brown at edges, less than 1 minute.
4. Increase the heat to high and add the chicken. Cook until nearly cooked through, a minute or so, stirring frequently. Add the rice noodles and cook, stirring almost continuously until heated through, another minute or so.
5. Clear a space on one side of the wok. Working quickly, crack the eggs into the wok and roughly scramble and toss with the noodles for a few moments. Add the reserved sauce and toss to combine. Add the peanuts, bean sprouts, and chives, stirring and tossing to incorporate all the ingredients. Divide between plates and garnish with lime wedges and additional bean sprouts, peanuts, and chile paste.

NOTE: Tamarind concentrate is available at most Asian markets and works well in pad thai. However, it is a convenience product intended to stand in for the real thing: homemade tamarind water. Tamarind water—a thin paste made from tamarind pulp (also found at Asian markets)—is easy to make and tastes superior to concentrate. Here's how: Cover a small portion of tamarind pulp with an equal amount of warm water and let soak for a few minutes to soften. Work the pulp with your fingers to help dissolve the paste and separate it from the seeds within. Strain the mixture, pushing on the mass of solids to release the pulp and leave the seeds behind. You should be left with a slightly fluid paste.

Chinese Chicken Salad

This is a refreshing dish that showcases chicken, cucumber, and a unique Asian ingredient called agar-agar (see Note). A great start to any hot-weather meal, this salad can be served at room temperature or chilled. To serve chilled, first prepare the agar-agar and cucumber and keep them in the refrigerator for an hour or more. About 1 hour before serving, marinate and then cook the chicken. Once the chicken has cooled to room temperature, assemble the salad.

SERVES 4

1/2	cup soy sauce
1/4	cup rice wine vinegar
2	tablespoons sugar
2	teaspoons Asian sesame oil
2	teaspoons Asian hot chili oil
2	large cloves garlic, minced
One	2-inch piece fresh ginger unpeeled, halved crosswise and crushed
1	pound skinless boneless chicken breasts
1/2	teaspoon kosher salt
1 1/2	ounces agar-agar in strips (see Note)
2	medium cucumbers
1	tablespoon cornstarch dissolved in 1 tablespoon cold water
2	tablespoons peanut oil
2	teaspoons toasted sesame seeds
1/2	cup coarsely chopped fresh cilantro leaves

1. Combine the soy sauce, vinegar, and sugar in a small mixing bowl, whisking to dissolve the sugar. Whisk in the sesame oil, chili oil, garlic, and ginger. Set the dressing aside.
2. Trim all fat from the chicken. Remove the strip of "fillet" from the underside of the breast halves. Expose one end of the sinew running down the center of the fillet and, using your fingers (or with the help of the tip of a paring knife), pull out the sinew and discard.
3. Lay the breast halves flat on a work surface, and with your knife parallel to the work surface, cut each breast piece in half, lengthwise, into thin cutlets. Cut these cutlets into strips of equal thickness between 1/8 inch and 1/4 inch and 1 to 2 inches long. Cut the fillets into similar-size strips. Put the chicken strips in a medium mixing bowl.
4. Dissolve the salt in 1 tablespoon of water and toss this mixture with the chicken strips to coat. Set aside for 30 minutes.
5. Meanwhile, pass the agar-agar briefly under running water to make it pliable but still firm (this makes it easier to cut). Using scissors, snip it into about 1½-inch lengths, letting them fall into a large mixing bowl as you work. Cover the agar-agar with abundant hot water and soak until softened and easy to chew, 5 to 15 minutes, swishing them around a few times (test frequently as they soak and don't let them stay in the water beyond when they first become tender; they'll get too limp). Drain. Working in 2 or 3 batches, roll agar-agar up in a clean kitchen towel or a triple thickness of paper towels and squeeze until completely dry. Return to the large mixing bowl and put in the refrigerator.
6. Peel the cucumbers and quarter them lengthwise. Cut or scrape the seeds away and discard. Cut the cucumber quarters crosswise into 1/8-inch-thick slices and place on top of the agar-agar in the bowl; return the bowl to the refrigerator.
7. After the chicken has marinated for 30 minutes, mix in the dissolved cornstarch mixture, stirring to coat the chicken completely. Heat the peanut oil in a wok or large skillet over medium-high heat. When the oil is hot but not smoking, swirl it to coat the wok and add the chicken, spreading it out in a single layer; cook for 45 seconds. Begin stirring to encourage the pieces to separate and continue cooking until the chicken is just barely cooked through, 1 minute or so, stirring regularly (the chicken should cook through with little or no browning; reduce the heat as necessary). Transfer to a plate and spread out to cool.

8. Add the chicken to the bowl with the agar-agar and cucumber. Remove the ginger from the dressing, squeezing the pieces to release juices back into the bowl. Whisk the dressing and pour half of it over the salad, tossing well to distribute. Divide the salad among serving plates or put it on a serving platter. Sprinkle with sesame seeds and scatter the cilantro over. Serve with the remaining dressing on the side for diners to add more if they'd like.

NOTE: Agar-agar is a translucent gelatin made from seaweed that is available at Asian markets. It comes in a powdered form for use as a setting agent and in long, grassy-looking strips that are used in salads like this one. These are usually sold bound in 3-ounce bundles sealed in plastic (avoid the artificially colored red and green types). The strips are soaked in water until tender and then squeezed dry before use. Half of a 3-ounce bundle is enough for this recipe.

Stir-Fried Chicken with Peanuts and Chiles

This dish is probably the inspiration for the famous Chinese-American kung pao chicken. Called gong bao chicken in its homeland, this is far less sweet and more tangy and spicier than the Chinese-American version. Read through the recipe a few times and have all your ingredients measured, close at hand, and arranged in the order each (or each group) is to be added to the wok. Serve with white rice and bok choy or another Chinese green vegetable.

SERVES 2

1 pound skinless boneless chicken breast or thigh meat, cut into 3/4-inch cubes

MARINADE

1 tablespoon cornstarch
1 large egg white
1 teaspoon dark soy sauce
1 teaspoon Shaoxing wine (Chinese rice wine) or medium-dry sherry
1 tablespoon water

SAUCE

1 tablespoon sugar
2 teaspoons cornstarch
1/4 cup Chicken Stock (page 299), canned low-sodium chicken broth, or water
1 tablespoon Chinkiang vinegar (Chinese black rice vinegar)
2 teaspoons dark soy sauce
1 teaspoon Asian sesame oil

STIR-FRY

2 tablespoons peanut oil
2 teaspoons Szechuan peppercorns
Eight to twelve 2- to 3-inch-long dried red Chinese or Japanese chiles, halved crosswise with seeds removed
3 large cloves garlic, minced
1 tablespoon finely grated peeled fresh ginger root
5 large scallions, cut into 1/2-inch lengths (both white and green parts)
1/2 cup unsalted blanched peanuts
Sprouts or pea shoots for garnish (optional)

1. To make marinade: Toss the chicken pieces with the cornstarch in a large mixing bowl. Add the egg white, soy sauce, rice wine, and water, stirring to coat the chicken.

2. To make the sauce: Combine the sugar and the 2 teaspoons cornstarch in a small bowl; whisk in the stock to dissolve the solids. Whisk in the vinegar, 2 teaspoons soy sauce, and sesame oil, and set aside.

3. For the stir-fry: heat a 14-inch wok over high heat for a few minutes. Have all the ingredients measured and close at hand. When the wok is very hot, add the peanut oil, swirling to coat the surface of the wok. (It should be smoking.) Working quickly, add the Szechuan peppercorns and chiles and toss for no more than 5 seconds; don't burn. Add the reserved chicken and its marinade. Stir almost constantly, separating the chicken pieces from one another, until golden at the edges but still raw within, 1 minute or so.

4. Add the garlic, ginger, and scallions, continuing to stir until the chicken is just about cooked through, 1 minute or so more. Add the reserved sauce, tossing until all the ingredients are coated and the liquid has reduced to a few tablespoons, no more than 45 seconds. Stir in the peanuts and remove from the heat. Serve immediately. Garnish if desired.

NOTE: Any of the unfamiliar ingredients are available at a good Chinese or Asian market.

Chicken Kababs with Cilantro-Lime Chutney

In our take on a well-known Indian dish, cubes of chicken breast are flavored and tenderized in a spice-laden yogurt marinade. The skewered and grilled meat is served with a complex and brightly flavored Cilantro-Lime Chutney. Serve over a pile of steamed basmati rice.

SERVES 4 AS A MAIN COURSE; 8 AS AN APPETIZER

4	tablespoons fresh lime juice
1	tablespoon vegetable oil
1/4	cup plain yogurt
One	1 1/2-inch piece 1-inch-thick fresh ginger, peeled and sliced into coins
3	large cloves garlic, peeled
1	tablespoon ground coriander seed
1 1/2	teaspoons ground cumin seed
1/2	teaspoon freshly ground black pepper
1/8	teaspoon cayenne pepper
3/4	teaspoon Garam Masala Spice Blend (page 296)
1	tablespoon kosher salt
2 1/4	pounds skinless boneless chicken breast cut into 1 1/2-inch cubes (see Note)
3	tablespoons melted unsalted butter, preferably ghee or clarified butter
	Fresh cilantro or mint leaves for garnish
1	recipe Cilantro-Lime Chutney (page 289)

1. Put 3 tablespoons of the lime juice, the oil, yogurt, ginger, garlic, coriander, cumin, black pepper, cayenne, garam masala, and salt in the bowl of a food processor. Process until smooth, or nearly so. Combine thoroughly with the chicken in a mixing bowl. Cover and marinate in the refrigerator for 4 to 12 hours, turning the pieces over in the marinade once or twice.
2. Thread pieces of chicken onto skewers, using about 4 per skewer, clustering the pieces together. Let the chicken sit at room temperature for about 30 minutes before cooking. Combine the melted ghee or butter and the remaining 1 tablespoon lime juice and reserve.
3. Grill the kababs on an oiled grill or grill pan over medium heat, turning to expose all 4 sides to the heat, until just cooked through, 9 to 12 minutes total. If the chicken threatens to burn, reduce the heat or move to a cooler part of the grill. During the last few seconds of cooking, brush the kababs with the reserved lime butter and arrange on a platter or serving plates. Garnish with the cilantro or mint leaves and serve with Cilantro-Lime Chutney spooned over the kababs or on the side.

NOTE: Because of the irregular shape of chicken breasts, it is not always possible to cut 2 pounds of perfect 1 1/2-inch cubes, as called for in this recipe. To ensure even cooking, cut any thinner parts a bit longer than the others and fold these pieces when placing them on the skewers to approximate the size of the properly cut cubes.

You'll want to use this trick on the tender strip of meat on the underside of each breast half. Detach the tender, pull out the tendon running down its center with the help of a paring knife (or just by grabbing it with fingers), and cut the tender into 2 or 3 pieces and fold as described.

If using wooden skewers, soak them in water for at least 30 minutes before threading them with the meat, and then wrap the long, exposed portion of wood with aluminum foil before putting them on the grill.

Moroccan-Style Chicken with Mixed Vegetables, Raisins, and Almonds

To our untraditional (but traditional-tasting) variation on a Moroccan classic, we add a marinating step that can be reduced in time or eliminated altogether if time is an issue. The chicken is so tender it falls from the bone, and is accompanied by an array of stewed vegetables, chickpeas, and raisins—all topped with fresh cilantro and crisp, honeyed almonds.

SERVES 4 TO 6

- 1½ teaspoons ground cinnamon
- 1½ teaspoons ground turmeric
- 1 teaspoon freshly ground black pepper
- ½ teaspoon ground nutmeg
- ⅛ teaspoon cayenne pepper
- 50 saffron threads (2 large pinches), briefly toasted in a pan and crumbled
- 2 cloves garlic, peeled and mashed into a paste with the broad side of a chef's knife
- 2 tablespoons grated peeled fresh ginger
- Kosher salt
- ¼ cup plus 3 tablespoons extra-virgin olive oil
- 8 chicken thighs (about 2½ to 3 pounds), trimmed of excess fat
- 1 pound seeded, peeled butternut, acorn, or similar squash, cut about ¾-inch square by 3 inches long
- 4 medium carrots, peeled (halved lengthwise at thick ends) and cut into 2- to 3-inch lengths
- 2 small to medium zucchini, quartered lengthwise and cut crosswise into 2- to 3-inch lengths
- 4 tablespoons unsalted butter, cut into 6 pieces
- ¾ cup unsalted roasted almonds
- 2 tablespoons honey

1. Mix together the cinnamon, turmeric, black pepper, nutmeg, cayenne, and saffron in a large, nonreactive bowl. Divide the spice mixture in two and remove half to a small dish; cover and set aside. Add the garlic and ginger, 1½ tablespoons of salt, and ¼ cup of the oil to the large bowl with the spices and mix well. Add the chicken and coat well with the mixture. Add the squash, carrots, and zucchini and gently toss to coat. Cover with plastic wrap and allow the chicken and vegetables to marinate for 2 hours at room temperature or overnight in the refrigerator.
2. Meanwhile, melt 2 tablespoons of the butter in a small skillet over medium-low heat. Add the almonds and cook, tossing them regularly, until they are darkened somewhat and toasted, 4 to 6 minutes. Don't let them burn. Add the honey and cook for 1 minute more, stirring well. Let the almonds cool on a plate. Break apart those stuck together chop coarsely and set aside.
3. Heat the remaining 3 tablespoons oil in a wide, 10- to 14-quart heavy pot over medium-high heat. Remove the chicken from the marinade (blot with paper towels if very wet) and sprinkle with additional salt on each side. When the oil is hot, and working in batches if necessary, add the chicken pieces, skin-side down, and cook until golden brown on both sides, 6 to 8 minutes per side, reducing the heat if they threaten to burn. Remove the chicken to a plate and set aside.
4. Pour off all but 3 tablespoons fat from the pot and return the pot to the stovetop. Reduce the heat to medium-low and add the remaining 2 tablespoons butter. When it's melted, add the onion and cook, stirring occasionally, until softened, about 5 minutes, scraping up any browned bits on the bottom of the pot with the help of the onion's moisture. Stir in the reserved spice mixture, then add the tomatoes, cilantro bundle, 4 cups water, and 2 teaspoons salt. Add the chicken, skin-side up, and any juices on the plate. Bring to a boil over high heat. Cover the pot and reduce the heat so that the stew maintains a bare simmer and cook for 1 hour, stirring occasionally.
5. Add the chickpeas and the reserved squash and carrots, nestling them between the chicken and beneath the surface of the liquid. Cover the pot and continue simmering for 15 minutes. Add the zucchini and the raisins in the same fashion and simmer for 15 minutes more.

1	large onion, chopped
One	15-ounce can tomatoes, drained and coarsely chopped
5	sprigs fresh cilantro tied in a bundle, plus 1/4 cup chopped fresh cilantro for garnish
One	15-ounce can chickpeas, drained
3/4	cup golden raisins
	8 to 12 cups freshly cooked couscous (instant or long-cooking)
	Lemon wedges for serving (optional)

6. At this point, the broth should taste richly of chicken, spices, and vegetables; if you feel it could be a bit more concentrated in flavor (or if the vegetables aren't yet tender), continue to simmer uncovered, for an additional few minutes (liquid should remain abundant and broth-like; it is not a sauce). Add salt to taste. Pour 1/3 of the broth into a sauceboat and keep warm. Spoon 1 to 2 cups couscous in the center of each serving plate and make a well in the center. Using a slotted spoon, place the chicken and vegetables attractively in each well and spoon the remaining broth over the servings. Garnish with the reserved almonds, chopped cilantro, and lemon wedges, if you like. Serve, passing the sauceboat of broth at the table.

Malaysian Spice-Fried Chicken

This is a wildly flavorful way to cook chicken. Thighs are our choice for this recipe, but you can use any part of the chicken (or cut up a whole bird as long as the pieces are similar in size).

SERVES 4

1	cup thinly sliced shallots (about 3 ounces)
One	1-inch piece fresh ginger, peeled and thinly sliced
1	tablespoon ground coriander seed
2	teaspoons ground turmeric
2	teaspoons ground cinnamon
2	teaspoons ground fennel seed
1	teaspoon ground cumin seed
1	teaspoon freshly ground black pepper
½	teaspoon cayenne pepper
¼	teaspoon ground cloves
1	tablespoon kosher salt
2	teaspoons sugar
½	cup unsweetened coconut milk (shaken before use)
3	pounds chicken thighs, cut in half across the bone (16 to 18 pieces) (see Note)
	Peanut oil or vegetable oil for frying
	Malaysian Chicken Dipping Sauce (page 292)

1. Put the shallots, ginger, coriander, turmeric, cinnamon, fennel seed, cumin, black pepper, cayenne, cloves, salt, and sugar in the bowl of a food processor. Process to a coarse paste, scraping down the sides of the bowl as needed. Add the coconut milk and process briefly to incorporate. Combine the spice paste and the chicken in a large bowl, mixing to coat the chicken thoroughly. Marinate in the refrigerator for at least 3 hours and up to 24. Let sit at room temperature for 1 hour or so before frying.
2. Preheat the oven to 200°F.
3. Heat ½ to 1 inch of oil to 365°F in a 12-inch, straight-sided heavy skillet over high heat. Working in two batches, slip the spice-coated chicken skin-side down into the hot oil and fry the first side until deep reddish brown at those places where the spices adhere to the chicken and a bit lighter elsewhere, 4 to 5 minutes. Turn the chicken and repeat until just cooked through, about 4 minutes more (the final color may be very dark brown—nearly black—in spots but it shouldn't burn or overcook).
4. Drain the chicken on a paper towel–lined dish or baking sheet and keep the first batch warm in the oven while you fry the second. Serve with bowls of Malaysian Chicken Dipping Sauce.

NOTE: The chicken pieces should be nearly uniform in size and not too large: 2 to 3 inches long and 1½-inches thick and wide is a good size. If you have a cleaver, this is a snap to do at home. If not, ask your butcher to do the work for you.

Braised Guinea Hen with White Wine, Rosemary, and Chile Pepper

This is a simple dish from central Italy that shows off the uniqueness of guinea hen.

SERVES 2 TO 3

4	tablespoons extra-virgin olive oil
One	3-pound guinea hen, butterflied with backbone, wing tips, and necks removed and chopped into 1-inch pieces; gizzard and heart reserved; and the butterflied bird cut into 4 leg-thigh pieces and 4 bone-in breast pieces of roughly equal size
½	cup dry white wine
2	cups Chicken Stock (page 299), or canned low-sodium chicken broth
	Kosher salt
	Freshly ground black pepper
	All-purpose flour for dredging
1	medium onion, ends removed, halved lengthwise and thinly sliced
3	large cloves garlic, thinly sliced
1	tablespoon tomato paste
2	tablespoons fresh lemon juice
¼	teaspoon crushed red pepper flakes
1	teaspoon finely chopped fresh rosemary

1. Heat 1 tablespoon of the oil in a medium saucepan over medium-high heat. When hot, add the 1-inch hen pieces and the giblets (the reserved gizzard and heart) and cook until deeply browned on two sides, 10 to 12 minutes, regulating the heat if they threaten to burn. Drain the oil while holding back the pieces and return to the heat. Add the white wine and bring to a simmer, scraping the bottom of the pan with a spatula to loosen any browned bits. Reduce the heat and gently simmer until the liquid is reduced by half, about 4 minutes. Add the stock and simmer very gently until reduced by half (¾ cup) again, about 30 minutes. Pass the sauce through a fine-mesh strainer set over a bowl, pressing hard on the solids to extract all their flavors. Set reduced hen stock aside.

2. Season the hen pieces generously with salt and pepper. Heat the remaining 3 tablespoons oil in a 10- to 12-inch lidded skillet over medium-high heat. When the oil is hot, and working in batches if necessary, dredge the hen pieces in the flour, shaking off any excess, and cook until deep golden brown on two sides, about 5 minutes per side. Remove to a plate (if any of the floury bits have burned excessively, drain the oil, scrape up any burned bits and heat a few fresh tablespoons of oil). Warm serving plates in a low oven.

3. Reduce the heat to medium and add the onion and garlic. Cook until the onion is translucent, about 5 minutes, stirring occasionally. In a small bowl, dissolve the tomato paste in the lemon juice along with 2 tablespoons warm water and add to the skillet. Stir in the crushed red pepper, ½ teaspoon of the rosemary, ¼ teaspoon salt, and the reserved reduced hen stock. Return the thigh and legs to the skillet and bring just to a simmer. Cover and reduce the heat to very low. Cook at a bare simmer for 10 minutes. Add the thicker two breast pieces; cover and cook for 5 minutes. Add the remaining breast pieces and any juices on the plate; cover and cook until all the breast pieces are just cooked through, about 20 minutes more.

4. Divide the guinea hen among warmed serving plates. Add salt to the braising liquid if necessary and spoon the liquid and onions over the guinea hen. Sprinkle with the remaining ½ teaspoon rosemary and serve.

Turkey Osso Buco with Fava Beans

This traditional dish hails from the region of Campania in Italy. If the turkey legs you find are on the smaller and taller side, brown them also on their skin sides. If you can't find favas, peas or cooked artichokes are delicious, too. This is good with rice, either plain white or a simple *risotto bianco* made with onion, turkey or chicken broth, Parmesan cheese, and a bit of butter. Note that fresh turkey legs are much more tender than frozen ones.

SERVES 3 TO 4

4	tablespoons extra-virgin olive oil, plus more for finishing the dish
3	ounces pancetta (sliced 1/8 inch thick) and cut into 1/4-inch pieces
2 1/2	to 3 pounds turkey legs, cut crosswise as for osso buco, about 1 1/2 inch thick
	Kosher salt
	All-purpose flour for dredging
1	large onion, finely chopped
3	large cloves garlic, minced
3/4	cup dry white wine
2	cups Turkey Stock (page 299), Chicken Stock (page 299), or canned low-sodium chicken broth
8	ounces (3/4 cup) fresh or 1 cup canned tomatoes, coarsely chopped and drained
3	cups blanched and peeled fresh or frozen fava beans
1/2	teaspoon finely chopped fresh rosemary
3	large fresh sage leaves, finely chopped
3	tablespoon finely chopped fresh flat-leaf parsley
	Finely grated zest of 1 1/2 lemons

1. Warm the oil in a 10- to 12-quart pot over medium heat. Add the pancetta and cook until crisp and golden, stirring occasionally, for 4 to 6 minutes. Remove with a slotted spoon and reserve.

2. Salt the turkey generously on all sides and dredge in the flour. Raise the heat to medium-high; add the turkey to the pot and cook until golden brown on both cut sides, for 10 to 12 minutes. Remove to a plate and reserve.

3. Reduce the heat to medium and add the onion and garlic. Cook until softened but without browning, stirring occasionally, for 6 to 8 minutes. Add the wine, scraping the bottom of the pot with a spatula to loosen any browned bits, and gently simmer until the liquid has reduced by half. Add the rosemary, sage, and 1 tablespoon of the parsley. Stir in the stock, tomatoes, ½ teaspoon salt, the reserved pancetta, and the reserved turkey and any juices remaining on the plate. Bring to a simmer; cover and cook at a bare simmer for 1½ hours.

4. Taste the sauce. If it seems a bit too liquid and lacking in flavor, simmer uncovered until slightly thickened and concentrated. Stir in the fava beans and salt to taste. Divide the turkey among serving plates and top generously with the sauce. Mix together the remaining 2 tablespoons of parsley and the lemon zest and sprinkle over each serving. Drizzle with a bit more oil and serve.

Rabbit with Sherry and Garlic Sauce

When making this Spanish favorite it's important to toss the rabbit with the garlic-sherry sauce before transferring it to the oven. It should also be tossed again with the sauce when the baking dish comes out of the oven, just before serving. These small pieces of rabbit should be rolled around in the seasonings as much as possible to help bind the flavors in the dish. Serve with the same sherry, well chilled, that is used in the dish.

SERVES 3 AS A MAIN COURSE; 6 AS AN APPETIZER (OR TAPA)

6	tablespoons extra-virgin olive oil, or more as needed
One	3-pound rabbit, cut into 18 to 20 small pieces, rinsed, blotted dry, and at room temperature
	Kosher salt
	All-purpose flour for dredging
1	large head of garlic, cloves peeled and thinly sliced
2	large sprigs fresh thyme, plus additional sprigs for garnish
1	cup fino or manzanilla sherry

1. Heat the olive oil in a large skillet over medium-high heat. Working in two batches, generously salt the rabbit pieces on all sides and dredge them in the flour, shaking off any excess. When the oil is hot, add the rabbit and cook until golden on all sides (even the larger end surfaces), 3 to 4 minutes per side, adding more oil if needed. Transfer to a plate and reserve.
2. Preheat the oven to 350°F.
3. Let the skillet cool slightly. Pour off all but 3 tablespoons oil and set over low heat (if the skillet or any flour has blackened excessively, pour off the oil and/or scrape off any black spots; add 3 tablespoons of fresh oil and return it to medium-low heat for a minute or two, reduce heat to low, and proceed with recipe). Stir in the garlic and thyme. Cook gently, until the garlic is pale gold at the edges, 1 to 3 minutes, stirring occasionally. Add the sherry and bring to a simmer. Reduce the heat to medium-low and simmer gently for 3 minutes, scraping up any browned bits stuck to the skillet with a spatula.
4. Return the rabbit to the skillet along with any juices on the plate and toss thoroughly to coat with the garlic-sherry mixture. Transfer the mixture to an 8-by-12-inch earthenware or glass baking dish. Cover tightly with lid or aluminum foil and bake for 20 minutes.
5. Remove from the oven and place the baking dish, uncovered, over low heat (glass may crack if heat is any higher than low). Turn the rabbit pieces over in the gently simmering sauce to coat the pieces and to slightly concentrate the flavor of the sauce, 1 to 3 minutes (there may not be a lot of sauce, but it should be flavorful and mostly cling to the pieces of rabbit; keep turning the rabbit until well coated).
6. Divide the rabbit among serving plates; spoon over any sauce remaining in the baking dish (a rubber spatual helps) and garnish each serving with a small cluster of thyme sprigs. Serve immediately.

Rabbit with Dijon-Mustard Sauce

Here is a French Burgundian standard—simple and really good. If you've never prepared rabbit, this is a great introduction. Serve the dish with a leafy, green vegetable, like spinach or chard, and a side of potatoes.

SERVES 4

One	3- to 3 1/2-pound rabbit cut into 12 to 14 pieces, saddle pieces wrapped in their belly flaps and secured with a toothpick (see Note), at room temperature
	Kosher salt
	Freshly ground black pepper
2	tablespoons vegetable oil
2	tablespoons unsalted butter
8 to 10	large sprigs fresh thyme
10 to 12	large cloves garlic, unpeeled, loose papery bits removed
3	tablespoons minced shallots
1	cup dry white wine
1	cup crème fraîche
3	tablespoons Dijon mustard, or more as needed
1	heaping tablespoon finely chopped fresh flat-leaf parsley for garnish (optional)

1. Preheat the oven to 375°F.
2. Generously salt and lightly pepper the rabbit pieces on all sides. Heat the oil and butter in a deep ovenproof skillet large enough the hold the rabbit in a single layer (at least 12 inches across) over medium-high heat. After the butter melts and its foam subsides, add the rabbit, in batches if necessary, and cook until pale golden brown on two sides, 3 to 4 minutes per side, reducing the heat if it threatens to burn. Remove the rabbit to a plate and pour off all but 2 tablespoons of the fat in the skillet.
3. Return the 6 leg pieces to the skillet; scatter the thyme and garlic cloves over and around the rabbit. Cover the skillet tightly; place in the oven and cook for 30 minutes. Remove from the oven and distribute the remaining rabbit pieces around the skillet along with any juices on the plate. Cover and return to the oven for 15 to 20 minutes more, or until an instant-read thermometer inserted in the meaty center of the saddle section registers 140°F to 150°F. Turn off the oven.
4. Attractively arrange the rabbit, garlic, and thyme sprigs on a serving platter; cover with foil and place the platter in the oven to keep warm (rabbit will continue to cook somewhat even as the oven cools). Place a sauceboat in the oven to warm.
5. Working with potholders, return the skillet to medium heat and add the shallots. Cook, stirring occasionally, until softened but without color, about 3 minutes. Increase the heat to medium-high and add the wine; simmer until reduced to about ½ cup, about 4 minutes, scraping the bottom of the skillet to loosen any browned bits. Stir in the crème fraîche and mustard and bring just to a simmer. Reduce the heat to medium-low and simmer gently until slightly thickened but still quite fluid, stirring occasionally, 3 to 4 minutes more. Taste the sauce and add a bit more mustard and/or salt if you feel it needs it. (The sauce should strike a pleasing balance of mustard and cream.) If the rabbit has given off any juices after resting in the oven, stir these into the sauce.
6. Pour half the sauce into the warmed sauceboat and drizzle the remaining sauce over the rabbit. Garnish with the parsley, if you like, and serve, passing the sauceboat at the table.

NOTE: You may want to reserve the rabbit's liver, kidneys, and heart to serve with the finished dish. Salt them and quickly pan-fry them just before serving. When removing these innards from the body of the rabbit, leave behind the tenderizing and tasty fat that lines the cavity and encloses the kidneys. When rolled up within the belly flaps, this fat mostly melts away but helps keep the loin meat within the saddle moist and flavorful during cooking.

TURKEY SAUSAGE
GOOSE
EY
TS
ULTRY
ABBIT
CKEN WINGS

OSTRICH

PHEASANT

SCOTCH GROUSE

SQUAB

WILD DUCK

R

WILD TURKEY

GAME BIRDS AND GAME

PARTRIDGE

SQUIRREL

"GLOVE BONED"
QUAIL

BUFFALO

EINDEER

WOOD
PIGEON

Wild
Goose

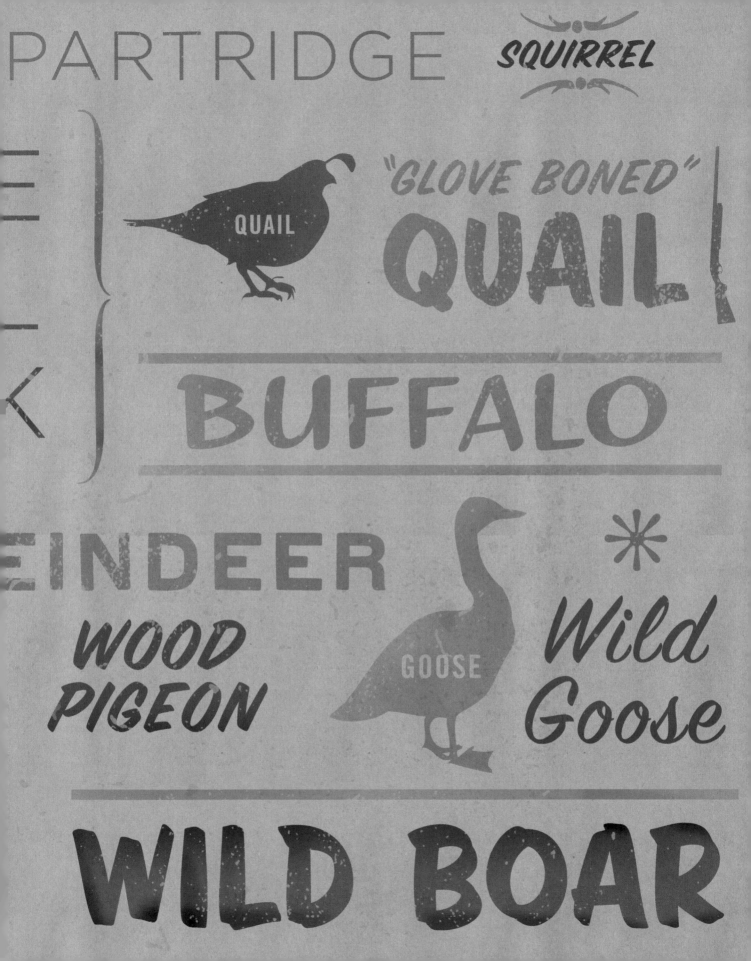

WILD BOAR

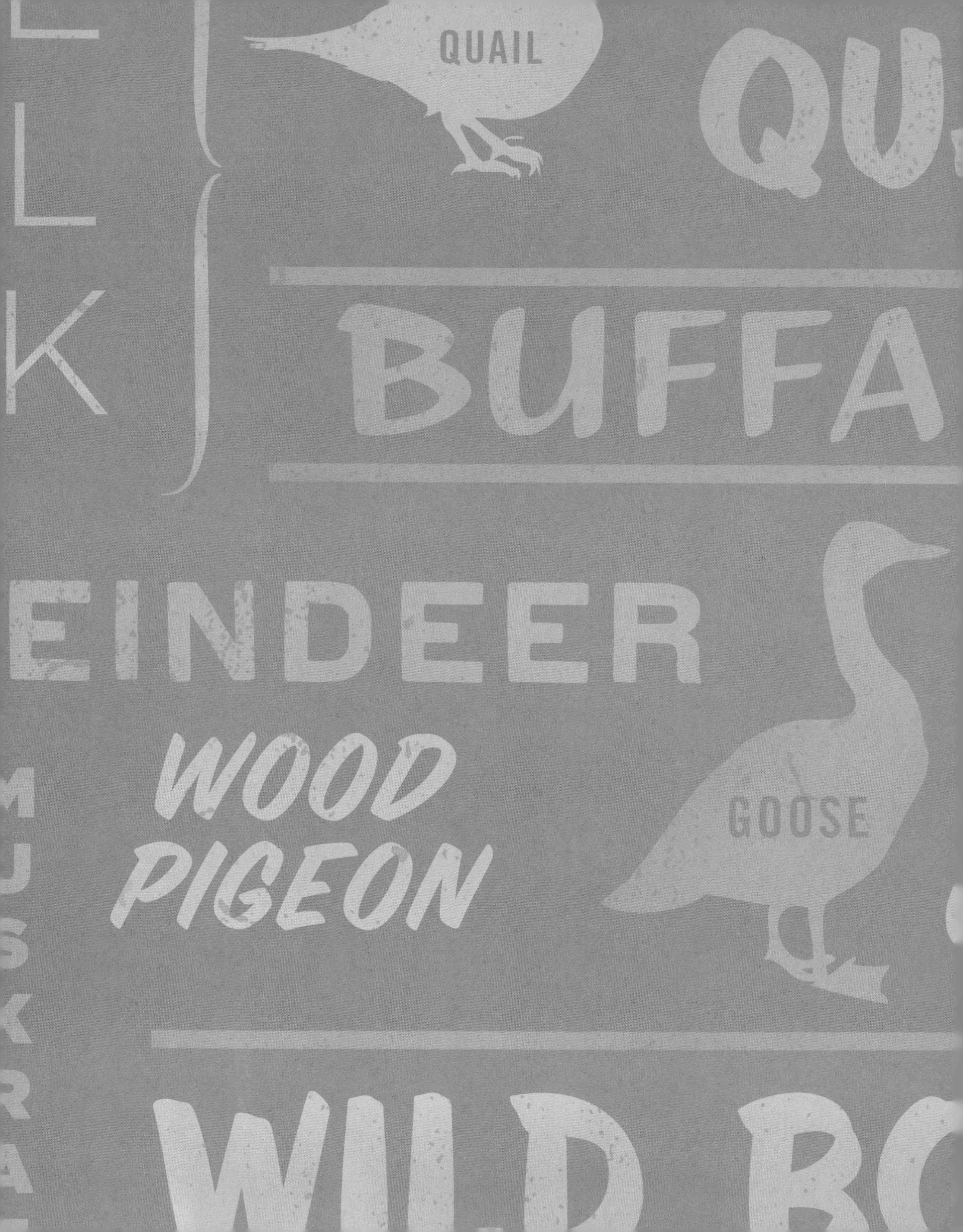
QUAIL
BUFFA
EINDEER
WOOD PIGEON
GOOSE
WILD BO
MUSKRA

CHAPTER SIX

Game Birds & Game

Wild birds are often the quarry of autumn hunters, but you don't have to be a hunter to enjoy them. Most can be special ordered from a good butcher, or you can always get them from us. Ostrich is popular in some parts of the country, where these large birds are raised on farms. Their lean meat is tasty and satisfying—some liken it more to beef than to poultry. Arguably, it is not a game bird as it is not hunted in the United States, but we included ostrich in this chapter because they are considered exotic.

There is a lot of game available, too, but only a few kinds appeal to popular tastes. The others must be special ordered, usually in large minimum amounts. For example, reindeer from Alaska and boar from New Zealand must be ordered well in advance, and so must elk, buffalo, and bear from the western states. But few people want to buy a complete animal of that size. Wild boar from Texas is readily available in some parts of the country. Smaller animals, such as squirrels and muskrats, can also be ordered. Venison is what our game meat lovers request most, so we keep it on hand.

GAME BIRDS

GROUSE

This tasty bird is sometimes erroneously called pheasant in the South and partridge in New England. In other sections of the country it may be referred to as quail. Scotch grouse is hunted in Scotland from late August to November. It is similar to the American variety but weighs less: Scotch grouse is about ½ pound, while the American type is usually ¾ to 1 pound.

PARTRIDGE

Partridge comes from the Himalayas and became a favorite with the English when they were stationed in India. The birds were then transported to other countries, including the United States, to be bred and raised. Many game-bird devotees consider the partridge to be the aristocrat of wild birds. An individual serving weighs only about 8 ounces, including the weight of the bones, so two birds are often necessary for each serving.

QUAIL

This bird weighs from 4 to 6 ounces, so two quail should constitute a single serving. Their meat is delicately flavored but pretty skimpy; the white meat is pretty much nonexistent. They are sold whole or partially boned with their wings and legs intact, and called "semi boneless" or "glove boned." It's a good idea to use poultry shears or a small knife to clip the bony first two joints on the end of the wings, although this is not crucial. Quail may require special ordering, depending on the butcher, but are never difficult to get.

SQUAB

These birds do not require the usual Conservation Department inspection that other game birds do. They may fit into the wild-bird category, but the squab you buy at a butcher shop, which are young pigeons, have been raised on farms and get the same USDA inspection as poultry. Squab, with its dark, rich meat, are luscious little morsels that usually weigh about a pound. When they weigh as much as 1¼ pounds, they are called pigeon, and when they weigh only ¾ pound, they are called doves. Hunters bag wild squab, which often are called wood pigeons.

To butterfly squab or any small bird, cut along either side of the backbone with poultry shears or a sharp chef's knife. Lay the bird, breast-side up, on a work surface and push firmly on the breastbone with the palm of your hand to crack the backbone lightly and flatten the bird.

WILD DUCK

As nearly every duck hunter knows, there are at least 24 varieties of duck available for shooting. More than half of these are diving ducks, while the rest are surface feeders. The diving types have a lobed hind toe and they sometimes feed on fish. This gives them a fishy flavor and renders them inedible. Of all the varieties of wild duck, mallard is preferred over all others, and it is outstanding. Surface feeders, mallards are raised in private preserves. This is the only type of wild duck we handle, and all our customers rave about it. Its average weight is 2 to 3 pounds.

WILD GOOSE

Just like wild turkeys, wild geese have less fat than domesticated geese. This makes them easier to cook, as there is less fat to drain off. The meat of this bird is quite lean and has an appealing, gamy flavor. A wild goose weighs from 10 to 14 pounds.

WILD TURKEY

Although wild turkeys bear a distinct resemblance to their domesticated cousins, they do not have the same amount of juicy fat. Domestic turkeys are not encouraged to exercise and they are also overfed. The wild turkey, on the other hand, gets a lot of exercise and lives on nuts, berries, and seeds—a lifestyle and diet that give the meat a gamy flavor. Few butchers carry wild turkeys, but some hunters kill them. Wild turkeys can weigh as much as 14 pounds.

OSTRICH

The meat from the world's largest bird—albeit a flightless one—is considered red meat, and many say it tastes very much like steak. It's high in protein and iron and quite low in calories, cholesterol, and fat, even when compared to chicken and turkey.

Ostrich meat is sold in some specialty shops and butcher shops but very often has to be special ordered. It's sold as fillet steaks, loin, and ground and regardless of what it is called, the meat is cut from the thigh and leg section of the bird. Cook it as you would beef: grill, broil, roast, or pan-cook it. There are also sausages made from ostrich meat. We offer a winning recipe for Ostrich Medallions with Foie Gras and Three-Onion Jam on page 250.

GAME

VENISON

The venison you buy in a butcher shop always comes from a private preserve, although the venison many Americans eat is shot by sport hunters during deer season in the fall. We prefer farmed deer for its milder flavor and appealing texture; most of it is imported from New Zealand. Farmed deer are kept in natural enclosures so that they can live and eat as if in their natural habitat, but they are protected from human predators and are monitored for illness and injury. These deer do not become domesticated, but taste milder than wild game. The males, called bucks, are heavier than the females, called does. During their first year, both bucks and does are referred to as fawns.

We buy the complete carcass of deer, which weighs from 60 to 150 pounds, and butcher it for our customers. Our customers are most interested in steaks and chops from the loin section, which tends to be more tender and mild than meat from the shoulder, rump, or round. The steaks and chops are broiled or grilled in much the same way that beef steaks and chops are. Other venison meat should be braised to render it tender. Properly cooked, venison is juicy and delicious.

WILD BOAR

Wild boar is similar to pork but has less fat. Anyone who likes pork will love wild boar for its rich, deeply satisfying flavor. Try our Braised Wild Boar with Figs on page 247. The meat is darker and the marbling is more compact looking. Because of this, it should be cooked carefully so it won't be dry. What fat it has should be trimmed because, while it's not inedible, it is not as pleasant as the fat from domestic pigs. Wild boar may need to be special ordered although it's becoming increasingly available in markets and butcher shops, particularly wild boar from Texas. Boar is cut and cooked just like pork is and small young boar are great barbecued whole.

VENISON
“quack!”
DUCK
WILD DUCK

RECIPES

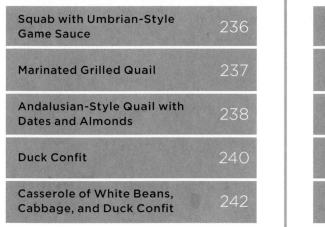

Squab with Umbrian-Style Game Sauce

If the livers or kidneys are included with any of the birds when you get them from your butcher, substitute them for a portion of the chicken livers in the recipe. This dish can also be cooked in a grill pan or on an outdoor grill for roughly the same amount of time. If you do cook the birds over a live fire, they should be cooked entirely over moderate coals or a combination of medium-hot coals and indirect heat, so as not to burn the skin.

SERVES 2 AS A MAIN COURSE; 4 AS AN APPETIZER

2/3	cup extra-virgin olive oil
5	large cloves garlic, chopped
1/2	teaspoon finely chopped fresh rosemary
1	tablespoon chopped fresh sage leaves
1	teaspoon fresh coarsely ground black pepper
2	squabs (about 1 pound each), backbone and wing tips removed; birds butterflied as shown on page 211
1/3	pound chicken livers, chopped
1	heaping tablespoon capers, rinsed
3	large anchovy fillets
2 1/2	ounces prosciutto di Parma or similar ham, finely chopped
4	juniper berries, crushed
1/8	teaspoon crushed red pepper flakes
2	cups dry white wine
	Kosher salt
2 to 3	teaspoons white wine vinegar

1. Mix 3 tablespoons of the oil, half the garlic, half the rosemary, half the sage, and the black pepper in a small bowl. Thoroughly massage the squabs all over with this mixture. Set aside for 1 to 2 hours at room temperature, covered.
2. Chop the chicken livers very finely—they will appear loose and watery, but continue chopping until they form a coarse paste. Chop and mash the capers and anchovies to a coarse paste. Reserve.
3. In a medium skillet, heat 2 tablespoons of the oil over medium-high heat. When the oil is hot, add the reserved livers, spreading them out in a thin layer, and cook until browned on one side, 1 to 2 minutes. Flip with a thin spatula and brown the other side, for 1 minute more. Separate the livers into small pieces with the spatula or a fork. Stir in the reserved caper-anchovy paste, the prosciutto, the remaining garlic, the remaining sage, the remaining rosemary, the juniper berries, and red pepper. Add the wine and bring to a simmer, scraping the skillet to loosen any browned bits. Reduce the heat and simmer very gently until the wine has reduced by at least two-thirds and the sauce is flavorful but still fluid, with a slushy texture, 15 to 20 minutes. Remove from the heat and stir in ¼ teaspoon salt, a few grindings of black pepper, 2 teaspoons of vinegar, and 3 tablespoons olive oil. Taste and adjust with more salt and vinegar if you like and set the skillet aside. Warm serving plates in a low oven.
4. Preheat one large or two small skillets big enough to accomodate the butterflied squabs over medium-high heat. Generously salt the squabs on all sides. Add enough oil to make a thick film in the skillet(s). When the oil begins to smoke, add the birds breast-side down and weight each with an aluminum foil–covered brick or skillets, adding a large can of tomatoes, etc., to increase the weight. Reduce the heat to medium and cook the squabs until deeply golden brown, 5 to 7 minutes. Turn and weight the squabs and cook for about 5 minutes more. Turn and weight the squabs once more to recrisp the breast side, 1 minute more. Squabs should be medium-rare (make a small incision in the thickest part of the breast and peek, if necessary). Remove the squab to a cutting board and let rest for about 3 minutes.
5. Reheat the sauce and cut each squab in half (cut between the breasts, directly through the breastbone); prop the halves attractively against each other on warmed serving plates. Add the juices on the cutting board to the sauce, spoon sauce around each portion, and serve.

Marinated Grilled Quail

This simply made and delicious dish is popular throughout the Middle East. If you prefer, the quail can also be pan-fried over medium-high heat in a heavy skillet following the same instructions.

SERVES 2

2	large cloves garlic, peeled and crushed
1	tablespoon finely chopped fresh thyme
1/2	teaspoon freshly ground black pepper
1	tablespoon fresh lemon juice
2	tablespoons extra-virgin olive oil
4	quail, butterflied, or 4 semi-boneless quail, wing tips removed
	Kosher salt
	Pomegranate, Pepper, and Walnut Purée (page 282; optional)
	Lemon wedges for garnish

1. Whisk together the garlic, thyme, black pepper, lemon juice, and oil in a small bowl and set the marinade aside to let the flavors develop for at least 10 minutes.
2. Lay the quail out in a medium, nonreactive baking dish and drizzle the marinade over the birds. Turn the birds to coat and, using your fingers or a brush, rub (or baste) the quail to help flavor them. Cover and set aside to marinate at room temperature for up to 2 hours or overnight in the refrigerator, basting with the marinade every so often. Bring to room temperature before proceeding.
3. Prepare a medium-hot charcoal fire. When it's ready, generously salt the quail on both sides. Grill quail, turning once and pushing gently on the birds with a spatula to make sure they make contact with the grill, until just cooked through and the juices run clear at the thigh when the skin is pricked, 3 to 4 minutes per side. Move the birds to a cooler spot on the grill if they threaten to burn. Do not overcook.
4. Serve with a few tablespoons of Pomegranate, Pepper, and Walnut Purée on the side, if you like, or with lemon wedges.

NOTE: To butterfly whole quail, cut along either side of the backbone with poultry shears or a sharp chef's knife and remove the strip of backbone (discard or reserve for stock). Lay each bird breast-side up on a work surface and push firmly on the breastbone with the palm of your hand to lightly crack the backbone and flatten the bird.

Andalusian-Style Quail with Dates and Almonds

Like much of the food of Spain's southernmost region, the flavors of North Africa are present in this dish. Here, onions and carrots are enriched with a sherry-spiked quail stock and the sweetness of dates and spices. The finished quail are arranged on top of the vegetables and scattered with toasted almonds. To make the quick quail-sherry stock, we use the chopped up backbones, necks, and wing tips of the butterflied quail as well as an additional fifth quail. As always, your butcher can do the butterflying and chopping, if you prefer. You also can pan-fry quail in a skillet instead of grilling them. For additional flavor, the quail can be marinated as on page 237.

SERVES 2 AS A MAIN COURSE; 4 AS AN APPETIZER

- 2 tablespoons olive oil or vegetable oil
- 5 quail: 4 quail with backbone removed and butterflied, wing tips and necks removed and, along with backbone, cut into 1-inch pieces; 1 quail cut into 1-inch pieces
- 1 cup medium-dry amontillado sherry
- 2 cups Chicken Stock (page 299), or canned low-sodium chicken broth
- 2 medium onions, chopped, plus ½ small onion, cut in half
- Kosher salt
- 3 ounces pitted dates (8 to 16 dates, depending on size), each cut into 5 or 6 lengthwise strips
- 4 tablespoons extra-virgin olive oil
- ⅓ cup blanched slivered almonds
- 4 large cloves garlic, finely chopped
- 2 medium carrots, peeled and chopped
- 1 teaspoon ground cumin seed
- ¼ teaspoon ground nutmeg
- ¼ teaspoon ground cinnamon
- 1 tablespoon finely chopped fresh flat-leaf parsley

1. Heat the 2 tablespoons oil in a medium saucepan over medium-high heat. When hot, add the quail pieces and cook until deeply browned on two sides, 10 to 12 minutes, regulating the heat if they threaten to burn. Drain the oil while holding back the quail and return to the heat. Add the sherry and bring to a simmer, scraping the bottom of the pan with a spatula to loosen any browned bits stuck to the bottom of the pan. Reduce the heat and gently simmer until reduced by half, about 4 minutes. Add the stock, 1 cup water, the half small onion, and the ¼ teaspoon salt and bring to a simmer. Cover the saucepan, leaving the lid ajar ½ inch or so, and simmer very gently over low heat for 45 minutes.
2. Pass the sauce through a fine-mesh strainer over a medium bowl, pressing hard on the solids to extract all their flavors. Skim the fat, if you like, and return the liquid to the saucepan (you should have about 1 cup; reduce the liquid or add a bit of additional chicken stock as necessary). (The quail-sherry stock can be made a day or two ahead, cooled, and kept in the refrigerator.)
3. Soak the dates in a small bowl of hot tap water for 5 or 10 minutes until no longer brittle or dry; drain.
4. Heat 1 tablespoon of the extra-virgin olive oil over medium-low heat. Add the almonds and cook until pale golden, stirring or tossing regularly, about 4 minutes. Sprinkle and toss with salt; transfer to a plate.
5. Heat the remaining 3 tablespoons extra-virgin oil in a 10- to 12-inch skillet over medium-high heat. Add the chopped onion, and cook, stirring occasionally, until pale golden at the edges, 6 to 8 minutes. Reduce the heat to medium-low and stir in the garlic and carrots. Cook gently, stirring regularly, until the onions are a deeper gold, very soft, and reduced in volume, 10 to 12 minutes. Stir in the cumin, nutmeg, cinnamon, and ½ teaspoon salt. Remove from the heat and reserve until ready to serve.
6. Prepare a medium-hot charcoal fire; when it's ready, generously salt the quail on both sides. Grill quail, turning once and pushing gently on the birds with a spatula to make sure they make contact with the grill, until just cooked through and the juices run clear at the thigh when the skin is pricked, 3 to 4 minutes per side. Move the birds to a cooler spot on the grill if they threaten to burn. Do not overcook. (Quail can also be pan-fried in olive oil in a skillet over medium-high heat following the same cooking instructions.)
7. While the quail are cooking, add the reserved quail-sherry stock and the dates to the skillet of vegetables and warm over medium heat. As soon as it simmers (you don't want it evaporating too much), divide the sauce and vegetables among heated serving plates. Top the vegetables with quail and scatter the reserved almonds over all. Sprinkle with the parsley and serve.

Duck Confit

As unpromising as well-salted duck cooked and preserved in its own fat may sound to some, the French technique of making confit and other dishes like it made elsewhere in the world are some of the most venerable and delectable preparations of the modern kitchen. A whole bone-in leg of duck confit is classically served alongside a salad of bitter greens such as frisee, endive, escarole, and arugula tossed with piquant vinaigrette, but the preserved duck meat can also be shredded and added sparingly to pasta sauces and fillings, or to a cassoulet of beans and other meats (see recipe page 242). Duck confit can be enjoyed the day it is made, although it may be improved somewhat during its stay in fat for up to a month or more.

SERVES 6

- 1/4 cup kosher salt
- 2 teaspoons freshly ground black pepper
- 1/8 teaspoon ground cloves
- 1/4 teaspoon ground nutmeg
- 1/4 teaspoon ground allspice
- 1/4 teaspoon freshly grated cinnamon
- 4 bay leaves, crumbled
- 1 tablespoon finely chopped fresh thyme leaves
- 6 Pekin (or Long Island) duck legs, about 3 pounds, trimmed of excess fat (see Note)
- 2 heads garlic (about 24 cloves), cloves crushed and peeled
- 2 1/2 to 3 pounds rendered duck fat (see Note)

1. Thoroughly combine the salt, pepper, cloves, nutmeg, allspice, cinnamon, bay leaves, and thyme in a large, wide mixing bowl. Add the duck legs and toss to coat, pressing and rubbing all the salt and spices onto every surface of the legs, so all the mixture adheres to the duck.
2. Spread half of the crushed garlic across the surface of a glass or ceramic baking dish just large enough to hold the duck and arrange the legs in the dish in a single layer. Evenly distribute the remaining garlic (and any remaining bits of spice mixture) over the duck legs. Cover tightly with a double layer of plastic wrap, pressing the first layer directly on top of the duck. Refrigerate for 18 to 36 hours.
3. Bring the duck to room temperature. Arrange a rack in the lower middle portion of the oven and preheat the oven to 225°F.
4. Begin melting the duck fat in a 5- to 7-quart heavy casserole or ovenproof pot over medium-low heat. Brush the garlic and bay leaves off the duck; just when the fat is almost liquefied, but not yet very hot, slip the legs, skin-side up, into the casserole so they are completely submerged, adding a bit more fat if needed to cover. When the fat just begins to send up tiny bubbles, 20 to 30 minutes (the temperature of the fat when it begins to bubble should register 170°F on a deep-fat thermometer), cover the casserole and place in the oven. Cook for 2½ to 3 hours, or until a skewer slides very easily when inserted into the thickest part of the thigh. Check the casserole after 45 minutes in the oven to ensure that the fat is issuing just a few tiny bubbles and the temperature remains around 190°F to 200°F throughout the cooking. Do not allow it to boil; adjust the oven temperature as needed.
5. Carefully remove the duck legs (grasping the ends of the legs with kitchen tongs works well) and transfer to a glass, ceramic, or earthenware storage container or dish deep enough to accommodate the duck and sufficient fat to submerge them. Pass the fat through a fine-mesh strainer or cheesecloth into a large bowl, leaving behind any meat juices in the casserole. These juices can encourage spoilage; reserve them to flavor other dishes. Pour strained fat over the duck to cover by about 1 inch. Let cool to room temperature and store in the refrigerator for up to a month or so (cool and store any remaining fat in the refrigerator for up to about 6 months).
6. When ready to serve, place the container with the duck in a simmering water bath set over low heat until the fat has melted. Remove the desired number of duck legs by carefully grasping the end of each leg with tongs and remove to a plate. Rechill melted fat and duck legs if not cooking all at the same time.

7. To prepare whole, bone-in duck legs, heat 2 to 4 tablespoons of the melted duck fat over medium-low heat in a skillet large enough to comfortably hold the duck in a single layer. Cook the duck gently, skin-side down, until skin is crisp and deep golden brown, and the duck is heated through, 10 to 20 minutes on the skin side and then 2 or 3 minutes on the second side (again, a skewer should slide very easily through the thigh when warmed through). Drain briefly and serve.

NOTE: Pekin (or Long Island) duck legs are widely available, but if you can't find them, the slightly larger Muscovy duck legs, or considerably larger moulard legs, can also be used. For the first, assuming the weight of 6 whole Muscovy duck legs will be closer to 4 pounds, increase the quantity of salt by 1 scant tablespoon. For the second, assuming the weight of 6 whole moulard duck legs will be closer to 5 pounds, increase the salt by 1½ tablespoons.

Duck fat is available at gourmet food shops and by mail from D'Artagnan (www.dartagnan.com) in 7-ounce containers; you'll need five or six of these. Use leftover fat for making pan-fried potatoes and omelets.

Casserole of White Beans, Cabbage, and Duck Confit

A great use of our Duck Confit and reason enough to make a double batch. Serve with a tart salad of crisp, bitter greens or endive.

SERVES 6

1	pound dried white beans, such as cannellini, picked over and soaked overnight in water to cover; rinsed and drained
2	whole cloves
3	yellow onions, 1 peeled and halved with root end intact, 2 finely chopped
5	large cloves garlic
1	small carrot, peeled and halved
1	rib celery, halved
1	large sprig fresh thyme, plus 1 teaspoon finely chopped fresh thyme
1	bay leaf
3	ounces fatty salt pork, cut into 3 equal pieces
	Kosher salt
½	small head savoy cabbage, cored and cut into ¾-inch squares (about 4 cups)
7	tablespoons duck fat (from duck legs confit, see below) or extra-virgin olive oil
4	duck legs confit (page 240), or enough to yield 2 cups coarsely shredded meat (see Note)
1	cup dry white wine
One	15-ounce can peeled whole tomatoes, drained and chopped
4	tablespoons finely chopped fresh flat-leaf parsley
	Freshly ground black pepper
⅔	cup plain dried bread crumbs, preferably homemade (see Note on page 131)

1. Put the beans and 7½ cups water into an 8- to 10-quart pot. Stick 1 clove into each onion half and add to the pot. Add the garlic, carrot, celery, thyme sprig, bay leaf, and salt pork. Bring just to a boil over high heat. Reduce the heat and cook at a bare simmer, stirring occasionally, or until the beans are just tender but still whole, about 45 minutes. (Cooking time will vary depending on the type and age of the beans and soaking time.)

2. When the beans are nearly done, stir in 1½ to 2 tablespoons of salt, making sure it is well mixed. When the beans are just tender, remove from the heat and let them rest for at least 15 minutes.

3. Drain the beans in a colander set over a large bowl and reserve both the beans and the cooking liquid. Pick out the salt pork, bay leaf, thyme sprig, and the vegetables from the beans and discard.

4. While the beans are cooking, bring a large pot of well-salted water to a boil; add the cabbage and cook until crisp-tender, about 3 minutes. Drain in a colander and cool under running water. Drain again and reserve in a mixing bowl.

5. Heat 4 tablespoons of the duck fat over medium-low heat in a skillet large enough to hold all the duck legs in a single layer. When hot, add the duck skin-side down and cook gently until the skin is crisp and deep golden brown and the duck is heated through, 10 to 20 minutes (don't rush this), regulating the heat if the duck threatens to burn. Transfer the duck to a plate. Remove 1 tablespoon duck fat from the skillet and use it to grease a 9-by-12-inch earthenware or glass baking dish and set aside. Pour off all but 2 tablespoons of duck fat in the skillet.

6. Add the chopped onions to the skillet and cook gently until pale golden at the edges, stirring occasionally, about 10 minutes. Increase the heat to medium-high and add the wine; simmer for 2 minutes, scraping the bottom of the skillet to loosen any browned bits. Add the tomatoes, chopped thyme, 2 tablespoons of the parsley, 3 cups of the reserved bean cooking liquid, and a few generous grindings of pepper (if you have less than 3 cups of bean liquid, add water or chicken broth as needed). Bring just to a simmer.

7. Meanwhile, position a rack in the middle of the oven and preheat the oven to 350°F.

8. Remove the crisp skin from the duck legs and chop into small bits; spread out on a small, paper towel–lined plate and reserve. Coarsely shred the duck meat from the bones into bite-size pieces and combine with the reserved cabbage, discarding the

bones. Spread half of the beans in the greased baking dish and distribute the duck-cabbage mixture on top of the beans. Top with the remaining beans.

9. When the bean liquid comes to a simmer, carefully pour it over the duck and beans, spreading the onion and tomatoes evenly across the top. Sprinkle the bread crumbs over the entire surface and drizzle with the remaining 3 tablespoons duck fat (heat the fat briefly in the microwave or a small skillet if not fluid).

10. Bake for 30 minutes. Reduce the oven temperature to 325°F and continue baking until the thickened liquid has evaporated about three-fourths of the way to the bottom of the baking dish, about 1½ hours longer. Adjust the oven temperature as needed to maintain a bare simmer. In spite of the level of evaporation in the baking dish, it will often appear that the liquid is still bubbling at the surface of the beans, so if you're unsure just how much liquid remains, peek down into the baking dish toward the end of cooking.

11. Let the casserole rest for 15 minutes, and if the bread crumbs are not crisp and browned, preheat the broiler and just before serving, slip the casserole briefly beneath it to brown and crisp the top (and if reserved bits of duck skin have gone limp, recrisp them in a small skillet with a bit of duck fat). Serve the casserole, spooning any liquid at the bottom of the baking dish around each portion and garnishing each with reserved bits of crisp duck skin and the remaining parsley.

NOTE: If your confit is made with the smaller Pekin (or Long Island) duck legs, you'll probably need 4 or 5 legs to yield the 2 cups shredded duck called for in the recipe. If you purchase muscovy duck legs confit, you'll need just 4; with the larger moulard legs, 3½ or so should be enough.

Spanish Holiday Duck with Pears

At the center of this special dish are two flavorful slow-roasted ducks that are served alongside a light but savory stuffing laced with pancetta, ground pine nuts, and herbs—it's sure to appeal to any lover of American-style stuffing. Alongside the duck and stuffing are pears poached in white wine and rich oloroso sherry. The pears can be cored and quartered or left whole. The trio is served with two sauces: one made from the duck giblets, and the other from the pear poaching liquid. As outlined in the recipe, each of the sauce components can be made well ahead of time.

SERVES 6

2	whole Pekin ducks, about 5 pounds each, liver, neck, and giblets reserved
	Kosher salt
2	tablespoons olive oil
1/4	cup dry oloroso sherry
4	cups Chicken Stock (page 299), or canned low-sodium chicken broth
1	sprig fresh thyme
1/2	bay leaf
2	teaspoons cornstarch

STUFFING

2	tablespoons olive oil
3/4	pound thinly sliced pancetta, or similar unsmoked bacon, finely chopped
2	medium onions, finely chopped
4	ribs celery, finely chopped
6	large cloves garlic, finely chopped
2	apples, peeled and cut into 1/4-inch pieces
1 1/2	cups pine nuts, ground into coarse bits using a mortar and pestle or pulsed in a food processor
1/3	cup chopped fresh flat-leaf parsley
8	cups very coarse, fresh bread crumbs (see Note, page 131)
	Kosher salt
	Fresh coarsely ground black pepper

CONTINUED>

1. Preheat the oven to 250°F. Trim the fatty deposits and some, but not all, of the excess skin at either end of the ducks' cavities. Using a sharply pronged fork (a cocktail fork or carving fork works well), prick the duck's skin down through the layer of fat beneath 30 or 40 times all over each duck, taking care not to pierce the flesh beneath the fatty layer (if it's difficult to pierce the skin at a 90-degree angle, it may be easier to work the fork in at 45 degrees or less). Salt the ducks generously inside and out.

2. Put the ducks, breast-side up and side by side, but not touching, on a roasting rack set in a roasting pan. Roast for 1½ hours. Transfer the roasting pan to the stovetop and prick the exposed top and sides of the ducks all over with the sharp fork about 30 times, again taking care not to puncture the flesh beneath (you'll see bloody juices if you've hit the flesh) and focusing especially on the areas where the fat looks thickest. Turn the birds breast-side down and roast for another 1½ hours. Remove the roasting pan and prick the bottom and sides of the birds in the same way as before. Turn ducks breast-side up and roast 1 hour, for a total of 4 hours. Increase the heat to 400°F and roast until deep golden brown and crisp, 45 minutes to 1 hour more, 4¾ to 5 hours total.

3. While the duck roasts, cut the reserved giblets into 10 or 12 pieces (except the liver—reserve it for the stuffing); chop the necks into 8 or 10 pieces. Heat the oil in a medium saucepan over medium-high heat. When the oil is hot, add the giblet and neck pieces and cook until golden brown on at least two sides, about 10 minutes. Pour off the fat while holding the pieces back with a slotted spoon and return to the heat. Add the sherry and simmer until reduced to 1 tablespoon. Add the chicken stock, 2 cups of water, the thyme sprig, and the bay leaf. Bring to a boil, scraping up any browned bits stuck to the bottom of the pan. Reduce the heat to maintain a very gentle simmer and cook until reduced to 1½ cups, about 1½ hours. Pass the sauce through a fine-mesh strainer set over a bowl, pressing hard on the solids to extract all their flavors. The sauce can be made up to this point up to 2 days ahead and stored in the refrigerator. Return the stock to the saucepan and set over medium-low heat. Dissolve the cornstarch in a ladleful of the stock and whisk into the saucepan. Simmer until just slightly thickened, 2 to 3 minutes. Season to taste with salt; remove from the heat and set aside.

4. To make the stuffing: Put the olive oil and pancetta in a deep 12- to 14-inch skillet or shallow pot and set over medium heat. Cook until some of the fat has rendered and the pancetta begins to brown, about 5 minutes, stirring occasionally. Add

1½	teaspoons finely chopped fresh thyme
¼	cup fresh lemon juice
3	large eggs, beaten

POACHED PEARS

2	cups dry white wine
2	cups dry oloroso sherry
1	cup sugar
One	2-inch stick cinnamon
1	sprig fresh thyme
6	ripe Comice or Bartlett pears, peeled and rubbed with half a lemon

the onions, celery, and garlic and cook until translucent, about 7 minutes, stirring regularly. Make a little room in the skillet and add the reserved duck livers and cook, turning once, until just slightly pink inside. Remove the skillet from the heat; transfer the chopped livers to a cutting board and chop them finely. Add the liver to the skillet along with the apples, ground pine nuts, parsley, bread crumbs, 2 teaspoons salt, 8 to 10 generous grindings of black pepper, and the chopped thyme. Return the skillet to medium heat. Toss and stir for a couple minutes to mix all the ingredients thoroughly. Remove from the heat and let cool in the skillet. Toss the mixture with the lemon juice and the eggs. Spread the stuffing out in a glass or ceramic baking dish just large enough to contain it. Cover tightly with aluminum foil. (The stuffing can be made up to a day ahead and stored in the refrigerator.) Cook with the duck for the last hour of its cooking at 250°F; remove from the oven and set aside. Reheat the stuffing during the last 10 to 15 minutes the duck is in the oven at 450°F, taking care not to let it burn.

5. To make the poached pears: Add the wine, sherry, sugar, cinnamon, and thyme in a pot just large enough to contain the pears (about 4-quart capacity). Add the pears to the pot and, if necessary, add enough water to cover the pears by ½ inch. Bring to a simmer over medium heat. Reduce the heat to maintain a bare simmer until the pears are tender when tested with a knife tip or a skewer, 30 to 50 minutes depending on the type and ripeness of the pears (if the liquid drops much below the pears, add small amounts of water or wine or partially cover the pot). Using a slotted spoon, carefully transfer the pears to a plate. Return poaching liquid to a brisk simmer and cook until reduced to a thin but flavorful syrup, for 20 to 40 minutes. (The poached pears can be made up to two days ahead and stored in the refrigerator. Reheat the pears and syrup together in a larger, covered pot.)

6. Remove the finished duck from the oven and proceed in one of the following ways. For presentation on a platter: Spread the stuffing out on the center of a large, heated platter and rest the ducks on top. Surround with the pears. Serve the giblet sauce and reduced pear poaching liquid in warmed sauceboats. For serving on individual plates: The duck can be cut, pulled, and/or hacked into serving-size portions; place a large spoonful of stuffing on heated plates and top with a portion of duck. Place a poached pear alongside the duck and spoon a generous portion of giblet sauce on each plate. Drizzle a tablespoon or two of the reduced poaching liquid over the pear and serve the remaining sauces on the side. In either case, make sure every diner gets a portion of crisp duck skin.

Braised Wild Boar with Figs

Here is a Rioja wine country classic that shows off the rich flavor of wild boar. Its earthy succulence is enhanced by a handful of truly complementary ingredients: rich red wine, nutty cured ham, tangy sherry, and sweet figs.

SERVES 4

1/4	cup extra-virgin olive oil
2 1/2	pounds well-trimmed wild boar shoulder or pork shoulder, cut into 2- to 3-inch roughly rectangular chunks
	Kosher salt
	All-purpose flour for dredging
1	medium onion, chopped
2	medium carrots, peeled and chopped
6	large cloves garlic, peeled and sliced
3	ounces thinly sliced Serrano or similar cured ham with a large rim of fat, finely chopped
1	tablespoon tomato paste
2	cups dry red wine
1/4	cup dry oloroso sherry (or substitute amontillado sherry)
2	cups Pork Stock (page 301), Chicken Stock (page 299), or canned low-sodium chicken broth
1	large sprig fresh thyme
1	bay leaf
2	whole cloves
	Freshly ground black pepper
12	large dried figs, stemmed and quartered
2	tablespoons finely chopped fresh flat-leaf parsley for garnish

1. Heat the oil in a 10-to 12-quart pot over medium-high heat. Generously salt the boar on all sides and dredge in the flour, knocking off any excess. When the oil is hot, add the boar and cook until deep golden brown on two sides, 5 to 6 minutes per side, reducing the heat if the meat threatens to burn and adding a bit more oil if needed. Transfer the boar to a plate and scrape up and discard any blackened bits in the pot.
2. Add the onion, carrots, garlic, and ham and cook until pale gold at the edges, 8 to 10 minutes, stirring occasionally. Add the tomato paste and cook for 1 minute, stirring. Add the wine and sherry, whisking to dissolve the tomato paste and then scraping up any browned bits stuck to the bottom of the pot. Reduce the heat and simmer for 5 minutes. Stir in the stock, 1 cup water, the thyme, bay leaf, cloves, a few generous grindings of black pepper, and 2 teaspoons salt.
3. Add the boar and any juices on the plate and bring just to a simmer. Cover pot and reduce the heat to maintain the barest possible simmer; cook until very tender, about 4 hours. Stir in the figs and gently simmer, uncovered, until the cooking liquid has thickened slightly and concentrated in flavor, about 30 minutes. Add salt to taste and let sit off the heat for 5 minutes or so.
4. Serve the boar and its sauce on plates or in wide, shallow bowls, garnished with parsley.

Rack of Venison with Warm Shallot-Apple Relish and Wild Mushrooms

This recipe makes more of the shallot-apple relish than you'll need, but the relish is great with other game, poultry, foie gras, or even tucked into a grilled cheese sandwich. You can use any dried wild mushroom you like, but black trumpets and porcini are our favorites. Of course, you can use fresh wild or cultivated mushrooms, too. If you decide to go with fresh mushrooms, figure about a half-pound total and chop or slice any large mushrooms. Be sure to increase the butter, chopped shallot, and salt with which they're sautéed by about half. Serve the venison with roasted acorn or butternut squash.

SERVES 4

3/4	cup sugar
4	tablespoons extra-virgin olive oil
2	cups sliced shallots, plus 2 tablespoons finely chopped shallots
3	firm tart apples, such as Granny Smith, peeled, cored, and cut into about 1/2-inch pieces
2	tablespoons whole mustard seeds
2	teaspoons ground mustard
1/2	teaspoon ground ginger
1/4	teaspoon crushed red pepper flakes
	Kosher salt
3	tablespoons white wine vinegar
1 1/2	ounces dried black trumpet or porcini mushrooms, soaked in 1 1/2 cups warm tap water until softened
2	tablespoons unsalted butter
One	8-rib rack of venison loin, about 2 1/2 pounds, frenched and trimmed of fat and silverskin, at room temperature
	Freshly ground black pepper
3	tablespoons vegetable oil or olive oil
1/2	cup Mustard Seed Vinaigrette (page 279), plus more to taste

1. Put the sugar and 2 cups water in a small saucepan and bring to a simmer over high heat, stirring to dissolve. Remove from the heat, cover, and set aside. Heat the oil in a 10- to 12-inch skillet over medium-low heat. Add the sliced shallots and cook until translucent, about 5 minutes, stirring occasionally. Stir in the apples and cook for 3 minutes. Add the reserved sugar syrup and stir in the mustard seeds, ground mustard, ginger, crushed red pepper, ½ teaspoon salt, and the vinegar. Simmer the mixture, stirring regularly, until a thick, slightly fluid syrup surrounds the apples, 10 to 15 minutes (note that the syrup will thicken as it cools). The shallot-apple relish can be made up to a week ahead and stored, covered, in the refrigerator. You'll need about 2 cups to finish the dish.

2. Remove the mushrooms from their soaking liquid; squeeze most of the liquid from them and set aside. Strain the soaking liquid through a fine-mesh strainer or paper towel to catch any grit. In an 8- to 10-inch skillet, melt the butter over medium-low heat. Stir in the chopped shallots and cook for 2 minutes. Add the mushrooms and increase the heat to medium; cook for 4 minutes, stirring regularly. Add the strained mushroom soaking liquid and ½ teaspoon salt. Simmer briskly until just 1 to 2 tablespoons of liquid remain, 6 to 8 minutes. The mushrooms can be made up to 6 hours ahead and kept at room temperature.

3. Preheat the oven to 400°F and arrange an oven rack in the middle of oven. If the venison is damp, blot dry and generously salt and lightly pepper all over. Heat the vegetable oil over medium-high heat in an ovenproof skillet large enough to hold the venison. When the oil is very hot, add the venison and cook, turning with tongs, until deeply browned around its circumference, 8 to 10 minutes. Transfer the skillet to the oven and roast bone-side down for 15 minutes. Turn the venison over and roast until an instant-read thermometer inserted in the middle of the venison registers 125°F for medium-rare, about 5 minutes more, 20 minutes total. Transfer the venison to a cutting board. Cover loosely with aluminum foil and let rest for 5 to 10 minutes.

4. Reheat the mushrooms and the shallot-apple relish separately, covered, over medium-low heat, stirring occasionally. Spoon ⅓ to ½ cup relish in a mound just off center of serving plates. Cut the venison between the bones into 8 chops. Prop 1 or 2 chops attractively against the relish on each plate. Whisk the vinaigrette and drizzle about 2 tablespoons of it around and over the venison. Scatter the mushrooms around each plate and serve.

Ostrich Medallions with Foie Gras and Three-Onion Jam

Reminiscent of both venison and beef, the flavor of ostrich has its own distinctive and mild gaminess. Although ostrich is typically very lean, this is a decadent dish in which each steak is topped with a slice of seared foie gras and accompanied by slightly bitter endive, a mustard-seed vinaigrette, and a dollop of a sweet-tart onion jam. This recipe is relatively easy to complete, but there is a lot going on in the last four steps, especially if you've never seared slices of foie gras before. Read through the recipe a few times so that you're comfortable with the mechanics of these steps.

SERVES 4

3/4	cup sugar
2	cups water
1	cup white wine vinegar
1/2	cup good-quality balsamic vinegar
	Kosher salt
1/4	teaspoon crushed red pepper flakes
1 1/2	medium onions, ends removed, halved lengthwise and cut into 1/4-inch-thick slices
1	cup sliced shallots
2	large leeks, white and pale green parts only, halved lengthwise, rinsed and cut crosswise into 1/4-inch-thick slices
6	large cloves garlic, thickly sliced
1	firm tart apple, such as Granny Smith, peeled, cored, and chopped into about 1/8-inch pieces
5	tablespoons extra-virgin olive oil
4	medium Belgian endives, quartered lengthwise
Four	4- to 5-ounce 3/4-inch-thick slices of fresh duck or goose foie gras (see page 269 about handling foie gras), kept covered in the refrigerator
	Fresh coarsely ground black pepper

1. Combine the sugar, water, vinegars, ¼ teaspoon salt, and the crushed red pepper in a saucepan and bring to a simmer, stirring to dissolve the sugar. Cover and keep warm.

2. Combine the onions, shallots, leeks, garlic, and apple in a bowl. Heat 3 tablespoons of the olive oil in a 10- to 12-inch skillet over medium-high heat until just smoking. Add the onion mixture to the skillet and cook until golden brown at the edges, 6 to 8 minutes, stirring regularly. Reduce the heat to medium-low and cook, stirring regularly, until the onions are reduced in volume but still a bit crisp to the bite, about 5 minutes more.

3. Stir the warm sugar-vinegar syrup into the onions and bring to a simmer. Adjust the heat to maintain a gentle simmer and cook until just a small amount of syrupy liquid remains and the mixture resembles a slightly runny jam, 45 minutes to 1 hour, stirring occasionally (note that the jam will thicken as it cools). Do not rush this step. Remove from the heat and let cool. Measure ⅔ cup for use in the recipe and store the remainder in the refrigerator for another use (it's great with cheese and crackers). The Three-Onion Jam can be made up to a week ahead.

4. Heat the remaining 2 tablespoons olive oil in a 10- to 12-inch skillet over medium-high heat. When the oil is hot, add the endive quarters cut-side down and reduce the heat to medium-low. Cook until partially golden brown, 3 to 4 minutes. Sprinkle lightly with salt; turn and cook the second cut side until partially golden brown, pressing lightly on the endive to spread the leaves in a slightly fanned pattern. The endive should be crisp-tender; let cool in the skillet and transfer to a paper towel–lined plate until ready to serve.

5. When ready to finish the dish, preheat the oven to 200°F. Remove the foie gras from the refrigerator and salt and pepper the slices on both sides. Warm the reserved onion jam over low heat in a covered saucepan, stirring occasionally to prevent scorching. Place 4 endive quarters on each serving plate (if you like, cluster the stem ends in the center and partially spread the leaves in a fan pattern; that way, when topped with the ostrich, the pattern will be visible). Put plates in the oven to warm. Salt and pepper the ostrich steaks and reserve.

6. Heat the vegetable oil in a 10- to 12-inch skillet over medium-high heat until just smoking. Add the ostrich steaks and cook until browned on both sides and cooked to medium-rare, about 3 minutes per side. Transfer the steaks to a plate to hold them and cover loosely with foil.

Four	6-ounce ostrich fan steaks cut 3/4 inch thick
2	tablespoons vegetable oil
1/4 to 1/2	cup Mustard Seed Vinaigrette (page 279)
1/3	cup cut fresh chives in 1/2-inch lengths

7. Preheat a dry 10- to 12-inch skillet over medium-high heat until just smoking. While the skillet heats, remove the warmed plates with the endive from the oven (keep them clear of the stovetop so plates don't get greasy while searing the foie gras). Whisk the vinaigrette and, for each serving plate, spoon about 1½ tablespoons over the endive. Lay the ostrich steaks on top of the endive and spoon 2 generous tablespoons of warm onion jam on each steak, along with any juices given off by the meat.

8. When the skillet just begins to smoke, add the foie gras (with the help of a spatula, if you like) and cook until seared dark golden brown on the first side, 30 to 45 seconds. Flip the slices with a spatula and cook until dark golden brown on the second side and just warmed through and custard-like within, 30 to 45 seconds more.

9. Divide the foie gras among the plates, placing the slices attractively on top of, or leaning them against, the ostrich steaks. Scatter the chives over all and serve.

BEEF LIVER

TRIPE

BRA

CALF'S TONG

Sweetbr

LAMB TONGUE

PORK LIVER

B
HE

KIDNEYS

P
KI

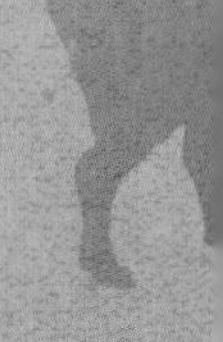

VARIETY MEATS

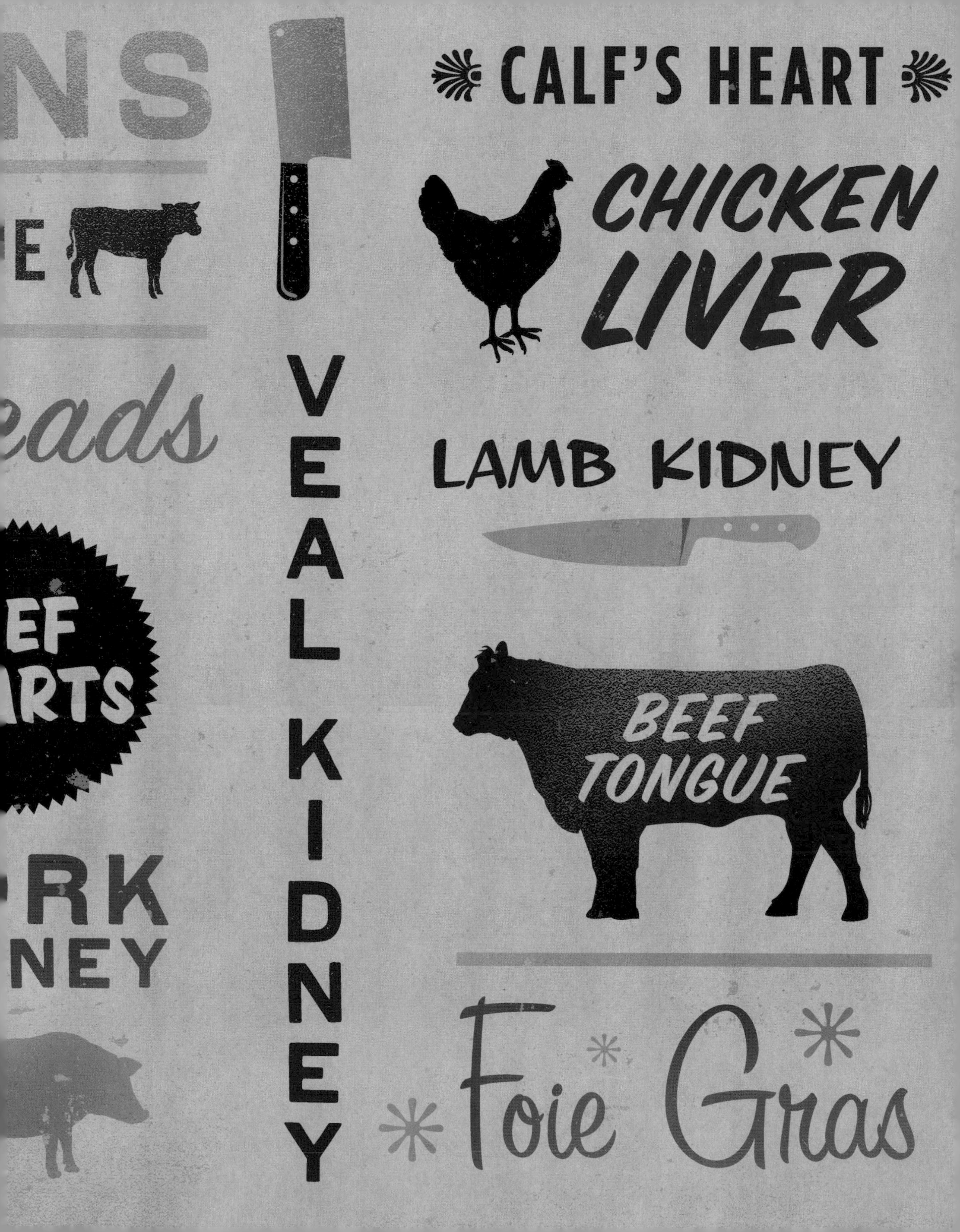
CALF'S HEART
CHICKEN LIVER
LAMB KIDNEY
VEAL KIDNEY
BEEF TONGUE
Foie Gras

NS
ads
CALF'S HEAR
CHICKE
LIVE
LAMB KIDNE
VEAL KIDN
BEEF
TONGUE
RK
EY

CHAPTER SEVEN

Variety Meats

Some people call these meats offal, a term that describes those parts of the animal that do not include bones or other skeletal matter. While it is also used to refer to the entrails only, its meaning has expanded to include just about anything that does not fit neatly into another category. We prefer the term "variety meats," which has a much more positive and—deservedly—appetizing ring to it.

Many people, Americans in particular, are aghast at the idea of eating a beef heart or tongue, but there were times when these organs were valued and nothing of the animal that gave its life for food was wasted. Today, the only variety meat commonly eaten is liver—mostly chicken or calf's liver. One of the most luxurious meats of all is foie gras, which is goose or duck liver.

We hope some readers will change their minds about variety meats. They are tasty, rich, and full of vitamins and minerals. In England, there is a vibrant movement to bring them back into the home kitchen, and even here they turn up on restaurant menus far more than they have in the past.

LIVER

Liver has great nutritive values, especially when it is not overcooked. We sell mainly calf's, beef, and chicken livers, which seem to be the most appealing to customers. Liver can be cooked in butter, oil, or, for a distinctive flavor, in bacon fat. Restaurants specializing in hearty, old-fashioned meals frequently tout liver cooked in bacon fat.

To prepare liver for cooking, peel the tissue from the surface of the meat and trim off any large, gristly tubes. Use a very sharp knife to cut up the liver. The different livers are:

CALF'S LIVER

This is the most delicate, the sweetest, and the tastiest of all animal livers. The entire liver weighs from 3 to 6 pounds. To mellow out the flavor of this and any liver, soak it in milk for about 1 hour before cooking.

BEEF LIVER

Even though this is not as tender as calf's liver, beef liver's nutritional value is much higher. It has a stronger, more liver-like taste and so is not as appealing to as many people as calf's liver is. The whole liver weighs from 10 to 16 pounds, but its price per pound is less than that for calf's liver.

CHICKEN LIVER

Chicken livers have exceptional flavor and texture. Buy them from a shop that sells them fresh and sells a lot of them. When they are fresh, they look glossy, stand solidly, and hold a firm shape. Chicken livers should have no discernible odor.

LAMB LIVER

This tiny liver weighs from ¾ to 1½ pounds. It is delightfully tender but not as flavorful as calf's or beef liver.

PORK LIVER

Pork liver sometimes is used to make pâté. It is similar in size and weight to lamb liver, but it is not a popular cut because of its strong flavor. It is used extensively in Chinese cuisine.

FOIE GRAS

We sell both duck and goose foie gras, but it needs to be special ordered. Foie gras is made from the livers of ducks and geese fattened with a special diet that renders the livers sweet and succulent. Goose foie gras is richer than duck foie gras, but both are adored by those who favor the decadent delicacy. Foie gras often is sliced and cooked quickly in a hot pan.

When you buy foie gras, look for beige, evenly colored, firm meat. Try to buy only grade A livers and cook them within a day or so of purchasing. If it's packed in Cryovac, foie gras will keep in the refrigerator for up to a week, although it should be used as soon as possible. It's important to buy foie gras from a purveyor you trust because unless it is fresh and of high quality, it is not worth the money. Always ask for "fresh" foie gras because otherwise, you may get foie gras pâté or terrine, which are cooked products.

Both goose and duck foie gras are common in France, but duck livers are far more available than goose livers in the United States. Luckily, they are largely interchangeable in recipes. Exceptional duck foie gras is produced in upstate New York and in Sonoma County, California.

The liver is formed by two lobes, one slightly smaller than the other, and usually weighs about 1½ pounds. Before use, simply rinse the foie gras and pat it dry. If it has veins and sinews, remove them with a sharp knife or tweezers. Let the liver sit at room temperature for 20 minutes to warm slightly, which makes it easier to work with. Handle the liver carefully so that it doesn't crack or tear. To slice foie gras, put it on a clean kitchen towel to prevent it from sliding on your work surface. Then, using a sharp knife that's been run under hot water to warm it, gently slice the lobe crosswise into thick slices.

KIDNEYS

The English love beef and kidney pie; in some English novels kidney stew is served for breakfast in handsome Sheffield silver pots over hot water. In the United States, broiled kidneys are a specialty in restaurants that cater to meat eaters, but otherwise are not especially popular. In addition to their unusually distinctive taste and flavor, kidneys are extremely nutritious.

VEAL KIDNEY

These are the most delicate and sweetest of all kidneys. They are delicious when split and broiled. One of our specialties is to put a veal kidney into a rolled loin or rump of veal.

BEEF KIDNEY

Much larger then veal kidneys, these are sizable pieces of meat, and have a very strong flavor and pungent odor when cooked. They are sometimes used for stews but demand a long cooking period—and stink up the kitchen.

LAMB KIDNEY

Small and delicious, lamb kidneys can be cooked in many ways. We tuck them into loin chops, and for special occasions, we insert them into a rolled leg of lamb. They can be split (butterflied) and broiled, grilled as a shish kebab, or cut up and added to a fantastic casserole with mushrooms, onions, and sherry. Lamb kidneys are sometimes included with English lamb chops.

Lamb kidneys are not as popular as they were years ago, although they are still available fresh or frozen. We only sell them fresh. The inner vein should be removed so that they don't smell and taste strong.

PORK KIDNEY

Even though these have a strong flavor, they are delicious inserted into a loin pork chop. They are about the same size as a lamb kidney.

TONGUE

Tongue is surprisingly tender, excellent for a cold buffet. We also like leftover tongue for sandwiches. You have a wide choice when you buy tongue; its size depends on the animal it comes from. You have a choice of fresh, pickled, or smoked tongue.

BEEF TONGUE

A beef tongue from a steer usually weighs from 3½ to 5 pounds (except pickled tongue, which weighs more because of the brine). We sell only first-quality tongue, which is gray to pink in color and completely blemish-free.

Fresh tongue requires slow, moist cooking. Pickled tongue must be simmered about 3 hours, and then cooked a little longer to remove the saltiness. After 3 hours of slow simmering, the tongue will be tender and the skin will be easy to peel off. (The tongue has to be peeled of the skin when still hot.) Smoked tongue, which has a rich and smoky flavor, has to be cooked slowly, too. Tongue shrinks a lot as it cooks; beef tongue serves from four to six people.

CALF'S TONGUE

Veal, or calf's, tongue weighs only ¾ to 2 pounds. It is more tender and less fatty than beef tongue and is excellent when braised or cooked in a sweet-and-sour dish. A medium-size veal tongue serves two to four people. Veal tongues are always sold fresh and are encased with a tough skin. The tongues soften with braising, which makes the skin easy to peel off.

LAMB TONGUE

A tiny delicacy, lamb tongue weighs ¾ to 1 pound. It is always sold fresh, has a light, gamy flavor, and must be braised.

PORK TONGUE

This is about the same size and weight as lamb tongue, but has a strong flavor. It, too, must be braised.

SWEETBREADS

Sweetbreads are the thymus glands and pancreas of the calf. You can also buy beef or lamb sweetbreads, but we recommend veal sweetbreads, which are tender, creamy, and rich. Thymus-gland sweetbreads have two lobes. Pancreas sweetbreads are called stomach sweetbreads or *noix*. Veal sweetbreads weigh from 1 to 1¾ pounds; beef sweetbreads are slightly heavier. Sweetbreads should be odor-free, rosy pink, covered with membrane, and look moist and fresh. It's critical to remove the membrane surrounding both lobes of the sweetbreads, which is easily accomplished after they have been parboiled. At times, the membrane will be easy to remove without boiling; in this case the butcher will be able to it for you.

Most people consider veal sweetbreads a delicacy and serve them sautéed or broiled, accompanied by a creamy sauce. Beef sweetbreads, because of their size, are a little tougher and not as tender and sweet but can be prepared the same way. Beef sweetbreads can tolerate slightly longer, slower cooking, but nearly always require parboiling to make them tender. Sweetbreads are sometimes soaked in milk before they are cooked, which mellows their taste and makes them more tender.

BRAINS

Calves' brains are the most flavorful, tender, delicate, and most commonly eaten of any brains. These are prepared in a similar fashion to sweetbreads, in that they are sautéed. They are also good poached and deep fried. When you buy them, they should be reddish, visibly bright, and clear looking. Brains are composed of two attached lobes.

HEART

Calves' and beef hearts are the most commonly eaten hearts, although very few people eat them nowadays. Calves' hearts are delectably sweet with a fine taste and texture; they weigh from 1½ to 2 pounds, which makes one just right for four people. Beef hearts are heavier than calves' hearts and more strongly flavored. Some people are drawn to their bold flavor and chewiness.

TRIPE

Tripe is the stomach lining of the animal, usually beef. Nowadays, it is usually sold "preblanched" and ready to cook. Ask the butcher to cut the tripe into small cubes for you; it's slippery and a little rubbery, which makes it tricky to slice. Try our recipe for Tripe and Red Chile Stew on page 261.

BEEF
LIVER
TRIPE
BRA
CALF'S T
Sweet
AMB TONGUE
IDNEYS
PORK L

RECIPES

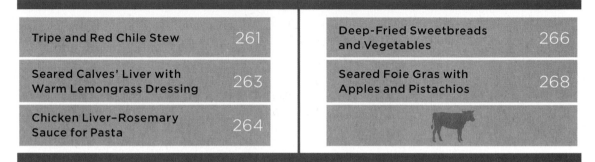

Tripe and Red Chile Stew

A silky, vibrant orange chile-spiked bowl of *menudo rojo*—courtesy of Mexico—is one of the world's most deliciously satisfying ways of enjoying tripe. This stew is great served with an icy cold beer.

SERVES 4

	About 2 ½ pounds (preblanched) honeycomb beef tripe to yield 2 pounds after trimming
1	pig's foot, split lengthwise by your butcher (about 1 pound)
1 ½	pounds beef oxtail, cut crosswise into a number of pieces
1	medium yellow onion, halved lengthwise
12	large cloves garlic, 6 peeled and lightly crushed, 6 unpeeled
	Kosher salt
1 ½	ounces dried New Mexico chiles (4 to 5 medium)
1	teaspoon dried oregano, preferably Mexican
½	teaspoon ground cumin seed
One	15-ounce can white hominy, drained

GARNISHES

1 chopped white onion, 2 or 3 chopped hot green chiles, half a bunch of chopped cilantro, 8 lime wedges, and 12 warmed, fresh corn tortillas

1. Working in the sink, place the tripe in a large bowl and cover with cold water. Rinse the tripe by swishing it around in the water for 30 seconds or so. Cover with fresh cold water and repeat the process until water runs clear, or nearly so. Drain and place the tripe on a work surface. Cut off or pull away and discard any excessively fatty deposits. If the tripe has a few areas that are bunched up and much thicker than the rest, use a small knife and butterfly these areas, cutting into their thickness and opening them up—so the tripe is of a more even thickness throughout. Put the rinsed tripe and the split pig's foot in a 10- to 12-quart pot; cover with cold water by a couple of inches and bring to a boil over high heat. Drain and rinse the meats under cold water. Cut the tripe into strips about 2 inches long by ½ inch wide.
2. Wipe out the pot and add the tripe, pig's foot, and the oxtail. Cover with 3 quarts water. Bring to a simmer over high heat, thoroughly skimming any impurities that rise to the surface. Add half the yellow onion, the crushed garlic, and 1 tablespoon salt. Reduce the heat and cook, uncovered, at the barest possible simmer (no more than a few bubbles breaking the surface) until the tripe is very tender, about 3 hours.
3. Meanwhile, preheat a skillet over medium heat and toast the chiles by pressing them lightly with a spatula against the hot skillet until fragrant, no more than 1 minute per side. Transfer to a bowl, cover with hot water, and soak until well softened, about 30 minutes. Stem and seed the chiles; chop coarsely and set aside.
4. Cut the remaining half onion lengthwise in half again. Heat a small skillet over medium heat and add the two onion quarters, cut-side down, and the remaining 6 cloves garlic in their skins. Cook, turning occasionally, until the onion is blackened on the cut sides, and the garlic is blackened and softened somewhat, 5 to 10 minutes. Transfer to a bowl, cover, and set aside.
5. After the meats have cooked for 3 hours, turn off the heat and, using kitchen tongs or a slotted spoon, remove the pig's foot and onion pieces and discard. Remove the oxtail pieces and set aside on a plate until cool enough to handle. While the meat cools, measure the volume of the tripe and the cooking liquid together. If less than 10 cups, add enough water to measure 10 cups and return the tripe and cooking liquid to the pot. Pick the meat from the oxtail and shred it back into the pot, discarding all fat and bones.

CONTINUED>

6. Peel and discard the skins of the charred garlic cloves. Put the peeled cloves in the jar of a blender along with the charred onion, softened New Mexico chiles, oregano, cumin, and 2 teaspoons salt. Add 2 cups of the cooking liquid (free of tripe) and blend on high speed until a smooth paste forms that is free of all but the tiniest bits of chile skin.

7. Stir the chile paste and hominy into the pot and bring just to a boil. Reduce the heat to maintain a moderate simmer (livelier than before) and cook until the liquid has thickened somewhat and the mixture resembles a soupy stew, about 1¼ hours, stirring occasionally. Add salt to taste and let stew rest off the heat for 5 minutes.

8. Ladle the stew into wide, shallow bowls and serve with spoons. Accompany the stew with a platter of garnishes: chopped white onion, green chiles, cilantro for scattering over the top, lime wedges to squeeze over each bowl, and warm corn tortillas to mop it all up.

Seared Calves' Liver with Warm Lemongrass Dressing

If you like the flavors of Thai cooking, here's an unusual and really fine way to enjoy calves' liver. Quickly seared pieces of liver are bathed in a piquant, aromatic dressing made with lemongrass, hot chiles, and ginger. The liver cooks quickly, so be sure to familiarize yourself with the recipe beforehand and have all your ingredients and utensils at hand. Because you have 12 individual pieces of liver to put in a hot skillet, it helps to add the pieces in a systematic order so you can remember which ones went in first, so as not to over cook them. Serve with jasmine rice on the side.

SERVES 2 AS A MAIN COURSE; 4 AS AN APPETIZER

- 4 tablespoons fresh lime juice
- 4 tablespoons Thai or Vietnamese fish sauce (*nam pla* or *nuoc nam*)
- 1/4 cup very thinly sliced scallions (white and pale green parts only)
- 1 generous tablespoon minced fresh lemongrass (working with the lower 5 inches or so, peel the toughest outer leaves; quarter lengthwise and then finely slice crosswise. Continue chopping until finely minced)
- 1/2 teaspoon fresh peeled grated ginger
- 1 to 2 thinly sliced fresh red Thai bird chiles or other very hot small chile
- 2 1/2 teaspoons sugar
- 1/8 teaspoon Asian sesame oil
- 1 tablespoon jasmine or other long-grain white rice
- 2 tablespoons finely chopped fresh mint
- 2 tablespoons peanut oil or vegetable oil
- 1 pound calves' liver, sliced just under 1/2 inch thick and cut into 12 roughly equal-size pieces

GARNISHES

Napa cabbage or iceberg lettuce (cut into thin wedges or coarsely chopped); Chinese long beans cut into 5-inch lengths or trimmed string beans (blanched until crisp-tender in boiling salted water); large sprigs of fresh mint and cilantro

1. Put the lime juice, fish sauce, scallions, lemongrass, ginger, chiles, sugar, and sesame oil in a small bowl, whisking to dissolve the sugar. Set the sauce aside.
2. Place the rice in a small skillet over medium heat and cook, shaking and swirling the pan regularly, until toasted and pale golden brown, 3 to 5 minutes. Let cool on a small plate and transfer to a mortar or spice grinder and grind to the consistency of fine cornmeal. Set aside.
3. When ready to cook, whisk the chopped mint and the reserved rice powder into the lemongrass sauce.
4. Heat the oil in a 10- to 12-inch skillet over medium-high heat. When the oil is very hot but not smoking, add the liver in a single layer and cook until nicely browned on both sides but still slightly pink in the center, no more than 1½ minutes per side. Turn off the heat and immediately pour the lemongrass sauce evenly over the liver in the skillet. Shake the pan to help the sauce heat through and to thicken it very slightly, 10 to 20 seconds.
5. Arrange the garnishes on one-half of each serving plate, leaving room for the liver and sauce.
6. Using kitchen tongs, arrange the liver on serving plates in overlapping slices. Spoon the sauce and flavorings over each portion and serve.

Chicken Liver–Rosemary Sauce for Pasta

From Piedmont, Italy, this dish will convert those who think they don't like liver. It works with any fresh pasta, though it's best with thin, flat, fresh egg noodles—such as tagliarini, tagliatelle, or pappardelle.

SERVES 2 TO 3 AS A MAIN COURSE; 4 TO 5 AS AN APPETIZER

- 3 tablespoons extra-virgin olive oil
- 1 small onion, finely chopped (about 2/3 cup)
- 1 1/4 pounds chicken livers, trimmed, blotted dry with paper towels, and cut into about 1/4-inch pieces (see Note)
- 1 large clove garlic, minced
- 1/2 cup dry white wine
- 1/2 cup Chicken Broth (page 299), or canned low-sodium chicken broth
- 1 tablespoon tomato paste dissolved in 1/2 cup hot water
- One 15-ounce can tomatoes, drained and finely chopped
- 3/4 teaspoon finely chopped fresh rosemary
- Kosher salt
- 1/2 teaspoon freshly ground black pepper
- 3/4 pound fresh thin egg pasta, such as tagliarini, tagliatelle, or pappardelle, fresh or dried
- 1 1/2 tablespoons unsalted butter
- 1 ounce Parmigiano-Reggiano or similar cheese, finely grated, plus more for serving

1. Heat the oil in a large skillet over medium-low heat and add the onion. Cook gently until softened, about 4 minutes, stirring occasionally. Slide the onion to one side of the pan so that almost all the cooking surface is visible and increase the heat to medium-high. Wait about 30 seconds for the pan to heat up (if the onion slides back to the center of the skillet, you can remove with a slotted spoon; return to the skillet with the garlic). Add the chicken livers in one layer and cook without disturbing until lightly browned on the first side, 3 to 4 minutes. Using the back of a thin spatula, scrape up the livers and flip them over; add the garlic and re-incorporate the onion. Cook for 2 to 3 minutes more, stirring occasionally.

2. Add the wine and cook until reduced to a few tablespoons, 2 to 3 minutes, scraping up any browned bits stuck to the bottom of the skillet. Stir in the broth, the tomato paste dissolved in water, the tomatoes, rosemary, 2 teaspoons salt, and the black pepper. Bring to a simmer; reduce the heat and cook at a gentle simmer, stirring occasionally, until the sauce has thickened and concentrated in flavor and just a small amount of liquid remains, about 30 minutes. Mash some of the liver pieces with the back of a spatula or wooden spoon to enrich the sauce. The sauce can be made a few hours ahead of time and reheated. Thin it with a few tablespoons of broth or water if it thickens excessively. Add salt to taste.

3. Cook the pasta in well-salted water until tender but still quite firm (al dente) and reserve ½ cup of the cooking water. Reheat the liver sauce, if necessary. Drain the pasta and return to the pot over very low heat. Add ⅓ cup of the reserved pasta cooking water, the butter, and cheese. Stir the pasta until the butter melts and the buttery sauce clings to the pasta, 30 seconds or so, adding a bit more cooking water if the pasta seems dry or too "tight." Divide the pasta among warmed serving bowls and spoon the liver sauce over each. Sprinkle with additional grated Parmesan, if you like, and serve immediately.

NOTE: Chicken livers should be trimmed of any connective tissue and fat, found mostly where each pair of livers is joined. After trimming, 1 1/4 pounds yields about the 1 pound needed for the dish.

Deep-Fried Sweetbreads and Vegetables

This recipe is a variation on Italy's *fritto misto*, or mixed fry. For people who might be hesitant to eat sweetbreads, this is a terrific way to serve them. You can prep the meat and vegetables a day ahead and store them tightly covered in the refrigerator, then bring them to room temperature before frying. A deep-fry test run with a small batch of vegetables is a good idea, even for experienced cooks. This way, you learn how many items can be put into the oil without overcrowding the pot, as well as see what "done" looks like—there's enough batter here to fry a little extra. This recipe can also be halved. Fritto misto looks great when piled on plates lined with newspaper.

SERVES 4 AS A MAIN COURSE; 6 AS AN APPETIZER

1 1/2	cups all-purpose flour, or more as needed
1 1/2	cups cake flour
1 1/2	tablespoons baking powder
	Kosher salt
3	cups seltzer water, or more as needed
1	pound veal sweetbreads
3	lemons, 1 squeezed to yield 2 tablespoons juice, 1 sliced into rounds just under 1/8 inch thick, 1 cut into wedges for garnish
2	large artichokes cleaned with some stem intact, each cut lengthwise into wedges 3/4 inch at the widest point (see Note, page 160)
	Extra-virgin or regular olive oil (or a combination) for frying (vegetable oil can also be used)
1	medium zucchini (about 1/2 pound), cut into 3/8-inch-thick rounds
2	small or 1 medium eggplant (about 1/2 pound), peeled and cut into 1/4-inch-thick rounds

1. Whisk together the two flours, baking powder, and a scant tablespoon salt in a large bowl. Make a well in the center and gradually whisk in the seltzer water, incorporating small amounts of flour from the inner edge of the well until all the flour is smoothly incorporated. The batter should be about the consistency of a thin milkshake. Thin with a bit of additional seltzer or whisk in small amounts of flour to thicken. Use immediately or cover and refrigerate for an hour or two.

2. Place the sweetbreads in a 2- to 3-quart pot and cover with 6 cups cold water. Add a tablespoon of the lemon juice and 2 teaspoons salt and bring to a simmer over medium-high heat. Reduce the heat to maintain a bare simmer and cook for 15 minutes, turning the sweetbreads halfway through the cooking. Drain the pot and plunge the sweetbreads into a bowl of ice water to cool. Peel the thickest layers of skin from the sweetbreads (not so much that the smaller nodes begin separating), and slice into 1- to 2-inch-long pieces about ¾ inch thick. Reserve.

3. Fill a 2- to 3-quart pot again with 6 cups of water and bring to a boil. Add 2 teaspoons salt, the remaining tablespoon of lemon juice, and the artichokes. Simmer until just tender, but still firm, about 10 minutes. Drain and reserve.

4. Heat 3 to 4 inches of oil in a large, heavy pot or deep-fat fryer to 375°F. Meanwhile, preheat the oven to 200°F and line two large baking sheets with a double layer of paper towel and set aside. Place serving plates or a platter in the oven to warm. Mix the vegetables, sweetbreads, and lemon slices in a large bowl and reserve.

5. When ready to fry, whisk the batter briefly and, working with ¼ to ⅙ of the vegetable-sweetbread mixture at a time, immerse them in the batter, coating the pieces well and separating any that stick together. Using a wide, flat strainer or large slotted spoon, scoop up the vegetable-sweetbread mixture (in two or three spoonfuls, if necessary) and let the excess batter run back in the bowl. Carefully transfer them to the hot oil and fry, again separating any pieces that stick together (if you work quickly, items can be dropped into the fryer a piece at a time, which insures they'll stay separated). Fry each batch until pale golden brown outside and tender (though not mushy) within, 4 to 6 minutes. Do not overload the pot; the vegetables should float freely. Transfer to a paper towel–lined pan and keep warm in the oven (try not to pile the pieces on top of one another). Repeat with the remaining vegetable-sweetbread mixture, allowing the oil to return to 375°F and scooping out stray bits of batter between batches. Add the herbs (if using) to the oil and fry until brittle, a minute or so. Drain.

- 1/2 small head cauliflower, large stems removed, broken into small florets about 1 inch across the top
- 1 red bell pepper, seeded and ribs removed, cut lengthwise into 3/4-inch-wide strips
- 1/3 pound green beans, stem ends snapped off
- 20 fresh sage leaves, or 10 small sprigs fresh rosemary, or a combination (optional)

6. Sprinkle salt over the vegetables and sweetbreads and pile attractively on warmed individual serving plates or a platter. Scatter the fried herbs over all, garnish with lemon wedges, and serve immediately.

Seared Foie Gras with Apples and Pistachios

In this dish, an easy-to-assemble "salad" of sautéed apple slices flavored with shallots, thyme, chives, and pistachio nuts complements the richness of seared foie gras, and the whole dish is surrounded by a drizzle of good balsamic vinegar. The apples are prepared first and served at room temperature so the cook's focus can remain squarely on the task of properly searing the slices of foie gras.

SERVES 4

- 1½ pounds whole fresh grade-A duck or goose foie gras (see Note)
- 2 tablespoons minced shallots
- ⅓ cup finely chopped celery (in about ¼-inch pieces)
- 4 firm tart apples, peeled and cut into wedges ¼ inch thick at the widest point
- 1 teaspoon finely chopped fresh thyme
- Kosher salt
- Freshly ground black pepper
- 1 generous tablespoon chopped/snipped fresh chives
- 3 tablespoons coarsely chopped pistachios
- ¾ ounce black truffle, very thinly sliced (optional)
- 2 to 2½ tablespoons traditional, artisan-made balsamic condiment or our Mock Balsamico (page 278)

1. Remove about 4 ounces of the irregularly shaped ends of the lobe of foie gras; chop the ends into about ½-inch pieces and set aside. Cut the remaining foie gras crosswise into ¾-inch-thick slices. Store the slices in the refrigerator, tightly covered with plastic, until ready to cook. The foie gras can be cut and chilled up to about 6 hours before cooking.

2. Put the 4 ounces of chopped foie gras in a 12- to 14-inch skillet (or divide between two smaller skillets) and set over low heat. Let the foie gras melt and render its fat, helping the process along by occasionally pressing on the pieces with a spatula. When all the fat has rendered and only sinewy bits of foie gras remain (this could take up to 15 minutes), discard the sinewy bits and add the shallots and celery and increase the heat to medium-low. Cook the vegetables, without coloring, for 2 minutes, stirring occasionally.

3. Add the apple, thyme, ½ teaspoon salt, and a few grindings of black pepper, stirring well to coat the apples. Cook, partially covered, until the apples are softened but still just slightly crisp, which, depending of the type of apple, usually takes from 4 to 8 minutes. Stir frequently to help the apples cook evenly. Stir in the chives, pistachios, and black truffle (if using). Remove the skillet from the heat and reserve.

4. Remove the foie gras from the refrigerator and salt and pepper the slices on both sides. Let sit at room temperature for 10 minutes. Select a skillet (or two) large enough to comfortably hold the slices of foie gras in a single layer and preheat it over high heat until just smoking. While the skillet heats, reheat the apple-pistachio mixture and divide it among 4 warmed dinner plates, setting the apples in a pile just off center.

5. When the skillet just begins to smoke, add the foie gras (with the help of a spatula, if you like) and cook until seared dark golden brown on the on the first side, 30 to 45 seconds. Flip the slices with a spatula and cook until dark golden brown on the second side and just warmed through and custard-like within, 30 to 45 seconds.

6. Divide the foie gras among the plates, laying the slices partially on top of the apples. Drizzle a few teaspoons of the balsamic condiment around the foie gras and serve.

NOTE: Before working with a whole lobe of foie gras, let it sit at room temperature for about 30 minutes to warm up slightly so that it is easier to work with. Put it on a clean kitchen towel to prevent it from sliding and, using a sharp knife that's been run under hot water to warm it, gently slice the lobe crosswise into thick slices, as called for in the recipe. The lobes can be presliced a few hours ahead, covered tightly in plastic and kept in the refrigerator.

If you've never seared slices of foie gras before, it's worth doing a trial run with a small piece of foie gras (preferably an end piece) cut to the same thickness as instructed in the recipe (3/4 inch). You want to sear the outsides to a deep golden brown while just warming the slices enough in the center that they turn soft and almost custard-like all the way through. If you're unsure whether the foie gras is cooked properly in Step 5, you can take a peek at the first slice you laid in the skillet—you can serve this slice to yourself. Since this all happens in less than 2 minutes in a hot skillet, it makes sense to have all your tools and serving plates close at hand and efficiently laid out. Your guests should be seated at the table, too. A last thought: You can't really overcook foie gras the way you can a steak, but you can leave it on the heat for long enough that the fat begins to render and the slices shrink. This results in slices that are a little less plump and succulent than they ought to be, but they'll still be delicious. And if you happen to undercook the foie gras slightly, it's even less of an issue; just return those pieces to the hot skillet until cooked through, usually no more than 15 seconds per side.

BÉARNAISE SAUC

ROMESCO SAUCE

Brine
FOR PORK OR POULTRY

Cilantro-Lim
CHUTNEY

QUICK TOMATO SAUCE

CHICKEN STOCK

GRE
POM

Mu
VIN

R
RE

SAUCES, CHUTNEYS, CONDIMENTS, AND STOCKS

E
OLIVE, WALNUT &
RANATE RELISH
tard Seed
AIGRETTE
ASTED
PEPPERS
MAYONNAISE
TOMATILLO
SALSA
Salsa
Mexicana
GARAM MASALA
SPICE BLEND
BEEF
STOCK

ALNUT &
RELISH
Seed
ETTE
ONNAIS
Sals
Mexic
GARAM M
SPICE B

CHAPTER EIGHT

Sauces, Chutneys, Condiments & Stocks

ARNAISE SA
Brine
FOR PORK
OR POULTRY
Cilantr
CHUT
QUICK
OMATO
SAUCE
CHICKEN
STOCK

RECIPES

Mayonnaise

MAKES ABOUT 2½ CUPS

We like store-bought mayonnaise just fine, but when you make your own it's richer and more satisfying than any you can buy. Here, we add a little very flavorful olive oil to neutral-flavored grapeseed or vegetable oil to perk it up.

3	large egg yolks at room temperature
1/8	teaspoon kosher salt
1/4	teaspoon fresh lemon juice
2	cups grapeseed oil or vegetable oil
3	tablespoons best-quality, fruity extra-virgin olive oil

1. In a large, very clean mixing bowl, whisk together the egg yolks, salt, and lemon juice. Whisking continuously, begin adding the grapeseed oil, gradually in a thin stream, until the mixture thickens considerably and a smooth emulsion forms.
2. Once emulsified, whisk in the remaining grapeseed oil in a thin stream until each is incorporated and the mixture thickens into a creamy and very thick mayonnaise. Whisk in the olive oil to incorporate. Transfer to a container and store tightly covered in the refrigerator for up to 1 week.

NOTE: The mayonnaise can also be made in a stand mixer with a whisk attachment: Begin adding the initial drops of oil with the machine on high speed, and as the mayonnaise thickens, reduce the speed of the whisk to medium or medium-slow, so as not to overbeat the mayonnaise.

Russian Dressing

MAKES ABOUT 2/3 CUP

1/2	cup mayonnaise
1/4	cup chili sauce or ketchup
1/2	teaspoon prepared horseradish
1/2	teaspoon fresh lemon juice
1/2	teaspoon Worcestershire sauce
1	tablespoon minced red onion
1	tablespoon minced dill pickle

Thoroughly combine all the ingredients in a bowl. Cover and chill before using.

Mock Balsamico

This is a tasty substitute for the exquisite, but savagely expensive, artisan-produced balsamic condiment (vinegar). Seek out the best of the cheaper kinds of balsamic vinegar, those that usually sell from $10 to $30 per bottle (depending on size and quality).

½ cup good-quality balsamic vinegar
1 tablespoon brown sugar

In a small saucepan, bring the vinegar and brown sugar to a boil over medium-high heat. Reduce the heat to medium and simmer, stirring occasionally, until the liquid is reduced to 2 to 2½ tablespoons. Transfer to a ramekin or small bowl to cool. When cool, Mock Balsamico should be the consistency of a very thin syrup. If necessary, thin with a few drops of balsamic vinegar.

Mustard Seed Vinaigrette

MAKES ABOUT 1 CUP

The Dijon mustard we use here is made from whole mustard seeds bound with just a tiny amount of smooth, "regular" Dijon mustard. The producers Maille, Bornier, Fallot, and some others make whole-grain Dijon mustards that are chock-full of seeds and perfect for this recipe; look for them. They are easy to find in most supermarkets. Avoid mustards that are smooth or that contain only a smattering of whole seeds.

2	tablespoons minced shallot
¼	teaspoon finely chopped fresh thyme
1	teaspoon kosher salt
	Fresh coarsely ground black pepper
2	tablespoons white wine vinegar
3	tablespoons whole-grain Dijon-style mustard
½	cup good-quality extra-virgin olive oil

In a small bowl, whisk together the shallot, thyme, salt, 3 to 4 generous grindings black pepper, vinegar, and mustard. Pour the oil into the bowl in a thin stream, whisking gently, to make a fairly thick vinaigrette (it is not necessary to fully emulsify the mixture). Whisk again before use.

Quick Tomato Sauce

MAKES ABOUT 4 CUPS

3	tablespoons extra-virgin olive oil
1	small onion, finely chopped
½	small carrot, peeled and finely chopped
2	large cloves garlic, minced
One	28-ounce can tomatoes in juice, coarsely chopped, ¾ cup juice reserved
½	teaspoon kosher salt
1	small sprig fresh rosemary, oregano, or marjoram, or one large sprig fresh thyme

1. Heat the oil in a medium skillet over medium heat. Add the onion, carrot, and garlic and cook, stirring occasionally, until just pale gold at the edges, 6 to 8 minutes. Stir in the tomatoes and the reserved juice, the salt, and rosemary. Bring to a simmer and reduce the heat to medium-low. Cook at a gentle simmer, stirring occasionally, until slightly thickened but still a bit fluid, 15 to 20 minutes. Add salt to taste.
2. If serving as a sauce spooned over meats, you may want to add a small amount of additional tomato packing juices or water to make the sauce a bit more fluid.

Béarnaise Sauce

MAKES ABOUT 1¾ CUPS

Béarnaise sauce has fallen into disrepute of late, primarily because it's not the healthiest of preparations. But there are times when you want to splurge, and since a little of this rich sauce goes a long way, why not? It's equally delicious served warm or at room temperature.

- ¼ cup tarragon wine vinegar
- 2 tablespoons dry white wine
- ¼ cup minced shallots
- ¼ cup finely chopped fresh tarragon
- ½ teaspoon freshly ground black pepper
- Kosher salt
- 3 large egg yolks
- ¾ pound (3 sticks) unsalted butter, well softened
- 1 tablespoon finely chopped fresh chervil or parsley

1. Combine the vinegar, wine, shallots, half the tarragon, and the black pepper in a small saucepan and bring to a simmer over medium heat. Reduce the heat to low and cook at a bare simmer until the liquid is reduced in volume to 1 tablespoon, 4 to 6 minutes. Immediately remove from the heat and pass the mixture through a fine-mesh sieve placed over a bowl, pushing firmly on the solids to release all their liquid. Stir in ½ teaspoon salt and let cool.
2. Bring an inch or two of water to a simmer in a medium saucepan and reduce the heat to very low. In a metal mixing bowl resting firmly on the saucepan with most of its bottom exposed to, but not touching, the water, vigorously whisk the egg yolks and the vinegar reduction until the mixture thickens to a creamy, pale yellow froth, increases in volume, and easily clings to the whisk, 1 to 3 minutes, making sure to whisk into the corners of the bowl. Take care that the underside of the bowl doesn't get hot enough to burn you when touched and that the barely simmering water is issuing just a wisp of steam; if the operation gets too hot, the eggs may scramble rather than thicken slowly; occasionally remove the bowl from the steam to control the heat.
3. Whisk in the softened butter, a tablespoon at a time in the beginning, until a few tablespoons have been absorbed and the sauce thickens. Continue adding butter in slightly larger amounts and whisk until the mixture is creamy and thick, taking care that the underside of the bowl remains hot but not scorching.
4. Stir in the remaining 2 tablespoons tarragon, the chervil, and salt to taste. If serving the sauce warm, keep it over hot (but not simmering) water, whisking occasionally and taking care that the bowl doesn't get too hot. If serving at room temperature, remove the bowl from the water bath and whisk gently until warm to the touch. Transfer to a sauceboat and serve.

NOTE: This recipe relies on whisking and emulsifying an egg-and-butter mixture set over simmering water (also called a water bath or *bain marie*). Béarnaise will be easier to make with a little preparation before you begin. First, you need a medium-to-small mixing bowl that will rest firmly on top of a saucepan of simmering water so that much of the belly of the bowl will be exposed to the water beneath while remaining above the level of the water itself. You can use a double boiler if you have one.

Second, since youw need a saucepan to reduce the vinegar mixture as well as a bowl into which you strain the reduction in Step 1, and, as you also need a saucepan and a bowl to make a water bath in Step 2, it makes sense that the same saucepan and bowl is used in both steps. We use a fairly wide 3-quart saucepan and an 8-inch-diameter mixing bowl for both steps. A little equipment experimentation beforehand will make the cooking go more smoothly.

Pomegranate, Pepper, and Walnut Purée

MAKES ABOUT 1½ CUPS

This boldly flavored purée—called *muhammara* in Syria—is delicious alongside all kinds of poultry, meats, and fish, especially when grilled. The purée can be used immediately, but its flavor improves if stored for a day or so.

2	red bell peppers
¾	cup shelled walnuts
¼	cup dried, fine bread crumbs, plus more as needed
1	tablespoon Aleppo pepper (see Note), or substitute 1 tablespoon sweet paprika and ¼ teaspoon cayenne pepper
2	teaspoons ground cumin seed
2	teaspoons ground coriander seed
½	teaspoon ground allspice
1	teaspoon kosher salt
1	tablespoon light or dark brown sugar
½	cup pomegranate molasses (see Note)
1	tablespoon tomato paste dissolved in 3 tablespoons hot water
2	teaspoons fresh lemon juice
2	tablespoons extra-virgin olive oil
⅓	cup pine nuts

1. Prepare a medium-hot charcoal fire or place each pepper on the burner of a gas range over a medium-high flame. Roast the peppers until blackened and blistered all over, 5 to 10 minutes, turning every few minutes to expose all surfaces to the flames (alternatively, preheat a broiler and put the peppers about 4 inches from the heat and handle as above). Enclose the blackened peppers in a paper or plastic bag (or cover in a bowl) and let them steam until cool enough to handle. Peel the peppers to remove blackened bits of skin but don't wash them. Stem, seed, and reserve.

2. Place the walnuts, bread crumbs, Aleppo pepper, cumin, coriander, allspice, salt, brown sugar, pomegranate molasses, dissolved tomato paste, lemon juice, and oil in the bowl of a food processor and process, scraping down the sides once or twice, until a thick, nearly smooth paste forms and the nut pieces have all but disappeared, about 30 seconds. Add the reserved roasted peppers and process to incorporate them completely. The result should be a thick but easily spreadable purée; thicken with small amounts of bread crumbs or thin with a bit of water if necessary. Fold in the pine nuts by hand and transfer to an airtight container.

NOTE: Aleppo pepper is a moderately spicy crushed red pepper with a deep crimson color; it's commonly available at Middle Eastern markets.

Pomegranate molasses, made from the concentrated juice of pomegranates and sold in glass bottles, is also available at Middle Eastern markets and well-stocked supermarkets and varies somewhat in thickness and intensity from producer to producer. The Cortas brand makes an excellent, widely available molasses, although the more common Al Wadi brand, along with others, works well too. A few types of pomegranate molasses are thicker and more intense than these and may require dilution with a little water for use in this recipe.

Green Olive, Walnut, and Pomegranate Relish

MAKES 2 TO 2½ CUPS

This is our take on a tasty condiment first introduced to us in Paula Wolfert's *The Cooking of the Eastern Mediterranean.* We think this is just the ticket served alongside Charcoal Grilled Lamb Chops with Garlic and Marjoram, page 153, our Grilled Ground-Lamb Skewers, page 164, and the Andalusian-Style Lamb Kababs, page 166.

- 7 to 8 ounces (about 2 cups) best-quality green olives, such as Picholine or Sicilian (see Note)
- ⅔ cup finely chopped unsalted walnuts
- ¼ cup finely chopped scallions
- ½ cup chopped fresh flat-leaf parsley
- 3 tablespoons extra-virgin olive oil
- 3 tablespoons pomegranate molasses, plus more as needed (see Note, facing page)
- 1 tablespoon fresh lemon juice
- Kosher salt
- ¼ teaspoon fresh coarsely ground black pepper
- ½ teaspoon Aleppo pepper (see Note, facing page) or generous pinch cayenne pepper plus ½ teaspoon sweet paprika
- ¾ teaspoon cumin seed, toasted briefly in a dry skillet and coarsely crushed
- ½ cup fresh pomegranate seeds, plus 2 tablespoons for garnish (optional)
- Sugar, as needed

1. To pit the olives, place them on a work surface and whack sharply with the broad side of a chef's knife to partially crush them and help free the pits (if the olives slide around excessively, place them between a kitchen towel before striking; if you're uncomfortable striking with the side of a knife, olives can be whacked with a mallet instead). Remove the pits with your fingers and discard. Tear or chop the olives into 2 or 3 coarse pieces and place in a mixing bowl.
2. To the olives, add the walnuts, scallions, parsley, oil, molasses, lemon juice, ¼ teaspoon salt, black pepper, Aleppo pepper, cumin, and the ½ cup pomegranate seeds (if using), mixing well to combine. The relish should taste quite sour but be balanced by a salty and sweet background. Depending on the brand of pomegranate molasses used, you may want to add an additional few teaspoons of molasses to intensify the pomegranate flavor and its sourness and/or stir in ¼ to ½ teaspoon of sugar to balance that sourness (some brands of pomegranate molasses are quite sweet, so adding more will boost both sweetness and sourness).
3. The relish can be used immediately, though the flavor improves if stored, covered, for a few hours or refrigerated for a day or so. Bring to room temperature before serving.

NOTE: Look for olives with little or no additional flavorings. Olives that are excessively salty or bitter can be rinsed a few times or soaked in a few changes of cool water for up to 1 hour or so, drained, and patted dry before use in the recipe.

Roasted Red Bell Peppers

2 red bell peppers, halved lengthwise, stemmed, seeded, any white ribs trimmed

Extra-virgin olive oil

1. Preheat the oven to 425°F. Place the pepper halves, cut-side down, on an aluminum foil–lined baking sheet. Drizzle with a few teaspoons of oil and rub all over the exteriors. Roast the peppers in the center of the oven until tender and the skins and cut edges have blackened somewhat, 35 to 45 minutes, rotating the pan halfway through cooking. Remove from the oven and let the peppers sit until cool enough to handle.

2. Peel off the skins with your fingers and discard, but leave most of the flavorful blackened bits attached to the cut edges. Reserve any juices released by the peppers. Store the peppers with any juices in a covered container in the refrigerator for up to 1 week.

Romesco Sauce

MAKES ABOUT 1½ CUPS

Romesco is a much-loved Spanish sauce made with peppers and almonds or hazelnuts. It tastes glorious with any number of meat and poultry dishes, especially those that are grilled or roasted.

1	large red bell pepper, halved lengthwise, stemmed and seeded
5	medium (or 3 large) canned tomatoes (about 12 ounces)
10	large cloves garlic, unpeeled, plus ½ small clove garlic, peeled and crushed
	Extra-virgin olive oil
1	ounce dried ancho chiles (about 1 large or 2 small peppers)
One	slice of crustless country-style bread, 3 by 3 by 1-inch thick
24	unsalted roasted almonds
1	teaspoon sweet paprika
⅛	teaspoon cayenne pepper
	Kosher salt
1	tablespoon sherry vinegar

1. Preheat the oven to 400°F. Place the red pepper halves, cut-side down, the tomatoes, and unpeeled garlic cloves on an aluminum foil–lined rimmed baking sheet, leaving some space between the items. Rub the peppers with a few teaspoons of oil and drizzle the tomatoes and garlic with a tablespoon or so of the oil, turning to coat. Roast in the center of the oven for 30 minutes. Remove the garlic to a plate to cool. Continue roasting until the peppers have blackened somewhat and the flesh is tender and the tomatoes have concentrated and sweetened, 15 to 30 minutes. When cool enough to handle, slip the garlic cloves from their skins and place in the bowl of a food processor along with the roasted tomatoes. Peel the skin from the red peppers and add to the food processor.
2. Place the ancho chiles in a small skillet over medium-low heat and gently toast until fragrant, about 2 minutes per side, pushing on them with the back of a spatula to help them make contact with the skillet. (Don't let them burn.) Transfer the chiles to a bowl and cover with very hot water; soak until soft, 15 to 45 minutes, turning once or twice. Stem and seed the chiles and add to the bowl of the food processor.
3. In the same skillet, warm 2 tablespoons of oil over medium-low heat. Add the bread and cook gently until toasted and colored a rich golden brown on both sides, 4 to 6 minutes. Add to the bowl of the food processor.
4. Add the almonds, paprika, cayenne, the ½ clove of crushed garlic, and 1 teaspoon salt. Pulse 5 or 6 times to coarsely chop ingredients; continuing to pulse, pour in ½ cup of oil to the bowl of the food processor, pausing to scrape down the sides of the bowl as needed, until the mixture is well incorporated but is still a bit coarse in texture, and the almonds are about the size of aquarium gravel. Add the vinegar and pulse to incorporate. Add additional salt and vinegar to taste, if needed, pulsing to incorporate (sauce should be just slightly tart from the vinegar). Transfer to a covered container and store in the refrigerator for up to 1 week.

Salsa Mexicana

MAKES ABOUT 2½ CUPS

- ½ medium white onion, finely chopped (generous ½ cup)
- 1¼ pounds ripe tomatoes, cut into ½-inch pieces (about 3 cups), or substitute drained canned tomatoes
- 3 to 4 medium serrano peppers, or 2 to 3 small green jalapeño peppers, finely chopped
- ½ cup loosely packed chopped fresh cilantro
- 1 teaspoon kosher salt
- ¼ teaspoon sugar
- 5 tablespoons fresh lime juice
- 1½ tablespoons vegetable oil

1. Soak the onion in cold water for 5 minutes; drain, blot dry, and transfer to a mixing bowl. Add the tomatoes, peppers, and cilantro and mix to combine. In a small bowl, whisk the salt and sugar into the lime juice until dissolved. Whisk in the oil.
2. Pour this dressing over the tomato-onion mixture and toss very thoroughly to coat. Salt to taste and serve.

NOTE: Depending on how much water is in the tomatoes, you may want to drain some of the excess liquid from the salsa before serving. May be stored in the refrigerator for up to 1 week.

Tomatillo Salsa

MAKES ABOUT 1½ CUPS

3	large cloves garlic, unpeeled
¾	pound tomatillos (about 6 medium), husks removed, washed and dried
3 to 4	medium green jalapeño peppers
½	teaspoon kosher salt
¼	teaspoon sugar
3	tablespoons finely chopped white onion, soaked in cold water for 5 minutes and drained
2	tablespoons finely chopped cilantro

1. Preheat a small skillet over medium heat. Add the garlic cloves to the skillet and toast them on all sides, until the skins are a bit blackened and the garlic has softened slightly, about 15 minutes. When cool enough to handle, slip the garlic cloves from their skins, trim any burned areas, and transfer them to the bowl of a food processor.

2. Meanwhile, preheat the broiler and line a baking sheet with aluminum foil. Distribute the tomatillos (stem-side down) and the jalapeños on the baking sheet and broil them on both sides until they're well charred and blackened in places, 4 to 8 minutes per side. If necessary, rotate the sheet to evenly expose them to the heat (tomatillos may collapse a bit but don't let them collapse completely, as it is important to retain most of their liquid).

3. Add the tomatillos to the bowl of a food processor. When cool enough to handle, peel the peppers, remove some or all of the seeds, and add them to the bowl of the processor along with the salt and sugar. Process until the mixture is smooth but still a bit chunky, about 20 seconds. Transfer to a mixing bowl. Stir in the onion and cilantro; salt to taste and serve. May be stored in the refrigerator in a tightly sealed container for up to 1 week.

NOTE: Salsa can be drained slightly to yield a thicker result.

Chimichurri Sauce

MAKES ABOUT 1¼ CUPS

This is our version of the tangy and well-loved Argentine parsley sauce and marinade. Though it's great as is, think of this recipe as a template, to which you can add or subtract flavors to make this sauce your own. A little oregano—fresh or dried—is often added to chimichurri and a good measure of black pepper can add kick; chopped onion can substitute for the scallion used here and fresh red or green chilies can replace some or all or the red pepper flakes; red wine vinegar can stand in for the distilled vinegar. And though it makes purists wince, some cooks substitute cilantro—and even mint—for some of the parsley.

- 1 cup tightly packed parsley leaves (some thin stems are fine)
- 3 large cloves garlic, coarsely chopped
- 2 scallions, coarsely chopped
- 3 bay leaves, crumbled
- ½ teaspoon paprika
- ¼ teaspoon crushed red pepper flakes
- ⅓ cup distilled white vinegar
- ⅓ cup water
- 1 teaspoon kosher salt
- ¼ teaspoon ground cumin
- ⅓ cup olive oil

1. Combine all the ingredients except the oil in the bowl of a food processor and process, scraping down the sides of the bowl once or twice, until mixture is smooth and no large bits remain, about 30 seconds. Add the olive oil and process for just a second or two to incorporate. Chimichurri can be served right away but it's best to let the flavors develop for a few hours. Though its color will fade somewhat, chimichurri keeps well for a week or so tightly covered in the fridge.

Cilantro-Lime Chutney

MAKES ABOUT 1¼ CUPS

One	1-inch piece 1-inch-diameter fresh ginger, peeled and sliced into coins
2 to 3	serrano peppers, or 2 small jalapeño peppers, seeded
Six	6-inch lengths of scallion greens (tops), chopped
2	cups very tightly packed fresh cilantro, with thin stems (about 2 very large bunches), coarsely chopped
½	cup tightly packed fresh mint leaves
½	teaspoon ground cumin seed
¾	teaspoon Garam Masala Spice Blend (page 296)
1	teaspoon kosher salt
½	teaspoon sugar
2 to 3	tablespoons vegetable oil
¼	cup fresh lime juice

1. Combine all the ingredients except the lime juice in the bowl of a food processor. Process until finely chopped, pulsing and scraping down the sides of the bowl as needed (this may take a few tries as the herbs can be stubborn). Add the lime juice and process until a bright green paste forms. It should be spreadable but not quite fluid.
2. Pulse in small amounts of lime juice, oil, or water to thin, if necessary. Serve or transfer to an airtight container and store in the refrigerator for up to 1 week.

Piquant Parsley Sauce

MAKES ABOUT 2 CUPS

- 3 cups lightly packed fresh flat-leaf parsley leaves
- 5 to 6 anchovy fillets
- 2 heaping tablespoons capers, rinsed
- 4 hard-boiled egg yolks
- 1 large clove garlic, peeled and sliced
- 2 tablespoons white wine vinegar
- ½ teaspoon kosher salt
- Generous pinch cayenne pepper
- 1 cup extra-virgin olive oil, plus more as needed

1. Combine all the ingredients except the olive oil in the bowl of a food processor. Pulse to chop, pausing to scrape down the sides of the bowl as needed. With the motor running, add the oil in a steady stream until a fluid, slightly thickened sauce forms and the ingredients are finely chopped. The mixture should be flecked with green, and thick but still quite fluid.

2. Process briefly with more oil as needed. Cover and refrigerate.

Cuban-Style Citrus-Garlic Sauce (Mojo)

MAKES ABOUT 5 CUPS

3	cups fresh orange juice
1 1/2	cups fresh lime juice
1/2	cup extra-virgin olive oil
1	large head of garlic (about 12 large cloves), cloves peeled and pushed through a garlic press or minced
5	bay leaves
1	medium onion, sliced crosswise into 1/4-inch-thick rings
	Kosher salt
1/2	teaspoon freshly ground black pepper

1. Put the orange and lime juices in a mixing bowl and reserve. In a medium saucepan, combine the oil, garlic, and bay leaves and bring to a simmer over medium heat; simmer gently but without browning the garlic, for 1 minute, stirring occasionally.

2. Stir in the onion, 1 tablespoon salt, and pepper; return to a simmer and cook for a minute or so more. Carefully pour the mixture into the reserved citrus juices, whisking to combine. Add salt to taste. Whisk again before serving. The sauce can be made up to two days ahead; it keeps for a few weeks, refrigerated in a tightly sealed container.

Malaysian Chicken Dipping Sauce

MAKES ABOUT 3/4 CUP

6	tablespoons Worcestershire sauce
2	tablespoons fresh lime juice
1	tablespoon plus 1 teaspoon soy sauce
1	tablespoon plus 1 teaspoon sugar
1 1/2	teaspoons ground (powdered) mustard
2 to 4	teaspoons Chile and Shallot Sambal (page 294), or 1 to 2 thinly sliced hot red chiles, such as Thai bird or serrano

Combine the Worcestershire sauce, lime juice, soy sauce, sugar, and mustard in a small bowl, stirring to dissolve the solids. Stir in the sambal or chiles, adding more to taste if desired. Serve in individual bowls with Malaysian Spice-Fried Chicken (page 222).

Thai Chile-Herb Dipping Sauce

MAKES ABOUT ⅔ CUP

1	tablespoon jasmine or other long-grain rice
6 to 8	dried whole Thai chiles (each about 2 inches long)
1	heaping tablespoon finely chopped scallion
2	tablespoons finely chopped fresh mint
2	tablespoons finely chopped fresh cilantro leaves
2	teaspoons sugar
3	tablespoons Thai or Vietnamese fish sauce (*nam pla* or *nuoc nam*)
⅓	cup fresh lime juice

1. Place the rice in a small skillet over medium heat and cook, shaking the pan, until fragrant and lightly toasted, less than 1 minute. Transfer the rice to a spice or coffee grinder and let cool. Process the cooled rice until almost powdered, transfer to a small bowl, and reserve.

2. Place the chiles in the same skillet and cook over medium heat until lightly toasted, 30 to 45 seconds, shaking the skillet to avoid burning. Transfer the chiles to a spice or coffee grinder and let cool. Pulse the grinder until the chiles are coarsely chopped. Transfer the chiles to the bowl with the rice (the rice and the chiles can also be ground separately with a mortar and pestle).

3. Add the scallion, mint, cilantro, sugar, fish sauce, and lime juice to the bowl, stirring to dissolve the sugar. Cover and reserve (the sauce can be made a few hours ahead and kept at room temperature). May be stored in a tightly sealed container in the refrigerator for up to 1 week; however, the bright colors will fade.

Chile and Shallot Sambal

MAKES ABOUT 1 CUP

Sambals are spicy chile-based condiments common throughout Indonesia, Malaysia, and Singapore. This one—at once fiery, tangy, and pleasantly funky—does double duty as both table condiment and recipe ingredient.

- 1 cup stemmed and chopped red Holland, jalapeño, cayenne, or other medium-hot, medium-size tapering red chiles (6 to 8 Holland or jalapeños)
- 1/4 cup stemmed and chopped red or green Thai bird chiles or other very hot small chile (10 to 15 Thai chiles)
- 1 cup thinly sliced shallots
- 2 large cloves garlic, sliced
- 2 firmly packed teaspoons dried shrimp paste (*belecan*), roasted (see Note, page 62)
- 2 teaspoons palm sugar or brown sugar
- 1/4 teaspoon kosher salt
- 2 tablespoons Thai or Vietnamese fish sauce (*nam pla* or *nuoc nam*)
- 2 tablespoons fresh lime juice

Combine all the ingredients in a food processor and blend, scraping down the sides of the bowl as needed, until a coarse sauce forms. Serve immediately or store, tightly covered, for up to a few weeks in the refrigerator.

Kafta Spice Mix

No two kafta spice mixtures are alike, but these are two of our favorites. The first emphasizes the flavors of allspice and black pepper; the second features the warm, sweet-spicy kick of cardamom. Feel free to concoct your own blends. The following quantities of each batch are suitable for the Grilled Ground-Lamb Skewers on page 164.

MIXTURE 1: In a small bowl, combine 1 teaspoon freshly ground black pepper, 1 teaspoon ground allspice, 1 teaspoon ground coriander seed, ½ teaspoon ground cinnamon, ½ teaspoon ground nutmeg, ½ teaspoon ground cumin, and ½ teaspoon ground cloves.

MIXTURE 2: In a small bowl, combine 1 teaspoon freshly ground black pepper, 1 teaspoon ground allspice, ½ teaspoon ground cinnamon, ½ teaspoon ground cloves, and ½ teaspoon ground cardamom.

Garam Masala Spice Blend

MAKES 1½ TEASPOONS

This Indian spice blend is best when homemade, although various mixtures of garam masala are sold commercially. Traditional mixtures usually include cinnamon, cloves, and cardamom, although there are many variations. We like this simple combination. It's especially great sprinkled on poultry and lamb, either before or after cooking.

- ½ teaspoon freshly ground black pepper
- ½ teaspoon ground cinnamon
- ¼ teaspoon ground cloves
- ¼ teaspoon ground cardamom

In a small bowl, combine all the spices and use immediately or store in an airtight container.

Pakora Batter

MAKES ABOUT 2 CUPS

- 1 1/2 cups chickpea flour (*besan*)
- 1/4 cup all-purpose flour
- 1 1/2 teaspoons kosher salt
- 1/2 teaspoon baking soda
- 1 1/2 teaspoons ground turmeric
- 1 to 2 cups water

Sift both flours into a mixing bowl and mix well with the salt, baking soda, and turmeric. Gradually add 1 cup water, whisking to incorporate and breaking up any lumps. Gradually add small amounts of remaining water by tablespoons, while still whisking, until the mixture is smooth and about the thickness of pancake batter (you may not use all the water). Test the thickness of the batter as described in Step 3 of Indian-Style Fritters with Lamb (page 174) and adjust as needed.

Corned Beef Pickling Spice

MAKES ABOUT 1/3 CUP

- 3/4 teaspoon mustard seed
- 3/4 teaspoon coriander seed
- 1/2 teaspoon fresh, coarsely cracked black pepper
- 1/4 teaspoon crushed red pepper flakes
- 1/4 teaspoon ground ginger
- 18 allspice berries
- 10 whole cloves
- 5 cardamom pods, cracked
- 3 bay leaves, crumbled
- One 1 1/2-inch-long cinnamon stick, cracked with a mallet or back of a skillet into small pieces

Combine all the ingredients and store tightly covered until use.

Chicken Stock

MAKES ABOUT 6 CUPS

3	pounds chicken wings, cut into 3 or 4 pieces each
8	cups cold water
½	large onion, halved
½	carrot, peeled and halved
½	rib celery, halved
2	large cloves garlic, crushed
2	sprigs fresh thyme
½	bay leaf
¼	teaspoon salt

1. In a 6-quart pot, combine the chicken wings with the water and bring to a simmer over medium-high heat. As it comes to a simmer, skim off any impurities that rise to the surface with a ladle or large spoon.
2. Add the onion, carrot, celery, garlic, thyme, bay leaf, and salt. Cook uncovered at a gentle simmer, stirring occasionally, for 1 hour.
3. Remove from the heat and let the stock rest for 15 minutes. Strain the stock through a large fine-mesh strainer or a colander double-lined with damp cheesecloth into a large bowl.
4. Fill a larger bowl or the sink with ice and water and nest the bowl of stock in it. Stir regularly until the stock has cooled.
5. Transfer the cooled stock to airtight containers, and refrigerate for up to 3 days or freeze for up to 3 months.

NOTE: To make turkey stock, substitute 3 pounds of turkey wings or turkey parts for the chicken wings.

Lamb Stock

MAKES ABOUT 4 CUPS

- 3 tablespoons vegetable oil
- 3 pounds meaty lamb bones, especially from the neck shoulder (alone or in combination), cut into large pieces
- 8 cups cold water
- ½ medium onion, halved
- ½ carrot, peeled
- ½ rib celery
- 2 large cloves garlic, crushed
- 2 small sprigs fresh thyme
- ¼ teaspoon salt

1. In a 6-quart pot, heat the oil over medium-high heat and cook the lamb in two batches until the meat is very deeply browned on at least two sides, 6 to 8 minutes per side. Reduce the heat if they threaten to burn. Remove the lamb to a plate and pour off the oil in the pot.
2. Return the pot to medium-high heat and add the water, scraping the bottom of the pot to loosen any browned bits stuck to the bottom of the pot. Return the lamb and any accumulated juices to the pot and bring to a simmer. As it comes to a simmer, skim off any impurities that rise to the surface with a ladle or large spoon.
3. Add the onion, carrot, celery, garlic, thyme, and salt. Cook uncovered at the barest possible simmer, stirring occasionally, for 2 hours.
4. Remove from the heat and let the stock rest for 15 minutes. Strain the stock through a large fine-mesh strainer or a colander double-lined with damp cheesecloth into a large bowl.
5. Fill a larger bowl or the sink with ice and water and nest the bowl of stock in it. Stir regularly until the broth has cooled.
6. Transfer the cooled stock to airtight containers, and refrigerate for up to 3 days or freeze for up to 3 months.

Pork Stock

MAKES ABOUT 5 CUPS

2	tablespoons vegetable oil
3 ½	pounds meaty pork spare ribs or neck bones (or a combination), cut into individual ribs or large pieces
8	cups cold water
½	medium onion, halved
½	carrot, peeled
½	rib celery
1	large clove garlic, crushed
1	small sprig thyme
¼	teaspoon salt

1. Heat the oil in a 6- to 8-quart pot over medium-high heat. When the oil is hot, add the pork in two batches, and cook until the meat is very deeply browned on all sides, including the meaty edges of the ribs, 6 to 8 minutes per side. Reduce the heat if they threaten to burn. Remove the pork to a plate and pour off the oil in the pot.

2. Return the pot to medium-high heat and add the water, scraping the bottom of the pot to loosen any browned bits. Return the pork (and any juices on the plate) to the pot and bring to a simmer. As it comes to a simmer, skim off any impurities that rise to the surface. Add the onion, carrot, celery, garlic, thyme, and salt. Partially cover and cook at the barest possible simmer (just a few bubbles breaking the surface) for 1½ hours, stirring once or twice.

3. Remove from the heat and let the stock rest for 15 minutes. Strain the stock through a large fine-mesh strainer or a colander double-lined with damp cheesecloth into a large bowl.

4. Fill a larger bowl or the sink with ice water and nest the bowl of stock in it. Stir regularly until the stock has cooled.

5. Transfer the cooled stock to airtight containers, and refrigerate for up to 3 days or freeze for up to 3 months.

Beef Stock

MAKES ABOUT 7 CUPS

Beef, veal, and pork bones are hard to come by, so ask your butcher to save any he removes for you. Take them home and freeze them for later use in stock. These days, the scarcest of beef products has to be the bones! In the old days, the butcher had plenty of bones to spare, but today's precut meat means fewer bones at the retail level.

4	tablespoons olive oil or vegetable oil
4	pounds meaty beef bones, such as ribs, shin, neck, or tail
16	cups cold water
1	onion, peeled and quartered
1	carrot, peeled
1	rib celery
2	large cloves garlic, crushed
2	sprigs fresh thyme
1	bay leaf
½	teaspoon salt

1. In a 10-quart pot, heat the oil over medium-high heat and cook the beef bones, in 2 batches if necessary, until very deeply browned on all sides, including the meaty edges of ribs, 6 to 8 minutes per side. Reduce the heat if they threaten to burn. Remove the beef to a plate and pour off the oil in the pot.
2. Return the pot to medium-high heat and add the water, scraping the bottom of the pot to loosen any browned bits. Return the beef bones, and any accumulated juices, and bring to a simmer. As it comes to a simmer, skim off any impurities that rise to the surface with a ladle or large spoon.
3. Add the onion, carrot, celery, garlic, thyme, bay leaf, and salt. Cook uncovered, at the barest possible simmer, with just a few bubbles breaking the surface, stirring occasionally, for 2½ hours.
4. Remove from the heat and let the stock rest for 15 minutes. Strain the stock through a large fine-mesh strainer or a colander double-lined with damp cheesecloth into a large bowl.
5. Fill a larger bowl or the sink with ice and water and nest the bowl of stock in it. Stir regularly until the stock has cooled.
6. Transfer the cooled stock to airtight containers, and refrigerate for up to 3 days or freeze for up to 3 months.

Veal Stock

MAKES ABOUT 8 CUPS

- 1/4 cup olive oil or vegetable oil
- 4 pounds meaty pieces of veal, with bone attached (see Note)
- 16 cups cold water
- 1 yellow onion, peeled and quartered
- 1 carrot, peeled
- 1 rib celery
- 2 large cloves garlic, crushed
- 2 sprigs fresh thyme
- 2 teaspoons tomato paste (optional; see Note)
- 1/2 teaspoon salt

1. In a 10-quart pot, heat the oil over medium-high heat and cook the veal, in 2 batches if necessary, until very deeply browned on all sides, including any meaty edges, 6 to 8 minutes per side. Reduce the heat if it threatens to burn. Transfer the veal to a plate and pour off the oil in the pot.
2. Return the pot to medium-high heat and add the water, scraping the bottom of the pot to loosen any browned bits. Return the veal and any accumulated juices to the pot and bring to a simmer. As it comes to a simmer, skim off any impurities that rise to the surface with a ladle or large spoon. Note the level of the liquid in the pot. Cook uncovered at the barest possible simmer, with just a few bubbles breaking the surface, stirring occasionally, for 2 hours. To compensate for the evaporating liquid, every so often add small amounts of hot water to keep the liquid at or near the level you noted. As the stock simmers, continue to skim the impurities that rise to the surface as carefully and thoroughly as you can.
3. Add the onion, carrot, celery, garlic, thyme, tomato paste (if using), and salt. Continue to simmer in the same way for 2 hours longer, skimming occasionally, although this time do not add any water so that the broth slowly concentrates and reduces in volume.
4. Remove from the heat and let the stock rest for 15 minutes. Strain through a large fine-mesh strainer or a colander double-lined with damp cheesecloth into a large bowl.
5. Fill a larger bowl or the sink with ice and water and nest the bowl of stock in it. Stir regularly until the broth has cooled.
6. Transfer the cooled stock to airtight containers, and refrigerate for up to 3 days or freeze for up to 3 months.

NOTE: Use veal breast cut into individual ribs; veal shoulder, neck, or shank cut into chunks; or any combination of these. If your butcher has veal bones in manageable sizes, add some of those, too.

The tomato paste adds a darker color, but it's not necessary.

Brine for Pork or Poultry

MAKES ABOUT 4 QUARTS

Experiment with various flavor combinations and brining times. The ratio of salt to water, however, should not stray too far from the proportions outlined in this recipe, although the quantity of sugar can be reduced, eliminated altogether, or be replaced by a roughly similar amount of brown sugar, maple syrup, or honey. The recipe can be halved or quartered to yield a smaller quantity of brine.

4 quarts (1 gallon) cool water
1 cup kosher salt
3/4 cup sugar
Herbs and seasonings of choice (see Note)

1. In a medium saucepan, combine 1 quart of the water with the salt, sugar, and your herbs and seasonings of choice. Bring to a boil over high heat, stirring to dissolve the salt and sugar. Pour into a large pot and stir in the remaining 3 quarts water. Cool to below 45°F in the refrigerator.
2. Use the brine in quantities sufficient to completely cover and surround whatever piece of meat is being brined. Brine pork or poultry, in the refrigerator, following individual recipe instructions or refer to the chart on facing page.
3. After removing meat from brine, blot dry and use in the recipe (if time permits, let meat rest in the fridge for a few hours—for smaller cuts—or up to a day—for larger cuts—to allow the brine to redistribute itself throughout the meat, which will yield a moister result.

NOTE: Brines can be flavored with any number of herbs, spices, and other aromatics. A bunch of sage, a few bay leaves, a head of crushed garlic cloves, and a tablespoon or so of peppercorns make a fine addition to the Italian-style Pork Chops with Peppers, Vinegar, and Black Olives on page 112. For the Rolled Roast Loin of Pork on page 116, thyme might replace the sage and a handful of fennel seeds might join the peppercorns, along with chopped onion, carrot, celery, and fennel tops. Exact quantities are not too crucial; be generous but not excessive when flavoring brines with herbs and spices—you want to flavor but not obscure the natural taste of the meat.

Brining Chart

Below are approximate timing guidelines for brining different cuts of meat. Smaller, thinner cuts of each item should be brined for the minimum times listed.

MEAT	TIME
Pork chops (1 to 1½ inch thick)	2 to 4 hours
Whole pork tenderloin	5 to 7 hours
Whole pork loin (3 to 5 pounds)	12 to 36 hours
Boneless chicken breasts	2 to 3 hours
Whole chicken (3 to 5 pounds)	6 to 12 hours
Boneless turkey breast (4 to 5 inches thick)	12 to 18 hours
Whole turkey (10 to 20 pounds)	18 to 36 hours

D

E

F

G

H

I

J

K

L

P

Q

T

V

W

Y

Z

Table of Equivalents

The exact equivalents in the following tables have been rounded for convenience.

Liquid/Dry Measurements

U.S.	METRIC
¼ teaspoon	1.25 milliliters
½ teaspoon	2.5 milliliters
1 teaspoon	5 milliliters
1 tablespoon (3 teaspoons)	15 milliliters
1 fluid ounce (2 tablespoons)	30 milliliters
¼ cup	60 milliliters
⅓ cup	80 milliliters
½ cup	120 milliliters
1 cup	240 milliliters
1 pint (2 cups)	480 milliliters
1 quart (4 cups, 32 ounces)	960 milliliters
1 gallon (4 quarts)	3.84 liters
1 ounce (by weight)	28 grams
1 pound	448 grams
2.2 pounds	1 kilogram

Lengths

U.S.	METRIC
⅛ inch	3 millimeters
¼ inch	6 millimeters
½ inch	12 millimeters
1 inch	2.5 centimeters

Oven Temperature

FAHRENHEIT	CELSIUS	GAS
250	120	½
275	140	1
300	150	2
325	160	3
350	180	4
375	190	5
400	200	6
425	220	7
450	230	8
475	240	9
500	260	10